THE CHINA-AUSTRALIA FREE TRADE AGREEMENT

This book provides readers with a unique opportunity to learn about one of the new regional trade agreements (RTAs), the China–Australia Free Trade Agreement (ChAFTA), which has been operational since December 2015 and is now at the forefront of the field. This new agreement reflects many of the modern and up-to-date approaches within the international economic legal order that must now exist within a very different environment than that of the late eighties and early nineties, when the World Trade Organization (WTO) was created. The book, therefore, explores many new features that were not present when the WTO or early RTAs were negotiated. It provides insights and lessons about new and important trade issues for the twenty first century, such as the latest approaches to the regulation of investment, twenty-first century services and the emerging digital/knowledge economy. In addition, this book provides new understandings of the latest RTA approaches of China and Australia. The book's contributors, all foremost experts on their subject matter within this field, explore the inclusion of many traditional trade and investment agreement features in the ChAFTA, showing their continuing relevance in modern contexts.

Studies in International Trade and Investment Law: Volume 18

Studies in International Trade and Investment Law
Recent titles in this series:

Redefining Sovereignty in International Economic Law
Edited by Wenhua Shan, Penelope Simons and Dalvinder Singh

Law and Ethics in International Trade and Environment Debates
Ilona Cheyne

Constitutionalism, Multilevel Trade Governance and Social Regulation
Edited by Christian Joerges and Ernst-Ulrich Petersmann

The Human Rights Impact of the World Trade Organisation
James Harrison

Developing Countries and the Multilateral Trade Regime: The Failure and Promise of the WTO's Development Mission
Donatella Alessandrini

Constitutionalism, Multilevel Trade Governance and International Economic Law
Edited by Christian Joerges and Ernst-Ulrich Petersmann

The Right to Development and International Economic Law: Legal and Moral Dimensions
Isabella Bunn

Free Trade and Cultural Diversity in International Law
Jingxia Shi

Tied Aid and Development Aid Policies in the Framework of EU and WTO Law: The Imperative for Change
Annamaria La Chimia

Balancing Human Rights, Environmental Protection and International Trade: Lessons from the EU Experience
Emily Reid

Public Procurement and Labour Rights: Towards Coherence in International Instruments of Procurement Regulation
Maria Anna Corvaglia

The China-Australia Free Trade Agreement

A 21st-Century Model

Edited by
Colin B Picker, Heng Wang and Weihuan Zhou

·HART·
PUBLISHING
OXFORD AND PORTLAND, OREGON
2018

Hart Publishing
An imprint of Bloomsbury Publishing Plc

Hart Publishing Ltd
Kemp House
Chawley Park
Cumnor Hill
Oxford OX2 9PH
UK

Bloomsbury Publishing Plc
50 Bedford Square
London
WC1B 3DP
UK

www.hartpub.co.uk
www.bloomsbury.com

Published in North America (US and Canada) by
Hart Publishing
c/o International Specialized Book Services
920 NE 58th Avenue, Suite 300
Portland, OR 97213-3786
USA

www.isbs.com

First published 2018

British Library Cataloguing-in-Publication Data
A catalogue record for this book is available from the British Library.

ISBN: HB: 978-1-50991-538-5
ePDF: 978-1-50991-539-2
ePub: 978-1-50991-540-8

Library of Congress Cataloging-in-Publication Data

Names: Picker, Colin, 1965- editor. | Wang, Heng (Law teacher), editor. | Zhou, Weihuan, editor.

Title: The China-Australia free trade agreement : a 21st-century model / edited by Colin Picker, Heng Wang, and Weihuan Zhou.

Description: Oxford [UK] ; Portland, Oregon : Hart Publishing, 2018. | Series: Studies in international trade and investment law ; 18 | Includes bibliographical references and index.

Identifiers: LCCN 2017045633 (print) | LCCN 2017046433 (ebook) | ISBN 9781509915408 (Epub) | ISBN 9781509915385 (hardback : alk. paper)

Subjects: LCSH: Foreign trade regulation—China. | Foreign trade regulation—Australia. | Free trade—China. | Free trade—Australia. | China—Foreign economic relations—Australia. | Australia—Foreign economic relations—China.

Classification: LCC KNQ3405 (ebook) | LCC KNQ3405 .C4525 2018 (print) | DDC 382.51094—dc23

LC record available at https://lccn.loc.gov/2017045633

Typeset by Compuscript Ltd, Shannon

Preface

Almost all the contributions in this book were presented at a conference sponsored by UNSW Law's China International Business and Economic Law (CIBEL) Initiative in June 2016. That conference, Chinese–Australian Economic Law Relations in the Post-ChAFTA World examined the consequence of ChAFTA—locally, regionally and internationally. The conference was held on 17 and 18 June 2016, the one-year anniversary of the signing of ChAFTA.

With over 30 presentations from some of the world's leading authorities the conference presented groundbreaking analyses on everything from the Australian constitutionality of ChAFTA to the facilitation of business under ChAFTA to the future of investment regulation in the region. The conference's keynote was delivered by the Honourable Andrew Robb, AO MP—as the Australian responsible for the negotiation of ChAFTA he was able to provide truly unique insights in ChAFTA's past, present and future. The conference was also honoured to hear from Ms Hongbo Wang, the Chinese Economic and Commercial Counsellor from the Consulate General of China in Sydney, who is also a renowned expert on international trade law.

The conference attracted over 90 attendees from across the region. The attendees represented the breadth of the professions that interact with or are affected by ChAFTA, with delegates from academia, legal and judicial practice, government departments, and trade and commerce. This diverse cohort along, with the distinguished presenters, contributed insightful thoughts and challenging debate on what this book will clearly show is a critical international agreement.

Contents

List of Contributors

Vivienne Bath

Vivienne Bath is Professor of Chinese and International Business Law, Director of the Centre for Asian and Pacific Law and Director of Research of the China Studies Centre at the University of Sydney. Her teaching and research interests are in international business and economic law, private international law and Chinese law. She has first class honours in Chinese and in law from the Australian National University, and an LLM from Harvard Law School. She has extensive professional experience in Sydney, New York, China and Hong Kong in international commercial law and foreign investment. Professor Bath speaks Chinese (mandarin) and German.

Eva Chye

Eva Chye is Principal Adviser for International Trade at PwC, and Research Associate at the University of Western Australia Law School. Her chapter draws upon 16 years of experience managing international education and research collaboration with Southeast Asia and China. Engagements with China which Eva has initiated and established include the first Confucius Institute in Australia, three joint research laboratories and 150 joint scholarships. Eva is also a certified translator with the National Accreditation Authority for Translators and Interpreters, and an accredited commercial mediator with the Australian Mediator Standards Board.

Lisa Burton Crawford

Lisa Burton Crawford is a Lecturer in the Faculty of Law at Monash University. Lisa teaches and researches in the field of public law, with a particular focus on the intersection of constitutional and administrative law. She has published widely in this field, in Australia and abroad. Her book, *The Rule of Law and the Australian Constitution*, was published by The Federation Press in 2017.

Patrick Emerton

Patrick Emerton is an Associate Professor in the Monash University Faculty of Law. He researches in constitutional law and theory, just war theory, human rights theory, and the philosophy of international law. His recent work includes contributions to the forthcoming *Oxford Handbook of the Australian Constitution* and to the *Oxford Handbook of Ethics of War*.

Henry Gao

Henry Gao is Associate Professor of Law at Singapore Management University and Dongfang Scholar Chair Professor at Shanghai Institute of Foreign Trade. With law degrees from three continents, he started his career as the first Chinese lawyer at the WTO Secretariat. He has advised many national governments as well as the WTO, World Bank, Asian Development Bank, APEC and ASEAN on trade issues. He sits on the Advisory Board of the WTO Chairs Programme, which was established by the WTO Secretariat in 2009 to promote research and teaching on WTO issues in leading universities around the world.

Jie (Jeanne) Huang

Jie Huang is a Senior Lecturer in the Faculty of Law, UNSW Sydney in Australia. She obtained her SJD degree from Duke University School of Law in the US. She was a Foreign Research Fellow at the Max Planck Institute for Comparative and International Private Law, Hamburg, Germany. She serves as a member on the International Law Association International Committee on Intellectual Property and Private International Law, an Arbitrator at the Hong Kong International Arbitration Center, Shanghai International Economic and Trade Arbitration Commission (Shanghai International Arbitration Center).

Emmanuel Laryea

Emmanuel Laryea is an Associate Professor in the Law Faculty, Monash University, and a member of the Monash Centre for Commercial Law and Regulatory Studies. Dr Laryea's teaching and research interest is in international economic law and African development. He is a Supervising Professor on UNCTAD's IIAs Mapping Project. He is the author of several publications, including *Paperless Trade: Opportunities, Challenges and Solutions* (Kluwer, 2002), and co-editor of *International Economic Law: Voices of Africa* (2012) and *International Economic Law and African Development* (2014) both published by Siber Ink, Cape Town, South Africa.

Ching-fu Lin

Ching-fu Lin is Assistant Professor of Law at National Tsing Hua University, where he teaches international health law, food law and policy, and international law and global governance. Professor Lin received his LLM and SJD from Harvard Law School, with the honours of John Gallup Laylin Memorial Prize (best paper in public international law) and Yong K Kim Memorial Prize (best paper in East Asian legal studies). He holds a double degree in law (LLB) and chemical engineering (BS) from National Taiwan University. Professor Lin has served as Visiting Fellow at the Graduate Institute of International and Development Studies in Geneva.

Han-wei Liu

Han-Wei Liu is Assistant Professor of Law at National Tsing Hua University, where he researches and teaches in international economic law, cyber-law, international law and global governance, and patent law, among others. Professor Liu received his PhD (summa cum laude) from the Graduate Institute, Geneva on a Kathryn Davis Scholarship, and his Masters from Oxford and Columbia on a Chevening Scholarship and Taiwan Government Scholarship, respectively. Prior to academia, he worked at Baker & McKenzie and Russin & Vecchi. Professor Liu holds visiting posts in Harvard and Columbia Law Schools and has served as a staff editor of the *Columbia Journal of European Law*.

Chang-fa Lo

Chang-fa Lo is Justice of the Constitutional Court of the ROC (Taiwan). He was Chair Professor and Lifetime Distinguished Professor at National Taiwan University (NTU); Dean of NTU Law; Director of the Asian Center for WTO and International Health Law and Policy of NTU; Commissioner of Taiwan's Fair Trade Commission & International Trade Commission. He received his SJD from Harvard Law. He was a panellist for two WTO disputes and is a member of the Permanent Group of Experts. He is chairman of the Asia WTO Research Network. He has authored 12 books and about 100 journal papers and book chapters and edited six books.

Nicholas Morris

Nicholas Morris is an Adjunct Professor in the Faculty of Law, UNSW Sydney; a Guest Professor at the China Executive Leadership Academy, Pudong (where he has lectured since 2004); and a Visiting Fellow at the Institute for New Economic Thinking in Oxford. In China, he has advised the Ministry of Finance on debt management and banking reform, and the Securities Investor Protection Fund (a subsidiary of the capital market regulator, CSRC) on securities regulation. He has also advised various Chinese development zones, the Chinese electricity and gas industries, and worked on the development of emissions trading schemes.

Shin-yi Peng

Shin-yi Peng is Professor of Law at National Tsing Hua University. Professor Peng has published articles in Asia, the United States and Europe. She is a frequent speaker at various international conferences, including the conferences organised by WTO Headquarters in Geneva. She is the Case Author of the Sixth EMC2 on WTO Law. Professor Peng has received a number of awards including the Outstanding Research Award from the National Science Council of Taiwan. She is a member of the Indicative List of Governmental and Non-Governmental Panellists for resolving WTO disputes. She is Co-Executive Vice President of the Society of International Economic Law (SIEL).

Colin B Picker

Professor Colin Picker (AB Bowdoin, JD Yale, PhD UNSW) is the Dean of the School of Law at the University of Wollongong in New South Wales, Australia. In addition to founding the CIBEL at UNSW when he was a professor, he was previously a founder and the first executive Vice-President of the Society of International Economic Law (SIEL). During that time, he helped create numerous regional networks for the field—in Africa, Latin America and in Asia. He has published widely in the areas of IEL, international law and comparative law. His numerous publications have appeared in leading publishers and journals around the world.

Takemasa Sekina

Takemasa Sekina is Associate Professor at Nagoya University of Commerce & Business (NUCB) in Japan. He received his legal education at Keio University, Japan (PhD and LLM) and was later engaged as a post-doctoral Research Fellow at the Japan Society for Promotion of Science (JSPS). He is currently a board member of the Government Procurement Review Board in Japan, and is on several research projects hosted by Japanese governmental institutions, such as the Ministry of Foreign Affairs of Japan and the Research Institute of Economy, Trade and Industry (RIETI).

Ken Shao

Ken Shao (PhD, LLM London, LLB Nanjing) is Professor of Law at the University of Western Australia. He specialises in Chinese culture and history, China's innovation economy and global knowledge governance issues. He has a leading teaching track-record in Chinese law education for the non-Chinese learner and is the founder of two Chinese law programmes in Australian universities. He is an education committee member of the Australia China Business Council (ACBC), an adjunct professor/fellow at the China University of Political Science and Law and the Centre for Studies of Intellectual Property Rights of Zhongnan University of Economics and Law.

Elizabeth Sheargold

Elizabeth Sheargold is a Legal Adviser at the Iran–United States Claims Tribunal and a PhD candidate with the Global Economic Law Network at Melbourne Law School. Previously, she worked in the Melbourne office of law firm Allens Arthur Robinson (now Allens Linklaters) and as Associate Director of the Center for Climate Change Law at Columbia University in New York. She completed her BA LLB (Hons) at the University of Melbourne, and her LLM at Columbia University.

Jingxia Shi

Jingxia Shi is Professor of International Business and Economic Law at the University of International Business and Economics (UIBE) Law School, China. She serves as the Director of UIBE International Law Institute (ILI) and UIBE Research Center for Unification of Commercial Law (RCUCL). She earned her BA, LLB and PhD in international law from Wuhan University. She also holds an LLM degree and JSD degree from Yale Law School. Her research focuses on international trade and investment law with many publications on trade in services and cross-border insolvency. She frequently counsels the Chinese government and large companies.

Tania Voon

Tania Voon is Professor at Melbourne Law School and was previously Associate Dean (Research). She is a former Legal Officer of the WTO Appellate Body Secretariat and has practised with King & Wood Mallesons and the Australian Government Solicitor and taught at the National University of Singapore, Georgetown University, the University of Western Ontario, the University of British Columbia, and other Australian universities. Tania undertook her LLM at Harvard Law School and her PhD at the University of Cambridge. She is a member of the Energy Charter Treaty's Roster of Panellists and the WTO's Indicative List of Governmental and Non-Governmental Panellists.

Heng Wang

Heng Wang is Associate Professor at UNSW Law, and co-director of UNSW Law's China International Business and Economic Law (CIBEL) Initiative. He is University Visiting Professorial Fellow at Southwest University Political Science and Law in Chongqing, China. His research has been quoted by scholars such as those from Oxford University and the Max Planck Institute. Heng has presented at WTO Headquarters and leading institutions including Harvard University, New York University and the LSE, and has taught in Australia, Canada, China, Japan and the US as a visiting professor. He was or is executive council member of one global, two Asian and all three Chinese societies of international economic law.

Junfang (Emma) Xi

Junfang Xi is Associate Professor of International Economics and Trade at Antai College of Economics and Management, Shanghai Jiao Tong University (SJTU) and a Fellow of UNSW Law's CIBEL initiative. Her research interests include international trade rules, WTO rules, and regional economic integration. She has been a visiting scholar at Marshall School of Business, University of Southern California (USC) and Sauder Business School, University of British Columbia (UBC), Canada. She is currently on secondment at UNSW Sydney as the Chinese Director of the Confucius Institute.

Shu Zhang

Shu Zhang is a Lecturer at the Deakin Law School and a fellow of the CIBEL Initiative, UNSW Law. Shu obtained her PhD degree from UNSW Law School in 2015. Before that Shu graduated from Law School, Peking University, China, and was an exchange student at Duke University School of Law. Shu's research interests focus on the law implementation and dispute resolution in trade, commerce and investment practices in the Asia-Pacific region and particularly, from China's perspective. Shu has conducted several research projects with the Beijing Arbitration Commission and the Australian Centre for International Commercial Arbitration.

Weihuan Zhou

Weihuan Zhou is a Senior Lecturer in the Faculty of Law, UNSW Sydney and a member of UNSW Law's CIBEL Initiative. He is a former legal consultant at the Institute for Training and Technical Cooperation of the WTO and has practised trade and commercial law with Corrs Chambers Westgarth. He has acted for governments and multinational companies in many major trade and investment matters. Weihuan obtained his LLM and PhD from the University of Sydney and has published widely on WTO law, trade remedies and free trade agreements. His work has been cited by research reports to the European Parliament and Australia's Productivity Commission.

List of Abbreviations

ASEAN–Australia-New Zealand FTA	AANZFTA
Australia–China Youth Association	ACYA
Association of Southeast Asian Nations	ASEAN
Bilateral Investment Treaty	BIT
China–Australia Millennial Project	CAMP
China–Australia Free Trade Agreement	ChAFTA
Communist Party of China	CPC
Australian Department of Foreign Affairs and Trade	DFAT
European Union	EU
Foreign Acquisitions and Takeovers Act 1975	FATA
Foreign Acquisitions and Takeovers Regulation	FATR
Free Trade Agreement	FTA
General Agreement on Trade in Services	GATS
General Agreement on Tariffs and Trade	GATT
International Centre for Settlement of Investment Disputes	ICSID
International Investment Agreement	IIA
Investor–State Dispute Settlement	ISDS
Australia-Japan Economic Partnership Agreement	JAEPA
Jiangsu Industrial Technology Research Institute	JITRI
Most-Favoured-Nation	MFN
Multinational Corporations	MNCs
Chinese Ministry of Commerce	MOFCOM
Chinese National Development and Reform Commission	NDRC
Regional Comprehensive Economic Partnership	RCEP
Trans-Pacific Partnership	TPP
Agreement on Trade-Related Investment Measures	TRIMS
Agreement on Trade-Related Aspects of Intellectual Property Rights	TRIPS
Chinese State Intellectual Property Office	SIPO
US Small Business Technology Transfer	STTR
Vienna Convention on the Law of Treaties	VCLT

Part I

An Introduction to ChAFTA

1

Australia, China and ChAFTA: Punching Above both Belt and Weight

COLIN B PICKER

I. INTRODUCTION

THIS BOOK PROVIDES readers with a unique opportunity to learn about a new regional trade agreement (RTA)—the China–Australia Free Trade Agreement (ChAFTA or the Agreement).[1] This new Agreement, which only came into operation in late 2015, reflects much of the most modern and up-to-date approaches within the international economic legal order (IELO)—at a substantive as well as formative/developmental level. Furthermore, it involves two important participants in the IELO—China and Australia. As such, it is an important modern and ongoing development that should be understood internationally as well as regionally and locally. This introduction will briefly make that case.

Substantively, ChAFTA is very typical of one type of the modern generation of RTAs, far removed from its earlier cousins that came into being decades ago. Many of those older RTAs were negotiated in the years before and in the decade after the World Trade Organization (WTO) was created in 1995—before it was known in what ways or how quickly (or slowly) the overlaying IELO architecture (mainly the WTO) would develop or how the new post-Cold War economic legal order would shape up.[2] Those early RTAs were created in the shadow of the Bretton Woods system (and specifically the subsequent International Trade Organization (ITO) and the General Agreement on Tariffs and Trade (GATT) negotiations) and

[1] Free Trade Agreement between the Government of Australia and the Government of the People's Republic of China (signed 17 June 2015, entered into force 20 December 2015) [2015] ATS 15 (ChAFTA).

[2] The vast majority of today's RTAs have been negotiated prior to 2005. See 'Facts and Figures: How Many Reginal Trade Agreements Have Been Notified to the WTO?' (WTO RTA Gateway, 2017), www.wto.org/english/tratop_e/region_e/regfac_e.htm.

out of the eventual compromise that led to Article XXIV of GATT 1947.[3] In contrast, more recent RTAs are now too far removed from that time and its contexts, and now may represent a new approach, one that begins to shift away from the conceptual confines of Article XXIV. Article XXIV when conceived was primarily concerned about trade diversion—and indeed, historically RTAs were often crafted so as to divert trade in a mutually beneficial way for the parties—to the harm of everyone else.[4] But, arguably today RTAs are more often born from the need to bypass the gridlock of the moribund WTO or for experimentation in liberalisation within the more specific contexts of bilateral or regional relationships. The concern today is less likely trade diversion and more likely the long-term harm to multilateralism as opposed to individual economic dislocations. If so, perhaps it is time to rethink Article XXIV and its equivalent under the General Agreement on Trade in Services (GATS)—Article V of GATS. In the meantime, the new generation of RTAs are leading the way. ChAFTA, as one of the newest of the modern generation RTAs, is also at the forefront of innovation, for example, through its built-in renegotiation commitments[5] and deliberately asymmetric commitments reflecting current realities that are expected to change going forward (eg, its inclusion of both positive and negative list approach to services commitments).[6] Given these and its other developments, the many different contributions in this book that explore ChAFTA's commitments are clearly relevant and important even outside China and Australia.

In addition to a move away from the original concerns of Article XXIV, modern RTAs reflect different geopolitical and economic realities from even 20 years ago—ones radically different from 1947, from 1995, and even from 2015. Today, unlike 1947 and even 1995 the IELO includes a strong and active China, which is now asserting itself regionally (eg, in the South China Seas) and globally (eg, through the One Belt One Road (OBOR) policy). Also, Australia is today not the subservient cousin of the United States it was in 1947, or 1995—and perhaps even significantly less than in 2015, as it slowly emerges from its post-war military reliance on the United States and given confused Trump national security and foreign policy signals. Similarly, the IELO would seem to no longer be led by either the Americans or the Europeans. The United States under Trump drifts in a

[3] See generally CB Picker, 'Regional Trade Agreements v the WTO: A Proposal for Reform of Article XXIV to Counter this Institutional Threat' (2005) 26 *University of Pennsylvania Journal of International Economic Law* 267, 280–81.

[4] ibid.

[5] See, eg, ChAFTA (n 1) Art 8.24.3. After the entry into force of this Agreement, at a time to be mutually agreed by the Parties, the Parties shall initiate the next round of the negotiation on trade in services in the form of negative listing approach, and conclude such negotiation as soon as they could.

[6] See the chapters in this book on services for detailed discussion of the differentiated commitments.

destructive manner through the world order (from undermining NATO to the WTO to NAFTA), while the EU is struggling with an existential crisis brought on by Brexit and other pressures (such as the refugee crisis). While ChAFTA was negotiated before all these most recent developments, it is nonetheless scheduled for further negotiations to extend and correct aspects of the current Agreement—with those negotiations taking place during this new post-Trump, post-Brexit, post-OBOR reality. Hence, following the development of ChAFTA may be akin to observing the conduct of an experiment, with the results of utility across the world—for new RTAs, for understanding China's future directions in the IELO, and for seeing how America's traditional allies operate in this new reality.

Therefore, this introductory chapter focuses on developing further this idea that ChAFTA represents something important for international economic law (IEL) scholars, practitioners and officials—supporting the very title of the book, 'The China–Australia Free Trade Agreement: A 21st-Century Model'. In other words, this chapter will develop the case that ChAFTA is worth exploring not only for the reasons already noted, but also due to the specific parties that are involved—parties whose historic and ongoing role and relationships are both critical in the development of the new IELO and also provide a counterpoint to the usual subjects of IEL analysis—the United States and Europe. In so doing, this introductory chapter will also consider how the book's individual chapters, focusing on specialised aspects of the Agreement, explore the many new features that were not present when the WTO or early RTAs were negotiated, providing insights and lessons about those new or more important trade issues for the twenty-first century, specifically, with focus on the latest approaches to the regulation of investment, twenty-first century services and the emerging digital/knowledge economy.

Finally, in addition to being important for IEL participants around the world wishing to understand the latest approaches and movement in IEL, early analyses of ChAFTA will be important locally and regionally. For, as noted above, ChAFTA has built-in commitments to further negotiations and therefore this book's contributions should also be critical for those ongoing and planned negotiations. In addition to providing deep level analyses of ChAFTA in general and in context, specific chapters will be of direct importance in those renegotiations. For example, the chapters exploring the investment provisions of ChAFTA are especially relevant given both parties have committed to begin discussing unfinished business, such as the investment provisions, and to work to further deepen and liberalise the Agreement.[7] This book is therefore both of local and current salience, as well as providing timeless analysis of features of the IELO for other states

[7] See, eg, ChAFTA (n 1) Art 9.9.3.

and IEL participants in the region and indeed around the world as they all develop their own approaches and find their way through the IELO.

II. AUSTRALIA AND CHINA: PUNCHING ABOVE WEIGHT AND WAISTLINE

It is legitimate to wonder why IEL practitioners, scholars, students or government officials would be interested in an RTA between the relatively empty and barren country of Australia and the newly emergent quasi-developed quasi-market economy of China. Similarly, the relevance of ChAFTA is not immediately clear to outside observers, but that is discussed in the next section of this chapter (the analyses and insights in the contributions to this book provide the evidence to make a strong case that ChAFTA's substantive aspects should be of more than local interest). This section, however, first focuses on the global, and specifically IELO relevance of the two parties. This section explores why their respective positions within the world are in fact significantly greater than would have been thought given their size (Australia—too small in the IELO) or 'youth' and behaviour (China—too newly joined to the IELO or too different in its behaviour).

A. Australia: 'Punching Above its Weight'

Australia is not the first country that comes to mind when considering IEL. While geographically impressive, being the only continent-size country, it is sparsely populated with a mere 24 million or so inhabitants.[8] Many cities in the world easily exceed that number (eg, Tokyo, Manila, Delhi, etc).[9] Much of the continent is inhospitable desert, while its climate fluctuates from flood to drought. Furthermore, it is somewhat off the main trade routes—located far down in the southern hemisphere. Nonetheless, it has a very high participation in the world's economy, both in relative and in absolute terms. Despite being fifty-first by population, it is ranked as the twelfth biggest economy in the world.[10] Its educational base is very well developed, especially in the fields relevant to the IELO—it has four law schools in the top 20 of the world, with corresponding significant contributions to IEL scholarship and activity.[11] That influence is also reflected at the governmental

[8] 'The World Factbook' (Central Intelligence Agency), www.cia.gov/library/publications/the-world-factbook/geos/as.html.

[9] See 'World's Largest Cities' *Worldatlas* (2016), www.worldatlas.com/citypops.htm.

[10] 'World in Figures: Rankings' *The Economist* (2017), worldinfigures.com/rankings/topic/7.

[11] QS Subject Rankings in 2017. See 'QS World University Rankings: Law' (QS Top Universities, 2017), www.topuniversities.com/university-rankings/university-subject-rankings/2017/law-legal-studies.

levels—with the Australian government taking a leading role in international activities around the world, and especially in IEL. Australia has been a major influence in the development of free trade agreements (FTAs) in the region.[12] It has also been exceptionally active in the development of mega-RTAs, as evidenced by its involvement in the Regional Comprehensive Economic Partnership (RCEP) and the Trans-Pacific Partnership (TPP) (and its likely successor). Although Australia is today not as active in the WTO's Dispute Settlement Body (DSB) as it used to be, that recent inactivity should not be a measure of its relevance to the IELO—for participation in the DSB is not just a factor of involvement in the IEL, but rather likely reflects cultural and political forces that either encourage or discourage participation in disputes or reflect a willingness to settle disputes rather than permit them to go to the panel stage. That being said, it has been involved in recent important disputes, most notably and currently in the seminal 'Plain Packaging' case.[13] Australia's role in IEL is thus well established—from its significant involvement in the creation of the ITO and GATT[14] to its creation of the Cairns Group[15] to frequent participation in the Doha Round as one of the 'group of five'.[16] To use a boxing metaphor, Australia truly does 'punch above its weight'.[17]

Australia is also geopolitically important. Since the Second World War it has been one of America's closest allies. The fact that Australia sent its own soldiers to fight in Vietnam, Iraq and Afghanistan alongside the United States' military is evidence of a commitment no other country has shown to their alliances with the United States. And yet—China has become a critical economic partner of Australia.[18] Furthermore, from a regional

[12] See T Sekine, chapter 5, section III, page 85 bottom.

[13] 'DS434: Australia—Certain Measures Concerning Trademarks and Other Plain Packaging Requirements Applicable to Tobacco Products and Packaging' (WTO, 7 July 2016), www.wto.org/english/tratop_e/dispu_e/cases_e/ds434_e.htm.

[14] See, eg, A Capling, 'The "Enfant Terrible": Australia and the Reconstruction of the Multilateral Trading System 1946–48' (2000) 40 (1) *Australian Economic History Review* 1, 1–21.

[15] See, eg, RA Higgott and AF Cooper, 'Middle Power Leadership and Coalition Building: Australia, the Cairns Group, and the Uruguay Round of Trade Negotiations' (1990) 44 (4) *International Organization* 589, 589–632. See also P Gallagher, 'Setting the Agenda for Trade Negotiations: Australia and the Cairns Group' (1988) 42 (1) *Australian Outlook* 3, 3–8.

[16] The group included the EU, the United States, Japan, Canada and Australia. See P Blustein, *Misadventures of the Most Favoured Nations: Clashing Egos, Inflated Ambitions, and the Great Shambles of the World Trade System* (New York, Public Affairs, 2009).

[17] To 'punch above weight' means '[i]f a country or business punches above its weight, it becomes involved in, or succeeds in, an activity that needs more power, money, etc. than it seems to have'. 'Meaning of "Punch Above Your Weight" in the English Dictionary' (*Cambridge Dictionary*, 2017), dictionary.cambridge.org/dictionary/english/punch-above-your-weight. The origin comes from boxing when contestants would only fight competitors of comparable weight—there being a heavy weight advantage when it comes to punches. See G Martin, 'The Meaning and Origin of the Expression: Punch Above One's Weight' (*The Phrase Finder*, 2017), www.phrases.org.uk/meanings/290900.html.

[18] It is Australia's number one export and import partner. See 'The World Factbook' (n 8).

perspective Australia has a strong belief and commitment to its future in Asia, and it does seem that Asia is likely of more relevance, especially in the long term, than North America.[19] Hence, Australia's interaction with both China and the United States can perhaps be viewed as a 'bell weather' of global geopolitics—especially in the post-Trump and in the current China Sea disputes environment. Eyes will be on Australia—and its economic relationship with China, especially when it comes time for the next round of negotiations of ChAFTA. At that time, the world will observe Australia's ability to navigate its complex and potentially conflict-ridden relationships with the United States and China.

B. China: 'Punching Above the Waistline'

While academic publications rarely focus on Australia's involvement with the IELO, it is a different matter with respect to China. Indeed, yet another book on China and its interaction with the IELO will come as no surprise and may also be viewed as not being all that worthy of attention (especially if it involves its interaction with a smaller country like Australia). But, many analyses of China in the IELO are concerned with China being the 'other'—as being outside the 'Club' due to its different characteristics and contexts and consequent perceived behaviours.[20] This is not surprising given how different China appears to the traditional power bases of the IELO (Europe and America). The perceived sources of China's difference include the fact that China: has the largest population in the world; is relatively newly industrialised/modernised; is a new superpower; is under tight internal political control, including restrictions on free speech; employs a centralised non-market economy structure; has perceived rampant corruption; is at least nominally a socialist system; has had historic and destructive instabilities (even in the second half of the twentieth century); and finally has strong and ancient non-Western characteristics. These traits are often viewed by many as obstacles to China having a 'regular' or 'normal' participation in the IELO. For some there is an even greater concern, that China's differences create a critical challenge to the established, largely Western, neo-liberal approaches of the modern international legal order. Many, rightly or wrongly, then believe China is a power that is outside what is considered normal or acceptable in the IELO. Those views are informed, rightly or wrongly, by

[19] See, eg, Australian Government, *Australia in the Asian Century* (White Paper, 2012), www.defence.gov.au/whitepaper/2013/docs/australia_in_the_asian_century_white_paper.pdf.

[20] See T Webster, 'China's Implementation of WTO Decisions' in C Picker, L Toohey and J Greenacre (eds), *China in the International Economic Order: New Directions and Changing Paradigms* (New York, Cambridge University Press, 2015) 98–102 (providing background of these sorts of views).

the perception that the IELO is mostly made up of middle-sized neo-liberal countries where governmental participation in the economy is viewed with disfavour. China is also often viewed, again—rightly or wrongly, as a rule breaker in the IELO, that it continually fails to honour its commitments—with abuses ranging from permitting violations of intellectual property to providing unfair subsidies to currency manipulation and so on. To extend the boxing metaphor, it is believed by many that China too often 'punches below the belt'.[21]

But, China today is perhaps no more of a rule breaker in the IELO than the other major powers. Indeed, many recent analyses of China's actions in the IELO suggest it is no worse than the other large powers. For example, recent studies suggest it behaves comparably in such critical measurements as WTO DSB compliance.[22] Furthermore, its domestic non-market centralised controls are diminishing more and more each year (via such initiatives as the Shanghai Free Trade Zone), and certainly may also suffer from decentralised provincial level challenges as opposed to centrally directed violations of IELO obligations. Certainly, there remain areas of concern for other members of the IELO, but then every complex economy provides areas of concern to others, just as many have provinces and other sub-federal entities with actions that lead to IEL liabilities for the federal or central government. So, while China may still occasionally 'punch below the belt', as do so many others in the IELO, it also can be viewed more and more as a party that now regularly 'punches above the belt' in the IELO arena—becoming a rule follower more than a rule breaker. Indeed, China is now much more active in the WTO's ongoing negotiations, in its DSB, in developing investment treaties, and in regional arrangements such as the RCEP. Hence, more and more it will be the case that China's interactions with the IELO will be viewed as 'normal'. Therefore, when it is innovative in the IELO, as is the case in ChAFTA, its actions should be worthy of emulation and attention from the rest of the world.

So—while both Australia and China are often viewed as largely irrelevant to the positive development of the IELO, one because of its size, the other because of its perceived character and behaviours, it may in fact be the case that both play a role different from expected—one punching above its weight, the other punching above the belt. As such, both deserve to be

[21] This phrase comes from boxing and other contact sports where it is not permitted to hit below the waist belt. It means, among other things, to act unfairly. See G Martin, 'The Meaning and Origin of the Expression: Below the Belt' (*The Phrase Finder*, 2017), www.phrases.org.uk/meanings/61100.html.

[22] Webster (n 20) 110–11. "China's compliance with the WTO, in contrast, has significantly exceeded its performance in other legal regimes. In many instances, China has made major revisions to its domestic legal system in order to comply with the DSB rulings. Moreover, China has done so typically within the reasonable period of time in which it agreed to do so." (footnotes omitted).

taken as seriously as the other major participants in the IELO. Accordingly, when they enter into a modern and innovative RTA, that RTA then deserves to be considered for it is likely to be of relevance to the development of the IELO. The next section further develops this idea as it draws on this book's contributions to show the many interesting and innovative approaches and issues for the larger IELO that are explicitly part of ChAFTA.

III. THE RELEVANCE OF CHAFTA'S APPROACHES FOR THE REST OF THE WORLD

As the contributors to this book note, ChAFTA has certain interesting features that can be explored to better understand the content of these new generations of RTA. ChAFTA also provides an example of an RTA that can be assessed to see how it may survive and thrive in the dynamic post-Brexit, post-Trump, post-OBOR economic legal environment—environments that are clearly both more dynamic and more static than anyone would have predicted at the birth of this modern international trade environment in 1995. As a result, a modern RTA needs to anticipate rapidly changing technologies and other forces even as it copes with the profound depression of a dysfunctional WTO in the IELO. Yet, these new RTAs must also navigate the turbulent waters caused by new and emerging mega-RTAs that engulf or encircle its participants. It is precisely issues such as these that the contributions in this book consider as they explore the many significant aspects of ChAFTA, from domestic constitutional concerns to encircling mega-RTAs to the challenges raised by pre-existing investment agreements to the role that ChAFTA will play in nurturing the dynamic 'innovation economy'.

In exploring these issues and the challenges to a modern RTA this book is divided into four main themes: (A) ChAFTA in its many contexts; (B) services; (C) investment issues; and (D) the knowledge economy. The first part focuses on the wider contexts of ChAFTA because the contexts provide both the rationale and fundamental environments within which ChAFTA will either succeed or fail. The next three parts then delve down into ChAFTA's details as the contributions address the themes raised above, for it is ChAFTA's approaches to services, investment and the knowledge economy which highlight its value as a lesson and harbinger of China's and other states' future RTAs and interactions with the wider IELO. Other subfields could also have been explored—such as its approach to goods or technical barrier to trade—but it is ChAFTA's consideration of these three other fields that are mostly novel or critical for the parties and the development of IEL.

But before those sections, this book also provides a second introduction to consider in detail ChAFTA's provisions—albeit from an analytical perspective. That chapter, by Heng Wang in 'An Analytical Introduction to ChAFTA: Features and Challenges', takes readers through ChAFTA's central components during which Wang notes the role of pragmatism and innovation in ChAFTA. Might this suggest that ChAFTA can serve as a safe opportunity for China to experiment with a developed Western country? The lessons from which could then be used in its later negotiations with other Western systems? Specifically, Wang's discussion of ChAFTA's scheduled approach—with renegotiation built in—suggests a model that might suit China as it permits the creation of an initial agreement even before reaching the confidence levels required for a more detailed and demanding RTA—one that can then be created as part of the later negotiations.

A. Contexts

Following the introductory chapters, the first part of the book then considers the contexts relevant to ChAFTA—from internal to regional to global contexts. The first explores a context insufficiently explored in most IEL works—the legal-cultural context.[23] Nicholas Morris' chapter, 'A Comparative Context: Ensuring Australian and Chinese Legal Systems Coexist to Facilitate Harmonious and Trustworthy Trade', explores the role of the Australian and Chinese legal cultures and in particular their impact on such critical issues as the trust needed to make the Agreement work. His examination and recommendations should be considered by those directly involved in the implementation and renegotiation of the Agreement. Given the levels of mistrust in the world with China's involvement in the IELO (the massive accession agreement, although now an old example, still reflects the lingering issue) and China's mistrust of the rest of the world's motivations for their approaches (such as the continuing de facto non-market status), the pathway Morris describes is one that should be taken on board as other countries work with China on RTAs and other IEL agreements.

Of course, ChAFTA does not take place in isolation—it must coexist in the larger region and among and within the various other IEL agreements existing and under consideration. Chang-fa Lo in his chapter, 'ChAFTA's External Impact on Related Mega-FTAs', explores the role of ChAFTA on other agreements, especially the TPP Agreement and the RCEP—and the role of those Agreements, whether ultimately enacted or not, on ChAFTA. The relationship between all these Agreements spans everything from the geopolitics of the TPP Agreement to more technical issues such as the overlap in commitments among all the agreements. Geopolitically, Lo notes the critical role that is played by ChAFTA—counteracting the United States' attempted containment of China, especially as Australia is such an ally of

[23] But see CB Picker, 'Comparative Legal Cultural Analyses of International Economic Law: Insights, Lessons and Approaches' (2014) 6 *The Indian Journal of International Economic Law* 54, 54–83.

the United States. ChAFTA is strategically a critical part of the geopolitical puzzle of the region. But, the fact that Australia can simultaneously enter into ChAFTA and play a more adversarial role with China strongly suggests that it can be possible to separate geopolitics and economics. This supports a long-held view that progress within the IELO is typically independent of geopolitics.[24]

A more specific example of the fact that ChAFTA cannot be considered in isolation is found in Takemasa Sekine's chapter, 'The Australia–China FTA and Australia's FTAs with Other Asian Countries: Their Implications for Future SOE Regulation'. In that chapter, Sekine explores the many different ways that RTAs have dealt with SOEs (state-owned enterprises), from strict to moderate to no regulation, and finds that ChAFTA, surprisingly, follows the last—essentially no regulation of SOEs. Sekine's detailed analysis dives deep into the regulations of SOEs in the ChAFTA parties' other RTAs. This leads him to the conclusion that an Australian-style competitive neutrality approach would be compatible with ChAFTA and that the parties should and can progressively work towards that goal. Thus, this wider context suggests the future direction that should be taken with respect to SOEs between the ChAFTA parties.

B. Services

After considering the different context surrounding and impacting ChAFTA, this book turns to one of the most critical areas of the modern IELO—trade in services. As states become ever more developed more of their economy ends up falling within the services sector, and indeed the share of their international trade will increasingly be dominated by services. This is already the case for the United States.[25] Australia too is significantly reliant on its services sector, with ChAFTA's main benefits perhaps being the potential opening up of China to Australian service exporters.[26] Four of the book's authors focus on services—covering very different perspectives and aspects of the Agreement—and correspondingly different insights and lessons for the parties, the region and the rest of the IELO.

First Jingxia Shi in her chapter, 'Services Liberalisation in ChAFTA: Progress Assessment and the Way Forward', presents an overview of the unprecedented market access commitments provided by ChAFTA. She then focuses on the unique mixed scheduling approach of ChAFTA—that

[24] See, eg, A Reich, 'The Threat of Politicization of the WTO' (2005) 26 *University of Pennsylvania Journal of International Economic Law* 779.

[25] See 'The World Factbook' (n 8).

[26] 'The services sector is the largest part of the Australian economy, accounting for about 70% of GDP and 75% of jobs'. ibid.

Australia has committed to a negative list approach while China makes its services commitments via a positive list approach. This bifurcated approach reflects the current fundamental differences in the two parties' trade in services—each at different points on the economic development ladder. Shi then discusses the anticipated eventual move of China to a negative list approach via the planned negotiations—a mechanism that has much to offer—within ChAFTA and as a model for other agreements that face similar asymmetric economic development challenges.

The services discussion in the book then proceeds to consider at a detailed level three service areas that are especially relevant to the parties and to the rest of the world: the movement of individual cultural services providers; legal services; and education services. Each of the analyses provides valuable insights to the states, the IELO and, most relevantly some might say, to our readers (typically being lawyers and/or educators). These contributions clearly show the critical nature of services in the IELO—especially to advanced economies and their IELO specialists!

The first analysis of a detailed area of services, by Shin-yi Peng, Han-wei Liu and Ching-fu Lin, considers cultural services in the chapter 'Culture-Oriented Mode 4 under ChAFTA: Policy Considerations'. There they note that cultural services are invariably associated with individuals—be they chefs or musicians, all of whom can deliver those services via their presence in another market (Mode 4 delivery). This chapter's analysis is especially critical in today's world given the prominence of immigration and foreign workers in domestic politics. Indeed, this is even more the case as it relates to participation in the IELO—as evidenced by the significant role that migration and immigrants played in the lead up to the Brexit referendum. The analysis in this chapter shows that ChAFTA has clearly approached the issue in light of this modern context, but did so in a culturally focused and respectful manner.

The next examination of services, by Weihuan Zhou and Junfang Xi in their chapter, 'Breakthrough or Standstill? China's Liberalisation of Legal Services under ChAFTA', is important in showing the relationship between real and illusory services gains from trade agreements. It explores the trade in legal services provisions of the ChAFTA and hence is also of personal relevance to the many legal services providers that would be the likely readers of this book! The chapter's examination finds that ChAFTA has not really provided greater market access to Australian legal professionals than has been extended by China to other foreign legal professionals through such Chinese domestic initiatives as the Shanghai Free Trade Zone. Perhaps it is going too far to describe it as an illusory liberalisation, but certainly the lack of tangible benefit does raise some serious concerns.

Finally, and perhaps most relevant for Australia's economy is a chapter by Eva Chye, 'Trade in Education Services under ChAFTA: What does it Mean for Australia?' As Chye notes, this chapter explores the number three export and the number one services export of Australia—education services.[27] ChAFTA's new treatment of this vital industry is especially important as the industry has changed greatly since GATS was launched in 1995—with a dramatic reliance by the universities now on revenue generated by international students. ChAFTA thus provides a timely approach for this vital industry—updating approaches from GATS and reflecting, as noted by Chye, the specific context that China is the primary supplier of foreign students to Australia. Thus, for Australia given the centrality of education services to the economy, they were always going to be considered front and centre—especially when its number one export market, China, was the counterparty. This chapter also allows examination of the very industry of which many of the readers (be they scholars or students) are members, as well as by readers that used to be in that industry, for all government and private practitioners were themselves trained in those very universities—often outside their own country and hence were participants in the trade itself.

Critically, all these chapters on services show how an intensive goods-exporting economy, such as China, can reach a fair deal with a services-strong modern Western economy, such as Australia, so that both feel they have got a fair deal. In a time when trade deals are much maligned, ChAFTA is a breath of fresh air, clearly showing the benefits to sophisticated, but different economies, and how they can gain from trade. In some sense, it is a perfect example of Ricardian comparative advantage being used properly (or perhaps the more modern factor theorem approaches at play).

C. Investment

The next section of the book focuses on one of the linchpins of the future of the Australia–China relationship—investment. Four of the contributors explore different aspects of investment regulation and ChAFTA and in so doing provide insights of universal applicability for the IELO in general, for other RTAs specifically, and for Australia and China individually.

As with the services section of this book, first an overview is provided. Vivienne Bath delivers an in-depth general overview of the investment provisions in her chapter, 'Substantive Provisions in ChAFTA's Investment Chapter'. But, she also rightly notes the fact that 'after 10 years of negotiation, completion of most of the substantive provisions of the Investment Chapter

[27] 'The latest figures firm up education's position as Australia's third-largest export after coal and iron ore, as well as its position as the largest services export, well ahead of tourism'. T Dodd, 'Education Revenue Soars to Become Australia's 20 Billion Export' *Australia Financial Review* (3 February 2016), www.afr.com/news/policy/education/education-revenue-soars-to-become-australias-20-billion-export-20160203-gmke3k#ixzz4jkkXtrs0.

has been deferred for later negotiations'.[28] As such, this chapter provides analysis of the many interesting possibilities that may result from the future negotiations of the parties. Consequently, for the parties this is a critical chapter for when they sit down to negotiate. For the rest of the world it is also important, for it shows that even when an agreement does not tackle hard issues, it does not need to totally abandon them. Rather, it can merely postpone them for a later agreed upon time, during which mutual trust and understanding can develop to provide a more fertile field for the negotiations.

The book's consideration of investment then moves to tackle a fundamental issue for new agreements—what to do about prior agreements. Specifically, Tania Voon and Elizabeth Sheargold in their chapter, 'Australia, China and the Coexistence of Successive International Investment Agreements' consider the role and function of ChAFTA's investment provisions in light of a pre-existing 1988 Australia–China BIT.[29] As they note, the fundamental problem is that ChAFTA is but a skeleton of an investment chapter[30] with its focus being national treatment and Most-Favoured-Nation (MFN) treatment, yet still reflecting the very modern approach of providing substantive and procedural protections for state policies. In contrast, the older and pre-existing BIT contains the usual investment protections (fair and equitable treatment and expropriation protections) but does not carve out policy exceptions. This chapter unfortunately concludes that ChAFTA's new provisions and approaches are unlikely to displace the applicability of the prior BIT, leaving Australia open to outdated Investor–State Dispute Settlement (ISDS) claims. Luckily, as noted above, the parties will be sitting down to negotiate more comprehensive investment provisions which will hopefully cure this issue.

Given investment is at its heart an action within a country, more so than trade which involves the movement across borders, it makes sense to consider the investment provisions from the internal perspectives of the two countries involved. Accordingly, Shu Zhang considers internal Chinese aspects of ChAFTA's investment provisions in her chapter, 'A Comparative Review of the Investor–State Arbitration Clause in ChAFTA from China's Perspective: Moving Forwards or Sideways?' The chapter at a fundamental level considers whether or not ChAFTA's investor–state arbitration clause reflects China's progression towards including more comprehensive investor–state arbitration provisions in its IEL relations. Ultimately the chapter suggests it is not, which is a step backwards from China's other recent agreements. This raises many questions, of course. Among them is

[28] V Bath, chapter 10, page 195.

[29] Agreement between the Government of Australia and the Government of the People's Republic of China on the Reciprocal Encouragement and Protection of Investments (signed 11 July 1988, entered into force 11 July 1988) [1988] ATS 14.

[30] T Voon and E Sheargold, chapter 11, 215.

whether this is an indication of increased Chinese investment regulation conservatism. Regardless, other states need to be aware of this regression if they are going to be seeking investment arrangements with China.

The last investment chapter then looks at the investment provisions from an Australian perspective—albeit one focused on the internal constitutional challenges presented by Agreements such as ChAFTA. Lisa Burton Crawford, Patrick Emerton and Emmanuel Laryea in their chapter, 'Investor–State Dispute Settlement and the Australian Constitutional Framework', situate their analyses completely within Australia's constitutional law as they consider the constitutionality of ChAFTA's ISDS provisions. While ultimately the chapter finds that the Australian executive is not necessarily permitted to enter into these sorts of agreements in the absence of explicit legislative authorisation, this procedural requirement is not insurmountable.[31] But, if legislative support is provided then the democratic legitimacy of ISDS would be bolstered and given the often negative view of ISDS it would seem to be worth ensuring that those sorts of provisions are as embedded in the democratic process as possible. The constitutional analysis here, while centred on Australia, is nonetheless instructive in a time of continued challenge to the legitimacy of many aspects of the IELO. Furthermore, this chapter presents some of the constitutional and democratic challenges that may arise in today's IELO for new 'players' in the IELO—for example, newly democratic states (eg, Myanmar) or states that are recently re-entering the IELO as independent participants (eg, Britain post-Brexit).

D. The Knowledge Economy

The last section of the book provides three chapters that focus on cutting-edge issues in IEL that result from the interaction of new technologies and globalisation—as part of e-commerce or the knowledge economy. As in the other sections, the first chapter of this section, by Henry Gao in his chapter, 'E-Commerce in ChAFTA: New Wine in Old Wineskins?', provides an overview of e-commerce provisions—in ChAFTA, other RTAs, especially those of Australia and China, as well as providing the background on the efforts to develop provisions within the WTO. Ultimately, using those comparisons Gao concludes with recommendations that would improve the e-commerce chapter of ChAFTA were it to be part of the renewed negotiations.

Jeanne Huang in her chapter, 'Expanding the E-Commerce Chapter in ChAFTA: A Green Box, Orange Box and Red Box Approach', takes the analysis of ChAFTA's e-commerce into even deeper detail and critique,

[31] L Burton Crawford, P Emerton and E Laryea, chapter 13, page 277.

employing a green, orange and red box form of analysis of what might be possible when the parties seek to renegotiate and improve ChAFTA's e-commerce provisions. In doing so, she draws on other agreements, such as the TPP Agreement, as examples of what might be possible. Nonetheless, she takes into account the other critical contexts that may stand as obstacles to the further liberalisation of e-commerce—especially for China. In particular, she notes that China's approach towards the internet, freedom of expression and national security may very well present some significant challenges to future change in some of the areas of e-commerce.

The book concludes with Ken Shao's chapter, 'The Ideas Boom: The Innovation Economy in the Post-ChAFTA Australia–China Relationship', which explores the role of ChAFTA's intellectual property provisions in the context of what is emerging to be perhaps one of the most critical parts of the economy around the world—the boom in what Shao calls the 'innovation economy'. While admitting that ChAFTA's intellectual property provisions do not really go beyond those already committed in other agreements, especially the WTO, he applauds its 'flexible approach' as being ideally suited to nurturing this critical sector in both economies.

IV. CONCLUSION

This book's contributions will be critical for the ongoing development of ChAFTA. Hopefully the insights from those contributions will play a role in the forthcoming negotiations to improve, deepen and extend ChAFTA. But, as noted above, this book and ChAFTA itself, may also have a larger role to play in the IELO. While ChAFTA may seem to regulate a far-off narrow part of the world's trade, it is in fact of great relevance and importance beyond the two countries involved. Its relevance and importance is related to many very different factors, including: the fact that it reflects recent innovations in trade regulation, includes unique and innovative aspects; concerns two important countries and their regions for the IELO; and presents a model for RTAs between such disparate countries (Western and non-Western, developed and developing, massive and medium/small, and so on).

While of course ChAFTA involves two powers not typically part of the traditional power bases of the IELO, it nonetheless reflects the importance of the Asia-Pacific region, especially North–South economic relationships. ChAFTA also reflects the needs of Western middle powers (Australia) and newly developed non-Western powers (China), an interesting and all too often neglected bilateral relationship form. Also, given the United States' withdrawal from multilateralism and IEL while Europe is in an extended period of instability, it remains for countries like Australia and China to help lead any progress in the IELO. Fortunately, the many lessons for the world are clear from the contributions here.

Finally, as ChAFTA shows, the IELO is a world project. All are players. All contribute. By focusing mainly on the European Union and America or on clusters such as developing states or the BRICS or on the mega-RTAs it is too easy to miss developments elsewhere. ChAFTA is thus excellent for showing that there are other parts of the IELO that include sophisticated development within the IELO. Indeed, it is good for scholars, practitioners and officials to focus on run of the mill 'old-school' RTAs instead of the usual focus on the mega-RTAs (many of which are doomed to not be ratified or where the substantive parts simply reflect the lowest common denominator of the many parties). Regular RTAs are here to stay, continuing to form the backbone of the trade system. It would be too easy for scholars and IELO officials and practitioners to miss the lessons and insights of an agreement such as ChAFTA. This book's value is thus both in its contribution to the further development of ChAFTA, the RCEP, the TPP, the regions other relationships (economic as well as geopolitical) but also to the wider IELO. True, while China's participation in the IELO is not normally the place that many would look for global models or for new innovations and while Australia is too little considered at all, as the contributions in this book suggest, the ChAFTA example may be a place to look as the world wends its way through this new IELO.

2

An Analytical Introduction to ChAFTA: Features and Challenges

HENG WANG

I. INTRODUCTION

IN THE CONTEXT of burgeoning free trade agreements (FTAs), China has increased the speed of concluding and updating FTAs,[1] including the China–Korea Free Trade Agreement and the China–Australia Free Trade Agreement (ChAFTA). The ChAFTA negotiation was initiated in 2005 and finalised in 2014.[2] After lengthy negotiations of around 10 years, the Agreement became effective on 20 December 2015 and was notified to the World Trade Organization (WTO). It is the first FTA reached by China with a major developed economy 'with large economic aggregates',[3] and is deemed to be 'one of the free trade agreements signed by China so far with the highest level of trade and investment liberalization'.[4]

ChAFTA is among the high-level FTAs of China regarding the coverage of the FTA and depth of commitments. For instance, it contains chapters dedicated to issues of intellectual property and e-commerce, which are absent in China's early FTAs such as the China–Pakistan and China–Singapore trade

[1] For instance, China has no FTA concerning the services trade that came into effect during 2005–06. However, usually one or more of China's FTAs were concluded or upgraded in the years since 2007.

[2] 商务部国际司[Department of International Trade and Economic Affairs, Ministry of Commerce (DITEA), '中华人民共和国政府和澳大利亚政府自由贸易协定解读'['A Reading of the Free Trade Agreement Between the Government of Australia and the Government of the People's Republic of China'] (中国自由贸易区服务网[China FTA Network], 24 April 2017), fta.mofcom.gov.cn/article/chinaaustralia/chinaaustralianews/201506/22176_1.html (in Chinese) (DITEA).

[3] Ministry of Commerce (MOFCOM), 'Interpretation for the China–Australia Free Trade Agreement' (19 June 2015), english.mofcom.gov.cn/article/policyrelease/Cocoon/201510/20151001144954.shtml.

[4] 'Ministers of Commerce of China and Australia Officially Sign the Free Trade Agreement' (*China FTA Network*, 25 June 2015), fta.mofcom.gov.cn/enarticle/enaustralia/enaustralianews/201506/22317_1.html.

pacts. In particular, ChAFTA contains a number of new rules such as an electronic commerce chapter that is absent in previous FTAs, such as the China–New Zealand FTA. ChAFTA also contains deeper services commitments than earlier ones in areas such as legal and financial services.

However, ChAFTA is not comparable with deep FTAs such as the EU–Canada Comprehensive Economic and Trade Agreement (CETA) and the Trans-Pacific Partnership Agreement (TPP Agreement). It is particularly the case regarding non-trade concerns. ChAFTA does not deal with labour and state-owned enterprises (SOEs), while other issues (eg environment and competition) have only been touched upon. In contrast, the TPP Agreement develops special chapters to address each of these issues and many of these rules are subject to the dispute settlement system under the FTA.

ChAFTA supports not only the development of trade and investment but also the stable development of the Asia-Pacific region and the liberalisation of world trade.[5] ChAFTA fosters a stronger economic partnership between China and Australia. Eventually, the strong Australia–China trade and investment relationship will contribute to the stable development of the region and to the development of world trade.

ChAFTA will lay the groundwork for future and ongoing negotiations and development of other trade and investment agreements, including the Regional Comprehensive Economic Partnership (RCEP) to which Australia and China are parties. ChAFTA is also of strategic importance. For China, Australia is a valuable bridge between the trade interests of the US and China, since Australia is a major US ally and China is Australia's top trading partner.[6] Australia was also the first developed country to propose the negotiation of an FTA with China.[7] Australia not only has concluded an FTA with the US and China, but also is a party to the TPP and RCEP negotiations. Notably, ChAFTA is a dynamic and work-in-progress type agreement that envisages subsequent negotiations. Therefore, ChAFTA could carry considerable implications for China's future FTAs including China's response to the trade approach of the US, since ChAFTA could be used by China to test the waters for new approaches.

Notably, there is inherent pragmaticism in ChAFTA. Meanwhile, it pushes the envelope substantively and geopolitically, and provides a model for China and Australia in their future trade relationships with other countries, even as it is critical for both. In this context, this chapter will analyse two

[5] C Li, J Wang and J Whalley, 'China's Regional and Bilateral Trade Agreements' (January 2014) NBER Working Paper No 19853, www.nber.org/papers/w19853.

[6] N Salidjanova, 'China's Trade Ambitions: Strategy and Objectives behind China's Pursuit of Free Trade Agreements' (28 May 2015), www.uscc.gov/sites/default/files/Research/China's%20Trade%20Ambitions%20-%2005.28%2015.pdf, 33.

[7] K Deere, 'Saving Face after Seven Years: Australia–China FTA Negotiations and Lessons from New Zealand' (2013) 16 *International Trade and Business Law Review* 295.

questions, so far under-explored: what are the key features of ChAFTA? What are the challenges to ChAFTA? Sections II and III will discuss these questions respectively. Section IV will analyse the implications of ChAFTA for the two countries and beyond, and then conclude.

This chapter argues first that ChAFTA adopts a problem-solving approach to harvest 'low-hanging fruit' (eg, tariff cuts). Containing WTO-based and WTO-friendly rules, it focuses on trade and investment facilitation through market liberalisation and carefully written good governance norms. In spite of its short form investment chapter, the Agreement is not as shallow as one may first think. It stimulates development concerning, among other things, regulatory issues (eg, regulatory transparency and cooperation in financial services, regulatory autonomy in investment); the negative list approach for services and investment; investor–state dispute settlement; and the investment facilitation arrangement. Second, ChAFTA will meet challenges in implementation and future negotiations. The former includes the considerable need for wide-ranging cooperation, and in its usage. The latter probably includes managing the complexity of legal issues, as well as internal and external uncertainties (including the uncertain development of WTO law and the US–China Investment Treaty negotiations). Finally, the future of ChAFTA depends on bilateral cooperation in FTA implementation, and the political willingness to develop a rule-based system. If properly managed, ChAFTA might bring an incremental paradigm shift of China's FTAs, which will carry vast implications for China's participation in the international economic legal order.

II. THE FEATURES OF CHAFTA: A PROBLEM-SOLVING APPROACH?

ChAFTA is a pragmatic Agreement, focusing on 'pet peeves' and generally not 'rocking the boat'. It adopts a problem-solving approach to harvest 'low-hanging fruit' (eg, tariff cuts). China is the largest trading partner of Australia in terms of both imports and exports of goods, and Australia is China's second largest outbound investment destination.[8] China is Australia's top overseas market for services exports, and investment grows strongly between the two countries.[9] It is natural that ChAFTA highlights the importance of market liberalisation. Regarding tariff reduction, from day one of its implementation ChAFTA set Chinese and Australian import tariffs at zero for over 86 and 82 per cent of exports by the other

[8] DITEA (n 2).

[9] Department of Foreign Affairs and Trade, Australian Government (DFAT), 'Outcomes at a Glance' (13 February 2017), dfat.gov.au/trade/agreements/chafta/fact-sheets/Pages/key-outcomes.aspx.

party respectively, and this proportion will eventually increase to 96 and 100 per cent.[10] Included among this liberalisation is Australia's exports of agricultural produce, resources and energy, for which China is Australia's largest market.[11] Investment and services trade is also facilitated through, for instance, services market opening[12] and the increased thresholds of investment review.[13] Among developed countries, Australia receives the largest number of Chinese professionals.[14] Meanwhile, Australian private equity and fund investors are welcomed to participate in the Chinese market as qualified foreign investors, and the bilateral cooperation is to be strengthened to promote 'greater Australian mid-market size funds investment participation in China, as well as options to strengthen Australia–China Renminbi (RMB) fund partnerships in China'.[15]

Meanwhile, ChAFTA manages to innovate and extend what one considers typically to be the scope and coverage of FTAs. ChAFTA consists of 17 chapters and pertinent annexes. Most of the rules are found in the main text of ChAFTA. Besides four annexes to the Agreement (ie, Annexes I–IV), there are 11 annexes in various ChAFTA chapters (eg, Annexes 2-A to Chapter 2). Among them, Annex IV includes five side letters dealing with skills assessment and licensing, financial services, education, legal services, and transparency rules applicable to investor–state dispute settlement (ISDS). Moreover, the following related documents were concluded 'as part of the overall ChAFTA package but do not form part of the Agreement':[16] a side letter on traditional Chinese medicine; two Memorandums of Understanding (MOUs) on an investment facilitation arrangement, and on a work and holiday visa arrangement. These related documents were signed together with ChAFTA. Generally speaking, side letters in Annex IV as well as the relevant documents are relatively short. Many provisions of the annexes and related documents are not commonly found in early FTAs of China.

ChAFTA provisions, including services trade rules, are usually WTO-inspired. Although ChAFTA builds on WTO norms, it contains

[10] DFAT, 'Guide to Using ChAFTA to Export and Import Goods' (26 May, 2016), dfat.gov.au/about-us/publications/Documents/guide-to-using-chafta-to-export-and-import-goods.pdf.

[11] DFAT, 'Outcomes at a Glance' (n 9).

[12] DFAT, 'Factsheet: Trade in Services' (20 December 2016), dfat.gov.au/trade/agreements/chafta/fact-sheets/Pages/fact-sheet-trade-in-services.aspx. (China has made new commitments in sectors such as manufacturing services and aged care services.)

[13] DITEA (n 2). (Investment screening threshold in Australia has been increased from AUD$0.248 billion to AUD$1.078 billion.)

[14] ibid.

[15] Free Trade Agreement between the Government of Australia and the Government of the People's Republic of China (ChAFTA) (signed 17 June 2015, entered into force 20 December 2015) [2015] ATS 15, Side Letter on Financial Services.

[16] DFAT, 'FTA Text and Tariff Schedules', dfat.gov.au/trade/agreements/chafta/official-documents/Pages/official-documents.aspx.

innovations regarding investment and services trade that often highlight good governance. Several major and interrelated features of ChAFTA will be discussed below.

A. WTO-Based Rules

At its heart, ChAFTA is a WTO-inspired and traditional FTA, building on the rules of and commitments under the WTO regime. ChAFTA has similar coverage with WTO law except for a few of its chapters, such as that on investment. While trade in goods, trade in services, intellectual property and dispute settlement are among the major issues covered in ChAFTA, non-trade concerns are not addressed in a robust way. It is similar with the WTO norms in this respect.

WTO law significantly affects the shaping of the substantive rules and the state-to-state dispute settlement system (SSDS) under ChAFTA. Similar with other FTAs involving China, a free trade area is established under ChAFTA consistent with the WTO disciplines on FTAs, namely Article XXIV of the General Agreement on Tariffs and Trade 1994 (GATT 1994) and Article V of the General Agreement on Trade in Services (GATS).[17] The SSDS under ChAFTA is modelled on the WTO dispute settlement understanding. However, unlike the WTO ChAFTA does not establish the appeal system. A number of fundamental WTO rules are incorporated into ChAFTA, including general exceptions clauses (ie, GATT Article XX,[18] and GATS Article XIV).[19] In most cases, ChAFTA rules closely follow or rely on the WTO norms, particularly in the WTO covered areas such as services trade, technical barriers to trade (TBT Agreement) and sanitary and phytosanitary (SPS) measures, and trade remedies. For instance, ChAFTA contains nearly identical provisions to GATS.[20] Key terms of technical regulation, standards and conformity assessment procedures also have the same meaning in ChAFTA as those in Annex 1 of the TBT Agreement.[21]

In particular, ChAFTA builds on the Agreement on Trade Facilitation (TFA Agreement), the latest development of WTO law. Several key provisions of the TFA Agreement are reflected in ChAFTA.[22] Some examples could be given here. Interested persons can get responses to their enquiries on

[17] ChAFTA (n 15) Art 1.1.
[18] ibid Art 16.2.1.
[19] ibid Art 16.2.2.
[20] ibid Art 1.1; General Agreement on Trade in Services (GATS) (15 April 1994) LT/UR/A-1B/S/1 Art VI:6, docsonline.wto.org.
[21] ChAFTA (n 15) Art 6.3(b).
[22] DFAT, 'ChAFTA Summary of Chapters and Annexes' (26 August 2016), dfat.gov.au/trade/agreements/chafta/fact-sheets/Documents/chafta-summary-of-chapters-and-annexes.pdf, 2.

customs matters, with the relevant procedures published on the internet.[23] ChAFTA also resembles the TFA in obliging the parties, in the event they decline to issue an advance ruling on tariff classification and origin, to promptly send the written notification to the applicant including the basis of its decision.[24] As a WTO-plus trade facilitation measure, ChAFTA provides for 'duty- and tax-free temporary admission of containers, pallets and packing material used in the transportation of goods', which is not provided for in the WTO norms.[25]

In addition to substantial alignment with the WTO, WTO rules are highly relevant to the operation and enforcement of ChAFTA rules. WTO rules could be regarded as the standard or basis for the operation of ChAFTA. For instance, the enforcement of intellectual property rules is crucial and is closely connected with the Agreement on Trade-Related Aspects of Intellectual Property Rights (TRIPS Agreement). ChAFTA mandates that countries 'provide for criminal procedures and penalties in accordance with the TRIPS Agreement to be applied at least in cases of wilful trademark counterfeiting or copyright piracy on a commercial scale'.[26] It highlights the alignment with the TRIPS Agreement and is nearly identical to the WTO counterpart.[27] Here ChAFTA stands in contrasts with the TPP Agreement, which specifically notes the criminal procedures and penalties for the protection of intellectual property right.[28] The transparency of subsidy measures under ChAFTA also relies on notifications to the WTO.[29] Additionally, both parties are prohibited from applying or maintaining a bilateral safeguard measure on a product if the measure has been applied in accordance with GATT Article XIX and the WTO Agreement on Safeguards.[30] On a related note, measures taken under certain WTO rules are explicitly recognised. For example, ChAFTA does not affect the adoption of TBT measures by both parties pursuant to the rights and obligations under the TBT Agreement.[31]

Furthermore, many rights and obligations under the WTO law are affirmed or retained in ChAFTA. ChAFTA has not elaborated the difference between

[23] ChAFTA (n 15) Art 4.7.2; Agreement on Trade Facilitation (11 December 2013) WT/L/911; WT/MIN(13)/36 Arts 1.2, 1.3, docsonline.wto.org.

[24] ChAFTA (n 15) Art 4.9.3; Agreement on Trade Facilitation (n 23) Art 3.1.

[25] Free Trade Agreement between Australia and China (Goods and Services): Note on the Meeting of 7–8 November 2016 (24 November 2016) WT/REG369/M/1 para 1.18, docsonline.wto.org.

[26] ChAFTA (n 15) Art 11.21.2.

[27] Agreement on Trade-Related Aspects of Intellectual Property Rights (15 April 1994) LT/UR/A-1C/IP/1 Art 61, docsonline.wto.org.

[28] eg, Trans-Pacific Partnership Agreement (TPP Agreement) Arts 18.68.1 (criminal penalities relating to technological protection measures); 18.69.1 (criminal penalities concerning rights management information), ustr.gov/trade-agreements/free-trade-agreements/trans-pacific-partnership/tpp-full-text.

[29] ChAFTA (n 15) Art 7.10.2.

[30] ibid Art 7.3.4.

[31] ibid Art 6.2.4.

'affirmed' and 'retained', although they are common in upholding the WTO norms. For the former, they include the rights and obligations under the Agreement on the Application of Sanitary and Phytosanitary Measures (SPS Agreement),[32] and the TBT Agreement.[33] For the latter, WTO rights and obligations are retained, such as those under GATT Article XIX and the Agreement on Safeguards,[34] the Agreement on Implementation of Article VI of the General Agreement on Tariffs and Trade 1994,[35] and the Agreement on Subsidies and Countervailing Measures.[36] The most typical example is that ChAFTA does not 'confer any additional rights or impose any additional obligations' on both sides regarding measures applied under GATT Article XIX and the Agreement on Safeguards.[37] It explicitly emphasises that ChAFTA follows exactly the WTO norms here. That said, WTO-extra (eg, investment) and WTO-plus (eg, certain trade facilitation provisions) rules exist in ChAFTA. In such a situation, the WTO-plus rules of ChAFTA often build on the WTO commitments of both parties as is the case with people mobility, services trade, SPS and TBT measures.[38]

Although the reliance on the WTO is common in FTAs, it reflects the pragmaticism of ChAFTA since the WTO rules are easily accepted by both nations. Moreover, both sides are committed to WTO approaches by affirming and using them in ChAFTA. Pragmaticism is also reflected in the coverage of ChAFTA that resembles the WTO law in many respects. In contrast, ChAFTA has narrow coverage compared with deep FTAs (eg, the TPP) and even the China–Korea FTA. Unlike the China–Korea FTA, stand-alone chapters on competition and environment are missing in ChAFTA, though ChAFTA does touch upon competition in a short article, which calls for cooperation rather than imposing stringent requirements. Such competition cooperation is to be promoted through information exchange, enforcement coordination and technical cooperation.[39] Environment rules are absent in ChAFTA. The narrow scope of ChAFTA helps to reach the consensus on the trade pact.

B. Innovative Investment and Services Rules

In comparison to China's WTO commitments and other FTAs, ChAFTA innovates in a number of investment and services rules. In ChAFTA, a substantial part, if not most, of the rule development occurs in services and

[32] ibid Art 5.4.
[33] ibid Art 6.4.
[34] ibid Art 7.8.1.
[35] ibid Art 7.9.1.
[36] ibid Art 7.10.1.
[37] ibid Art 7.8.1.
[38] DFAT, 'ChAFTA Summary of Chapters and Annexes' (n 22) 3, 5.
[39] ChAFTA (n 15) Art 16.7.

investment. The innovation is reflected not only in the current rules of ChAFTA, but also in its plan for further negotiations. It reflects the inherent pragmatism of ChAFTA, which highlights investment and services trade, a key area of bilateral economic relationships. Services and investment will play an increasingly important role in the Australia–China economic relationship. As discussed below, the liberalisation of financial services in China is understandable since banking and wealth management is the leading area of Australian investment in China.[40] ChAFTA contains innovative rules and new commitments in this respect to address the barriers. Again, it does not focus on the thorny issues of non-trade concerns to finalise the deal.

i. Services

ChAFTA is innovative among China's FTAs regarding services, including its approach to services trade commitments, GATS-plus obligations, cooperation on services and China's specific services trade commitments. Regarding the approach to services trade, Australia is the first country to provide China with commitments on a negative list approach, which adopts the North American Free Trade Agreement approach. China is expected to move to the same approach from the current positive list approach of GATS as part of the scheduled continuing negotiations.[41] If this occurs, it will be a remarkable development of China's approach to services trade.

GATS-plus obligations are developed further in ChAFTA regarding transparency, domestic regulation and cooperation on qualification recognition, to name a few. In the ChAFTA negotiations, 'GATS-plus' stipulations were a top priority for Australia, including the extended scope of commitments, heightened requirements for regulators and rules for behind-the-border barriers to services trade.[42] GATS-plus transparency obligations, which will be discussed later, are also imposed.[43] As a GATS-plus obligation concerning domestic regulation, ChAFTA requires one party to permit services providers of the other party to use enterprise names under which they can trade in the other party.[44] Both sides also agreed on qualification recognition cooperation,[45] which is more detailed than GATS.

ChAFTA is also innovative in terms of cooperation in services trade. The cooperation contemplated in ChAFTA will promote good governance and enable businesses from both sides to have an equal footing with counterparts from other countries. The cooperation on financial services is a typical example, which includes the processing of applications and the recognition

[40] DFAT, 'Outcomes at a Glance' (n 9).
[41] ChAFTA (n 15) Art 8.24.3.
[42] DFAT, 'ChAFTA Summary of Chapters and Annexes' (n 22).
[43] ChAFTA (n 15) Art 8.18.
[44] ibid Art 8.13.7.
[45] ibid Art 8.15.

of regulation. The Australian Prudential Regulatory Authority (APRA) and the China Banking Regulatory Commission (CBRC) will cooperate on issues under the Side Letter on Financial Services, which may involve the development of prudential frameworks of both parties. In particular, both sides will expeditiously process applications filed by financial institutions for the establishment of subsidiaries, branches and sub-branches on 'an equitable, non-discriminatory and good faith basis'.[46] It is worth noting that both sides will promote the cooperation in areas such as the recognition of regulation and the consideration of qualification. Australia and China will promote the recognition of each other's over-the-counter derivatives regulation to encourage cross-border activities.[47] For the knowledge and skill assessment of Chinese people nominated as 'responsible managers' of branches or subsidiaries of Chinese banks in Australia, the Australian Securities and Investment Commission (ASIC) will consider the nominee's relevant qualifications and experience obtained in China and according to the same criteria applicable to other jurisdictions.[48] It is also confirmed that Chinese institutions are eligible to supply payment services (including clearing payments) in Australia.[49] Related to this, Chinese financial institutions could apply for membership of the Reserve Bank Information and Transfer System on a national treatment basis.[50]

Related to the innovative rules, China provides more specific commitments in services trade under ChAFTA compared with most of its previous FTAs. For services trade commitments, China offers Australia its best ever FTA commitments (except for the agreements with Hong Kong, China and Macau, China).[51] China's Most-Favoured-Nation (MFN) treatment commitments cover 10 service sectors,[52] 'three more than the best commitments China has made in any other FTA'.[53] China has given the first ever FTA commitment on commercial association between law firms,[54] manufacturing

[46] ChAFTA (n 15) Side Letter on Financial Services.
[47] ibid.
[48] ibid.
[49] ibid.
[50] ibid.
[51] Free Trade Agreement between Australia and China (Goods and Services) (n 25) para 1.15.
[52] ChAFTA (n 15) Annex 8-A.
[53] DFAT, 'ChAFTA Summary of Chapters and Annexes' (n 22). The recent 100-day trade talks between the US and China may bring more liberalisation in services such as card payment services, which could go beyond ChAFTA.
[54] Meanwhile, it is observed that ChAFTA does not provide extra market access for Australian legal practices as it recognises current practice in the Chinese market and the same market access granted to Australian firms is also available to other foreign legal practices. It should be noted that the China–Korea FTA contans essentially the same commitments on legal services with ChAFTA. These two Agreements were signed on the same day. W Zhou and J Xi, 'China's Liberalisation of Legal Services under the ChAFTA: Market Access or Lack of Market Access for Australian Legal Practices' (2017) 51 *Journal of World Trade* 233, 233–64.

services and aged care services.[55] It enables Australian businesses to have greater access to service sectors including healthcare, tourism and financial services. In China, Australian firms are allowed to, inter alia, operate wholly owned subsidiaries in tourism, establish profit-making aged care institutions throughout the nation and wholly Australian-owned hospitals in selected provinces, and have a majority stake in joint ventures supplying services in agriculture, forestry, hunting and fishing.[56] For the first time, China gave Australia a quota of RMB 50 billion under the RMB Qualified Foreign Institutional Investor Programme, under which Australian financial institutions could invest offshore RMB in Chinese onshore financial instruments.[57]

ii. Investment

A number of ChAFTA investment rules are innovative, particularly in areas of China's expected transition to the negative list approach, regulatory autonomy, ISDS and investment facilitation. For the scheduling of investment commitments, China will shift to the negative list approach,[58] which seems to be affected by the US–China bilateral investment treaty (BIT) negotiations. It will be a fundamental change for China regarding the approach to investment. The negative list will happen, since China is to adopt the market access negative list approach nationwide from 2018 onwards.[59] This approach will facilitate investment, since investment will be allowed except for that listed in the negative list. It will boost investor confidence and enhance predictability.

While a lot of ink has been spilled regarding the right to regulate, ChAFTA dives in and contains a number of provisions to ensure regulatory autonomy, such as the exclusion of certain regulatory measures from ISDS, the public welfare notice and the provision on general exceptions. The ISDS mechanism does not apply to claims against non-discriminatory measures for lawful public welfare objectives (ie, health, safety, environment, public morals or order),[60] and claims relating to foreign investment screening, such as the review by the Foreign Investment Review Board (FIRB).[61] For the

[55] DFAT, 'Fact Sheet: Trade in Services' (n 12).

[56] 'China–Australia Free Trade Agreement: Pros and Cons' (Australian Broadcasting Corporation, 21 Oct 2015), www.abc.net.au/news/2015-06-17/china-australia-free-trade-agreement-pros-and-cons/6553680.

[57] DFAT, 'Factsheet: Financial Services' (13 December 2016), dfat.gov.au/trade/agreements/chafta/fact-sheets/Documents/fact-sheet-financial-services.pdf.

[58] ChAFTA (n 15) Art 9.9.3(c).

[59] 'China to Expand FTZ Negative List Model Nationwide' (*HKTDC*, 6 September 2016), hkmb.hktdc.com/en/1X0A7BW7/hktdc-research/China-to-Expand-FTZ-Negative-List-Model-Nationwide.

[60] ChAFTA (n 15) Art 9.11.4.

[61] DFAT, 'ChAFTA Summary of Chapters and Annexes' (n 22).

measures for legitimate public welfare purposes, the responding party in the ISDS processes could issue a public welfare notice, which will trigger consultation between treaty parties.[62] If both parties decide that the disputed measure is not a violation given its public welfare objectives, such decision is binding on an investment tribunal.[63] The general exceptions clause also supports the right to regulate by, inter alia, clarifying that environment measures are covered by general exceptions clauses when these measures protect human, animal or plant life or health, or relate to the conservation of exhaustible natural resources.[64]

For ISDS, ChAFTA innovates by ensuring treaty parties have more control over the ISDS processes and by strengthening the dispute settlement discipline. The ISDS rules include a great deal of detail regarding the selection of arbitrators and the interpretation of the schedule and provisions. ChAFTA employs a roster of arbitrators, permitting governments to choose the arbitrators as an initial matter, which differs from the current practice of the respondent government and investor appointing arbitrators ad hoc.[65] Specifically, within two years after the effective date of the FTA, a roster of ISDS arbitration panellists will be established, which shall consist of at least 20 individuals.[66] Each party is to choose at least five individuals, and both sides will jointly select at least 10 individuals as the tribunal chairpersons who are not Australian or Chinese nationals.[67]

The discipline of ISDS is strengthened to ensure greater transparency, accountability, and efficiency. The code of conduct for arbitrators is innovative and imposes more detailed requirements on arbitrators.[68] For the transparency of ISDS arbitral proceedings, a number of documents may be made publicly available, ranging from requests for consultation and decisions of the tribunal[69] to the disputing party's pleadings, minutes or transcripts of tribunal hearings or written submissions by the non-disputing party.[70] Although such publication is at the discretion of the respondent in the ISDS processes, such provision is not common in previous FTAs of China. It is noteworthy that the Side Letter on Transparency Rules Applicable to ISDS envisages further negotiations on transparency. Compared with other trade pacts of China, ChAFTA contains more advanced ISDS procedural provisions to improve efficiency and assist the adjudication. For instance, it provides for consolidation orders in the event of multiple claims

62 ChAFTA (n 15) Arts 9.11.5, 9.11.6.
63 ibid Art 9.18.3.
64 ibid Art 9.8.2.
65 ibid Art 9.15.5.
66 ibid.
67 ibid Art 9.15.6.
68 ibid Annex 9-A.
69 ibid Art 9.17.2(a).
70 ibid Arts 9.17.2(b), 9.17.2(c).

with common legal or factual issues arising from the same events.[71] It also stipulates that the tribunal may appoint experts to report in writing on factual issues involving 'environmental, health, safety, or other scientific matters' in the proceedings.[72] Overall, ChAFTA endeavours to strike a balance between the protection of investment and public interests.

Moreover, the parties may jointly interpret the Schedule of Non-Conforming Measures in ChAFTA Annex III, which is binding on the ISDS Tribunal.[73] It ensures that both countries could control the interpretation of the scheduled commitments. The parties could also exercise control on ISDS by a joint decision to declare their interpretation of FTA provisions, which will bind the ISDS Tribunal in ongoing and future cases.[74]

ChAFTA facilitates investment by Chinese investors in Australia through improved investment screening thresholds and conditions for labour mobility. For China, a major demand of the ChAFTA negotiations was a labour mobility clause enabling Chinese workers to work on Chinese-funded projects, and more liberal FIRB review thresholds for Chinese investors, particularly SOEs.[75] ChAFTA responds to these demands to a certain degree. For Chinese non-SOE investment in Australia's non-sensitive sectors, the FIRB investment screening threshold has been increased from AUD$0.248 billion to AUD$1.078 billion.[76] Furthermore, the MOU on an investment facilitation arrangement (IFA) is included in ChAFTA. Australia is the first developed country to provide China with such an arrangement regarding Chinese 'temporary skilled workers'[77] for qualified large projects,[78] which will facilitate the visa process for Chinese workers under the IFAs. Additionally, labour market testing is not required to enter into an IFA but may be relevant for the issue of visas under the IFAs.[79]

It is worth noting that ChAFTA is a work-in-progress type agreement and further development is planned. A number of provisions are forward looking. As discussed above, China will likely shift to a negative list approach regarding investment and services trade commitments. Further negotiation will be conducted for a more comprehensive investment chapter.[80]

[71] ibid Art 9.21.
[72] ibid Art 9.20.
[73] ibid Art 9.19.
[74] ibid Art 9.18.2.
[75] L He, 'Reassessing the China–Australia Free Trade Agreement Negotiation Process' (2015) 10 *Frontiers of Law in China* 714, 720.
[76] DITEA (n 2).
[77] See, eg, Memorandum of Understanding Between the Government of Australia and the Government of the People's Republic of China on an Investment Facilitation Arrangement (signed 17 June 2015) paras 8–11, dfat.gov.au/trade/agreements/chafta/official-documents/Documents/chafta-mou-on-an-investment-facilitation-arrangement.pdf.
[78] DITEA (n 2).
[79] 'Memorandum of Understanding' (n 77) paras 6, 8.
[80] ChAFTA (n 15) Art 9.9.3.

For example, to further enhance transparency ChAFTA envisages, within one year of the entry into force of the pact, that consultations will be conducted on the application of the United Nations Commission on International Trade Law (UNCITRAL) Rules on Transparency in Treaty-based Investor–State Arbitration to ISDS arbitrations.[81] Furthermore, within three years after the effective date of ChAFTA, negotiations will be started with the aim of establishing an ISDS appellate mechanism to resolve disputes on 'issues of law',[82] which could include substantive or procedural ones. This will go beyond any other Chinese trade agreements. Moreover, the MFN clause in ChAFTA's investment chapter enables the investors from both parties to benefit from investment rules of future agreements signed by either party, which covers pre-establishment and post-establishment stages.[83] If these future agreements contain innovative provisions that provide better treatment than those under ChAFTA, investors could enjoy such benefit under the MFN clause.

C. Increased Good Governance Norms

ChAFTA also incorporates good governance norms in selected areas such as services trade and non-tariff measures (NTMs). These are some of the major problems faced by businesses, but are not sensitive ones. ChAFTA avoids more difficult issues such as SOEs, labour and competition. Once again, it reflects a pragmatic approach to reach agreement as soon as possible.

The Agreement makes it clear right from the outset that both parties resolve to establish 'clear rules governing their trade which will ensure a predictable, transparent and consistent commercial framework for business operations'.[84] Good governance norms can be found in different chapters across ChAFTA. For instance, both sides will cooperate to streamline selected skills assessment processes for temporary skilled labour visas, to encourage the streamlining of pertinent licensing procedures, and to improve access to pertinent skills assessments.[85] Such provisions will benefit services trade and investment by providing enhanced predictability and reducing red tape.

Progress in good governance has been made particularly with respect to services and NTMs. For example, in financial services, China agrees to provide provisions on 'transparency, regulatory decision-making and

[81] ChAFTA (n 15) Side Letter on Transparency Rules Applicable to Investor–State Dispute Settlement. There seems to be no public information about the progress of the negotations in this respect.

[82] ibid Art 9.23.

[83] ibid Art 9.4.1.

[84] ibid, recital 7 of the Preamble.

[85] ChAFTA (n 15) Side Letter on Skills Assessment and Licensing.

streamlining of financial services licence applications'.[86] Notably, regulatory transparency is provided in the Annex on Financial Services, which requires regulators of one party to make administrative decisions on a completed application of a financial service provider of the other party within 180 days, and to notify the decision to the applicant.[87] As discussed earlier, both parties commit to expeditiously process applications filed by financial institutions for the establishment of subsidiaries, branches and sub-branches on 'an equitable, non-discriminatory and good faith basis'.[88] These commitments will help to improve the efficiency and fairness in the regulation of financial services.

Good governance provisions and commitments are also found in the rules on NTMs. Generally, the ChAFTA Committee on Trade in Goods will review NTMs to ensure that they 'do not constitute unnecessary obstacles' to bilateral trade.[89] In particular, good governance is highlighted in rules on trade facilitation. Equality of treatment is also provided, such as the requirement of the same treatment for importation of goods subject to the advance ruling irrespective of the identity of the importer or exporter if the facts and circumstances are the same 'in all material respects'.[90] Through an advance ruling, the customs administration could provide a ruling to traders on the tariff classification of goods before importation. Moreover, efficiency and cost-effectiveness are taken into account on a number of occasions,[91] which will also ease the burden of businesses. Both parties shall grant the release of perishable goods, in exceptional circumstances, outside the business hours of the customs and other authorities.[92] Another example is that under the ChAFTA origin rules, consignments of originating goods could be split up in non-parties for further transport,[93] and minor errors or discrepancies will be tolerated.[94] It remains to be seen how minor errors or discrepancies will be interpreted in the implementation of ChAFTA as the Agreement does not provide the definitions. In practice, a typical example of such minor errors or discrepancies would be a typo.

While many aspects of good governance have found their way into ChAFTA, transparency appears to have received the greatest attention. Transparency is highlighted in both a separate chapter and specific rules in other chapters. A special transparency chapter strives to address a number of issues that are relevant to businesses, including those in administrative

[86] DFAT, 'ChAFTA Summary of Chapters and Annexes' (n 22).
[87] ChAFTA (n 15) Annex 8-B, Art 5.
[88] ChAFTA (n 15) Side Letter on Financial Services.
[89] ChAFTA (n 15) 2.7.4.
[90] ibid Art 4.9.6.
[91] See, eg, ibid Art 4.6.1 (the application of information technology in customs procedures).
[92] ibid Art 4.11.1(b).
[93] ibid Art 3.13.3.
[94] ibid Art 3.17.

proceedings. The chapter incorporates rules on the publication of rules and administrative rulings,[95] the notification and provision of information,[96] the 'consistent, impartial, objective and reasonable' administration of rules and administrative rulings,[97] as well as review and appeal of final administrative actions regarding matters covered by ChAFTA.[98] If properly implemented, it will improve the transparency of the operation of trade regulations.

Specific rules on transparency include transparency of non-tariff measures (eg, SPS and TBT measures),[99] greater transparency in customs procedures through publication and enquiry points,[100] transparency of trade remedies,[101] regulatory transparency in financial services,[102] and transparency of measures relating to people mobility.[103] Under these rules, stakeholder participation is possible in areas such as trade in goods and intellectual property. Interested persons are afforded the opportunities to comment on draft laws and regulations regarding customs matters.[104] In the application of information technology in customs procedures, ChAFTA requires, 'to the greatest extent possible', consultation with relevant stakeholders including firms directly affected.[105] For intellectual property, ChAFTA obliges the parties to consider issues and questions 'of interest to private stakeholders',[106] which may be achieved through consultation with stakeholders.

Meanwhile, some transparency rules impose WTO-plus obligations, such as online publication of intellectual property rights (eg, granted or registered patents for invention),[107] and provision of reasons for the denial of preferential tariff treatment.[108] Among them, the GATS-plus transparency requirements for services trade and the transparency of NTMs deserve further attention. The former require, inter alia, prompt publication of regulatory decisions including their basis, and of the measures concerning public networks or services including the requirements for permits.[109] For the latter, a mechanism is in place to deal with the transparency and review of NTMs, which will be the responsibility of three committees—one each on trade in goods, SPS and TBT measures.[110] This mechanism suggests that

[95] ibid Art 13.2.
[96] ibid Art 13.3.
[97] ibid Art 13.4.
[98] ibid Art 13.5.
[99] ibid Arts 2.7.3, 2.12.
[100] ibid Art 4.7.
[101] See, eg, ibid Art 7.10.2.
[102] ibid Annex 8-B, Art 5.
[103] ibid Art 10.5.
[104] ibid Art 4.7.3; Agreement on Trade Facilitation (n 23) Art 2.1.1.
[105] ChAFTA (n 15) Art 4.6.3.
[106] ibid Art 11.23.2.
[107] ibid Art 11.6.1.
[108] ibid Art 3.22.2.
[109] ibid Art 8.18.
[110] ibid Art 2.12.

SPS and TBT measures attract special attention. In the same vein, ChAFTA imposes WTO-plus transparency obligations on TBT and SPS measures. For instance, a party must respond to comments received from the other party before the publication of final technical regulations or conformity assessment procedures.[111] Furthermore, ChAFTA allows at least 60 days for the other party to make comments on certain proposed SPS measures,[112] which set stricter rules than the SPS Agreement's requirement of 'reasonable time' for comments.[113]

D. Conclusion

The features of ChAFTA discussed above reflect the different positions of each side. WTO-based rules are favoured by China, and form the bases of its many trade pacts. Innovative investment and services rules, as well as increased good governance norms, in contrast, seem to be driven by Australia. Examples include ISDS, regulatory autonomy in investment and the duty-free movement of containers, pallets and packing materials. For investment, the ChAFTA approach reflects the position of Australia that recently seems to have taken a case-by-case approach.[114] Notably, Australia has faced the first investor–state dispute brought against Australia arising from the tobacco plain packaging legislation.[115] The duty- and tax-free temporary admission of containers and materials used in the transportation of goods also seems to be in ChAFTA at the instigation of Australia as the representative of Australia in the WTO suggested more liberalisation in this respect.[116]

These features of ChAFTA reflect a pragmatic approach that focuses on solving selective priority problematic issues between the two prior to ChAFTA (eg, particularly with respect to investment and services—the raised investment screening threshold, and regulatory transparency in financial services). Such an approach helped to close the deal, most likely representing the view that achieving something is better than nothing. This

[111] ibid Art 6.8.2.

[112] ibid Art 5.5.4.

[113] World Trade Organization, Agreement on the Application of Sanitary and Phytosanitary Measures Annex B, para 5, www.wto.org/english/tratop_e/sps_e/spsagr_e.htm.

[114] M Feldman, R Monardes and C Rodriguez-Chiffelle, 'The Role of Pacific Rim FTAs in the Harmonisation of International Investment Law: Towards a Free Trade Area of the Asia-Pacific' (Geneva, International Centre for Trade and Sustainable Development and World Economic Forum, March 2016) 6, papers.ssrn.com/sol3/papers.cfm?abstract_id=2761263.

[115] Attorney-General's Department, 'Tobacco Plain Packaging—Investor-State Arbitration', www.ag.gov.au/tobaccoplainpackaging.

[116] Free Trade Agreement between Australia and China (Goods and Services) (n 25) para 1.18.

approach is reflected in, among other ways, the exclusion of sensitive areas and the widespread utilisation of WTO-based rules. It is also reflected in ChAFTA's narrow coverage—for example, it does not address thorny WTO-extra issues such as labour and only touches upon sensitive issues such as the environment. In addition, taking trade in goods as an example, China has exempted certain agricultural products from tariff reduction (eg, cotton, sugar) or extended their tariff reduction period, while Australia has set a three- or five-year tariff reduction period for selected sensitive industrial products.[117] The approach of ChAFTA, as reflected in the features of ChAFTA, is likely to continue in the future trade agreements by China.

III. THE CHALLENGES TO CHAFTA

This section will analyse the challenges the two countries may encounter in the implementation and development of ChAFTA. It will help stakeholders to think of how to overcome the many and often new challenges faced. These challenges can also serve as examples for each and the rest of the world when these sorts of new issues arise, or when these types of joined parties are brought together.

A. The Implementation of ChAFTA

ChAFTA faces major challenges in its implementation and especially as it aims to launch and ensure successful further negotiations. The effective implementation of ChAFTA is crucial to a win–win outcome for Australia and China while the need for a successful next round is critical if this sort of approach is to be replicated by other parties. As a result, significant efforts have been made to implement ChAFTA through FTA mechanisms and domestic measures and it is hoped that similar efforts will be made to ensure successful negotiations.

However, challenges still exist in the implementation of ChAFTA. The implementation demands close cooperation across a wide range of areas and legal issues. Cooperation is crucial to the success of ChAFTA, including to the operation of newly established FTA committees. For instance, the review of NTMs require both sides' efforts through the ChAFTA committees, particularly those on SPS and TBT measures.[118] If the ChAFTA rules are unclear, the implementation will rely on cooperation, since history shows that dispute settlement systems are rarely utilised under FTAs.

[117] DITEA (n 2).
[118] ChAFTA (n 15) Art 2.12.

Furthermore, ChAFTA calls for cooperation in a wide range of areas such as intellectual property,[119] services trade (eg, taxation and traditional Chinese medicine (TCM) services)[120] and competition.[121] In particular, services trade rules demand wide-ranging cooperation. For example, financial services cooperation will be promoted in areas such as payments system oversight, Australia–China Renminbi (RMB) fund partnerships in China, information exchange on regulatory systems and policies, as well as measures against money laundering.[122] Cooperation will also extend to qualifications recognition in services trade. Both parties will encourage relevant bodies to develop standards and criteria for licensing and certification, and provide recommendations on mutual recognition in selected service sectors (eg, engineering and TCM).[123]

The cooperation required by ChAFTA could extend beyond or go deeper than under the WTO. One example is the consultation with stakeholders. The implementation of ChAFTA involves the consultation with relevant stakeholders including businesses.[124] The cooperation on intellectual property requires the parties to consider issues and questions 'of interest to private stakeholders',[125] which is not provided in the TRIPS Agreement and China's earlier FTAs such as the China–New Zealand FTA. It remains to be seen how this obligation will be fulfilled in practice, especially as the implementation of ChAFTA involves a large number of entities on both sides, including public and private ones. For instance, the ChAFTA side letters on skill assessment and financial services entail close cooperation between Australian (eg, Trades Recognition Australia, APRA and ASIC), and Chinese (eg, the China International Contractors Association, the CBRC and China's State Administration of Foreign Exchange) agencies. The coordination and cooperation among various agencies of two countries would likely not then be an easy job. The challenges include the efficiency of such coordination.

Moreover, other challenges include the FTA usage rate. It is important to ensure that businesses, particularly small businesses, are able to capitalise on the opportunities under ChAFTA. But, access to ChAFTA benefits alongside the 'noodle bowl' effect are among the problems that businesses may face. For the former, for instance, businesses outside first-tier cities may not be familiar with ChAFTA. Even businesses that know ChAFTA need expertise and experience to reap the benefits. In particular, small and

[119] ibid Art 11.23.
[120] ibid Art 8.25.
[121] ibid Art 16.7.
[122] ChAFTA (n 15) Side Letter on Financial Services.
[123] ChAFTA (n 15) Art 8.15.2.
[124] See, eg, ibid Art 4.6.3 (the application of information technology in customs procedures).
[125] ibid Art 11.23.2.

medium-sized enterprises (SMEs) could encounter many problems, such as insufficient opportunities, the complexity of rules, difficulties in interpretation and implementation, and remaining regulatory differences.[126] ChAFTA unfortunately has only a limited number of provisions that result in the engagement of businesses. Pitifully it does not explicitly provide special support for SMEs. On the noodle bowl effect, businesses in Australia and China already utilise a large number of other trade and investment agreements (eg, the TFA Agreement, and the RCEP in the future), which may contain different and complicated rules. To ensure that businesses take advantage of ChAFTA and other related agreements, the noodle bowl effect arising from overlapping agreements should be carefully addressed.

B. The Future Negotiations of ChAFTA

An interesting characteristic of ChAFTA was a commitment to further negotiations to upgrade ChAFTA. Subsequent negotiations will likely further develop ChAFTA, and in particular its rules on investment and trade in services. Tariff reduction, services market opening and investment rules are now among focuses of ChAFTA. Taking agriculture as an example, Australia enjoys a first-mover advantage in exports to China over major agricultural competitors (eg, the US, Canada and the EU) through ChAFTA.[127] It explains why tariff reduction would continue to be a key issue in subsequent negotiations of ChAFTA. Related to this, the just announced US–China trade deal also focuses on agriculture[128] given the large market in China. Besides the exports of commodities, a lot could be explored under ChAFTA to ensure the substantial growth of the Australia–China economic relationship. Differing from South–South FTAs, complementarity exists in the trade between China and Australia, with the former's advantage in labour-intensive manufacture and machinery and the latter's strength in agriculture and services.[129] It provides great opportunities for further development of the bilateral economic relationship.

Some of these developments have been envisaged in part by the failure to complete detailed or deep commitments in the original ChAFTA package. A number of sensitive issues are excluded or remain untouched under ChAFTA, ranging from labour mobility and SPS market access to

[126] H Wang, 'The Implications of the Trans-Pacific Partnership for SMEs: Opportunities and Challenges' (2016) 6 *KLRI Journal of Law and Legislation* 45, 65–73.

[127] DFAT, 'Outcomes at a Glance' (n 9).

[128] Office of Public Affaris, 'Joint Release: Initial Results of the 100-Day Action Plan of the US–China Comprehensive Economic Dialogue' (US Department of Commerce, 11 May 2017), www.commerce.gov/print/3122.

[129] Deere (n 7) 304.

investment. In Australia, for instance, the requisite skill levels for Chinese visa applicants remain unchanged; and SPS market access matters are set apart and negotiated separately from the FTA negotiations.[130] ChAFTA does not affect certain sensitive domestic systems such as Australia's biosecurity arrangement.[131] Regarding investment, the screening of investment from China is a delicate issue, and Australia will continue to review Chinese investments in agribusinesses at lower thresholds, in sensitive sectors (eg, media, telecommunications and defence-related industries) and by Chinese SOEs.[132] The review of foreign investment may be a potential issue for future negotiations. Moreover, ChAFTA incorporates underdeveloped investment treatment provisions, mainly national treatment and MFN treatment. The arbitration claim under ISDS is limited to the violation of national treatment.[133] Therefore, investment treatment provisions and the ISDS applicability are rather limited. To promote and protect investment, there will be a review of investment law framework within three years after the pact enters into force,[134] and both parties will start negotiations on a 'comprehensive' investment chapter.[135] A number of important investment provisions will be further negotiated, including the minimum standard of treatment, expropriation, transfers, performance requirements, and senior management and board of directors.[136] Subsequent negotiation plans also exist for possible appellate review in ISDS, which should be negotiated within three years of the FTA coming into effect.[137]

The major challenge to subsequent ChAFTA negotiations is probably that much that was left involves substantial levels of complexity and uncertainty. It is plain that the negotiations will involve complicated legal and political issues, since most of the easy jobs have been done. Among the obstacles to the renegotiations are the uncertainties within the political and economic environment in each country and in the wider region. For example, further liberalisation of services trade could be a delicate issue in China. The subsequent negotiations of ChAFTA will not be isolated from China's ongoing domestic reforms. China's ChAFTA commitments often seem to be linked to its (Shanghai) Pilot Free Trade Zone (SFTZ). Indeed, some services liberalisation measures in the SFTZ have been incorporated into ChAFTA, including those on telecommunications, legal services, construction

[130] DFAT, 'China–Australia FTA (ChAFTA): Myths Versus Realities' (29 July 2015), exportcouncil.kontribune.com/articles/6362.
[131] ibid.
[132] DFAT, 'Outcomes at a Glance' (n 9).
[133] ChAFTA (n 15) Art 9.12.2.
[134] ibid Art 9.9.1.
[135] ibid Art 9.9.3.
[136] ibid Art 9.9.3(b).
[137] ibid Art 9.23.

and maritime transport.[138] It is observed that most of ChAFTA's commitments by China are limited to selected types of services trade or to the SFTZ with frequent limitations on the types of commercial presence despite higher foreign equity.[139] It may be challenging to further liberalise the services trade market given China's gradual approach to services trade liberalisation and the significance of domestic interest groups.[140] Thus, China's domestic reforms and the FTZs, in particular, are likely to play a role in further negotiations of ChAFTA.

That said, ChAFTA does call for cooperation on sensitive issues. Among them, both sides will endeavour to further reduce the number of occupations subject to mandatory skills assessment for Chinese applicants for the relevant Australian visa, or eliminate the requirement in five years.[141] If there is the political willingness, ChAFTA presents the opportunity for China to test the commitment to market liberalisation for Australia, a middle power, before further opening up to larger economies (eg, the US).[142] How these sensitive issues will be handled in subsequent negotiations is yet to be seen.

In addition to the internal uncertainties that will impact the negotiations to update ChAFTA, there are forces within the larger international economic legal environment such as the development of WTO law, as well as relevant trade and investment agreements (eg, the RCEP, the US–China BIT and the China–Japan–Korea FTA). Future negotiations of ChAFTA will clearly be connected to these Agreements. For example, both sides will conduct negotiations on the commitments on government procurement after the finalisation of negotiations on China's accession to the WTO Agreement on Government Procurement.[143] Another example to show the role of other FTAs could be the role played by China's trade agreements with New Zealand[144] and Chile, which compete with Australia regarding agricultural products. For instance, New Zealand is key to China as it was the first country to approve a WTO accession agreement with China and the first advanced economy to conclude an FTA with China.[145] Under ChAFTA,

[138] DITEA (n 2).

[139] A Lumsden, L Knight and W Zhou, 'Free Trade with China–What Does this Mean for Australian Services Firms?' (25 March 2015), www.dynamicexport.com.au/export-market/articles-export-markets/Free-Trade-with-China-What-does-it-mean-for-services-firms/.

[140] Deere (n 7) 305, 316.

[141] ChAFTA (n 15) Side Letter on Skills Assessment and Licensing.

[142] Deere (n 7) 305.

[143] ChAFTA (n 15) Art 16.8.

[144] Relating to this, New Zealand was expecting Australia to obtain a much better result in market access under ChAFTA given the significant investment flows between China and Australia. A Berger, 'Investment Rules in Chinese Preferential Trade and Investment Agreements: Is China Following the Global Trend towards Comprehensive Agreements?' (2013) German Development Institute Discussion Paper 7/2013, www.die-gdi.de/uploads/media/DP_7.2013.pdf.

[145] Salidjanova (n 6) 33.

Australian products could benefit from tariff reductions under ChAFTA similar to those from New Zealand under the China–New Zealand FTA.[146] Another part played by relevant FTAs is that they may set a floor beyond which ChAFTA would seek to go in the new negotiations. Indeed, the influence of investment agreements is likely to play a role in China's adoption of the negative list approach, probably connected to China's BIT negotiations with the US in which China committed to taking the same approach. It partially explains why ChAFTA contains an MFN clause in its investment chapter, which then takes into account China's other investment agreements, such as the possible US–China BIT. Similarly, the negotiations on the ISDS appeal system might be affected by the practice of the EU, which first incorporates the ISDS appeal system in the CETA and the EU–Viet Nam FTA.

In future negotiations of ChAFTA, these existing trade and investment agreements (eg, the upgrade of the China–New Zealand FTA) and new agreements (eg, the RCEP) will probably impact ChAFTA negotiations. It remains to be observed whether ChAFTA will develop detailed rules in non-trade concerns (eg, environment and labour) and lean towards deep FTAs. Unless China has strong willingness to adopt stringent regulatory requirements, ChAFTA is likely to largely remain the status quo and the paradigm shift will be difficult. Regulatory improvement is more likely to involve sectors where the services market is liberalized, such as healthcare.[147] In the long term, it is interesting to observe whether and how ChAFTA may interact with deep FTAs.

IV. CONCLUDING REMARKS: THE IMPLICATIONS OF CHAFTA

Reflecting a pragmatic approach, ChAFTA focuses on trade and investment facilitation mainly through market liberalisation and a number of carefully written good governance norms. Different from the TPP, it does not intend to set a governance model or impose a large number of stringent regulatory requirements. ChAFTA is a WTO-based and WTO-friendly trade agreement that supports the multilateral trading system. It largely builds on the WTO rules and further develops them through innovative provisions (eg, a chapter on electronic commerce). ChAFTA has made substantial progress in several discrete but important areas, including tariff cuts, services trade and investment. The development often takes place through, inter alia, enhanced market access, non-discrimination treatment and regulatory cooperation. Overall, the innovations of ChAFTA exist in a narrow range of areas

[146] See, eg, DFAT, 'China–Australia Free Trade Agreement: A Snapshot', dfat.gov.au/trade/agreements/chafta/fact-sheets/Documents/chafta-snapshot.pdf.

[147] DFAT, 'Outcomes at a Glance' (n 9). (ChAFTA provides new or significantly improved market access for health and aged care services businesses in China.)

(eg, investment and services). The Agreement is not as shallow as one may first think as it touches upon, inter alia, regulatory transparency and regulatory cooperation (eg, cooperation in financial services, and the harmonisation of plant breeders' rights and administrative systems).[148]

ChAFTA is a work-in-progress type FTA. It is a dynamic pact in terms of its implementation (eg, the review of NTMs, the review of the implementation of services trade rules, and the consideration of intellectual property issues concerning private stakeholders) and further negotiations. It seems to take a two-step approach: first the conclusion and implementation of the FTA rules, and then the upgrade of ChAFTA (eg, comprehensive investment rules). ChAFTA needs to be further developed as it contains only short-form provisions, particularly on WTO-extra issues.

The future of ChAFTA depends largely on close cooperation between the parties in implementation, on the one hand, and their political willingness to further develop the rule-based system on the other. The desire to maintain the competitiveness of both parties regarding trade and investment is probably among the key driving forces of ChAFTA. ChAFTA has the potential of rule development, most notably regarding deeper regulatory cooperation and sophisticated investment rules. It may indicate an incremental shift to a more rules-based FTA focusing on good governance norms. If properly managed, the bilateral efforts could promote good governance and drive down trade costs.

The possible paradigm shift of ChAFTA, if there is political willingness for such paradigm shift in the future should carry vast implications not only for the China–Australia economic relations, but also for the Chinese model of FTAs and beyond. ChAFTA has indicated the flexibility of both sides in negotiating a trade agreement, and has wide and far-reaching implications for the cooperation between China and Australia. Meanwhile, the benefits under ChAFTA could be made available under other agreements, including China's BIT negotiations with the US and EU. Therefore, it will carry wider implications for China's interaction with other partners, particularly developed economies in terms of trade and investment agreements. In other words, ChAFTA may act as a 'pilot zone' for China's FTAs. It could lay a foundation for and contribute to the negotiations of mega FTA (ie, the RCEP). ChAFTA may even serve as a pathway to China's FTA model and have a demonstration effect for China's FTAs. The starting point is probably to address major challenges to ChAFTA in terms of its effective implementation and subsequent negotiations.

[148] ChAFTA (n 15) Art 11.16(a).

Part II

The Contexts within which ChAFTA exists

3

A Comparative Context: Ensuring Australian and Chinese Legal Systems Coexist to Facilitate Harmonious and Trustworthy Trade

NICHOLAS MORRIS

I. ESTABLISHING TRUSTWORTHINESS IN TRADE ARRANGEMENTS

MAKING THE CHINA–AUSTRALIA Free Trade Agreement (ChAFTA) work effectively requires that the Australian and Chinese legal and regulatory systems work together to create a harmonious and trustworthy trading environment.[1] At the state-to-state level, international law provides a framework, for example through the Vienna Convention on Treaties,[2] but at the level of the individuals and firms who implement trading arrangements the situation is less clear. Crucially, it is important that trading partners can rely on each other's trustworthiness over matters where one or the other party has superior information, expertise, market access or political clout. Good faith implementation of ChAFTA trading arrangements by the individuals, firms and officials involved is a necessary condition for continuing, and mutually beneficial, trade under the Treaty.[3] In this chapter, drawing on work which examines how the legal and regulatory system can enhance and encourage trustworthy behaviour in financial markets,[4] we explore how legal systems can promote, or undermine, trustworthy actions in the various aspects of trade covered by ChAFTA.

[1] In what follows, we use the term 'legal' to embrace both legal and regulatory arrangements.

[2] Vienna Convention on the Law of Treaties (adopted 23 May 1969, entered into force 27 January 1980) 1155 UNTS 331.

[3] Good faith and the *pacta sunt servanda* ('agreements must be kept') rule are explicitly referred to in the Vienna Convention, and are widely recognised as basic principles of common law. See American Society of International Law and the International Judicial Academy, 'Pacta Sunt Servanda' (September 2008), www.judicialmonitor.org/archive_0908/generalprinciples.html.

[4] N Morris and D Vines (eds), *Capital Failure: Rebuilding Trust in Financial Markets* (Oxford, Oxford University Press, 2014).

There are many different legal traditions in the world, with widely varying societal and philosophical underpinnings. Four types which are often identified are common law, civil law, religious law and technocratic/administrative law. Australian law largely follows the UK common law tradition. Chinese law, in contrast, mostly falls into the fourth category, although it also has imported elements from other systems, particularly civil law from continental Europe.[5]

Different societies have different methods of encouraging trustworthy behaviour. In Australia, good behaviour is rewarded through, for example, various types of recognition and bad behaviour is penalised through exclusion from public activities. Education instils a sense of public duty and moral values. Religious practices can also play an important role, as in the teachings of Christianity and in the prohibitions of Islam,[6] Hinduism[7] and Judaism.[8] Islamic Finance, for example, in its stricter forms seeks to prevent the excesses of usury. In China, *Guanxi* provides a support system for those who adhere to behavioural norms established over thousands of years.[9] '*Faithless Guanxi*' is penalised by exclusion from public and commercial opportunities.[10]

Convergence of legal and regulatory standards is an important step in the process of developing trust between trading partners. However, getting consensus as to legal standards between Australia and China will be difficult. It has been argued that international cooperation is most effective when there is a global regime in which 'concerted unilateralism' leads to a good outcome.[11] This is because any reforms to economic policymaking are driven by domestic political agendas. That means that national policymakers will not adopt policies which are in the global interest unless they are also in the national interest. In economic terms we cannot seek a cooperative

[5] For discussion of the recent evolution of Chinese law see, eg, Y Svetiev and L Wang, 'Competition Law Enforcement in China: Between Technocracy and Industrial Policy' (2016) 79(4) *Law and Contemporary Problems* 187; and C Li, 'The Rise of the Legal Profession in the Chinese Leadership' (2013) *China Leadership Monitor* 42.

[6] S Schwartz 'Islam and Communism' (Centre for Islamic Pluralism, 2009), www.islamicpluralism.org/documents/islam-communism.pdf.

[7] SA Desai and DF Mulla, *Principles of Hindu Law*, 20th edn (New Delhi, Butterworths India, 2007).

[8] N Schoon and J Nuri, 'Comparative Financial Systems in Judaism, Christianity and Islam: The Case of Interest' (1 June 2012), ssrn.com/abstract=2126503 or, dx.doi.org/10.2139/ssrn.2126503.

[9] Y Luo, Y Huang and S Wang, 'Guanxi and Organizational Performance: A Meta-Analysis' (2012) 8(1) *Management and Organization Review* 139.

[10] W Shi and XL Cui (2004) 'On Evaluation of Civil Servants and the Criteria of Morality, Competence, Hard Working, and Performance' Guangdong Social Science, 6, 70–75 石伟; 崔修利 (2004): 论公务员绩效考核与德能勤绩, 广东社会科学, 6, 70–75.

[11] D Vines, 'On Concerted Unilateralism: Raising the Global Growth Rate through Macroeconomic Policy Coordination' in T Bayoumi, S Pickford and P Subacchi (eds), *Managing Complexity: Economic Policy Cooperation after the Crisis* (Washington DC, Brookings Institution Press, 2016).

equilibrium which is not also, in technical terms, a 'Nash Equilibrium'.[12] National policymakers will tend to free ride on such an equilibrium, leading to breakdown where the required form of law does not comply with pre-established norms. Legal and regulatory cooperation therefore needs to make it possible for there to be different forms of regulation in different countries of a kind which reflect the different industrial, and cultural, forms which exist in different places.[13]

Contracts are often incomplete,[14] and imperfectly defined or conflicting laws and regulations can mean that they are hard to enforce,[15] especially when the relevant activities transcend jurisdictional boundaries. Without trustworthy relationships, the confidence to invest gets eroded, gains from trade become more difficult to achieve, and in due course the economic system becomes unsustainable.

The legal system, both at a national and at a global level, has a crucial role to play both in defining what behaviour is acceptable and in holding individuals, firms and countries to account for their actions and for the adverse externalities they create.[16] Without legal or regulatory constraints, it is easy for those with superior information, or with monopoly access to markets, resources or suppliers, or with superior political power, to take advantage of those who are less privileged. It has been argued that one of the roles of the law, including in bilateral and multilateral trading arrangements, is to ensure that relationships between market players and stakeholders are as fair and transparent as possible.[17]

II. RELEVANT SPECIFICS OF ChAFTA ARRANGEMENTS

ChAFTA contains a wide range of arrangements, which potentially require different legal approaches and where trustworthiness is required in different ways. Before turning to how the law can encourage trustworthy behaviour

[12] A 'Nash Equilibrium' is one in which movement away from the equilibrium point benefits neither party. See 'Nash Equlibrium' in the *International Encyclopedia of the Social Sciences*, 2nd edn (online) 540–42, www.columbia.edu/~rs328/NashEquilibrium.pdf.

[13] S Jaffer, S Knaudt and N Morris, 'Failures of Regulation and Governance' in N Morris and D Vines (eds), *Capital Failure: Rebuilding Trust in Financial Services* (Oxford, Oxford University Press, 2014).

[14] O Williamson, *The Economic Institutions of Capitalism* (New York, Free Press, 1985); WN Epstein, 'Facilitating Incomplete Contracts' (2014) 65(2) *Case Western Reserve Law Review* 297.

[15] C Winston, *Government Failure versus Market Failure* (Washington DC, Brookings Institution Press, 2006).

[16] J Armour, 'Enforcement Strategies in UK Corporate Governance: A Roadmap and Empirical Assessment' (2008) ECGI Working Paper No 106/2008, papers.ssrn.com/sol3/papers.cfm?abstract_id=1133542.

[17] F Fukayama, *Trust: The Social Virtues and the Creation of Prosperity* (New York, Free Press, 1995).

by officials, individuals and firms, we therefore explore some specific classes of arrangement. These include places where it is possible for officials to delay implementation of the Treaty; where common standards over measurement are needed; effective implementation of specific rules, such as 'Most-Favoured-Nation' status; issues related to ensuring effective competition; and, importantly, the basis on which foreign investment in each country may be undertaken.

Many of the agreed reductions in tariffs involve time frames which both countries are expected to honour, over periods ranging from immediately after ChAFTA's entry into force (eg, barley and sorghum, coking coal, most minerals) to four years (dairy, pork, wines, horticulture, processed foods, manufactured goods) to longer periods (orange juice, beef, sheep and goat meat). Once the Agreement is fully implemented, 100 per cent of Chinese exports to Australia will enjoy zero-tariff treatment.[18]

All these timetables require that relevant agencies in both countries allocate the time and resources to ensuring that the relevant processes are suitably adjusted, notwithstanding unforeseen political events. In his message to the then Australian Prime Minister when ChAFTA was signed, President Xi Jinping talked of an 'an improved institutional guarantee for the two countries' and how they would conduct 'close win–win cooperation' on an ongoing basis.[19] His remarks show clearly that, at least to the Chinese, trade agreements such as ChAFTA are not only about commercial relations, but also about cultural alignment.

Some of the changes in ChAFTA involve measurement of volumes, a process which relies on the fair and transparent collection of data. For example, China can apply additional customs duties for beef (in excess of 170,000 tonnes) and for milk powder products (17,500 tonnes). Australian wool exporters have been granted duty-free treatment for up to 30,000 tonnes of clean wool each year, increasing by 5 per cent per year.[20] These require trustworthy behaviour by the relevant officials and also allocation of the relevant allowances between traders.

In other cases, ChAFTA requires that relevant institutions in both countries honour specific parts of the Agreement. For example, ChAFTA includes Most-Favoured-Nation (MFN) clauses which prescribe that

[18] The full text of the Agreement may be found at dfat.gov.au/trade/agreements/chafta/official-documents/Documents/chafta-agreement-text.pdf; a helpful summary may be found at Ashurst, 'Introduction to the China Australia Free Trade Agreement (ChAFTA)' (30 June 2015), www.ashurst.com/en/news-and-insights/legal-updates/foreign-investment-update-introduction-to-the-china-australia-free-trade-agreement/.

[19] See M Salvacion, 'China, Australia to Mutually Benefit as Historic FTA Comes into Force' (21 December 2015), en.yibada.com/articles/96652/20151221/china-australia-benefit-historic-fta-comes-force.htm#ixzz4Z5CzZrhN.

[20] This is in addition to the 287,000 tonne existing WTO wool quota (which imposes a tariff of 1%). See 'Factsheet: Agriculture and Processed Food' (20 December 2016), dfat.gov.au/trade/agreements/chafta/fact-sheets/Documents/fact-sheet-agriculture-and-processed-food.pdf.

if China extends greater beneficial treatment to other trade partners in the sectors of education, tourism and travel, construction, engineering, securities, environmental, forestry, computer and certain scientific and consulting services, Australian service providers will also receive the same benefit.[21] A key Chinese Ministry of Education website is to be adjusted to help Australian education providers achieve a greater profile in China.[22] Australian businesses are intended to be given improved market access in China.[23] All these require 'good faith' (and hard to monitor) actions on a continuing basis by a variety of Chinese institutions, including governments, businesses and other stakeholders.[24]

China's entry into the World Trade Organization (WTO) in 2001 required the Chinese government to undertake wide-ranging economic reforms to the legal system, financial markets, state owned enterprises, bureaucracy and corporate governance. These reforms are ongoing and will continue in parallel with arrangements related to ChAFTA. However, Chinese government-owned entities remain active in various markets and the enforcement of competition law against state-owned enterprises and government departments will be a challenge.

ChAFTA has committed both countries to a 'Future Work Programme' which includes negotiations on protection from expropriation, imposing minimum standards of treatment for investments, the application of investment protection to services and Investor–State Dispute Settlement (ISDS) processes.[25] Importantly, the work programme also needs to cover the harmonisation of competition law, including the prohibition of cartels or anticompetitive agreements among firms such as agreements to exclude competitors from the market, boycotts and price fixing; the prohibition of abuses of dominant market power by large firms or monopolies; and the control and review of mergers and acquisitions and agreements between competitors (such as joint ventures) which may lead to the creation of a dominant firm or monopoly or have the purpose of lessening competition.

[21] For discussion of MFN in international law see OECD, 'Most-Favoured-Nation Treatment in International Investment Law' (2004) OECD Working Papers on International Investment 2004/02, dx.doi.org/10.1787/518757021651.

[22] The foreign education regulation website of the Ministry of Education, for explanation of China's commitment see MOFCOM, 'Interpretation for the China–Australia Free Trade Agreement' (19 June 2015) cl 25, english.mofcom.gov.cn/article/policyrelease/Cocoon/201510/20151001144954.shtml.

[23] For discussion, see, eg, Trade and Investment Queensland, 'China–Australia Free Trade Agreement' (2015), www.tiq.qld.gov.au/wp-content/uploads/2016/01/chafta-Fact-Sheet.pdf.

[24] S Reinhold, 'Good Faith in International Law' (2013) 2 *UCL Journal of Law and Jurisprudence* 40.

[25] See Department of Foreign Affairs and Trade (DFAT), 'China–Australia Free Trade Agreement (ChAFTA) Summary of Chapters' (2015) Annex 8-B (Financial Services), dfat.gov.au/trade/agreements/chafta/fact-sheets/Documents/chafta-summary-of-chapters-and-annexes.pdf.

ChAFTA also involves specific permissions for Australian businesses in China.[26] These include that Australian financial service providers will be allowed to establish joint venture companies with up to 49 per cent Australian ownership; that Australian insurance providers will be given more liberal access to China's motor vehicle insurance market;[27] that Australian companies will be able to construct, renovate and operate wholly-Australian-owned hotels and restaurants in China; that Australian travel agencies and tour operators will be able to establish wholly-Australian-owned subsidiaries in China;[28] and that Australian providers will be able to establish profit-making aged care institutions throughout China and wholly-Australian-owned hospitals in Beijing, Tianjin and Shanghai as well as the provinces of Jiangsu, Fujian, Guangdong and Hainan.[29] All these permissions clearly require that the relevant Chinese authorities facilitate such access on a timely basis.

The WTO Ministerial Declaration adopted in DOHA in 2001[30] highlighted the importance of 'transparency, non-discrimination and procedural fairness, and provisions on hardcore cartels; modalities for voluntary cooperation; and support for progressive reinforcement of competition institutions'.[31] Under ChAFTA, private (non-government) Chinese investors in Australia were accorded equal status with private investors from the US, New Zealand, Japan, South Korea and Chile. The Australian government will still review private Chinese investments in sensitive sector businesses; Australian urban land and entities; and Australian rural land, agriculture and agribusiness. ChAFTA also introduced improved access and mobility for a range of Australian and Chinese skilled personnel. Alongside ChAFTA, Australia and China have also completed negotiations on a Work and Holiday Arrangement (WHA) under which Australia will grant visas for up to five thousand Chinese work and holidaymakers annually.

[26] Trade outcomes of ChAFTA are summarised in the Senate Standing Committee on Foreign Affairs, Defence and Trade, 'China–Australia Free Trade Agreement' (6 November 2015) Ch 3, www.aph.gov.au/Parliamentary_Business/Committees/Senate/Foreign_Affairs_Defence_and_Trade/China-Aust_Free_Trade/Report/c03; while advantages and issues for Australian businesses are presented in the Joint Standing Committee on Treaties, 'Report 154: Treaty Tabled on 17 June 2015' (19 October 2015), www.aph.gov.au/Parliamentary_Business/Committees/Joint/Treaties/17_June_2015/Report_154.

[27] See DFAT, 'China–Australia Free Trade Agreement: Factsheet: Financial Services' (13 December 2016), dfat.gov.au/trade/agreements/chafta/fact-sheets/Documents/fact-sheet-financial-services.pdf.

[28] See DFAT, 'China–Australia Free Trade Agreement: Factsheet: Trade in Services' (20 December 2016), dfat.gov.au/trade/agreements/chafta/fact-sheets/Documents/fact-sheet-trade-in-services.pdf.

[29] For discussion of healthcare opportunities in China for Australian operators, see K Brown, 'Australia–China Healthcare Opportunities' (China Studies Centre, University of Sydney, 2006), sydney.edu.au/china_studies_centre/images/Business%20Forum/2015/reportchinesehealthcarereportfinal.pdf.

[30] Ministerial Declaration (14 November 2001) WT/MIN(01)/DEC/1, docsonline.wto.org.

[31] ibid para 25; Winston (n 15).

ChAFTA also covers bilateral investment, and intends that the host state treat investors from the other state no less favourably than it treats its own national investors.[32] However, there are still detailed provisions to be worked out, especially enforceable rights currently available under the existing Australia–China Bilateral Investment Treaty (the Australia–China BIT) of 1988. Dispute resolution processes remain unclear, and it is doubtful that arbitration at the International Centre for the Settlement of Investments Disputes (ICSID) is available for any claims, except expropriation claims, without China's express agreement. To date there have been no registered ICSID arbitrations under the Australia–China BIT.

ChAFTA arrangements also include affirmation of existing intellectual property commitments and provision of a framework for cooperation; co-ordination between respective regulators on competition policy; a framework for growth of e-commerce; provision for future negotiations on access to Chinese government procurement markets; and facilitation of trade through streamlined customs processes.[33]

III. DIFFERENCES BETWEEN LEGAL SYSTEMS

Different types of legal system vary in the mechanisms they contain to influence norms, and in their ability to hold those who behave in untrustworthy ways to account.[34] All also specify duties, which they impose in different ways.[35] Working out which type of law is likely to engender the most trustworthy behaviour depends on how well key items—such as duties, prohibition, regulation, labour laws and penalties—can be implemented in the relevant legal framework.[36] This varies from country to country, and also from sector to sector.

The international legal system has an important role to play in setting out acceptable standards of behaviour, defining responsibilities and obligations,

[32] Free Trade Agreement between the Government of Australia and the Government of the People's Republic of China (ChAFTA) (signed 17 June 2015, entered into force 20 December 2015) [2015] ATS 15, Ch 9.

[33] Announcement 57. See DFAT, 'China–Australia Free Trade Agreement' (2015) Q23, dfat.gov.au/trade/agreements/chafta/fact-sheets/Documents/chafta-faqs.pdf.

[34] For a helpful discussion, see M Svensson, 'Norms in Law and Society: Towards a Definition of the Socio-Legal Concept of Norms' in M Baier (eds) *Social and Legal Norms* (Farnham, Ashgate, 2013).

[35] A useful summary of the importance of duties in Australian law, for example, may be found in VP Shrivington, 'Ethics and Conflict of Interest and Duties' (Law Society of New South Wales, April 2006), www.lawsociety.com.au/cs/groups/public/documents/internetcostguidebook/026415.pdf.

[36] For discussion of regional and sectoral variations in business recognition of human rights, eg, see M Wright and A Lehr, 'Business Recognition of Human Rights: Global Patterns, Regional and Sectoral Variations' (Office of the United Nations High Commissioner for Human Rights, 12 December 2006), www.business-humanrights.org/sites/default/files/media/bhr/files/Business-Recognition-of-Human-Rights-12-Dec-2006.pdf.

and holding countries and multinational firms to account for their trustworthy adherence to international norms.[37] Consistency between legal systems, in a world in which many economic activities cross national boundaries, is crucial to the development of trading arrangements such as ChAFTA.[38] Effective coordination is needed to ensure that unsatisfactory behaviour does not migrate from one country system to another and that multinational companies do not engage in 'jurisdiction shopping' to evade their obligations. Piecemeal changes to legal systems on a national basis will merely lead to 'forum shopping' and arbitrage between systems.[39]

The evolution of legal systems in Western nations during the past 40 years has unfortunately had insufficient focus on enhancing trustworthiness.[40] This is partly because legislators and policymakers in various countries, including Australia, have sought to rely on 'market forces' to ensure that self-interested behaviour leads to a fair and sustainable outcome. In the aftermath of the 'Global Financial Crisis', it is now widely accepted that this reliance has been mistaken.[41] At the global level, and in the context of trade agreements such as ChAFTA, ensuring consistency between legal traditions is now essential if migration of undesirable attributes between systems is to be avoided.[42]

The development of an international legal framework which encourages and enforces pro-trust norms needs to be sensitive to the different traditions, philosophies and national practices which are embodied in each system. These factors are all important in the development of a harmonised legal system to underpin ChAFTA in the longer term, especially if the benefits of deeper integration are to be achieved.

International law has made some progress in seeking to clarify what constitutes acceptable, trustworthy, behaviour across national boundaries. In the area of contracts, for example, achievements during the past century include the Uniform Laws on the International Sale of Goods,[43]

[37] See R Murphy, 'Country by Country Reporting: Holding Multinational Corporations to Account Wherever They Are' (Washington DC, Task Force on Financial Integrity and Economic Development, 2009), www.financialtransparency.org/wp-content/uploads/2015/04/Final_CbyC_Report_Published.pdf.

[38] For an authoritative discussion of this issue, see TF Bathurst, 'The Importance of Developing Convergent Commercial Law Systems, Procedurally and Substantively' (speech at the 15th Conference of Chief Justices of Asia and the Pacific, Singapore, 28–30 October 2013), www.supremecourt.justice.nsw.gov.au/Documents/Publications/Speeches/Pre-2015%20Speeches/Bathurst/bathurst_2013.10.28.pdf.

[39] CA Whytock, 'The Evolving Forum Shopping System' (2011) 96 *Cornell Law Review* 481.

[40] T Bingham, 'The Rule of Law' (2007) 66(1) *Cambridge Law Journal* 67.

[41] Morris and Vines (n 4).

[42] M Busch, 'Overlapping Institutions, Forum Shopping, and Dispute Settlement in International Trade' (2007) 61(4) *International Organization* 735.

[43] Convention relating to a Uniform Law on the International Sale of Goods (1964, The Hague) (UNIDROIT, 30 September 2013), www.unidroit.org/instruments/international-sales/international-sales-ulis-1964.

the UNIDROIT Principles of International Commercial Contracts,[44] the Principles of European Contract Law,[45] and the Vienna Convention for the International Sales of Goods (CISG). However, the drafting of these international texts has been complex because of the need to embrace both civil law and common law systems.[46] China has been argued to have a major role to play as the international system develops further,[47] a matter we explore below.

IV. A FOUR-PART FRAMEWORK FOR IMPROVING TRUSTWORTHINESS

In order to understand the necessary developments in law and regulation which are needed for trustworthy trading relationships, I and colleagues at Oxford have developed a four-part framework which has been set out in a recent book, *Capital Failure: Rebuilding Trust in Financial Services*,[48] with the four parts listed as follows:

i. an appropriate specification of obligations;
ii. an identification of corresponding responsibilities;
iii. the creation of mechanisms by which these responsibilities can be carried out; and
iv. the holding to account of those involved, in an appropriate manner.

The relevance of this framework in the context of ChAFTA should be clear. A genuine concern about the outcomes for trading partners will lead to a set of well-defined obligations to those partners. The following three things—responsibilities, mechanisms and accountability—then flow from those obligations.

44 'UNIDROIT Principles of International Commercial Contracts 2010' (UNIDROIT, 2010), www.unidroit.org/english/principles/contracts/principles2010/blackletter2010-english.pdf.

45 'The Principles of European Contract Law 2001 (Parts I, I, and III)', www.transnational.deusto.es/emttl/documentos/Principles%20of%20European%20Contract%20Law.pdf.

46 CB Picker, 'International Law's Mixed Heritage: A Common/Civil Law Jurisdiction' (2008) 41(4) *Vanderbilt Journal of Transnational Law* 1083; CB Picker, 'China, Global Governance and Legal Culture: The Example of China and the WTO' in J Nakagaw (ed), *China and Global Economic Governance: Ideas and Concept* (ISS Research Series No 45) (Institute of Social Science, University of Tokyo, 2011) 77; CB Picker, 'China's Legal Cultural Relationship to International Economic Law: Multiple and Conflicting Paradigms' in C Picker, L Toohey and J Greenacre (eds), *China in the International Economic Order: New Directions and Changing Paradigms* (New York, Cambridge University Press, 2015) ch 5, 62–76.

47 F Allen et al, 'Law, Institutions and Finance in China and India' in B Eichengreen, P Gupta and R Kumar (eds), *Emerging Giants: China and India in the World Economy* (Oxford, Oxford University Press, 2010).

48 Morris and Vines (n 4).

The legal system affects these outcomes in numerous ways, and it is helpful to specify in some detail where this can occur. In principle, the legal system can affect behavioural outcomes in many ways, including:[49]

1. Providing guidance on what is regarded as acceptable behaviour.
2. Establishing duties, through, for example, rules imposed on agents, fiduciaries and trustees.
3. Cultural guidance.
4. Incentivising people and companies to act in a trustworthy manner.
5. Regulating specific aspects of commercial operations, eg, price, return, customs duties, licence fees, charges for public services, disclosure, compliance, etc.
6. Prohibiting certain actions, eg, murder, theft, insider trading and usury.
7. Shame and recognition, including exclusion, withdrawal of licences and honours.
8. Imposing penalties, typically fines or imprisonment, on those who break the law.

In terms of the four-part framework for improving trustworthiness, (1), (2) and (3) help with the definition of obligations and responsibilities; (4), (5) and (6) set out mechanisms whereby these can be encouraged and enforced; while (7) and (8) are important parts of holding to account.

It is helpful to think about how the legal system can contribute to encouraging the necessary trustworthiness using the spectrum of activities in the implementation diagram (Figure 1) below. The arrow in the diagram

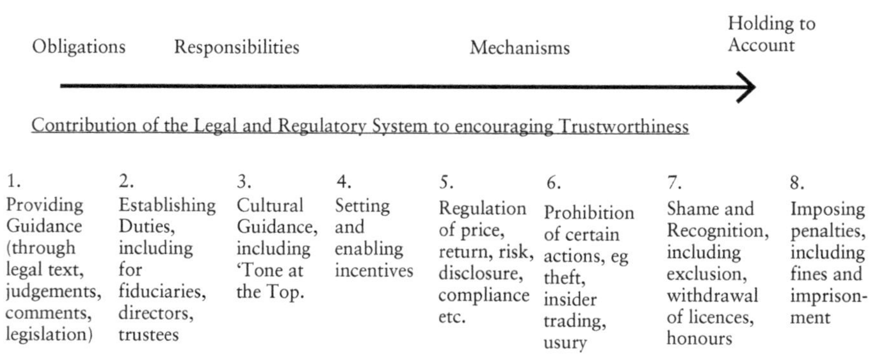

Figure 1: Implementing the Four-Part Framework

[49] There have been many attempts to define the role of an effective legal system. One of the more authoritative is that of Lord Thomas Bingham (2007), who sets out eight requirements which may be summarised as accessibility, effectiveness, equal access, protection of human rights, resolution of civil disputes, probity of those in authority, fairness, and compliance with international law.

emphasises, in general terms, the steps in the process which leads from defining obligations through to deterrence and the imposition of penalties. The numbers in the spectrum are steps in a process which can be followed in order to identify where and how the legal and regulatory system can best intervene to encourage trustworthy outcomes.

As the diagram illustrates, the legal system has many important roles to play in encouraging trustworthy behaviour. It is important that the legal system provides an ever-present threat of punishment for those who step over the line and behave in an unacceptable manner, and that it makes sure that liabilities are recognised and enforced. But the legal system also has a broader role to play. In their judgments, for example, judges have the opportunity to make clear the standards of behaviour which are expected of market participants.[50] And some legal activity consists explicitly of the writing of rules, and the development of standards, which the regulatory system can then enforce.

Capital Failure explores in some detail what makes individuals (and by extension, the leaders of firms) behave in a particular manner. As Gold puts it:

> A pre-requisite for deciding to abide by the norms of a particular relationship is seeing that they apply. Hence the considerations that motivate a person depend on the relationship that she takes herself to be in, how she 'frames' her situation, and hence the norms that govern her interactions. A person can fail to be trustworthy because she does not frame an inter-action as one that requires strong trust, even though she would have been motivated to be trustworthy had she framed it differently.[51]

Further, in that book we make the distinction between weak trust and strong trust. Weak trust is behaviour which is entirely driven by self-interest, while strong trust is based on a regard for the wellbeing of others (Adam Smith's 'Other-regarding behaviour').[52] If the trading relationship is based only on weak trust, then the trading partners need to construct and enforce contracts, arrangements and regulations containing clauses to cover every possible eventuality. If, however, they are motivated by strong trust, then an incomplete contract may suffice, and it may be possible to avoid costly legal processes. As Gold observes, 'it is clear from this that, where strong trust is available, it is more efficient than weak'.[53] In the main, trade arrangements

[50] M Gleeson, 'The Role of a Judge in a Representative Democracy' (speech to the Judiciary of the Commonwealth of the Bahamas, 4 January 2008), www.hcourt.gov.au/assets/publications/speeches/former-justices/gleesoncj/cj_4jan08.pdf.

[51] N Gold, 'Trustworthiness and Motivations' in N Morris and D Vines (eds), *Capital Failure: Rebuilding Trust in Financial Services* (Oxford, Oxford University Press, 2014).

[52] For a discussion of the relevant aspects of Adam Smith's work, notably expressed in his 'Theory of Moral Sentiments', see A Offer, 'Regard for Others' in N Morris and D Vines (eds), *Capital Failure: Rebuilding Trust in Financial Services* (Oxford, Oxford University Press, 2014).

[53] See Gold (n 51) 139.

mostly fall into the category of weak trust, with both parties seeking the best advantage from their own point of view. However, the rhetoric of President Xi's remarks suggests that, at least from the Chinese side, they seek something more, and are taking into account, at least in principle, the longer-term interests of their trading partners. In this way, trade agreements between partners with very different social, cultural and governmental structures, may play a wider role than, for example, trade agreements between two well-developed countries with similar cultural backgrounds.

Capital Failure also explores how law and regulation might be utilised to tilt the battleground of norm formation at the individual, organisational and national levels in favour of a more ethical culture. It explores the potential efficacy of both regulatory strategies (eg, process-oriented regulation) and governance strategies (eg, corporate objectives, directors' duties, ethics committees, and remuneration) as mechanisms for introducing a norm of 'other-regarding' behaviour into the decision-making processes of companies and governments.

V. THE AUSTRALIAN LEGAL SYSTEM

Australian laws and regulations are based on the common law system inherited from the UK.[54] Common law is quite flexible, relying on precedent and the latest set of judges to adapt to new situations.[55] In some areas, judges cite 'public policy' as a reason for changing their interpretation of the law, although there is some resistance to the judiciary usurping the role of legislators in this way.[56] Common law imposes fiduciary duties of loyalty,[57] but these are sometimes set aside where apparently well-informed consent is given, and the courts in many Western states have recently regarded contracts as taking precedence over common law fiduciary duties. Apparent fiduciary duties have also been eroded by the increasing ability of agents to 'contract around' such duties, as well as the development of corporate law to include, for example, the 'business judgement' rule.[58]

[54] For a general discussion of common law systems, and comparison with civil law systems, see 'The Common Law and Civil Law Traditions' (The Robbins Collection), www.law.berkeley.edu/library/robbins/pdf/CommonLawCivilLawTraditions.pdf.

[55] K Turcotte, 'Why Legal Flexibility is not a Threat to either the Common Law System of England and Australia or the Civil Law System of France in the Twenty-first Century' (2005) 1(2) *Hanse Law Review* 190.

[56] Gleeson (n 50).

[57] T Frankel, 'Fiduciary Law: The Judicial Process and the Duty of Care' (1993 Isaac Pitblado Lectures, University of Manitoba Law School, 1993).

[58] SS Arsht, 'The Business Judgment Rule Revisited' (1979) 8(1) *Hofstra Law Review* 93. The business judgement rule, which has been part of the common law for two centuries, recognises, at its simplest, that directors should not be held liable for honest mistakes or unpopular business decisions.

As a result, the ability of common law systems to define and uphold obligations and responsibilities, and hence encourage and enforce trustworthy behaviour, can be subject to pressure from both sides of the trading relationship. Some commentators have argued that there is now a need to clarify the nature of duties and remedies, and to re-establish the primacy of fiduciary requirements,[59] a matter which has received greater attention since the Global Financial Crisis. This is important in trading relationships, to ensure that those with greater access to information, to expertise, or to relevant knowledge do not use this in ways which are detrimental to the longer-term trading relationship.

Common law jurisdictions also often resist direct prohibition (eg, of unreliable or toxic financial services products), regarding this as infringing personal liberty and inhibiting free markets.[60] Regulation in such systems can be ineffective if it is limited to compliance and ensuring disclosure. Incentives for the enforcement of trustworthy behaviour are constrained by the high costs of bringing legal actions. Finally, penalties imposed on multinational corporations tend to be insufficient to deter untrustworthy behaviour. Unless these deficiencies can be overcome, the common law system will struggle to be effective in encouraging and enforcing trustworthy behaviour. Class actions are seen by some as a solution to this problem.[61]

Western legal tradition, both in common law and civil law jurisdictions, has sought to place boundaries between politics, morality and law, in order to protect individuals from abuse of power by the government.[62] Unfortunately, this has to some extent eroded the effectiveness of the law in encouraging trustworthy behaviour, as the lack of a moral basis for legal enforcement reduces its ethical basis.[63]

VI. CHINESE LAW AND PRACTICE

It has been argued elsewhere that China's superior performance in recent years reflects major differences in approach from most other countries,

[59] J Getzler, 'Financial Crisis and the Decline of Fiduciary Law' in N Morris and D Vines (eds), *Capital Failure: Rebuilding Trust in Financial Services* (Oxford, Oxford University Press, 2104).

[60] H Genn, 'Common Law Reasoning and Institutions' (Faculty of Laws, University College London, 2015), www.londoninternational.ac.uk/sites/default/files/documents/clri-subjectguide2015-ch1-4.pdf.

[61] Many of these problems also occur in civil law systems. For a detailed discussion of the relative effectiveness of common law and civil law systems, see GK Hadfield, 'The Quality of Law in Civil Code and Common Law Regimes: Judicial Incentives, Legal Human Capital and the Evolution of Law' (University of Southern California Law School, March 2006), law.yale.edu/system/files/documents/pdf/The_Quality_of_Law_in_Civil_Code.pdf.

[62] MA Glendon, P Carozza and C Picker, *Comparative Legal Traditions in a Nutshell*, 3rd edn (St Paul, MN, West Academic Publishing, 2008).

[63] S Shavell, 'Law versus Morality as Regulators of Conduct' (2002) 4(2) *American Law and Economics Review* 227.

and derives from fundamental philosophical attitudes developed during the long history of China.[64] The concept of moral values being needed to sustain social stability and prosperity can be traced back to Laotzu and Confucius in 500 BC,[65] and the concepts derived from both Taoism and Confucianism have provided guidance on how to ensure the trustworthiness of institutions, organisations and individuals.[66] We have already noted that the Chinese may have in mind not only the optimisation of commercial arrangements, but also the facilitation of cultural alignment between the two societies. This is akin to the development of strong trust between the two parties, which we have argued is potentially a more efficient basis for trade arrangements. Such alignment is consistent with Taoist and Confucian principles and with Chinese practice as evidenced by *Guanxi* relationships.

In the Taoist model, which was accepted by Confucianism in later years, Yin and Yang forces create five major subordinate forces (benevolence (*Ren*), propriety (*Li*), faithfulness (*Xin*), justice (*Yi*) and wisdom (*Zhi*)). Where legal and regulatory systems are weak or underdeveloped, the basis of trust embedded in the values of society can still be used to ensure a fair and efficient outcome. Today, value-based principles derived from the ethical framework of Taoism and Confucianism are generally accepted as underpinning the network of interpersonal relationship among leaders and followers in China that cooperate and support one another.[67]

Ancient Chinese legal traditions are still dominant in the Chinese system, and norms of behaviour are well understood in Chinese society. Chinese legal tradition is grounded in ethical principles so it is potentially capable of specifying duties. The planning, governmental control systems, and even informal arrangements that have been effective in China's development over the past four decades are, I believe, a direct result of these Taoist and Confucian philosophical underpinnings, which lead to a beneficial style of economic mechanism which has been called 'Economic Taoism'.[68]

Formal Chinese law is focused on supporting administrative systems, and often relies on persuasion and relationship-based penalties rather than

[64] XZ Bai and N Morris, 'Leadership and Virtue Ethics: A Daoist Approach' (2014) 16(2) *Public Integrity* 173.

[65] PSS Wong, PA Neck and B McKenna, *Spiritual Wisdom of Taoism in Business: Toward a General Theory of Action* (Cambridge, MA, Harvard University Press, 2013).

[66] XZ Bai and N Morris, 'The Significance of the Ethical Framework of Taoism and Confucianism in the Chinese Politics and Society' (Asia-Pacific Humanities and Social Sciences Conference, Shanghai, November 2014).

[67] S Lovett, LC Simmons and R Kali, 'Guanxi versus the Market: Ethics and Efficiency' (1999) 30(2) *Journal of International Business Studies* 231.

[68] XZ Bai and N Morris, 'China, Economic Taoism, and Development: Different Paradigms and Different Outcomes' in C Picker, L Toohey and J Greenacre (eds), *China in the International Economic Order: New Directions and Changing Paradigms* (New York, Cambridge University Press, 2015).

extensive codification or legal intervention.[69] Chinese legal practice also makes extensive use of arbitration, especially in labour disputes, and has a strong impact on social practice and cultural understandings of rights.[70] Whereas methodological individualism and utilitarianism in Western systems makes the job of the law in supporting trustworthiness difficult, the need to attend to relationships and the ability of an authoritarian regime to impose regulations and penalties potentially enhances the ability of the Chinese system to set and enforce appropriate norms.

VII. LONGER-TERM CONSIDERATIONS

In the development of the 'Sussex Framework' for the evaluation of trading agreements, researchers at Sussex University[71] make the distinction between 'Shallow' and 'Deep' integration. They provide the following, helpful, definition of what comprises 'Deep' integration:

> Deep, or positive, integration involves policies and institutions that facilitate trade by reducing or eliminating regulatory and behind-the-border impediments to trade, where those impediments may or may not be intentional. These can include issues such as customs procedures, regulation of domestic services production that discriminate against foreigners, product standards that differ from international norms or where testing and certification of foreign goods is complex and perhaps exclusionary, regulation of inward investments, competition policy, intellectual policy protection and the rules surrounding access to government procurement.[72]

President Xi's remarks, and the fact that ChAFTA contains numerous arrangements which, at least in intention, seek such deep integration suggest that the development of these longer-term arrangements is the intention of both parties. This reinforces the need to ensure that Australian common law-based laws and regulations harmonise well with Chinese legal and regulatory practice. The Sussex authors emphasise the need to create a 'common economic space', which involves 'both removal of barriers to trade that operate behind borders (eg, discriminatory taxes and regulations) as well as actions to undertake common policies needed for dealing with the existence of public goods and externalities'.[73]

In addition, compliance with the WTO arrangements in other respects is important, at least in the longer term. A number of authors have stressed the

[69] HP Glenn, *Legal Traditions of the World*, 4th edn (Oxford, Oxford University Press, 2010).

[70] NJ Diamant, BL Stanley and KJ O'Brien, *Engaging the Law in China: State, Society, and Possibilities for Justice* (Stanford, CA, Stanford University Press, 2005).

[71] Centre for the Analysis of Regional Integration at Sussex (CARIS).

[72] D Evans et al, 'Assessing Preferential Trading Agreements Using the Sussex Framework' (2007) Centre for the Analysis of Regional Integration at Sussex (CARIS) Working Paper No 1, www.sussex.ac.uk/webteam/gateway/file.php?name=cariswp01.pdf&site=261.

[73] ibid 8.

disadvantages of preferential trade agreements, such as ChAFTA, in trade facilitation and in dispute settlement.[74] One example of the problems raised is the need to establish the 'nationality' of each product for which preferential tariffs are agreed, a process which can be used politically:[75]

> What makes RoO (rules of origin) particularly relevant is that they are not a neutral instrument: given that RoO can serve as an effective means to deter transhipment, they can tempt political economy uses well beyond trade deflection. Indeed, RoO are widely described as a trade policy instrument that can work to offset the benefits of tariff liberalization.[76]

In the light of recent geopolitical changes, such as 'Brexit' and the election of Donald Trump as President of the United States of America, it is important that preferential trading arrangements such as ChAFTA take into account the difficulties of ensuring ongoing, trustworthy, implementation. This includes ensuring that other trading partners, both of China and of Australia, are not unduly disadvantaged by the arrangements.

VIII. LEARNING FROM CONFUCIUS

Confucian legal practice emerged from systems that had persisted for thousands of years. Confucius was the architect of the *li*, which believes that large populations can only be held together by informal and long-term agreement, and which denies the lasting and effective normativity of formal law and formal sanctions.[77] In developing this, he was reflecting the belief most recently expressed by the Chinese Planning Commission (National Development and Reform Commission (NDRC)),[78] that mutual trust and respect are crucial in the development of sustainable commercial relationships. In modern terms,[79] Confucius believed trustworthy actions could only emerge from strong trust, that is trust which genuinely emerges from concern for the welfare of others.

Nevertheless, there is a long tradition of formal law and formal sanctions, or *fa*, in Chinese law, dating back to the legalists of at least the eighth century

74 H Dieter, 'The Multilateral Trading System and Preferential Trade Agreements: Can their Negative Effects be Minimised?' (2008) German Institute for International and Security Affairs, Berlin, GARNET Working Paper No 54/08, www2.warwick.ac.uk/fac/soc/pais/research/researchcentres/csgr/garnet/workingpapers/5408.pdf.

75 A Krueger, 'Free Trade Agreements as Protectionist Devices: Rules of Origin' (1993) National Bureau of Economic Research Working Paper No 4352, ssrn.com/abstract=1852078.

76 A Estevadeordal, J Harris and K Suominen, 'Multilateralising Preferential Rules of Origin Around the World' (WTO–HEI Conference on Multilateralising Regionalism, Geneva, 10–12 September 2007), www.wto.org/english/tratop_e/region_e/con_sep07_e/estevadeordal_harris_suominen_e.pdf.

77 Glenn (n 69) 321.

78 For a description of its activities and importance, see 'Main Functions of the NDRC', en.ndrc.gov.cn/mfndrc/.

79 Gold (n 51).

BC (500 years before Confucius).[80] *Fa* means imposed standards, which are needed to deal with those who engage in criminal conduct or conduct which does not match the established order. The development of criminal/administrative codes continued through to the last of the dynasties, the Ch'ing, which terminated in 1911, and became greatly admired in Europe, where the final versions were translated into French, Russian and English.[81]

China's use of value-based leadership and its associated trustworthy relationship *Guanxi*, underpinned by Taoist and Confucian ethical values, have been used to drive trading arrangements for thousands of years.[82] Chinese politics and society today are still largely driven by focus on trustworthy relationships.[83] With the core values grounded in legislative mandates, national mission, vision statements of leaders, and in political and public will, the ethical framework of Taoism and Confucianism is playing an increasing role in harmonising Chinese society and keeping it sustainable.[84] The fact that the Chinese legal system is grounded in ethical principles arguably makes it a better system for the encouragement of trustworthiness, because it is potentially capable of specifying duties and prohibiting untrustworthy actions.

As a result, many of the problems with which Western capitalist systems are now struggling do not arise to the same extent in the Chinese system.[85] This is partly because Chinese society places a greater value on trustworthiness, and does not rely in the same way on markets to ensure ethical outcomes. Confucianism gives considerable attention to 'virtue, benevolence, social rightness and morality—with harmony as a central goal'.[86] It is also because the trustworthy relationship *Guanxi* system, reinforced by the apparatus of state control, including specification of 'honours and disgraces' for leaders, contains systems for holding 'faithless' individuals and companies to account that the incentives for trustworthy behaviour are stronger.[87]

[80] Books of punishment existed for at least three centuries before Confucianism became the official doctrine in China, around the late third century BC. Glenn (n 69) 323.

[81] ibid.

[82] W Ling and L Fang, 'The Chinese Leadership Theory' in *Advances in Global Leadership*, vol 3 (UK, Emerald Group Publishing Limited, 2003).

[83] Lovett, Simmons and Kali (n 67).

[84] J Liu, Y Wang and L Wu, 'The Effect of Guanxi on Audit Quality in China' (2011) 103 *Journal of Business Ethics* 621; Luo, Huang and Wang (n 9) 139–72; Shi and Cui (n 10).

[85] T Kuran, 'West Is Best? Why Civilizations Rise and Fall' (2011) 90(1) *Foreign Affairs* 159; J Whalley et al, 'China and the Financial Crisis' (CIGI/Chinese Academy of Social Sciences Task Force, 2009), citeseerx.ist.psu.edu/viewdoc/download?doi=10.1.1.357.8648&rep=rep1&type=pdf.

[86] Picker, 'China, Global Governance and Legal Culture' (n 46) 77.

[87] T Hu, 'To Set up Construct Socialist Concepts on Honors and Disgraces' (in Chinese) *The People's Press* (4 March 2006), politics.people.com.cn/GB/1024/4336318.html; 胡锦涛(2006)：牢固树立社会主义荣辱观，人民网>>时政>>高层动态，２００６年３月４日，politics.people.com.cn/GB/1024/4336318.html; DC Yang, 'The Present State of Evaluation of Civil Servants and the Policy Recommendation' (in Chinese) (2010) 6 *Journal of Chongqing University* (Social Science edn) 68; 阳东辰(2010): 中国公务员绩效考核制度的现状与改革对策，重庆大学学报(社会科学版).

IX. CONCLUSION

Sustainability of ChAFTA arrangements will, I believe, require that determining what can be achieved through consensus and long-term sustainable relationships, in the manner of Confucian *li*, is given precedence, and that resort to formal penalties and prohibitions, in the manner of Confucian *fa*, is limited to those cases where *li* is genuinely impossible or ineffective. The fact that there is an ongoing Work Programme for the Australian and Chinese governments to implement ChAFTA effectively respects this need. Understanding and taking into account differences both of legal and regulatory systems, and of local culture, is important in the development of a harmonised legal and regulatory system to underpin the China–Australia Free Trade Agreement. The development of strong trust between the two parties is likely, in the long run, to lead to trading arrangements which are more sustainable, and efficient, than if the arrangements simply reflect the maximisation of short-term commercial advantage.

4

ChAFTA's External Impact on Related Mega-FTAs

CHANG-FA LO

I. INTRODUCTION: THE NEED TO LOOK AT THE EXTERNAL IMPORTANCE OF CHAFTA TO OTHER REGIONAL AGREEMENTS

AUSTRALIA AND CHINA have a very close and important economic and trade relationship with each other: China is the largest export market for Australia's goods and services[1] and Australia is economically important to China.[2] The operation of ChAFTA will be a significant force in continuing and strengthening such economic and trade relations. But it must be noted that the importance of ChAFTA is not limited to its enhancement of the bilateral economic ties between the two economically and politically important countries. Hence in addition to looking at ChAFTA's economic significance for its parties, it is also important to look at the Agreement from a broader perspective to see whether it also has external implications or impacts, especially for the regional trade arrangements (RTAs), such as those RTAs which geographically cover either Australia or China. This chapter chooses two proposed RTAs, ie, the Regional Comprehensive Economic Partnership (RCEP) and the Trans-Pacific Partnership Agreement (TPP), as examples to illustrate ChAFTA's external significance.

There are good reasons to consider ChAFTA's external impacts–especially on the regional RTAs considered in this chapter. First, both of the proposed

[1] China is the world's second largest economy and is the largest export market for Australia's goods and services (accounting for nearly one third of total exports of Australia) and also a growing source of foreign investment in Australia. See Department of Foreign Affairs and Trade, 'China–Australia Free Trade Agreement', dfat.gov.au/trade/agreements/chafta/Pages/australia-china-fta.aspx.

[2] Australia is China's sixth largest trading partner (China's fifth biggest supplier and tenth biggest buyer). See A Holmes, 'Australia's Economic Relationships with China' (Parliament of Australia, December 2013), www.aph.gov.au/About_Parliament/Parliamentary_Departments/Parliamentary_Library/pubs/BriefingBook44p/China.

RTAs are going to be mega-FTAs (concerning their respective geographic coverages and their high percentages of global GDP) if they are created. These proposed RTAs include either one or both of the ChAFTA parties. China is a common party to ChAFTA and the RCEP. Australia is a common party to ChAFTA, the RCEP and the TPP. There are thus geographical overlaps between ChAFTA on the one hand and the RCEP/TPP on the other. Such overlaps could affect the respective operations of these Agreements. Second, the formation and negotiations of the RCEP and the TPP were initiated and supported by some leading countries with specific strategic goals in mind. It would be meaningful to examine whether ChAFTA has any implications for those strategic imperatives. Third, it is worth exploring whether ChAFTA could contribute to the survival of the TPP after the US' withdrawal from the partnership. Fourth, different FTAs have different standards/levels of trade liberalisation, intellectual property protection and investment liberalisation/protection. It would therefore be useful to reflect whether the standards adopted by ChAFTA will be an important benchmark for the further negotiations of the RCEP.

Section II of this chapter explains the geographic overlaps between ChAFTA on the one hand and the RCEP and the TPP on the other, as well as the impact arising from such overlaps. Section III of this chapter argues that the conclusion and implementation of ChAFTA has some implications for the strategic goals of the US with the TPP. The successful operation of ChAFTA can also serve as an incentive to encourage China to consider participation in the TPP. Section IV argues that there are possible positive effects of ChAFTA serving as a benchmark for the negotiations of the RCEP so as to make its liberalisation of higher quality. Section IV summarises the various external impacts of ChAFTA on the two identified mega-FTAs.

II. THE IMPACT OF THE GEOGRAPHIC OVERLAPS BETWEEN CHAFTA, THE RCEP AND TPP

A. ChAFTA's Geographic Overlaps with the RCEP and TPP

As an initial matter it should be noted that although the Trump Administration in the US has withdrawn from the TPP and that therefore some of the TPP participating countries are having serious doubt about the future of the TPP without the US,[3] some of the other TPP participating countries

[3] C Reichert, 'TPP: With Trump out, is China in?' (*ZDNet*, 27 January 2017), www.zdnet.com/article/tpp-with-trump-out-is-china-in/.

are still considering the creation of a TPP without the US.[4] For instance, the heads of the Japanese and Australian governments are still trying to bring some version of the TPP into force, although there are commentators saying that even such a revised or rebranded TPP will still not be enacted.[5] There are also views being disseminated about having some form of the TPP with China as an additional participating country.[6]

The TPP was originally concluded between 12 parties, including Australia, Brunei Darussalam, Canada, Chile, Japan, Malaysia, Mexico, New Zealand, Peru, Singapore, the United States and Viet Nam, though now the US has withdrawn from the proposed agreement. The RCEP, in contrast, is currently being negotiated between 16 parties, including the 10 ASEAN Member States[7] and six of the ASEAN's FTA Partners (Australia, China, India, Japan, Korea and New Zealand). Such mega-FTAs clearly will have geographic overlaps with other FTAs.

There are two kinds of geographic overlap between different FTAs (ie, different FTAs having common parties). The first kind is where one FTA (especially a mega-FTA) embraces all the parties of another FTA. The embracing one (such as the RCEP or the TPP) can be called the 'outer-FTA' and the embraced one can be called the 'inner-FTA' (such as the ASEAN–Australia–New Zealand FTA and the China–ASEAN FTA being inner-FTAs of the RCEP, and the US–Australia FTA being an inner-FTA of the TPP).[8] The overlapping situation between ChAFTA and the RCEP is of such a kind. Both China and Australia are parties negotiating the conclusion of the RCEP. Hence ChAFTA will become an inner-FTA of the RCEP when the RCEP is created.

In this context, it should be noted that this 'inner/outer-FTA' relation is somewhat similar with, and somewhat different from, an 'FTA/WTO' relation. The similar aspect is that an inner-FTA is geographically fully embraced by the outer-FTA, just like how an FTA (if its parties are WTO Members) is geographically fully embraced by the World Trade Organization (WTO). The difference is that an FTA is governed by the General Agreement on

[4] I Reynolds and M Heath, 'Australia Pushes for TPP without US after Trump Exits Deal' (24 January 2017), www.bloomberg.com/politics/articles/2017-01-24/australia-leads-push-for-tpp-without-u-s-after-trump-exits-deal.

[5] B McHugh, 'Trans Pacific Partnership on Trade Almost Defunct, But Regional Comprehensive Economic Partnership May Take Its Place' (*ABC News*, 16 January 2017), www.abc.net.au/news/2017-01-16/will-tpp-be-replaced-by-china-led-rcep/8180514.

[6] P Karp, 'Australia Open to China and Indonesia Joining TPP after US Pulls Out' *The Guardian* (23 January 2017), www.theguardian.com/australia-news/2017/jan/24/australia-open-to-china-and-indonesia-joining-tpp-after-us-pulls-out.

[7] The ten members are: Brunei, Cambodia, Indonesia, Laos, Malaysia, Myanmar, the Philippines, Singapore, Thailand and Vietnam (listed alphabetically).

[8] The concepts of the 'inner-FTA' and the 'outer-FTA' are used in C Lo, 'Coordinative Approach to Resolve Normative and Operational Conflicts between Inner and Outer-FTAs' (2016) 50 *Journal of World Trade* 147.

Tariffs and Trade (GATT) Article XXIV,[9] including the requirement that the duties and other regulations of commerce shall not be higher or more restrictive than the corresponding duties and other regulations of commerce existing in the same constituent territories prior to the formation of the FTA as provided in Article XXIV:5(b) and that the duties and other restrictive regulations of commerce (except, where necessary, those permitted under Articles XI, XII, XIII, XIV, XV and XX) are eliminated on substantially all the trade between the FTA parties in products originating in such parties as provided in Article XXIV:8(b). But an inner-FTA is not 'governed' by an outer-FTA through any provision stipulated in the outer-FTA. They are both governed by GATT Article XXIV. Having explained that the 'inner/outer-FTA' relation is different from the 'FTA/WTO' relation, it must also be noted that operationally speaking, an FTA's operation is basically not affected by the WTO. For instance, both parties can decide to have their dispute either resolved in the WTO or in an FTA, just like they can decide to have their dispute either resolved in the outer-FTA or in the inner-FTA. If a party decides to rely on the WTO's Dispute Settlement Mechanism (DSM) and if such action is against the provision in the FTA, the WTO's dispute settlement panel will have to decide whether to apply the good faith principle or the principle of estoppel to reject the complaint. This is similar to the situation where a party decides to rely on the outer-FTA's DSM in contradiction to the provision in the inner-FTA. The outer-FTA's adjudicator will also have to decide whether to apply the good faith principle or the principle of estoppel to reject the complaint.

The second kind of geographic overlap between different FTAs is where one FTA has partial common parties with another FTA. The overlapping situation between ChAFTA and the TPP is of such a kind. Australia is a negotiating party to the TPP. But China is not. If the proposed TPP is created, Australia will become a common party to ChAFTA and the TPP.

As will be explained below, the first kind of overlap (ie, the embracing-embraced or outer-inner situation) could affect the operation of both Agreements. A trade dispute between China and Australia could be resolved under ChAFTA or under the RCEP when the RCEP is concluded and becomes effective. But, the situation of partial common parties between two FTAs does not cause serious operational issue. A trade dispute between China and Australia can be resolved under ChAFTA, but the dispute cannot be resolved under the TPP (if the TPP finally becomes effective without China's participation). However, as will be explained, the TPP's substantive rules could still affect the implementation and operation of ChAFTA.

[9] If an FTA includes liberalisation in trade in services, it is also governed by the General Agreement on Trade in Services (GATS) Art V (especially para 1), which requires an economic integration to have substantial sectoral coverage and to eliminate all discriminations.

B. The Overlaps and the Operation of ChAFTA and the RCEP

Substantively, the obligations assumed by the overlapping parties (ie, China and Australia) under ChAFTA and the RCEP could be different. For instance, it is possible that China's commitment of trade liberalisation for a specific product or service under ChAFTA could be higher than its commitment for the same product or service under the RCEP—indeed that is not unlikely given that concessions narrowly tailored in a bilateral FTA may be deeper than those offered more widely in plurilateral FTAs, especially mega-FTAs.

As indicated above, ChAFTA and the RCEP have an 'inner and outer FTAs' relation. ChAFTA is definitely going to be a very important 'inner-FTA' to the RCEP. They will have operational interactions after the RCEP is created. Each one of these FTAs can impact the operation of the other. If a complaining party (either sporadically or consistently) prefers conducting its bilateral interactions under ChAFTA, instead of under the RCEP, the operation of the RCEP could certainly be undermined.

For instance, if there is a dispute between the two parties and if the substantive rules governing their respective rights and obligations (including their respective substantive commitments) in regard to the dispute are different in these two Agreements, the forum chosen by the complaining party would also decide the substantive rules to be applied. If ChAFTA's DSM is used, the substantive rules provided in ChAFTA will govern the dispute. Whereas if the RCEP's DSM is used, the substantive rules provided in the RCEP will govern the dispute. Since the RCEP does not have its text made available to the public yet, we can only look at ChAFTA's substantive provisions and dispute settlement provisions to examine the situation.

The substantive and consultation provisions to address the conflict between ChAFTA and other FTAs are provided in Article 1.2 of ChAFTA, which states:

> 1. The Parties affirm their existing rights and obligations with respect to each other under multilateral and bilateral agreements to which both Parties are party, including the WTO Agreement.
>
> 2. Nothing in this Agreement shall derogate from the existing rights and obligations of a Party under the WTO Agreement or any other multilateral or bilateral agreement to which both Parties are party.
>
> 3. In the event of any inconsistency between this Agreement and any other multilateral or bilateral agreement to which both Parties are party, the Parties shall immediately consult with a view to finding a mutually satisfactory solution.[10]

[10] Free Trade Agreement between the Government of Australia and the Government of the People's Republic of China (ChAFTA) (signed 17 June 2015, entered into force 20 December 2015) [2015] ATS 15, Art 1.2.

Since there is no indication in these provisions that the term 'existing rights and obligations' should refer only to the substantive rights and obligations, they therefore should include substantive and procedural rights and obligations under other multilateral and bilateral agreements. From the substantive aspect, the substantive rights and obligations of China and Australia under ChAFTA and the RCEP will be in parallel according to the above provisions. They coexist and do not affect each other. But this approach could become confusing and does not resolve problems in real cases. If a ChAFTA substantive obligation is in conflict with an RCEP substantive obligation, China or Australia will have to know which one to follow. Although both parties can consult, they might not be able to find a solution. Also, if a ChAFTA party's level of liberalisation of a product is higher than the same party's liberalisation commitment under the RCEP for the same product, it is possible that a dispute concerning the liberalisation commitment for such product being resolved under ChAFTA could result in a more favourable outcome for the complaining party than the outcome for the same dispute being resolved under the RCEP.

The procedural provisions to address the possible conflict between ChAFTA and the RCEP are also provided in Article 15.4 of ChAFTA:

> 1. Unless otherwise provided in this Article, this Chapter is without prejudice to the rights of the Parties to have recourse to dispute settlement procedures available under other international trade agreements to which they are both parties.
>
> 2. Where a dispute regarding any matter arises under this Agreement and under another international trade agreement to which both Parties are party, the complaining Party may select the forum in which to settle the dispute.
>
> 3. Once the complaining Party has requested the establishment of, or referred a matter to, a dispute settlement panel or arbitral tribunal, the forum selected shall be used to the exclusion of the others.[11]

Under these provisions in Article 15.4, both China and Australia maintain their right to have recourse to dispute settlement procedures under the future RCEP. The complaining party can select either the RCEP or ChAFTA as the forum to settle the dispute it has with the other party. Once a selection is made, the other dispute settlement procedure will be excluded. Such approach does not, however, solve the overlap issues between ChAFTA and the RCEP because it is possible that the result under the dispute settlement procedure of ChAFTA could be different from the result under the RCEP due to their different substantive obligations, as explained above.

There are also additional issues involved here. First, since Article 1.2 of ChAFTA has provided that the 'existing rights and obligations with respect

[11] ibid Art 15.4.

to each other under multilateral and bilateral agreements to which both Parties are party' are affirmed and since the 'existing rights and obligations' should include 'procedural rights', the consultation requirement under Article 1.2.3 logically should also include the consultation of the inconsistency between ChAFTA and another agreement concerning their DSMs. In other words, when parties have different views about the DSM to be used for a specific dispute, they shall also immediately consult each other with a view to finding a mutually satisfactory solution. Because of the provision in Article 1.2.3, the complaining party will have to consult the other party to resolve different views about the selection of the dispute settlement forum prior to the complaining party's exercise of rights under Article 15.4.2 to select the forum to be used to settle the dispute. Second, there is no immediate effect arising from the failure of conducting consultation based on Article 1.2.3. If the complaining party ultimately selects ChAFTA's DSM, supposedly the other party of ChAFTA should not have a problem with that (at least from the perspective of ChAFTA), because it is to maintain the function of ChAFTA. But if the complaining party selects the DSM under another agreement, Article 1.2.3 of ChAFTA will not be directly applied by the adjudicator of that DSM. In such a situation, there will be a question as to whether the responding party can argue that because of the complaining party's failure to conduct consultations to address the conflict of forum, it is not bringing the complaint in a good faith manner. Arguably, if the DSM in another agreement includes a 'good faith provision' to govern its whole dispute settlement procedure,[12] the good faith argument should be considered by the adjudicator in the procedure under another agreement. Third, under Article 15.4.3, when the complaining party has referred a matter to a DSM, the forum selected shall be used to the exclusion of the others. If the complaining party has referred the case to the DSM under another agreement, both the complaining party and the other party are not to bring the complaint under ChAFTA. Otherwise, the complaint should be dismissed based on Article 15.4.3. On the other hand, if the complaining party has referred the case to the DSM under ChAFTA, the other party is supposed to be prevented from submitting the case to the DSM under another agreement. But in case the other party disregards the provision of Article 15.4.3 and still brings the complaint under the DSM of another agreement, the adjudicator of the DSM under another agreement cannot directly apply Article 15.4.3

[12] eg, Art 3.10 of the Dispute Settlement Understanding of the WTO provides in part: 'It is understood that requests for conciliation and the use of the dispute settlement procedures should not be intended or considered as contentious acts and that, if a dispute arises, all Members will engage in these procedures in good faith in an effort to resolve the dispute'. Understanding on Rules and Procedures Governing the Settlement of Disputes (15 April 1994) LT/UR/A-2/DS/U/1 Art 3.10, docsonline.wto.org.

of ChAFTA. In such a situation, the adjudicator of another agreement could consider that the party should be prevented by estoppel from bringing the complaint.[13] However, it is uncertain as to whether the principle of estoppel can always be applied by the adjudicator under the DSM of another agreement.[14]

In addition to the legal technicalities discussed above, consideration must be taken from the broader perspective of the continuous relations between the two Agreements (ie, ChAFTA and the RCEP). If the bilateral disputes are constantly taken under ChAFTA, it could undermine the operation of the RCEP. Whereas if they are always taken under the RCEP, it could weaken the effectiveness of ChAFTA. The conflict can be eased if it can be ensured that ChAFTA and the RCEP are as consistently liberalised as possible and hence that the substantive rules and commitments will become similar to each other so that the outcomes will be consistent no matter whether the dispute is resolved under ChAFTA or under the RCEP.

C. The Impact on ChAFTA of its Overlap with the TPP

For the proposed TPP, China was not a negotiating party. But Australia was a very important player in the negotiation and final formation of the TPP text. Through the participation of Australia in the TPP, there is an overlap in the geographical coverage between the TPP and ChAFTA. Such geographical overlap could affect the implementation of ChAFTA if the TPP can survive the US withdrawal from the partnership.

The standards of treatment in an agreement can be heightened because of another agreement. For instance, if a standard of protection of investment in the TPP is higher than that in ChAFTA, China may be able to claim the higher standard of protection committed by Australia under the TPP based

[13] The term 'estoppel' is considered as a rule of international law which prevents a party from 'going back on its previous representations when those representations have induced reliance or some detriment on the part of others'. E Voyiakis, 'Estoppel' (*Oxford Bibliographies*, 23 March 2012), www.oxfordbibliographies.com/view/document/obo-9780199796953/obo-9780199796953-0058.xml.

[14] For instance, in *Argentina—Poultry Anti-Dumping Duties*, it is stated in the panel report that: 'Argentina considers that Brazil's conduct in bringing the dispute successively before different fora, first MERCOSUR and then the WTO, constitutes a legal approach that is contrary to the principle of good faith and which, in the case at issue, warrants invocation of the principle of estoppel'. Argentina-Definitive Anti-Dumping Duties on Poultry from Brazil-Report of the Panel (22 April 2003) WT/DS241/R para 7.18, docsonline.wto.org; see also ibid para 7.37. The panel did not refuse the possible application of the principle of estoppel. But it rejected Argentina's claim that Brazil is estopped from pursuing the WTO dispute settlement proceedings because Argentina failed to persuade that the requirements of applying the principle of estoppel have been met. ibid paras 7.37–7.39.

on the Most-Favoured-Nation (MFN) provision in ChAFTA's investment chapter.

For instance, under ChAFTA, negotiations are not yet completed concerning the minimum standard of treatment (such as fair and equitable treatment) for investors and investments and the requirements for an expropriation of investment.[15] However, under the TPP, there are detailed rules and requirements concerning minimum standards of treatment[16] and concerning expropriation.[17] A question arises as to whether China would be able to claim, based on the MFN treatment provided in Article 9.4.1 of ChAFTA, that its investors should be entitled to fair and equitable treatment as well as to the compensation for expropriation granted to other TPP parties by Australia under the TPP. This particular Article reads:

> Each Party shall accord to investors of the other Party, and covered investments, in relation to the establishment, acquisition, expansion, management, conduct, operation, and sale or other disposition of investments in its territory, treatment no less favourable than that it accords, in like circumstances, to investors and investments in its territory of investors of any non-Party.[18]

From this perspective, the TPP (if it becomes effective) could affect the implementation of ChAFTA, notwithstanding that China is not party to the TPP, especially when the level of trade/investment liberalisation or investment protection in the TPP is higher than that in ChAFTA.

III. ChAFTA'S IMPLICATIONS FOR THE TPP

A. ChAFTA's Implications for the Strategic Goals of the US

Some have argued that the TPP was developed and supported by the US substantially in order to 'contain' and isolate China, to counteract China's increasingly greater dominance in Asia. The TPP was thought by some people to be a geopolitical victory and 'a pillar of Washington's "pivot" to Asia' and 'a testament to America's staying power in the region'.[19] There were also claims made that the Chinese-led RCEP and the US-led TPP were competing geopolitical tools of the two competing powers.[20] However,

[15] See ChAFTA (n 10) Art 9.9.3.

[16] See Trans-Pacific Partnership Agreement (TPP Agreement) Art 9.6, ustr.gov/trade-agreements/free-trade-agreements/trans-pacific-partnership/tpp-full-text.

[17] See ibid Art 9.8.

[18] ChAFTA (n 10) Art 9.4.1.

[19] M Meidan, 'The TPP and China: The Elephant That Wasn't in the Room' (15 October 2015), thediplomat.com/2015/10/the-tpp-and-china-the-elephant-that-wasnt-in-the-room/.

[20] GG Chang, 'TPP vs RCEP: America and China Battle for Control of Pacific Trade' (6 October 2015), nationalinterest.org/feature/tpp-vs-rcep-america-china-battle-control-pacific-trade-14021.

there were also contrary views. For example, it was argued that the TPP's raison d'être being the containment of China was both counterproductive and incorrect. American officials had also made remarks about the TPP not being an 'exclusive club' and about the US welcoming nations which were willing to meet the TPP's standards.[21] Since the TPP has not become 'a thing of the past', it is helpful to consider the implication of ChAFTA for those strategic aspects of the TPP.

From China's perspective, ChAFTA can be considered as an important step in breaking any US-led containment and counteracting the US' attempted rebalance in the Asia-Pacific region. Though, there have already been other breaks of the US containment policy, such as the China–Korea FTA[22] and the proposed China–Japan–Korea FTA.[23] But ChAFTA is of even higher importance to China for many reasons: first, Australia and the US have long been close allies—some have argued that Australia has been America's closest ally (serving with the US in numerous geopolitical conflicts, such as the Vietnam conflict during the 1960s and 1970s, and more recently with the US in Iraq and Afghanistan—even when other supposed close allies, such as the UK, were absent). The conclusion and the successful operation of ChAFTA mean that the US is not able, through a regional agreement (such as the proposed TPP), to confine China's policy in pursuing and establishing a close tie with the US' long-time close economic/strategic partner.[24] From this perspective, ChAFTA has a very important external implication for China in counterbalancing the US' relations in the Asia-Pacific region.

Second, although Australia was not the first Western country to sign an FTA with China,[25] it was the first 'major' Western developed country to create an FTA relationship with China. Hence, in addition to the economic impacts which could contribute to both parties, the conclusion of ChAFTA also indicates that it is possible and practicable for the major Western powers to establish an FTA with China. These sorts of relationships are thus symbolic for China and could serve as an encouragement for other major Western countries (including those which also closely cooperate with the US' geopolitics) to establish a closer economic relation with China. Broadly

[21] P O'Connor, 'The Trans-Pacific Partnership: A Trade Agreement of Inclusion, Not Containment' (Center for Strategic & International Studies, 6 January 2016), www.csis.org/analysis/pacnet-2-trans-pacific-partnership-trade-agreement-inclusion-not-containment.

[22] The text of the China–Korea FTA can be found at fta.mofcom.gov.cn/topic/enkorea.shtml.

[23] The progress of the proposed China–Japan–Korea FTA can be found at fta.mofcom.gov.cn/topic/chinarh.shtml.

[24] Australia is considered as the US' vital ally economically, in defence and security, and in many other aspects.

[25] China has its FTAs with New Zealand in 2008, with Iceland in 2013 and with Switzerland in 2014. See China FTA Network, 'China's Free Trade Agreements', fta.mofcom.gov.cn/english/fta_qianshu.shtml.

speaking, this also contributes to China's response to the US' 'chilly' position towards China.

Third, although ChAFTA is not necessarily a model for Western countries to consider or to follow when negotiating an FTA with China, it is certain that the packages which are contained in ChAFTA will be constantly looked at so as to see whether there are examples to be followed or things to be avoided when negotiating their FTAs with China. For instance, in some areas (such as the area of trade in goods mentioned below), the respective commitments of Australia and China are of a relatively high standard, but in some other areas (such as the area of trade in services entering into China mentioned below), their respective commitments are relatively moderate. In the area of trade in goods, 85.4 per cent in value of their trade has been subject to tariff-free status upon the entry into force of the Agreement. Upon the implementation of their commitments, Australia and China will have 100 per cent and about 97 per cent of their respective goods exports by value enjoying zero tariff. In the area of trade in services, Australia's commitments to China are made in its 'negative list'. But China still maintains a 'positive list' approach, though that may be changed during the scheduled renegotiations. In the area of investment, they grant MFN status to each other. Australia also commits to lower its approval threshold for Chinese investment.[26] It is likely that other Western countries pursuing their FTAs with China could consider China's commitments in ChAFTA as the basis, starting point or benchmark to make their requests in their future negotiations.

In some other areas, ChAFTA only reiterates the parties' rights and obligations under various WTO agreements. For instance, Article 7.9, paragraph 1, of ChAFTA provides that:

> Except as otherwise provided for in this Article, each Party retains its rights and obligations under the Agreement on Implementation of Article VI of the General Agreement on Tariffs and Trade 1994 (the Anti-Dumping Agreement) contained in Annex 1A to the WTO Agreement.[27]

It does not specifically mention whether Australia can still identify China as a non-market economy when conducting a 'specific anti-dumping investigation'. Although China had been given 'market economy status' by Australia in 2005 before both countries entered into ChAFTA negotiations,[28]

[26] China FTA Network, 'China–Australia FTA Officially Signed' (23 June 2015), fta.mofcom.gov.cn/enarticle/enaustralia/enaustralianews/201506/22255_1.html.

[27] ChAFTA (n 10) Art 7.9, para 1.

[28] 'Chapter 11—The Proposed Australia–China Free Trade Agreement' (Parliament of Australia, July 2004), www.aph.gov.au/Parliamentary_Business/Committees/Senate/Foreign_Affairs_Defence_and_Trade/Completed_inquiries/2004-07/china/report01/c11.

'surrogation' (which is a way to decide the normal value for the non-market economy in an anti-dumping investigation) was still introduced in investigations against some Chinese products when the Australian government was under pressure from domestic industries, especially during the period of the Australian dollar's appreciation between 2009 and 2014. Australia considered it had the right to make such a dumping calculation directly based on the Anti-Dumping Agreement. Of course, China strongly criticised the practice.[29] Nevertheless, that did not prevent both countries from concluding their bilateral FTA. This approach—of putting difficult and sensitive issues aside—definitely could be a very good example for other countries when negotiating their FTAs with China and hence help make their negotiations easier.

If US Western partners can establish closer trade ties with China more easily, the US would have a higher level of difficulty when seeking to economically or strategically confine China—through an FTA (such as the TPP) or other means.

B. ChAFTA's Implications for the Survival of the TPP

As mentioned above, there are differing views concerning the TPP's next steps after the withdrawal of the US from the partnership. One view is the possibility of including China in the TPP. This chapter argues, for a number of reasons, that the successful operation of ChAFTA can serve as an incentive to encourage China to consider participation in the TPP (which appears that it will be without the US).

First, one of the original ideas of promoting the TPP by the US (as suggested by many commentators) was to use it to confine China.[30] Now the US is out of the TPP game. The 'major' obstacle for China's consideration in participating in the TPP does not exit any more. But it needs to be noted that whether or not some rules in the current text of the TPP (such as those provisions in Chapter 14 of the TPP concerning freedom of cross-border flows in Article 14.11 and general prohibition against data localisation in Article 14.13, as well as those provisions in Chapter 17 of the TPP (ie, state-owned enterprises SOE), such as the non-discrimination and commercial consideration in Article 17.4 and the non-commercial assistance in

[29] Moulislegal, 'Aggressive Anti-Dumping Protection—The Dark Side of Australia's FTA Romance' (26 October 2015), moulislegal.com/aggressive-anti-dumping-protection-the-dark-side-of-australias-fta-romance/.

[30] See, for instance, World Economic Forum, 'Mega-regional Trade Agreements: Game-Changers or Costly Distractions for the World Trading System?' (July 2014), www3.weforum.org/docs/GAC/2014/WEF_GAC_TradeFDI_MegaRegionalTradeAgreements_Report_2014.pdf, 37 (especially concerning the discussion of the 'China containment' argument).

Article 17.6) would be acceptable to China is yet to be seen. Second, it is indeed hard to specifically compare the respective levels of liberalisation in the TPP and ChAFTA. But since ChAFTA is of 'relatively' high quality or high level with respect to liberalisations, it should be of less difficulty for China to achieve the level of liberalisation required in the TPP based on its existing commitments under ChAFTA (except for those areas sensitive to China, such as the SOE provisions mentioned above). Third, China already has experiences with plurilateral FTAs. For instance, it already has the China–ASEAN FTA, the parties of which include China and 10 ASEAN countries. Now China is also negotiating the RCEP, which adds onto its experiences in negotiating a plurilateral FTA. China also has considerable experience of having FTAs with smaller countries. Its previous FTA partners are mostly with relatively small economies. Its experiences under ChAFTA fill the gap, providing experience in cooperating with a major economy under an FTA. Such negotiating and working experiences could help build its capacity in negotiating with the remaining major economies under the TPP (including Canada, Japan and Mexico).

All these could increase the possibility of including China in a new version of the original proposed TPP. If China is ultimately brought to the TPP's negotiation table, it would seem that the TPP has a greater chance of being reborn even though the original leading player—the US—is not there.

IV. THE IMPLICATIONS OF ChAFTA ON THE RCEP'S NEGOTIATIONS

Although there might be different views about the level of the quality of commitment made by both parties in ChAFTA, it is at least considered by both sides that the Agreement is of a high standard as 96.8 per cent of China's tariff lines are subject to linear tariff reduction, mostly to be implemented within five years; that all products coming to Australia from China will be subject to zero tariff, mostly to be implemented upon entry into force of the Agreement; that Australia makes its service commitments in the form of a negative list, with only a limited number of sectors being excluded; and that China's service commitments were built upon its WTO commitments, with additional sectors included in its positive list. From some perspectives (such as the shorter length of time to implement the tariff reductions and the wider scope of service commitments), ChAFTA might be considered as even more advanced than some other FTAs concluded by Australia with its other trading partners.[31]

[31] China's Ministry of Commerce, 'Interpretation for the China–Australia Free Trade Agreement' (19 June 2015), english.mofcom.gov.cn/article/policyrelease/Cocoon/201510/20151001144954.shtml.

In addition to the current commitments, there are also some built-in mechanisms to ensure further liberalisation in bilateral trade and further protections for their investments. For instance, concerning service commitments made in the form of a positive listing approach, Article 8.24, paragraph 3, provides that:

> After the entry into force of this agreement, at a time to be mutually agreed by the Parties, the Parties shall initiate next round of the negotiation on trade in services in the form of negative listing approach, and conclude such negotiation as soon as they could.[32]

Also concerning investment commitments, ChAFTA requires the parties to 'commence negotiations on a comprehensive Investment Chapter, reflecting outcomes of the review referred to in paragraphs 1 and 2, immediately after such review is completed'. ChAFTA's requirement of continuously enhancing the mutual commitments also serves as a benchmark for the other FTA negotiations with China.

For the ongoing negotiation of the RCEP, the higher standards of trade liberalisation and the incremental approach of investment protection in ChAFTA are also examples for the RCEP negotiations. Due to the diverse backgrounds and levels of development among RCEP countries, it is likely that some negotiating parties will look for exceptions or exclusions from the trade and investment liberalisation. Hence, it is never the goal for the RCEP negotiations to have a very high standard of liberalisation. Although each FTA has its own negotiation scenario, the levels of commitment in other FTAs are constantly looked at and compared in the negotiation of an FTA. The commitments made by both parties in ChAFTA can be a good example to consider, partly because of the fact that both parties of ChAFTA are also parties to the RCEP and partly because of the fact that ChAFTA was newly concluded. At least (or presumably), China and Australia are not supposed to make commitments which are less attractive to each other in the RCEP context. ChAFTA is a good benchmark to the RCEP negotiation also because ChAFTA is concluded between a developed country and a developing country. It is very positive that they were able to include a 'relatively' impressive list of commitments which are to be further added by some built-in mechanisms for 'progressively' enhancing their respective commitments. Hence, it is fair to say that ChAFTA should be a positive role model for the RCEP to achieve relatively higher standards in the trade/investment liberalisation and commitments as well as in investment protections.

[32] ChAFTA (n 10) Art 8.24, para 3.

V. SOME CONCLUDING REMARKS

Australia is one of a few developed countries having concluded an FTA with China. Among these developed countries, Australia is the economically largest and most important country for China. To Australia, China is also a trading partner with geographical and economic significance. There is no doubt about the high economic importance of ChAFTA to their bilateral trade relations.

But ChAFTA is not merely an FTA concluded by Australia or China to enhance their bilateral economic relations. It has implications beyond the enhancement of the already close economic ties between the two major countries.

There are certain possible external implications of ChAFTA for the mega-FTAs, including the proposed RCEP and the TPP. Such implications include the possible positive effects of ChAFTA serving as a benchmark for negotiations of the RCEP so as to make the liberalisation in the RCEP of higher quality; the possible operational interactions with the RCEP (especially when there is a dispute between China and Australia which can presumably be dealt with in both FTAs); and the possible contribution to the survival of the TPP. Such external implications should not be neglected when reviewing ChAFTA.

5

The China–Australia FTA and Australia's FTAs with Other Asian Countries: Their Implications for Future SOE Regulation

TAKEMASA SEKINE

I. INTRODUCTION

AUSTRALIA HAS RECENTLY enhanced its presence in East Asia in terms of trade relations. This is best illustrated by the series of free trade agreements (FTAs) it concluded, between 2014 and 2015, with China,[1] South Korea[2] and Japan.[3] It also joined the Trans-Pacific Partnership (TPP),[4] which also embraces some Asian countries.

However, regarding the content of trade agreements, Australia's approach is not always consistent and prominent differences can be seen in the regulation of state-owned enterprises (SOEs) in its agreements with other states. Australia partially succeeded in including a provision based on the concept of 'competitive neutrality'—in the current context, this mainly implies the internal policy that Australia has developed to regulate its own SOEs—in the Singapore–Australia FTA (SAFTA),[5] the Korea–Australia FTA (KAFTA)[6] and the Japan–Australia Economic Partnership Agreement (JAEPA).[7]

[1] Free Trade Agreement between the Government of Australia and the Government of the People's Republic of China (signed 17 June 2015, entered into force 20 December 2015) [2015] ATS 15 (ChAFTA).

[2] Free Trade Agreement between the Government of the Republic of Korea and the Government of Australia (signed 8 April 2014, entered into force 12 December 2014) [2014] ATS 43 (KAFTA).

[3] Agreement between Japan and Australia for an Economic Partnership (signed 8 July 2014, entered into force 15 January 2015) [2015] ATS 2 (JAEPA).

[4] Signed on 4 February 2016.

[5] Singapore–Australia Free Trade Agreement (signed 17 February 2003, entered into force 28 July 2003) [2003] ATS 16 (SAFTA).

[6] KAFTA (n 2) Art 14.4.

[7] JAEPA (n 3) Art 15.4.

These SOE-related provisions are distinguishable from those included in the FTAs concluded by the North American Free Trade Agreement (NAFTA)[8] Members.[9] While the provisions in two recent Australian FTAs—KAFTA and JAEPA—are somewhat toned down compared with SAFTA, those three Agreements as a whole serve as an effective stepping stone for dissemination of a broad and flexible approach in internationally regulating SOEs.

Conversely, the China–Australia FTA (ChAFTA) did not establish any rules on the behaviours of SOEs beyond those prescribed in the World Trade Organization (WTO) agreements. This is more notable given that other FTAs concluded by China shortly before ChAFTA—for example, the Switzerland–China FTA—require application of competition law to all undertakings of the parties, including undertakings with special and exclusive rights.[10]

Amid those developments, the TPP Agreement, embedded with SOE regulation, was signed in February 2016. Although the TPP itself is unlikely to come into force due to US opposition, it is likely that a successor agreement involving many of the other TPP signatories and much of the substance of the TPP will eventually come into force; hence the relevance of the detailed discussion of the TPP in this chapter. Indeed, the TPP has succeeded in incorporating not only the traditional disciplines inherited from the General Agreement on Tariffs and Trade (GATT) and NAFTA, ie, non-discrimination and commercial considerations, but also the new legal framework labelled as non-commercial assistance (NCA). Some of the new rules set forth under the NCA framework are quite ambitious and without precedent.

We can therefore see at least three options for transnationally regulating SOEs: the strict regulation invented in the TPP Agreement; the more moderate and flexible approach incorporated in SAFTA, KAFTA and JAEPA; and no additional regulation.[11] Among these, ChAFTA chose the third option, despite other possibilities—in particular the second option. This chapter will investigate the implications of this policy selection in ChAFTA, taking into account the evolution of the other options. Section II of this chapter considers Australia's overall approaches in its FTA to SOE regulation. Sections III and IV examine more specifically SOE regulations in SAFTA, KAFTA and

[8] North American Free Trade Agreement (signed 17 December 1992, entered into force 1 January 1994) 32 ILM 289 (1993) (NAFTA).

[9] See, eg, ibid Arts 1502, 1503; see also, Free Trade Agreement between Canada and the Republic of Korea (signed 22 September 2014, entered into force 1 January 2015) Arts 15.2, 15.3.

[10] Free Trade Agreement between the Swiss Confederation and the People's Republic of China (signed 6 June 2013, entered into force 1 July 2014) (Switzerland–China FTA).

[11] With regard to FTAs concluded between countries outside the Asia-Pacific region, the Canada–EU FTA, for instance, explicitly confirms the application of competition law to SOEs (Art 17.3) in addition to provisions directly addressing SOEs' behaviours that are comparable to those in NAFTA (n 8) Arts 18.4, 18.5.

JAEPA, and consider the trends in these Agreements. Section V examines the peculiarity of ChAFTA in light of the other FTAs. Section VI considers the SOE chapter of the TPP Agreement which may influence, in some way, future SOE regulation under trade agreements. With these in mind, section VII considers how ChAFTA and other FTAs can contribute to the development of SOE regulation in the Asia–Oceania region.

II. AUSTRALIA'S FTAS AND SOE REGULATIONS

Although Australia is perceived as having succeeded in becoming an exemplar of SOE regulation in the domestic market,[12] its same efforts in regulating SOEs in the international space are not yet so innovative. The contents of SOE regulation in its FTAs are comparatively less demanding than the US approach and are inconsistent. SOE regulation in Australia's FTAs can be roughly divided into two categories: NAFTA-style and competitive neutrality style (Table 1).

Table 1: SOE Regulations included in Australia's FTAs

Name of Agreement	Provision(s) relating to SOE	Approach
Australia–Papua New Guinea	–	
SPARTECA	–	
ANZCERTA	–	
Singapore–Australia FTA	Ch 12, Art 4	Competitive neutrality
Thailand–Australia FTA	–	
US–Australia FTA	Arts 14.3 and 14.4	NAFTA-style, with competitive neutrality applicable to Australia
Australia–Chile FTA	Arts 14.4 and 14.5	NAFTA-style
ASEAN–Australia–New Zealand FTA	–	
Malaysia–Australia FTA	Art 14.4(3)	Application of competition laws

(continued)

[12] M Rennie and F Lindsay, 'Competitive Neutrality and State-owned Enterprises in Australia: Review of Practices and Their Relevance for Other Countries' (2011) OECD Corporate Governance Working Papers No 4, 44 www.oecd-ilibrary.org/governance/competitive-neutrality-and-state-owned-enterprises-in-australia_5kg54cxkmx36-en?crawler=true.

Table 1: *(Continued)*

Name of Agreement	Provision(s) relating to SOE	Approach
Korea–Australia FTA	Art 14.4	Competitive neutrality
Japan–Australia EPA	Art 15.4	Competitive neutrality
China–Australia FTA	–	No competition chapter; no specific SOE regulation
TPP	Ch 17	Commercial considerations and non-commercial assistance

The NAFTA-style agreements' regulation of SOEs is founded on the concept of 'non-discrimination and commercial considerations', rooted in the prescriptions of GATT Article XVII. The first two subparagraphs of Article XVII provide:

> 1. (a) Each contracting party undertakes that if it establishes or maintains a State enterprise, wherever located, or grants to any enterprise, formally or in effect, exclusive or special privileges, such enterprise shall, in its purchases or sales involving either imports or exports, act in a manner consistent with the general principles of non-discriminatory treatment prescribed in this Agreement for governmental measures affecting imports or exports by private traders.
>
> (b) The provisions of subparagraph (a) of this paragraph shall be understood to require that such enterprises shall, having due regard to the other provisions of this Agreement, make any such purchases or sales solely in accordance with commercial considerations, including price, quality, availability, marketability, transportation and other conditions of purchase or sale, and shall afford the enterprises of the other contracting parties adequate opportunity, in accordance with customary business practice, to compete for participation in such purchases or sales.

According to the Appellate Body in *Canada—Wheat Exports and Grain Imports*, GATT Article XVII:1(b) should be interpreted in accordance with paragraph 1(a), which means that the former must be understood as clarifying the scope of the latter.[13] Therefore, the requirement of commercial considerations becomes relevant only when the transaction at issue is discriminatory (including the treatment of dissimilar situations in a formally identical manner). In other words, the commercial considerations requirement will be taken into account when examining whether discriminatory behaviour can be justified under GATT Article XVII.[14] It does not

[13] Appellate Body Report, *Canada—Measures Relating to Exports of Wheat and Treatment of Imported Grain* 89, WT/DS276/AB/R (30 August 2004) (*Canada—Wheat Exports and Grain Imports AB Report*).

[14] ibid 110–12.

require state trading enterprises (STEs)[15] to act commercially in any transactions.

Another notable interpretation given by the Appellate Body in the above case was that paragraph 1(b) 'refers to purchases and sales transactions where: (i) one of the parties involved in the transaction is an STE; and (ii) the transaction involves imports to or exports from the Member maintaining the STE'.[16] Given this interpretation, GATT Article XVII:1 will not be applied to an STE's transaction when no foreign enterprises are directly involved in the transaction. For instance, an STE's sale of goods to domestic enterprises with non-commercial low prices that are to the detriment of imports *competing with* the STE, falls outside the scope of GATT Article XVII:1.[17]

While SOE regulation under NAFTA shares basic elements with GATT Article XVII, the former's detail differs slightly, in particular from the above interpretation given by the Appellate Body. NAFTA contains two provisions pertinent to the regulation of SOEs: the first addresses monopolies (Article 1502) and the second applies to state enterprises (Article 1503). Article 1502(3) prescribes as follows:

> Each Party shall ensure, through regulatory control, administrative supervision or the application of other measures, that any privately owned monopoly that it designates and any government monopoly that it maintains or designates:
>
> (a) acts in a manner that is not inconsistent with the Party's obligations under this Agreement wherever such a monopoly exercises any regulatory, administrative or other governmental authority that the Party has delegated to it in connection with the monopoly good or service, such as the power to grant import or export licenses, approve commercial transactions or impose quotas, fees or other charges;
> (b) except to comply with any terms of its designation that are not inconsistent with subparagraph (c) or (d), acts solely in accordance with commercial considerations in its purchase or sale of the monopoly good or service in the relevant market, including with regard to price, quality, availability, marketability, transportation and other terms and conditions of purchase or sale;
> (c) provides non-discriminatory treatment to investments of investors, to goods and to service providers of another Party in its purchase or sale of the monopoly good or service in the relevant market; and

[15] While there is no definition of STEs in GATT, the Understanding on the Interpretation of Article XVII of the General Agreement on Tariffs and Trade 1994 adopted a 'working definition', in which STEs are described as: 'Governmental and non-governmental enterprises, including marketing boards, which have been granted exclusive or special rights or privileges, including statutory or constitutional powers, in the exercise of which they influence through their purchases or sales the level or direction of imports or exports'.

[16] *Canada—Wheat Exports and Grain Imports AB Report* (n 13) 157.

[17] However, the Appellate Body's decision intimates a different interpretation may be adopted in a different situation. ibid 160.

(d) does not use its monopoly position to engage, either directly or indirectly, including through its dealings with its parent, its subsidiary or other enterprise with common ownership, in anticompetitive practices in a non-monopolized market in its territory that adversely affect an investment of an investor of another Party, including through the discriminatory provision of the monopoly good or service, cross-subsidization or predatory conduct.

Article 1503 stipulates that the parties must ensure that any state enterprise[18] (a) acts in a manner that is not inconsistent with the concerned party's obligations under NAFTA regarding investment and financial services when the said enterprise exercises its delegated governmental authority;[19] and (b) accords non-discriminatory treatment in the sale of its goods or services to investments of investors of the other party.[20] These have become standard requirements in NAFTA Members' subsequent FTAs.[21]

One of the main differences between the provisions in NAFTA and GATT concerns the scope of a transaction that needs to be based on 'commercial considerations'. As detailed above, the Appellate Body has ruled that 'commercial considerations' are required when the transaction at issue is between an STE and an enterprise of the other Member. However, Article 1502(3)(b) of NAFTA does not imply such a limitation.[22] Consequently, inconsistency with Article 1502 would result when a foreign enterprise, which is competing but not directly contracting with a certain government monopoly, is excluded from the market due to non-commercial practices of the SOE.

Among agreements to which Australia is a party, the US–Australia[23] and Australia–Chile FTAs[24] adopted this NAFTA-style SOE regulation (the Australia–Chile FTA requires commercial considerations only when the state monopoly exercises special or exclusive rights).[25] Nevertheless, these

[18] 'State enterprise' is defined as 'an enterprise owned, or controlled through ownership interests, by a party.' NAFTA (n 8) Art 1505.

[19] ibid Art 1503(2).

[20] ibid Art 1503(3).

[21] Examples are the Free Trade Agreement between the Republic of Korea and the United States of America (signed 30 June 2007, entered into force 15 March 2012) (Korea–US FTA); the Canada–Peru Free Trade Agreement (signed 29 May 2008, entered into force 1 August 2009); and the Free Trade Agreement between the State of Israel and the United Mexican States (signed 10 April 2000, entered into force 1 July 2000).

[22] While the transactions contemplated in para (c) presuppose the direct involvement of another party's enterprises, para (b) broadly addresses any transactions other than those for complying with the terms of its designation that are consistent with para (c).

[23] Australia–United States Free Trade Agreement (signed 18 May 2004, entered into force 1 January 2005) [2005] ATS 1 (US–Australia FTA).

[24] Australia–Chile Free Trade Agreement (signed 30 July 2008, entered into force 6 March 2009) [2009] ATS 6 (Australia–Chile FTA).

[25] ibid Art 14.4(2). This discussion regarding the *exercise* of exclusive or special rights or privileges may have a strong connection with the similar discussion over this phrase under GATT Art XVII and the Understanding on the Interpretation of Article XVII of GATT 1994. On this point, see EU Petersmann, 'GATT Law on State Trading Enterprises: Critical

Agreements also entertain competitive neutrality in the final paragraphs of provisions regarding state enterprises, which thus appears to have only a secondary role.[26]

Apart from NAFTA-style agreements, Australia has introduced competitive neutrality as a main framework for SOE regulation in several agreements, in particular with Singapore (SAFTA), South Korea (KAFTA) and Japan (JAEPA). The significance of this will be analysed in the following sections, in addition to the China–Australia FTA.

III. SOE REGULATIONS UNDER SAFTA, KAFTA AND JAEPA

In terms of concluding FTAs, Australia is one of the most proactive countries penetrating the Asia region; to date, in addition to SAFTA, KAFTA, JAEPA and ChAFTA, it has concluded agreements with ASEAN (the ASEAN–Australia–New Zealand FTA)[27] and individually with some of its Members (Thailand[28] and Malaysia).[29,30] In light of these FTAs, Australia seems to have exerted a strong influence in constructing the basic framework of FTAs in this region. Among those Australian FTAs, this chapter focuses on SAFTA, KAFTA and JAEPA in this section, since they embrace the concept of competitive neutrality in regulating SOEs.

A. SAFTA

SAFTA was signed on 17 February 2003 and entered into force on 28 July 2003.[31] A provision regarding SOEs is included in the competition policy chapter (Chapter 12) and prescribes as follows:

> Article 4 Competitive Neutrality
>
> 1. The Parties shall take *reasonable measures* to ensure that governments at all levels do not provide any competitive advantage to any government-owned businesses in their business activities simply because they are government owned.

Evaluation of Article XVII and Proposals for Reform' in T Cottier et al (eds), *State Trading in the Twenty-First Century* (Ann Arbor, MI, University of Michigan Press, 1998) 88.

[26] Australia–Chile FTA (n 24) Art 14.5(4); US–Australia FTA (n 23) Art 14.4(3).

[27] Agreement Establishing the ASEAN–Australia–New Zealand Free Trade Area (signed 27 February 2009, entered into force 1 January 2010) [2010] ATS 1.

[28] Australia–Thailand Free Trade Agreement (signed 5 July 2004, entered into force 1 January 2005) [2005] ATS 2.

[29] Malaysia–Australia Free Trade Agreement (signed 22 May 2012, entered into force 1 January 2013) [2013] ATS 4.

[30] Moreover, agreements with India and Indonesia are under negotiation.

[31] WTO, 'Welcome to the Regional Trade Agreements Information System (RTA-IS)' (2016), rtais.wto.org/UI/PublicShowMemberRTAIDCard.aspx?rtaid=60.

2. This Article applies to the business activities of government-owned businesses and not to their non-business, non-commercial activities (emphasis added).

As is apparent from the title and its contents, this provision is distinguishable from previous SOE regulation in trade agreements, such as that in GATT or NAFTA. Under SAFTA, the parties are required to adopt reasonable measures to ensure a level playing field of enterprises in their domestic markets. In what conditions would such 'reasonable measures' be enforced? There is no guidance in SAFTA. If it is assumed that these 'reasonable measures' or the provision itself are established with Australia's competitive neutrality framework in mind,[32] such measures would be applicable when required to ensure: taxation neutrality, debt neutrality, commercial rate of return, regulatory neutrality, and that prices charged by SOEs (government-owned businesses) reflect full cost attribution.[33] However, some of these obligations demanding fairness in competition overlap with the Agreement on Subsidies and Countervailing Measures (SCM Agreement)[34] or national treatment obligations and other obligations provided under either SAFTA[35] or the WTO agreements.[36] Therefore, the prime benefit of this provision might be that it can require appropriate measures to be taken regarding the activities of SOEs that would not be caught by other provisions in SAFTA or the WTO agreements: the most plausible situation would be when activities relating to trade in services are concerned, given that subsidies connected to the services are comprehensively excluded from the scope of the services chapter in SAFTA.[37]

B. KAFTA

KAFTA was signed on 8 April 2014 and entered into force on 12 December 2014.[38] For Australia, South Korea is its third largest export market and

[32] For detail, see below section IV.

[33] Commonwealth Competitive Neutrality Policy Statement (1996), archive.treasury.gov.au/documents/275/PDF/cnps.pdf, 16–19.

[34] SAFTA (n 5) Art 7(2), Ch 2 confirms that the parties will abide by the provisions of the SCM Agreement. In addition, the Agreement on Implementation of Article VI of the General Agreement on Tariffs and Trade 1994 (Anti-Dumpling Agreement) may also be applied in certain cases.

[35] SAFTA (n 5) Art 2, Ch 2; Art 12, Ch 7.

[36] As these rules are more effective because disagreements can be referred to the dispute settlement mechanism of either the WTO or SAFTA, application of these rules would be preferred over this catch-all competitive neutrality clause, which is excluded from the scope of the dispute settlement mechanism under SAFTA. SAFTA (n 5) Art 8(2), Ch 12.

[37] SAFTA (n 5) Art 2(2)(a), Ch 7. However, subsidies provided in relation to services supplied by SOEs might also be excluded from the scope of SAFTA, under Art 8(3), Ch 12 thereof. The relationship between Art 4, Ch 12 and Art 2(2)(a), Ch 7 is ambiguous.

[38] WTO (n 31).

fourth largest overall trading partner.[39] It was the first FTA to be concluded by Australia with a major trading partner in North Asia.[40]

Regarding the SOE regulation, KAFTA embraces the concept of competitive neutrality. Article 14.4 prescribes as follows:

> Article 14.4: Competitive Neutrality
>
> The Parties *recognise the importance* of ensuring that governments at all levels in their territories do not provide any competitive advantage to any state enterprise in its business activities as a result of it being a state enterprise. This Article shall apply to the business activities of state enterprises and not to their non-business, non-commercial activities. The application of this Article shall not obstruct the performance of the particular public tasks assigned to them (emphasis added).

This provision is somewhat modest compared with its equivalent in SAFTA discussed above since it only confirms the *common recognition* that the creation of a level playing field among state enterprises and private enterprises is important. Nonetheless, it is notable in view of the previous practices that South Korea has preferred to adopt a competition law-based approach towards SOE regulation (Table 2).[41] Those Agreements have typically prescribed that a party's competition laws should be applied to state enterprises and designated monopolies.

Table 2: SOE Regulations included in South Korea's FTAs

Name of Agreement	Provision(s) relating to SOE	Approach
Korea–Chile FTA	Art 14.8	Application of competition laws
Korea–Singapore FTA	Art 15.4	Competitive neutrality
EFTA–Korea FTA	Art 5.1(2)(b)	Application of competition laws
ASEAN–Korea FTA	–	–
Korea–India CEPA	–	–
EU–Korea FTA	Arts 11.4 and 11.5	Application of competition laws, non-discrimination
Peru–Korea FTA	Art 15.9	Application of competition laws
Korea–US FTA	Arts 16.2 and 16.3	NAFTA-style
Korea–Turkey FTA	Framework Agreement Art 3.8	Application of competition laws

(continued)

[39] Australian Government, 'KAFTA: A Snapshot', dfat.gov.au/trade/agreements/kafta/fact-sheets/Pages/kafta-a-snapshot.aspx.

[40] ibid.

[41] For examples of exceptions see, eg, Korea–US FTA (n 21) Arts 16.2, 16.3.

Table 2: *(Continued)*

Name of Agreement	Provision(s) relating to SOE	Approach
Colombia–Korea FTA	Art 13.9	Application of competition laws
Korea–Australia FTA	Art 14.4	Competitive neutrality
Canada–Korea FTA	Arts 15.2 and 15.3	NAFTA-style
China–Korea FTA	Art 14.5	Application of competition laws
Korea–Viet Nam FTA	Art 11.4	Application of competition laws
Korea–New Zealand FTA	Art 12.1(2)(a)	Application of competition laws

The competition law-based approach can be characterised as moderate and deferential compared with the competitive neutrality or NAFTA approach. This is because SOEs may readily be excluded from competition laws at the discretion of competent government; and if this occurs, FTAs could no longer require a party to take any measures to regulate the behaviours of SOEs. Contrary to this, the NAFTA approach, ie, requiring commercial considerations in a government monopoly's transactions, may warrant more coercive control over the conduct of SOEs, since commercial considerations can be required irrespective of the SOE concerned being excluded from the application of domestic competition laws. Competitive neutrality may stand in between these approaches. Although competitive neutrality may share the same deficit with the competition law approach, it has an additional advantage in that—if it is constructed somewhat similarly to the Australian policy—it could include matters that are usually not captured by competition laws.[42] However, it is not clear from the text of KAFTA to what extent South Korea gave serious consideration to a competitive neutrality policy. At any rate, the fact that South Korea has deviated from its previous practices suggests that, despite the weakness of the provision in KAFTA, South Korea has indicated its readiness to adopt an alternative approach in its FTA with Australia.

Moreover, it is intriguing to note that the Korea–Singapore FTA includes a provision regarding competitive neutrality.[43] Unlike KAFTA, yet like SAFTA, the competitive neutrality provision in the Korea–Singapore FTA is more straightforward: parties are required to take reasonable measures to

[42] OECD, 'Roundtable on Competition Neutrality: Issues Paper by the Secretariat' (2015) DAF/COMP(2015)5, www.oecd.org/officialdocuments/publicdisplaydocumentpdf/?cote=DAF/COMP(2015)5&docLanguage=En, 17.

[43] Free Trade Agreement between the Government of the Republic of Korea and the Government of the Republic of Singapore (signed 4 August 2005, entered into force 2 March 2006) (Korea–Singapore FTA) Art 15.4.

ensure a level playing field among government-owned businesses and non-government-owned businesses. In light of this, it is a fair observation that Korea is showing a positive attitude towards disseminating the concept of competitive neutrality through trade agreements, while not adopting the concept as a standard discipline for SOE regulation. The impact of KAFTA will be examined after analysis of JAEPA in the next subsection.

C. JAEPA

JAEPA was signed on 18 July 2014 and entered into force on 15 January 2015.[44] While, for Australia, it is the third agreement to incorporate the concept of competitive neutrality,[45] this agreement is notable for Japan since it is the latter's first agreement that explicitly introduced a provision intended to regulate the behaviours of SOEs. As demonstrated in Table 3, despite its large number of FTAs, Japan had never previously incorporated specific SOE regulation in its FTAs. At best, Japan's preceding agreements contained provisions regarding monopoly service suppliers, which merely replicates Articles VIII and IX of the General Agreement on Trade in Services (GATS).[46]

Table 3: SOE Regulations included in Japan's FTAs

Name of Agreement	Provisions relating to SOE			
	State trading enterprise (GATT XVII)	Monopoly supplier of a service (GATS VIII and IX)	Original Provisions	Approach
Japan–Singapore EPA	–	Arts 65 and 66	–	–
Japan–Mexico EPA	–	–	–	–
Japan–Malaysia EPA	–	Art 105	–	–
Japan–Chile EPA	–	–	–	–

(continued)

[44] WTO (n 31).

[45] Recall that the US–Australia FTA and the Australia–Chile FTA both incorporated the competitive neutrality policy, but only gave it a secondary role.

[46] Previous Japanese FTAs can be understood as requiring the application of competition laws to SOEs, but they do not clearly indicate so.

Table 3: *(Continued)*

Name of Agreement	Provisions relating to SOE			
	State trading enterprise (GATT XVII)	**Monopoly supplier of a service (GATS VIII and IX)**	**Original Provisions**	**Approach**
Japan–Thailand EPA	–	Art 83	–	–
Japan–Indonesia EPA	–	Art 86	–	–
Japan–Brunei EPA	–	Art 83	–	–
Japan–ASEAN EPA	–	–	–	–
Japan–Philippines EPA	–	Art 80	–	–
Japan–Switzerland EPA	–	Arts 51 and 52	–	–
Japan–Viet Nam EPA	–	Art 67	–	–
Japan–India EPA	–	Art 67	–	–
Japan–Peru EPA	–	–	–	–
Japan–Australia EPA	–	Art 9.10	Art 15.4	Competitive neutrality
Japan–Mongolia EPA	–	Arts 7.10 and 7.11	–	–
TPP	Art 17.4	Art 17.4	Art 17.6–8	Commercial considerations and non-commercial assistance

JAEPA contains the following provision on SOEs:

> Article 15.4: State-Owned Enterprises
>
> In addition to Article 15.3, bearing in mind the relationship between the promotion of competition and other policy objectives, the Parties *recognise* that seeking to ensure that governments do not provide competitive advantages to state-owned enterprises simply because they are state owned can contribute to the promotion of competition (emphasis added).

As with KAFTA, this Article seems to be based on the concept of competitive neutrality, although it does not spell out the term anywhere in the provision.

Meanwhile, it remains to be seen whether Japan will promote this principle in its other FTAs since Japan did not include equivalent provisions in its EPA with Mongolia, which was concluded in the same period as JAEPA. Moreover, the Japan–Singapore FTA[47] did not contain any provisions pertaining to competitive neutrality, in contrast with the Korea–Singapore FTA.[48]

IV. COMPETITIVE NEUTRALITY IN THE ASIA-OCEANIA NETWORK

As revealed in the previous section, Australia is diffusing the concept of competitive neutrality[49] in East Asia countries; it appears that these attempts have partially succeeded, as those countries agreed to include this concept in FTAs even though some of those provisions were limited to 'recognition' of the concept. It is possible, therefore, that the concept of competitive neutrality will evolve cooperatively through the relationship between Australia and its Asian FTA partners.

Australia's competitive neutrality policy[50] has advantages compared with the existing SOE regulation under GATT, NAFTA, or the WTO agreements. First, it encourages an ex ante resolution.[51] For instance, where a certain government activity of a commercial nature (significant government business activity) is exempted from taxation and this is liable to disadvantage competing private entities, such an SOE may pay, to the Official Public Account, an amount required to ensure parity with the tax levied upon their competitors (taxation equivalent regime, TER),[52] or alternatively, with regard to particular activities, adjust its price to that which would be

[47] Agreement between Japan and the Republic of Singapore for a New-Age Economic Partnership (signed 13 January 2002, entered into force 30 November 2002) (Japan–Singapore EPA).

[48] However, this absence of a provision pertinent to SOEs is understandable because the Japan–Singapore EPA was concluded very early (in 2002) in both countries' ventures into FTAs. The outcome might be different if the Agreement had been concluded more recently.

[49] The concept of 'competitive neutrality' may take various forms. In the following sections, the term will be used with the system akin to the Australian policy in mind. This is because the present chapter analyses the concept based on that contained in the trade agreements between Australia and Asian countries.

[50] For a comprehensive description of the Australian competitive neutrality policy see, eg, D Healey, 'Competitive Neutrality: Addressing Government Advantage in Australian Markets' in J Drexl and V Bagnoli (eds), *State-Initiated Restraints of Competition* (Cheltenham, Edward Elgar, 2015) 3.

[51] OECD, 'Roundtable on Competition Neutrality' (n 42) 17; D Healey, 'Competitive Neutrality: The Concept' in D Healey (ed), *UNCTAD Research Partnership Platform, Competitive Neutrality and its Application in Selected Developing Countries* (Geneva, United Nations, 2014) 14.

[52] Australian Government, 'Australian Government Competitive Neutrality Guidelines for Managers' (2004), consult.treasury.gov.au/market-and-competition-policy-division/competitive-neutrality-review/supporting_documents/2004%20Competitive%20Neutrality%20Guidelines%20for%20Managers%20AGCN_guide_v4.pdf, 18.

determined in the absence of the tax deduction (taxation neutrality adjustment, TNA).[53] Under this framework, distortion of competition can be prevented before the infliction of actual harm. Although the SCM Agreement's procedures may be applied, for instance, in the case of threat of material injury to domestic industry,[54] it does not deviate from the basic framework designed for ex post response to the actual injury.[55] Second, it may have broader coverage compared with the approach adopted under GATT, the WTO, or NAFTA. Certainly, under the current WTO system (and FTAs based on the WTO system), SOEs' market distorting conduct or the competitive advantages that SOEs may gain from government assistance may be eliminated, to some extent, through certain disciplines and mechanisms provided in GATT (eg, Article XVII), the SCM Agreement, and GATS (eg, Articles VIII and IX). However, several scenarios fall outside the scope of the existing WTO rules.[56] Apart from the rules regarding subsidies connected to trade in services, which are largely absent from the WTO agreements,[57] subsidies (pertinent to trade in goods) provided to an SOE by another SOE, for instance, will not necessarily be regulated under the SCM Agreement. This is due to the Appellate Body's current interpretation of the SCM Agreement, which presumes SOEs that do not possess, exercise, or have vested in them any governmental authority are outside the definition of 'public body' in Article 1.1(a) of the SCM Agreement.[58] The Australian model, encapsulating a flexible approach to government's assistance, may address the loophole in the WTO system (as well as FTAs based on the WTO system)[59]

[53] ibid 19.

[54] GATT Art VI, and fn 45 SCM Agreement.

[55] OECD, 'Roundtable on Competition Neutrality' (n 42) 19. F Kawashima, 'Competitive Neutrality Principles in Australia: Lessons for the TPP Negotiation on Disciplines over State-Owned Enterprises' (2015) RIETI Discussion Paper Series 15-J-026, www.rieti.go.jp/jp/publications/dp/15j026.pdf, 23 (in Japanese).

[56] This was obviously the biggest motivation for creating new rules in the TPP Agreement, which will be discussed in section VI below.

[57] However, some obligations under GATS, eg, the Most-Favoured-Nation (MFN) obligation and, to a limited extent, the national treatment obligation, will be applied to subsidies pertaining to trade in services. P Sauvé and M Soprana, 'Learning by Not Doing: Subsidy Disciplines in Services Trade' (E15 Initiative, International Centre for Trade and Sustainable Development (ICSTD) and World Economic Forum, 2015), e15initiative.org/wp-content/uploads/2015/04/E15_Subsidies_Sauve-and-Soprana_final.pdf, 6. See also, General Agreement on Trade in Services (GATS) (15 April 1994) LT/UR/A-1B/S/1 Art XV docsonline.wto.org.

[58] See, eg, Appellate Body Report, *United States—Antidumping and Countervailing Duties (China)* (15 March 2011) WT/DS379/AB/R, docsonline.wto.org, 317–18. See also, Appellate Body Report, *United States—Countervailing Measures on Certain Hot-Rolled Carbon Steel Flat Products from India* (8 December 2014) WT/DS436/AB/R 4.54, docsonline.wto.org.

[59] Many FTAs, including those concluded by the US, do not usually contain any supplementary rules (so-called 'WTO-plus' provisions) regarding subsidies or countervailing measures (eg, US–Australia FTA (n 23); JAEPA (n 3) Art 2.12). As such, FTAs' rules do not normally differ from WTO disciplines. TJ Prusa, 'Trade Remedy Provisions' in JP Chauffour and JC Maur (eds), *Preferential Trade Agreement Policies for Development: A Handbook* (Washington DC, World Bank Publications, 2011) 185; T Voon, 'Eliminating Trade Remedies from the WTO: Lessons from Regional Trade Agreements' (2010) 59 *International & Comparative Law*

and enable comprehensive treatment of the anticompetitive situation caused by SOEs. Third, it takes an educative approach.[60] According to an OECD report, this is because the 'competitive neutrality policy and enforcement bodies work with governments to achieve implementation'.[61]

As discussed above, the Australian competitive neutrality policy also has advantages over the simple application of competition laws, the only policy tool that can be discerned as a formal competitive neutrality policy in most countries. This is a corollary of Australia's policy since it was developed based on the premise that (traditional) competition laws alone are insufficient to address the issues stemming from the participation of government businesses in a competitive market.[62]

Nevertheless, a comprehensive competitive neutrality policy founded on the basic principles adopted in Australia is not widely supported by other countries in their international agreements. Perhaps this is because the policy is not 'designed for internationalization'.[63] As the Australian competitive neutrality policy depends heavily on the regulating government's ambition and capacity, it provides no means for impacted countries to prevent their private competitors from being driven out of the market if the governmental institutions in charge of regulating SOEs are reluctant in meeting their duties.[64] This appears to be one of the core reasons why the system incorporating straightforward and explicit provisions proscribing certain practices relating to SOEs, such as those stipulated in Articles 1502 and 1503 of NAFTA, being preferred over competitive neutrality policy in the TPP negotiations (see the discussion in section VII below).[65]

Quarterly 625, 638; R Teh, TJ Prusa and M Budetta, 'Trade Remedy Provisions in Regional Trade Agreements' (2007) WTO Staff Working Paper ERSD-2007-03, www.wto.org/english/res_e/reser_e/ersd200703_e.pdf, 21.

[60] A Capobianco and H Christianse, 'Competitive Neutrality and State-Owned Enterprises: Challenges and Policy Options' (2011) OECD Corporate Governance Working Papers No 1, www.oecd-ilibrary.org/governance/competitive-neutrality-and-state-owned-enterprises_5kg9xfgjdhg6-en?crawler=true, 15.

[61] ibid.

[62] FG Hilmer et al, 'National Competition Policy' (Canberra, Australian Government Publishing Service, 1993) 6–7.

[63] D Scissors, 'Why the Trans-Pacific Partnership must Enhance Competitive Neutrality' (2013) Backgrounder 2809, thf_media.s3.amazonaws.com/2013/pdf/bg2809.pdf, 3. Accordingly, during the TPP negotiation, Australia has proposed an internationalised version of its competitive neutrality policy. Under this proposal, while the primary responsibility would fall on domestic institutions, an affected country may initiate state-to-state dispute settlement proceedings when it is not satisfied with the implementation of a system. Inside US Trade, 'Business Groups Wary of Australian Approach on SOE Disciplines in TPP' (24 May 2013).

[64] Scissors (n 63) 4. It is also highlighted that some developing countries do not have the capacity to implement a similar system to that required under the Australian competitive neutrality policy. T Kawase, 'Trans-Pacific Partnership Negotiations and Rulemaking to Regulate State-owned Enterprises (Policy Update 053)' (22 April 2014), www.rieti.go.jp/en/special/policy-update/053.html.

[65] Inside US Trade (n 63).

Despite this opposition, the ex ante and flexible approach contemplated in the Australian competitive neutrality policy still warrants consideration in securing equal competitive conditions throughout the Asia-Oceania region, and furthermore the foundation for such an approach seems to be in place. For instance, in Japan, competition-distorting subsidies provided by the local government may be withheld through ex ante consultation with the Japanese Fair Trade Commission (JFTC). In 2007, the JTFC published its consultation cases with local governments.[66] Among them was a case regarding a subsidy provided by an anonymous city (City A) for promotion of a co-generation system. City A, which was simultaneously a distributor of co-generation systems, ie, an 'enterprise' under the Antimonopoly Act,[67] considered introducing a policy providing a subsidy to residents who purchased a co-generation system from City A, whereas the same subsidy would not be offered to residents who purchased the same system from private companies. According to the JFTC, this subsidy was likely to distort competition among co-generation distributors, thereby infringing the Antimonopoly Act. More specifically, it would fall within the definition of 'Below-cost Pricing'[68] if the provision of this subsidy resulted in the retail price being reduced to far below the cost incurred to supply the services at issue.[69] Including this example, the JFTC's consultation records imply that an ex ante and flexible approach may prevail in Japan.[70] Although there is no comprehensive policy dealing with competitive neutrality at this stage in Japan,[71] it would be possible to construct a system that is harmonic and supplemental to the Australian competitive neutrality policy, or to develop a system more appropriate for the international implementation of competitive neutrality framework. Eventually, such a system may be embraced by other Asian countries.[72]

[66] JFTC, 'Consultation Cases from local government' (2007), www.jftc.go.jp/houdou/pressrelease/kako/07062001.files/07062001-tenpu.pdf, 1 (in Japanese).

[67] Act on Prohibition of Private Monopolization and Maintenance of Fair Trade (Japanese Act No 54 of 14 April 1947).

[68] Antimonopoly Act, Arts 2(9)(iii) 19; Designation of Unfair Trade Practices (Fair Trade Commission Public Notice No 15, 18 June 1982) para (6); The Guidelines for Exclusionary Private Monopolization under the Antimonopoly Act 2009, pt II:2.

[69] JFTC (n 66) 2.

[70] Under the consultation procedure, it is possible to take a more flexible approach in preventing the distortion of competition. Indeed, in some consultation cases, the JFTC exhibits concerns over the adverse effects on competition without indicating any infringement of specific provisions of the Antimonopoly Act.

[71] OECD, 'Roundtable on Competitive Neutrality in Competition Enforcement: Note by Japan' (2015) DAF/COMP/WD(2015)6, www.oecd.org/officialdocuments/displaydocument/?cote=DAF/COMP/WD(2015)6&docLanguage=En, 2.

[72] See also, S Gaur, 'Competitive Neutrality Issues in India' in D Healey (ed), *UNCTAD Research Partnership Platform, Competitive Neutrality and its Application in Selected Developing Countries* (Geneva, United Nations, 2014) 159. It notes that India may espouse Australian-style competitive neutrality policy in some form.

V. CHAFTA AND OTHER FTAS CONCLUDED BY CHINA

Against this background, Australia and China concluded ChAFTA: signed on 17 June 2015, it came into force on 20 December 2015. However, the Agreement did not contain any explicit regulations regarding SOEs.

At first glance, this outcome might be attributed to China's concerns about the regulation of SOEs. One can imagine that the SOEs in China resisted the introduction of SOEs-related provisions.[73] However, this assumption is at odds with China's typical practices. China has already introduced forms of SOE regulations in its FTAs (Table 4). For instance, the Iceland–China FTA provides that the Agreement's competition chapter will be applied to undertakings with privilege and exclusive rights authorised by law.[74] An obligation to apply either party's respective competition laws is also prescribed in the same Article.[75] Hence, both parties may not exclude their SOEs from the application of competition law (to the extent that the competition chapter's application does not prevent the SOEs fulfilling their legal functions).[76] A similar provision was inserted in the Switzerland–China FTA, with slightly more succinct expression: this Agreement's competition chapter applies to *all undertakings* of the parties.[77]

Table 4: SOE Regulations included in China's FTAs

Name of Agreement	Provisions relating to SOE			
	State trading enterprise (GATT XVII)	Monopoly supplier of a service (GATS VIII and IX)	Original Provisions	Approach
China–Macao CEPA	–	–	–	–
China–Hong Kong CEPA	–	–	–	–

(continued)

[73] Y Jiang, 'Australia–China FTA: China's Domestic Politics and the Roots of Different National Approaches to FTAs' (2008) 62(2) *Australian Journal of International Affairs* 179, 183. See also, G Song and WJ Yuan, 'China's Free Trade Agreement Strategies' (2012) 35(4) *The Washington Quarterly* 107, 115. It exhibits several examples of SOEs hampering or affecting several FTA negotiations.

[74] Free Trade Agreement between the Government of Iceland and the Government of the People's Republic of China (signed 15 April 2013, entered into force 1 July 2014) (Iceland–China FTA) Art 62(2).

[75] ibid Art 62(4).

[76] ibid Art 62(2).

[77] Switzerland–China FTA (n 10) Art 10(2). Again, such application will be required insofar as it does not hinder those undertakings from exercising their special and exclusive rights.

Table 4: *(Continued)*

Name of Agreement	Provisions relating to SOE			
	State trading enterprise (GATT XVII)	**Monopoly supplier of a service (GATS VIII and IX)**	**Original Provisions**	**Approach**
ASEAN–China FTA	–	Services Agreement, Arts 7 and 8	–	–
Chile–China FTA	–	–	–	–
China–New Zealand FTA	–	Art 123	–	–
Pakistan–China FTA	–	Services Agreement, Arts 7 and 8	–	–
China–Singapore FTA	Art 9	Arts 69 and 70	–	–
Peru–China FTA	Art 17	–	–	–
China–Costa Rica FTA	–	–	–	–
Iceland–China FTA	–	Arts 76 and 77	Art 62(2)	Application of competition laws
Switzerland–China FTA	Art 2.6	Arts 8.10 and 8.11	Art 10(2)	Application of competition laws
China–Korea FTA	Art 2.11	Art 8.12	Art 14.5	Application of competition laws
China–Australia FTA	–	Art 8.23	–	–

Even more noteworthy is the China–Korea FTA.[78] This Agreement contains a competition chapter that, in terms of the number and detail of the provisions, is far more sophisticated than previous agreements concluded by China, and the SOE-related provision is incorporated in the context of this holistic competition policy, which seems to have reflected South Korea's intentions.[79] After affirming that the competition chapter will be applied to

[78] Free Trade Agreement between the Government of the People's Republic of China and the Government of the Republic of Korea (signed 1 June 2015, entered into force 20 December 2015) (China–Korea FTA).

[79] Most of Korea's FTAs emphasise the application of competition laws to state enterprises through a separate provision, rather than simply noting the equal application of competition

all undertakings of each party[80] and confirming that the same chapter does not prevent a party from establishing or maintaining public enterprises,[81] this Agreement requires each party not to adopt or maintain, regarding public enterprises, any measure contrary to the principles contained in its prevailing provision that advocates the proper implementation of competition laws,[82] and to ensure that those enterprises are subject to competition laws.[83]

In sum, China is amenable to a certain level of SOE regulation in FTAs.[84] Moreover, it may be inferred from China's agreed rules to date on the application of competition laws that those rules would be included in its future trade agreements. The prime benefit—though, in certain cases, it is actually a weakness—of the competition law-based approach is that it does not curtail the regulating country's discretion in conducting SOE regulation. Considering the current status of SOEs and their role in the Chinese economy, the competition law-based approach can be seen as the more realistic and acceptable, and thereby more effective, option for regulating conduct by SOEs that affects trade with China.[85] Indeed, China seems to be gradually applying its Antimonopoly Law (AML) to SOEs, although the AML's enforcers still appear hesitant to enforce the law against big SOEs.[86] The concept of competitive neutrality policy nurtured in Australia does not intrinsically conflict with this premise of autonomy.[87] Therefore, it is regrettable that

laws to all enterprises in general terms. See, eg, Free Trade Agreement between the Republic of Colombia and the Republic of Korea (signed 21 February 2013, entered into force 15 July 2016) Art 13.9.

[80] China–Korea FTA (n 78) Art 14.5(1).

[81] ibid Art 14.5(2).

[82] ibid Art 14.5(3)(a).

[83] ibid Art 14.5(3)(b).

[84] This suggests that Australia, rather than China, felt reluctant to introduce SOE-related provisions, in particular those demanding the application of competition laws to SOEs, in ChAFTA. One reason for this speculation is the limited scope and enforceability of competition law-based regulation. The effectiveness of the competition law-based approach highly depends on the regulating country's ambition; another potential constraint is where its scope does not extend to SOEs' conduct not usually captured under competition laws, such as subsidies or preferential arrangements provided to SOEs by the government. Considering that ChAFTA's negotiation was partially in parallel with the TPP negotiations, omitting SOE-related provisions was probably the better choice to avoid infecting the outcome of the TPP negotiations, since the latter Agreement is obviously concerning as regards Chinese SOEs, despite the non-participation of China.

[85] B Jin, 'Competitive Neutrality in the Trans-Pacific Partnership (TPP) Negotiations on International Investment' (2015) 1 *Transnational Dispute Management* 30–31. It argues that China is not prepared to accept the SOE regulation that the US seems to have advocated during the TPP negotiations.

[86] H Chen and J Whalley, 'The State-Owned Enterprises Issue in China's Prospective Trade Negotiations' (2014) CIGI Papers No 48, 3.

[87] See, eg, X Shiying, 'Competitive Neutrality of SOEs in China' in D Healey (ed), *UNCTAD Research Partnership Platform, Competitive Neutrality and its Application in Selected Developing Countries* (Geneva, United Nations, 2014) 76. It recommends that a complaints process

ChAFTA does not contain any provisions regarding the treatment of SOEs, even in the modest way that can be found in KAFTA and JAEPA.[88]

VI. SOE REGULATION UNDER THE TPP AGREEMENT

Despite the fact that it will not formally come into effect, the likelihood of a very similar successor agreement including similar approaches suggests that there is great value in considering the relevant approaches of the TPP in this chapter. Critically, the conclusion of the TPP Agreement (signed 4 February 2016) has paved the way to widen the application of SOE regulation under trade agreements in general.[89] The TPP Agreement established an independent chapter concerning SOEs, accomplishing the incorporation of not only the traditional disciplines inherited from GATT and NAFTA—ie, concepts of non-discrimination and commercial considerations—but also the new framework labelled as non-commercial assistance (NCA). While some of these rules are completely novel, the SOE chapter as a whole would essentially be evaluated as an expansion of the WTO-based approach. This is because the new NCA rules espouse the basic disciplines of the SCM Agreement and simultaneously extend those disciplines, without significant modification, to fields that are not covered under the SCM Agreement, such as non-commercial assistance provided with respect to trade in services. Considering this generic concordance with previous rules, it is not unreasonable to expect that the SOE disciplines in the TPP Agreement should become standard rules, rather than being limited to the Pacific Rim.[90]

in China should not be established, due to the government's lack of motivation to weaken the economic advantages of SOEs, while advocates the strict enforcement of competition law in controlling exclusive business conduct by SOEs.

[88] See, eg, R Tomasic and P Xiong, 'Chinese State-Owned Enterprises in Australia: Legal and Investment Challenges' (2015) 30(2) *Australian Journal of Corporation Law* 151, 176. It submits the necessity of regulating SOEs within the China–Australia relationship, focusing particularly on investment issues; but see, M Bowman et al, 'The Australia–China Free Trade Agreement and the Growing Acceptance of Chinese State Capital Investment' (2015) 8(1) *Asian Journal of Public Affairs* 1, 11. It predicts the future softening of investment review policy towards Chinese SOEs by the Australian government.

[89] At the time of writing, the fate of the TPP Agreement is unclear. While the US administration has formally announced its 'withdrawal' from the Agreement, some of the remaining TPP signatories are considering the possibility of establishing TPP-11, ie, the TPP Agreement without the US. In addition, there is the potential for SOE-related provisions in the TPP Agreement to become a template for SOE regulation and transplanted into other FTAs. Inside US Trade, 'Language in NAFTA Draft Notice Similar to TPP Text on Investment, IP, SOE' (7 April 2017) In light of these developments, the present chapter's discussion assumes that SOE-related provisions established in the TPP Agreement may survive in some form in the future.

[90] It is noteworthy that the TPP Agreement appointed a committee specifically to consider SOE matters; one of its tasks is to contribute to the dissemination of TPP-style SOE disciplines. Trans-Pacific Partnership Agreement (TPP Agreement) Art 17.12.2(c), ustr.gov/trade-agreements/free-trade-agreements/trans-pacific-partnership/tpp-full-text. See also, MK Lewis,

Conversely, the TPP rules are not without concerns and problems. First, the new rules are, by their nature, coercive. Under the TPP rules, if a certain form of non-commercial assistance is causing adverse effects or injury to another party, the providing country needs to take appropriate action to remove those effects or withdraw the assistance concerned; otherwise, it will be confronted with the countermeasures permitted under the TPP dispute settlement procedure.[91] While the TPP rules do not contain a mechanism of countervailing duty, they also do not clearly specify a more flexible approach. For instance, they do not contain a mechanism somewhat akin to the undertakings system envisaged under Article 18 of the SCM Agreement.[92] In essence, the complaining party is given discretion and control over all the counteracting processes and the providing party will be directly condemned through the rules in the TPP Agreement.[93] Second, and on the contrary, some lacunae remain under the new rules, even when they are combined with the SCM Agreement. For instance, although the TPP Agreement NCA rules seek to cover non-commercial assistance that may not be caught by the SCM Agreement (eg, assistance provided by SOEs not vested with governmental authority),[94] they do not contemplate the situation where assisted exports adversely affect the domestic industry of another TPP party operating within that party's domestic market, ie, the case that would be subject to countervailing duties under the SCM Agreement.[95]

'The TPP and the RCEP (ASEAN+6) as Potential Paths toward Deeper Asian Economic Integration' (2013) 8(2) *Asian Journal of WTO and International Health Law and Policy* 359, 370. It suggests that the conclusion of the TTIP would raise the TPP's SOE rules as a global standard, since it is likely that the former would incorporate the latter.

[91] TPP Agreement (n 90) Arts 28.19, 28.20.

[92] Steinbach acknowledges the difficulty of monitoring, and casts doubt on the effectiveness of price undertakings in eliminating the injurious effects of dumping practices. These deficiencies might explain why this mechanism was not introduced under the TPP NCA rules. See, eg, A Steinbach, 'Price Undertaking in EU Anti-dumping Proceedings: An Instrument of the Past?' (2014) 29(1) *Journal of Economic Integration* 165, 174. See also, L Rovegno and H Vandenbussche, 'A Comparative Analysis of EU Antidumping Rules and Application' (2011) IRES Discussion Paper 2011–23, 18. It briefly portrays, in the context of anti-dumping procedures, the US' limited willingness to engage in price undertakings measures. However, it seems that the TPP Agreement does not a priori exclude such 'mutually satisfactory resolution'. TPP Agreement (n 90) Art 28.2. In addition, the TPP Agreement embraces the system of monetary payments: TPP Agreement (n 90) Arts 28.20.7–15.

[93] By contrast, apart from the FTAs concluded by NAFTA Members, most countries have conventionally adopted a system that: (i) is based on the application of competition law; and (ii) excludes the competition chapter from the scope of their FTAs' dispute settlement procedures. This demonstrates more deferential attitudes towards SOE regulation predicated on domestic legislation.

[94] TPP Agreement (n 90) Art 17.6.2. Regarding the meaning of 'government' under Art 1.1(a) SCM Agreement, see above section IV.

[95] Art 17.7.1(b)(i) TPP Agreement only stipulates the situation where sales of a covered investment (namely, a third TPP party's investment) or imports from a third TPP party, but not products of the domestic industry of an importing party, are displaced or impeded from the market of the party importing assisted products.

Therefore, if assistance is provided to the SOE in a form that does not fulfil the definition of 'subsidy' under the SCM Agreement, the importing party may have no means to address the adverse effects upon its domestic industry emanating from assisted exports.[96] Third, the new TPP rules do not properly respond to the public services concerns.[97] In this respect, services provided by SOEs are excluded from certain provisions in the SOE chapter of the TPP Agreement when 'supplied in the exercise of governmental authority'.[98] The meaning of this phrase is clarified under GATS,[99] enunciated as 'any service which is supplied neither on a commercial basis, nor in competition with one or more service suppliers'.[100] However, this exception is narrow, especially when considered at face value. Services that fit this definition are very limited as most public services contain commercial aspects or (potentially) compete with other suppliers.[101] Moreover, according to the TPP Agreement, 'a service supplied by [an SOE] of a party within that party's territory shall be deemed not to cause adverse effects';[102] thereby, NCA rules will not be applied to assistance given in relation to those services. However, this exception is too broad. It muddles all domestic services, irrespective of whether they have public purposes.[103] Admitting that this represents a compromise in the negotiation and, hence, tentatively the best solution for all parties, it is nonetheless, at least theoretically, not ideal.[104]

[96] It should be noted, however, that under the TPP NCA rules, if the assistance leads to significant price undercutting, significant price suppression, price depression, or the phenomenon of lost sales, an importing party may react to the importing of goods produced by assisted SOEs. Art 17.7.1(c)(i) refers to 'the market of a Party' (and 'in the same market'), with no limitation upon what constitutes the affected market, suggesting that the importing party may claim, under the TPP's dispute settlement procedure, the existence of adverse effects if one of the aforementioned phenomena occurs in its domestic market. However, in the case of significant price undercutting, the same provision explicitly stipulates that the comparison of price must be between the price of the good at issue and the price of 'imports of a like good of another Party' or 'a like good that is produced by an enterprise that is a covered investment in the territory of the Party'. In short, the comparison is not between the price of the good at issue and that of like goods produced by the domestic industry (unlike under Art 17.8.2).

[97] M Yun, 'An Analysis of the New Trade Regime for State-Owned Enterprises under the Trans-Pacific Partnership Agreement' (2016) 20(1) *Journal of East Asian Economic Integration* 3, 27.

[98] TPP Agreement (n 90) Art 17.2.10.

[99] TPP Agreement (n 90) Ch 17, fn 11.

[100] GATS (n 57) Art I:3(c). See also, above (n 11); TPP Agreement (n 90) Ch 17.

[101] R Adlung, 'Public Services and the GATS' (2005) WTO Working Paper ERSD-2005-03, 8–12. It explores, simultaneously, the possibility that GATS Art I:3(c) would be interpreted more broadly than its literal meaning.

[102] TPP Agreement (n 90) Art 17.6.4.

[103] There is also the concept of the 'public service mandate' in Arts 17.1, 17.4 TPP Agreement and the public policy/public interest exceptions for competition laws in Art 16.1.2.

[104] Y Tojo, 'International Discipline on SOEs: Development of Fair Competition Rules' (2016) RIETI Discussion Paper Series 16-J-011, 23 (in Japanese). There are some additional exceptions. For instance, in certain circumstances, the supply of financial services by an SOE pursuant to a government mandate will be deemed not to give rise to adverse effects under certain provisions in the TPP Agreement where the party in which the financial service is supplied requires a local presence to supply those services. See TPP Agreement (n 90) Art 17.13.3.

On balance, there are fears that SOE regulation under the TPP Agreement may come under heavy fire from both sides: it could be blamed as too weak from the proponents of strong SOE regulation and too bold from those who view SOEs as important instruments in developing societies.

VII. FUTURE SOE REGULATION AND CHAFTA

Currently, there are variations in SOE regulation provided under FTAs. At one end of the spectrum, there is the TPP Agreement, which enables direct regulation of SOEs based on the rules it deploys with viable enforcing mechanisms. At the opposite end is ChAFTA, which does not contain any particular SOE regulations and the conduct of SOEs are principally not condemned beyond the existing WTO framework. SAFTA, KAFTA and JAEPA, those that can be labelled as the competitive neutrality group, are located between those two poles (Figure 1).

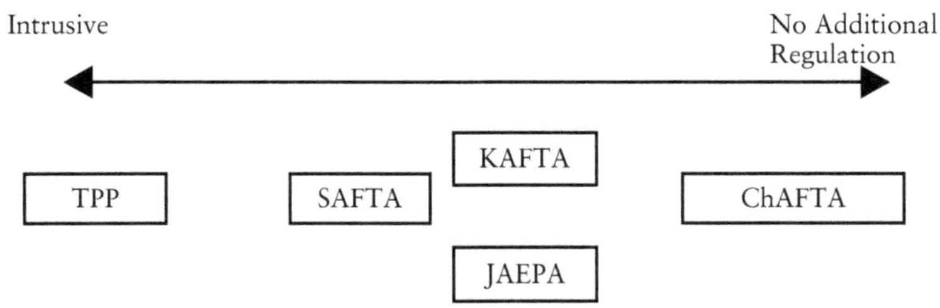

Figure 1: Spectrum of SOE Regulation under Australia's FTAs

At the time of writing, the fate of the TPP Agreement is undetermined though looking less likely to come into effect. On one hand, if the TPP Agreement or a TPP-like agreement enters into force, it would serve as a strong driving force for toughening SOE regulation in the Asia-Pacific region. Not only would it refine existing SOE regulation under the trade agreements that are already in force, but it would also affect future agreements by tempting TPP parties to use its framework as a template when concluding new agreements with other countries. On the other hand, the demise of the TPP will result in most operative SOE regulations being confined to no or small-scale regulations, ie, concentrating on the right side of Figure 1 above.[105] ChAFTA's omission of specific provisions addressing the behaviours of SOEs would

[105] The SOE chapter established under the TPP Agreement might survive, even with the failure of the Agreement, by the adoption of a similar chapter in future bilateral agreements concluded by TPP Members, in particular the US. Nevertheless, such attempts may not have the same impact as the TPP Agreement, which involves 12 countries and nearly 40% of the global GDP.

send a negative signal regarding the development of SOE regulation to the region or international community, and may entrench this custom of indifference. This is the scenario that needs to be avoided.

Bearing this in mind, it is necessary to revisit the strategy for proper SOE regulation. As discussed herein, China's FTAs are gradually introducing competition law-based SOE regulation. This approach is not in conflict with Australia's competitive neutrality policy. Therefore, the first option for a new strategy may be to create new principles or rules on SOE regulation, either inside or outside ChAFTA. The hardest approach would be to amend ChAFTA and insert the provisions focusing on the behaviours of SOEs. This can be achieved through the review and amendment processes provided in the Agreement.[106] The more tempered approach is to append a side letter or to create cooperative agreements. The former may either be integrated into the Agreement, analogous to the current side letters attached as Annex IV to the Agreement,[107] or isolated from the Agreement, such as the side letter regarding Chinese Medicine[108] or the several memorandums of understanding associated with the Agreement.[109] The creation of a cooperative agreement, on the other hand, can be achieved via the mechanism prepared within ChAFTA that aims to enhance collaboration in competition matters. Pursuant to Article 16.7 of ChAFTA, Australia and China will devise new or use existing mechanisms to cooperate in enforcing competition laws and policies. This commitment could serve as a stepping stone for future development of comprehensive cooperation in competition matters. Furthermore, it would be more constructive if the concept of competitive neutrality is clearly recognised as a part of competition policy for the purpose of this cooperation.

Another route for the development of SOE regulation is to create rules in different frameworks that could involve both Australia and China, such as the Regional Comprehensive Economic Partnership (RCEP). However, introducing SOE regulation in the RCEP might be too ambitious, with the existence of ChAFTA operating as a hurdle to that end. The first step that Australia should take, therefore, is to develop SOE regulation in bilateral agreements, to generate an atmosphere that would embrace a certain degree of cross-border SOE surveillance in the region. This will require Australia to further develop a competitive neutrality concept with Singapore, South

[106] ChAFTA (n 1) Arts 16.5, 17.3.

[107] Side letters included in Annex IV are binding, in principle (ChAFTA (n 1) Art 17.1). However, as some provisions in the Agreement are excluded from the application of dispute settlement procedures established under the Agreement, side letters connected to those provisions will be dealt with in the same manner.

[108] Side Letter on Traditional Chinese Medicine.

[109] eg, Memorandum of Understanding between the Government of Australia and the Government of the People's Republic of China on an Investment Facilitation Arrangement.

Korea and Japan under the current FTAs, and to foster competition cooperation among other Asian countries through new FTAs. The same would be true for China and countries that are candidates for counterparts in China's FTAs. From this perspective, the China–Korea FTA can be praised, since it advanced cooperative regulation for the behaviour of SOEs, and this effort should be continued with expectations of spilling over to other FTAs.

In any event, ChAFTA, as it stands, represents a missed opportunity to diffuse more flexible methods of regulating SOEs. However, there remains a path to develop SOE regulation that may suit the Asia-Oceania region.[110] If this is achieved, in particular within the framework of ChAFTA, it may be said that SOE regulation in ChAFTA has contributed to developing SOE regulation in the region. Alternatively, proper SOE regulation may be established via a different path. While an ideal way may be through plurilateral FTAs, steady effort through bilateral agreements also contributes to such a goal. It is important to keep up the effort to pursue proper cross-border or region-wide SOE regulation irrespective of the fate of the TPP Agreement, and ChAFTA should have a role to play in such endeavours.

VIII. CONCLUSION

As analysed herein, there is no comprehensive SOE regulation in ChAFTA, despite strong interest in that topic on the part of Australia, which has succeeded in diffusing the concept of competition neutrality to some Asian countries, such as Singapore (SAFTA), South Korea (KAFTA) and Japan (JAEPA). Even compared with China's previous FTAs, ChAFTA may be assessed as taking a step backwards; the Agreement does not even mention the application of competition laws to SOEs. Nevertheless, there remains a possibility to elaborate comprehensive SOE regulation within the Australia–China relationship. A competitive neutrality policy may work harmoniously with existing competition laws, as well as entailing additional advantages derived from its flexibility and ex ante nature that cannot be attained in the simple application of competition laws. Therefore, both countries need to continue their efforts to enhance cooperation and develop mechanisms with Australian competitive neutrality policy in mind, to ensure equal opportunity for competition between private and public enterprises; such a course can eventually contribute to the development of appropriate SOE regulation in the Asia-Oceania region. Concurrent with this, it may also be sensible to

[110] P Kowalski and K Perepechay, 'International Trade and Investment by State Enterprises' (2015) OECD Policy Papers No 148, 25. It suggests that stringent regulation at the international level, such as that in the TPP Agreement, does not always fit the circumstances of individual countries.

embrace other countries that can afford to share the spirit of Australian-style competitive neutrality policy, such as Singapore, South Korea and Japan. As economic integration is evolving, thanks to the enhancement of trade agreements in the Asia-Oceania region, it also needs to create cross-border cooperative mechanisms to properly ensure a level playing field among various competitors, so that the signatories are not deprived of the benefits of free trade. It is expected that the cooperative relationship between Australia and China will achieve this, through long-term effort.

Part III

Insights and Lessons for Trade in Services

6

Services Liberalisation in ChAFTA: Progress Assessment and the Way Forward

JINGXIA SHI

I. INTRODUCTION

AFTER 10 YEARS of marathon negotiations, the China–Australia Free Trade Agreement (ChAFTA) was officially signed in Canberra on 17 June 2015.[1] Thereafter, the two parties respectively carried out their domestic approval procedures and brought the Agreement into force on 20 December 2015.

As one of China's key economic and trade partners, with its GDP ranking twelfth worldwide, Australia is also an important member of the Organisation for Economic Co-operation and Development (OECD) and the G20 and has a mature market economy and governance model. The foreign direct investment between China and Australia has increased dramatically in recent years.[2] The signing of ChAFTA reflects China's continuous efforts to deepen domestic reform and establish closer trade relations with developed economies. On the other hand, China is Australia's largest partner of trade in goods, the largest source of imports and the largest destination of exports. Thus, for Australia, reaching a free trade agreement (FTA) with its number one trading partner is a historic accomplishment for Australian exporters.

While ChAFTA is one of the most progressive FTAs that China has entered into, the negotiation of ChAFTA was exceptionally hard and was suspended

[1] Gao Hucheng, the Minister of Commerce of the People's Republic of China, and Andrew Robb, the Minister for Trade and Investment of Australia, on behalf of their respective governments, officially signed the Free Trade Agreement between the Government of Australia and the Government of the People's Republic of China in Canberra, Australia. Chinese President Xi Jinping and Australian Prime Minister Tony Abbott exchanged congratulatory letters on the official conclusion of ChAFTA on that day.

[2] See, eg, Department of Foreign Affairs and Trade (DFAT), 'Which Countries Invest in Australia?' (October 2016), dfat.gov.au/trade/topics/investment/Pages/which-countries-invest-in-australia.aspx; see also, DFAT, 'Where Does Australia Invest?' (October 2016), dfat.gov.au/trade/topics/investment/Pages/where-does-australia-invest.aspx.

on several occasions.[3] There are several reasons for the protracted negotiations. First, the lack of an FTA did not seem to have prevented a burgeoning trade relationship between China and Australia. Second, economic modelling of an FTA between the two showed that the benefits to be gained are actually somewhat limited.[4] This may be a result of the inherent limitation of bilateral trade deals as opposed to a multilateral one. Further, there was a concern that a bilateral deal with China might lead to welfare losses for Australia.[5] Despite the various difficulties, the political will in both countries played a pivotal role in pushing forward the conclusion of ChAFTA. The final Agreement achieves its basic objective for a comprehensive and high-standard agreement with a group of relatively balanced interests.

ChAFTA comprehensively enhances the bilateral economic relations between Australia and China in a lasting and deep manner. Among other things, ChAFTA significantly lowers the threshold for bilateral trade and investment and has made more open, convenient and standard institutional arrangements for the future development of economic relations. Furthermore, given that both China and Australia are great powers in the Asia-Pacific region and the world's major economies, the conclusion of ChAFTA lays a solid foundation for the process of building the Asia-Pacific Free Trade Area, as well as a deeper integration of the Asia-Pacific economies.[6]

This chapter focuses on the liberalisation of trade in services under ChAFTA. The central idea is that services commitments in ChAFTA deserve more attention not only because of the creation of unprecedented market access compared with the previous FTAs China and Australia

[3] In October 2003, China and Australia signed the Trade and Economic Cooperation Framework and decided to carry out a joint feasibility study in FTA. In March 2005, the joint study was completed and ChAFTA was deemed feasible and would, on the whole, bring real benefits to two countries. Then the negotiations were officially launched in April 2005. From the launch to the announcement of the conclusion of substantive negotiations in November 2014, 21 rounds of negotiations and dozens of small-scale consultations were conducted. For more details on the negotiation, see, dfat.gov.au/trade/agreements/chafta/negotiations/Pages/about-the-negotiations.aspx.

[4] A piece in the *Australian Financial Review* referred to modelling performed by the Centre for International Economics and commissioned by the Australia–China Business Council, which 'suggested that Australia's GDP stood to gain an annual boost of 0.7% over two decades with an FTA in the bag'. The estimated increase in China's GDP over the same time horizon was just 0.1%. See, eg, J Laurenceson, 'Why an Australian FTA with China Has Never Stacked Up' (22 October 2013), theconversation.com/why-an-australian-fta-with-china-has-never-stacked-up-19299; see also, Centre for International Economics, 'Estimating the Impact of An Australia–China Trade and Investment Agreement—2008 Economic Modeling Update, Prepared for Australia China Business Council' (November 2008), acbc.com.au/admin/images/uploads/Copy3report_fta_modelling.pdf.

[5] ibid.

[6] The 22nd APEC Economic Leaders Meeting decided to launch the process of building the Asia-Pacific Free Trade Area. APEC, '2014 Leader's Declaration at the 22nd APEC Economic Leaders' Meeting' (11 November 2014) text and Annex A (The Beijing Roadmap for APEC's Contribution to the Realization of FTAAP), apec.org/Meeting-Papers/Leaders-Declarations/2014/2014_aelm.aspx.

have signed, but also due to the creative scheduling methods and further upgrading arrangements. The author maintains that it is the right time for China to gradually adopt a negative list approach in negotiating FTAs and accordingly to build its capacity in this respect as well. Following this introduction, section II then examines the current situation of the services sector and trade of the two countries and analyses the potential impact of services liberalisation under ChAFTA on the two parties' domestic services industries and trade. Section III gives an overview of the services commitments made by Australia and China in ChAFTA. China's key sectoral commitments are highlighted as well. Section IV contemplates the creative mixed or hybrid services scheduling methods adopted by ChAFTA. It first summaries the basic features of the positive list and negative list approaches and then analyses the challenges that China faces in upgrading its services commitments through a negative list approach. The analysis in this regard is conducted in the wider context of China's recent acceptance of a negative list approach in its other FTAs and bilateral investment treaty (BIT) negotiations.

II. ChAFTA AND THE SERVICES INDUSTRY AND TRADE BETWEEN CHINA AND AUSTRALIA

An 'enabler' permitting the productive engines to move forward smoothly, services are both the backbone and the growth engine of economies in the twenty-first century, developed and developing alike, including Australia and China. Higher GDP growth often goes hand-in-hand with the growth of service sectors.[7] In recent decades, services trade continues to be the most dynamic part of world trade, and the services sector has long been the largest recipient of foreign direct investment (FDI).[8] The massive potential gains to be reaped through greater liberalisation of services trade and investment take various forms including job creation, greater economic efficiency, more

[7] See, eg, Office of Policy Development, Economics and Statistics Administration, US Department of Commerce, 'Services Industry and Economic Performance' (March 1996), www.esa.doc.gov/sites/default/files/serviceindustries_0.pdf. The report addresses three questions: whether services-oriented economies can sustain high rates of output growth; whether they can generate large numbers of good jobs; and whether they can compete efficiently in global markets. See also, D Park and K Shin, 'The Service Sector in Asia: Is it an Engine of Growth?' (2012) ADB Economics Working Paper Series No 322, www.adb.org/publications/service-sector-asia-it-engine-growth; JW Lee and WJ McKibbin, 'Service Sector Productivity and Economic Growth in Asia' (2014) ADBI Working Paper No 490, ssrn.com/abstract=2471430 or dx.doi.org/10.2139/ssrn.2471430.

[8] See, eg, S Descheemaeker, 'Ubiquitous Uncertainty: The Overlap between Trade in Services and Foreign Investment in the GATS and EU RTAs' (2016) 43 (3) *Legal Issues of Economic Integration* 265; K Fukao and K Ito, 'Foreign Direct Investment and Services Trade: The Case of Japan' in T Ito and AO Krueger (eds), *Trade in Services in the Asia Pacific Region* (Chicago, University of Chicago Press, 2003).

variety and lower costs of doing business.[9] Both China and Australia have achieved high-level negotiation outcomes with mutual benefits in their services sectors in ChAFTA. This part contemplates the potential impact of ChAFTA on the two countries' services industry and trade.

A. ChAFTA and Australia's Services Industry and Trade

Australia, as a developed economy, has a higher development level in the services industry. Australia's important services sector includes financial services, legal and professional services, education, telecommunications and electronic commerce, followed by mining and energy services, environmental services and construction.[10] Total trade in services accounted for 21.3 per cent of Australia's total trade in 2015 (up from 19.7 per cent in 2014). Australia's exports of services rose by 10.0 per cent to AUD$66.2 billion in 2015, while its imports of services rose by 8.4 per cent to AUD$76.3 billion in 2015.[11] The Services Trade Restrictiveness Index (STRI) score compiled by the OECD is often employed to evaluate the degree of openness/restrictiveness of a country's services market.[12] It is found that Australia has a lower score on the STRI than the average in 18 of 22 sectors, reflecting the generally pro-trade regulatory environment in Australia.[13]

With the commodities boom becoming a distant memory, the Australian government is looking to promote services exports to maintain sustainable growth. This was also reflected in the negotiation of ChAFTA where services constituted a key part of Australia's interests and concerns.

China was the largest exporter of services to Australia, up 2.2 per cent to US$286.5 billion and the second largest importer of services from Australia, up 3.5 per cent to US$468.9 billion in 2015.[14] ChAFTA tries to lay a firmer

[9] See, eg, GC Hufbauer, JB Jensen and S Stephenson, 'Framework for the International Services Agreement, Policy Brief' (2012) Peterson Institute for International Economics No PB12-10, piie.com/publications/pb/pb12-10.pdf; see also, S Kurtishi-Kastrati, 'The Effects of Foreign Direct Investments for Host Country's Economy' (2013) 5(1) *European Journal of Interdisciplinary Studies* 26.

[10] A Lumsden, L Knight and W Zhou, 'What Does the China FTA Mean for Australian Services Firms?' *The Australian* (13 March 2015), www.theaustralian.com.au/business/business-spectator/what-does-the-china-fta-mean-for-australian-services-firms/news-story/5fadc5a9594efef20ac2307b121aa6ba.

[11] DFAT, 'Trade in Services Australia 2015' (August 2016), dfat.gov.au/about-us/publications/Documents/trade-in-services-australia-2015.pdf, 2–4.

[12] International trade in services is often impeded by trade and investment barriers and domestic regulations. The Services Trade Restrictiveness Index (STRI) developed by the OECD helps identify which policy measures restrict trade. It provides policymakers and negotiators with information and measurement tools to open up international trade in services and negotiate international trade agreements. It can also help governments identify best practice and then focus their domestic reform efforts on priority sectors and measures. For more information, visit OECD, 'Services Trade Restrictiveness Index' (2017), www.oecd.org/tad/services-trade/services-trade-restrictiveness-index.htm.

[13] ibid.

[14] ibid.

foundation for much faster export growth across many services sectors. Now for Australia, ChAFTA delivers the best ever services opportunities going back the other way, including new or enhanced access to the Chinese market. The market access China has offered to Australia in ChAFTA provides Australian firms with a competitive advantage over many other foreign services suppliers. It is thus expected that ChAFTA will further boost the development of Australia's services industry and trade with China.

B. China's Shift from Resources to Services and ChAFTA

The conventional wisdom seems to be that developing countries have to pass through stages of manufacturing and/or agricultural comparative advantage before gaining proficiency in the production of services;[15] however, even low-income economies today have services sectors that account for nearly half of their economic output, and some of their services arms are competitive in international markets.[16] Indeed the share of developing countries in world services exports has increased in recent decades. Services thus may well serve as a conduit for leapfrogging traditional paths of economic growth.

This is of particular importance to China. As widely noted, China has been undergoing a welcome but rocky transition from an economy driven by inward investment and exports to one in which services are the major factor in economic expansion.[17] The so-called economic 'new normal' in China has captured the world's attention. In the past China was a hyper growth economy in a catch-up phase, driven by inbound investment and exportation. It has now been in the process of moving towards a more mature economy, with slower but still significant growth and a much bigger role for services consumption.[18] In fact, the services industry and trade have played a key role in China's transition from its hyper growth phase to a more sustainable and services-led economy.

China exported commercial services worth US$232.4 billion in 2014 with its commercial services imports amounting to US$381.6 billion. In addition to the huge deficit of services trade, services account for only about 48 per cent of the Chinese economy, significantly lower than the average for middle-income countries. Services also account for a relatively low share of total Chinese trade (14 per cent of imports and 9 per cent of exports).[19]

[15] Hufbauer, Jensen and Stephenson (n 9).

[16] ibid.

[17] Peterson Institute for International Economics, 'China's Economic Transformation: Lessons, Impact, and the Path Forward' (October 2015), piie.com/publications/piie-briefings/chinas-economic-transformation-lessons-impact-and-path-forward, 3.

[18] Blackrock, 'China's Shift to Services: A Commercial Property Perspective' (2016), www.blackrock.com/institutions/en-gb/literature/whitepaper/china-services-transition.pdf.

[19] See, eg, 商务部(Ministry of Commerce (MOFCOM)), '中国服务贸易统计报告2015' ('China Statistics of Trade in Services 2015)' (25 October 2016), tradeinservices.mofcom.gov.cn/c/2016-01-26/284930.shtml.

China scores above average on the STRI in all sectors. The STRI reports that Australia's services barrier accounts for 16.12 per cent, while China's services barrier accounts for 67.93 per cent.[20] These figures illustrate that there is great room for China to remove its services and investment barriers in order to improve the performance of services industry and trade.

To this end, China has been concluding new agreements on trade and investment with other economic partners, further opening up its services market. However, given that China has not previously invested much in its domestic services industry, it does not have the infrastructure in place to rapidly grow its services sector to meet the internal demand. To fill the gap, China has been making appropriate decisions in light of its growing internal services economy. Its shift from resources-based towards a stronger consumer-led growth is bringing balance to its services sector and stabilising it against potential volatility in domestic markets. China is now Australia's second biggest trading partner, only second to New Zealand. With the entry into force of ChAFTA, China's services industry may face new opportunities and challenges. Even without ChAFTA, the financial transactions between the two countries have increased, with, for example, China's outbound investment in Australia growing significantly. It is expected that ChAFTA will play an important role in promoting China's further services liberalisation.

III. SERVICES LIBERALISATION IN CHAFTA: HORIZONTAL AND SECTORAL COMMITMENTS

The importance of services liberalisation to overall trade growth is often overlooked. For many reasons, there has been little progress in multilateral talks to liberalise services trade and investment.[21] This has made Regional Trade Agreements (RTAs) a major forum for services liberalisation over the past decade.[22] While many RTAs codify the status quo for regulatory systems and foreign access to local services markets, some have managed to go further in selected sectors.[23] ChAFTA is of the latter type—further to

[20] OECD, 'OECD Services Trade Restrictiveness Index (STRI) of People's Republic of China' (December 2016), www.oecd.org/tad/services-trade/STRI_CHN.pdf.

[21] The liberalisation of services at the multilateral level has been stuck in the ill-fated Doha Development Round for many years now. Services trade has become a hostage both of institutional deficiencies in the General Agreement on Trade in Services (GATS) and of political dissent over the broader Doha agenda. Hufbauer, Jensen and Stephenson (n 9).

[22] The recent decades have witnessed a surge of FTAs. As of 1 July 2016, some 635 notifications of RTAs (counting goods, services and accessions separately) had been received by GATT/WTO. Of these, 423 were in force. These WTO figures correspond to 460 physical RTAs (counting goods, services and accessions together), of which 267 are currently in force. WTO, 'Welcome to the Regional Trade Agreements Information System (RTA-IS)' (2017), rtais.wto.org/UI/PublicMaintainRTAHome.aspx.

[23] For more analysis on services commitments in the RTAs, see, eg, J Marchetti, M Roy and Laura Zoratto, 'Is there Reciprocity in Preferential Trade Agreements on Services?' (October 2012) WTO Staff Working Paper ERSD-2012-16. See also, WTO, 'WTO Dataset of Services Commitments in Regional Trade Agreements (RTAs)' (2017), www.wto.org/english/tratop_e/

promote services liberalisation, given the fact that Sino-Australian trade in services has been developing rapidly in recent years.[24]

Note that any comprehensive deal, including FTAs negotiation, generally involves a balance of significant interests and thus it was believed that for an FTA with China to be economically meaningful for Australia, China's concessions in the area of services should be included.[25] This is both due to the strengths and comparative advantage enjoyed by Australian services providers and the room for the Chinese services market to open further in the context of the Chinese 'new normal'.[26]

This section first gives an overview of horizontal services commitments in ChAFTA and then highlights key sectoral commitments; the mixed scheduling methods are discussed in section IV. It finds that China and Australia both made unprecedented horizontal and sectoral services commitments compared with their previous FTAs.

A. Horizontal Services Commitments in ChAFTA

ChAFTA includes the text and annexes. In addition to the Preamble, the text consists of 17 chapters, among which several chapters directly or indirectly concern trade in services, including: Trade in Services (Chapter 8); Investment (Chapter 9); Movement of Natural Persons (Chapter 11); Electronic Commerce (Chapter 12); Dispute Settlement (Chapter 15) etc. Also included within ChAFTA are eight annexes, including a Schedule of Specific Commitments on Services (China, Annex III-2) and five side letters (Annex IV) on skills assessment, financial services, education services, legal services and the Rules on Transparency in Treaty-based Investor–State Arbitration.

serv_e/dataset_e/dataset_e.htm. The dataset shows the level of market access committed by parties to each RTA, by mode of supply and by sector, in comparison with achievements in services in the WTO. The dataset also shows the highest level of market access commitments by each WTO Member across all its RTAs.

[24] Particularly, the scale of trade in services between the two countries expanded from US$8.443 billion in 2008 to US$16.716 billion in 2014, with an average annual growth rate of 14%. Currently, there is a big deficit of services trade between China and Australia. China's service exports to Australia reached US$3.665 billion, while Australia's service exports to China reached US$13.05 billion. MOFCOM, 'Interpretation for the China–Australia Free Trade Agreement' (19 June 2015), english.mofcom.gov.cn/article/policyrelease/Cocoon/201510/20151001144954.shtml.

[25] Likewise, for a deal to be struck, Chinese concessions with respect to services need to be balanced by Australian concessions. To this end, China pushed for Australian concessions with respect to inward investment. In particular, the threshold for most Chinese investment proposals currently stands at AUS$0. This is in contrast to the AUS$1 billion threshold for most investment proposals from the US and New Zealand. See, eg, Laurenceson (n 4).

[26] Much ink has been spilled over the Chinese economy entering a stage of 'new normal' after many years of high-speed growth. See, eg, F Green and N Stern, 'China's "New Normal": Structural Change, Better Growth and Peak Emissions (Policy Brief)' (June 2015), www.lse.ac.uk/GranthamInstitute/wp-content/uploads/2015/06/Chinas_new_normal_green_stern_June_2015.pdf.

In addition, ChAFTA contains two Memorandums of Understanding (MOUs) on the Investment Facilitation Arrangement (IFA) and the Work and Holiday Visa Arrangement (WHVA), as well as cooperative side letters on traditional Chinese medicine services.[27] All these directly or indirectly relate to trade in services between the two parties.

Overall, the breakthroughs in services liberalisation are mainly reflected in two aspects: first through liberalization, and second through measures impacting movements of people. First, with respect to liberalisation: ChAFTA is the first Agreement for China in which its FTA partner makes services commitments through a negative-list approach, *and* who provides China with the comprehensive non-discriminatory treatment and market access, subject to a few exceptions.[28] China, for its part, and based on its WTO accession commitments, further opens its services sector for Australia in the form of positive list, and takes some autonomous and open measures of the (Shanghai) Pilot Free Trade Zone (SFTZ).[29] ChAFTA contains measures of autonomous liberalisation taken in the SFTZ,[30] which embodies the 'reproducibility and generalisability' of reform experience. Some open measures taken in the SFTZ in respect of sectors such as telecommunications, legal services, construction and maritime transport are included in ChAFTA, which not only creates more market opportunities for Australian services providers, but also provides China with valuable experience in reform experiment. Furthermore, through a Most-Favoured-Nation (MFN) clause, Australia's competitive position into the future is also secured if China extends any more beneficial treatment to other trade partners in services sectors.[31] On the other hand, the level of openness of Australia to China's services is higher than that of the Japan–Australia FTA[32] and the South Korea–Australia FTA recently reached.[33] This hybrid scheduling methodology is rather creative in the sense that it takes into account the

[27] For the text of ChAFTA, see fta.mofcom.gov.cn/Australia/australia_special.shtml or dfat.gov.au/trade/agreements/chafta/official-documents/Pages/official-documents.aspx.

[28] These exceptions are listed in the Annex III—Part I: Schedule of Non-Conforming Measures, referred to in Ch 8 (Trade in Services) and Ch 9 (Investment) Schedule of Australia.

[29] China's services commitments are contained in the Annex III—Part 2: Schedule of Specific Commitments on Services, referred to in Ch 8 (Trade in Services) and Ch 10 (Movement of Natural Persons) Schedule of the People's Republic of China.

[30] The SFTZ is at the forward position in China's economic reform process.

[31] Free Trade Agreement between the Government of Australia and the Government of the People's Republic of China (ChAFTA) (signed 17 June 2015, entered into force 20 December 2015) [2015] ATS 15, Art 8.7 (Most-Favoured-Nation Treatment).

[32] The Japan–Australia Economic Partnership Agreement (JAEPA) entered into force on 15 January 2015. The conclusion of negotiations on JAEPA was announced in Tokyo on 7 April 2014. The texts of JAEPA are available at dfat.gov.au/trade/agreements/jaepa/official-documents/Pages/official-documents.aspx.

[33] The Korea–Australia Free Trade Agreement (KAFTA) entered into force on 12 December 2014. The texts of KAFTA are available at dfat.gov.au/trade/agreements/kafta/Pages/korea-australia-fta.aspx.

different developmental stage of the services industry and markets of the two parties, to be discussed in more detail in section IV.[34]

Second, major breakthroughs have been made on movements of people related to services. Article I of the General Agreement on Trade in Services (GATS) spells out, in brief language, four modes of delivering services across borders. Among these modes, liberalisation of the temporary movement of natural persons—customarily called Mode 4—has proven to be the most contentious.[35] Because of the great sensitivity of immigration policy, even for the temporary movement of highly skilled and bonded persons, Mode 4 commitments are very limited and have focused primarily on professional service suppliers.[36] ChAFTA has gone further to include market access for more service workers. Specifically, for example, Australia has agreed to establish an investment facilitation mechanism to provide a 'Green Channel' for Chinese workers to apply for Australian visa and work permits so as to promote Chinese investment in Australia. Australia especially establishes a mechanism for engineers and technicians to go to Australia as part of Chinese investment activities.[37] Furthermore, Australia unilaterally provides work and holiday visas for 5,000 Chinese youth to go to Australia each year and reside in Australia for 12 months.[38] This is helpful in strengthening cultural exchanges and promoting the development of relations between the two countries.

Australia also offers an annual entry quota of 1,800 people for occupations with Chinese characteristics, including traditional Chinese medicine (TCM) practitioners, Chinese language teachers, Chinese chefs and martial arts coaches, who can stay in Australia for up to four years, and may extend the term of stay upon expiration.[39]

To sum up, ChAFTA aims to further enhance the liberalisation level of bilateral trade in services, delivering China's best ever services commitments, including the provision of new or significantly improved market access not

[34] For more analysis on this hybrid scheduling method, see below section IV.

[35] The language of Mode 4 reads: 'Provision of services by a service supplier of one Member, through presence of natural persons of a Member in the territory of any other Member'. The words are few while the perceived implications are broad. A commitment to Mode 4, although involving only temporary movement—meaning limited stays of specific categories of service providers—is often mistakenly viewed as a form of permanent migration. Therefore, commitments to temporary movement are sensitive, as they are negotiated in collaboration with national immigration officials.

[36] See, eg, LA Winters et al, 'Liberalizing Temporary Movement of Natural Persons: An Agenda for the Development Round' (August 2003), siteresources.worldbank.org/INTRES/Resources/liberalising_temporary_movement_LAW.pdf. This paper discusses the issues, difficulties and routes to further liberalising Mode 4 under GATS, particularly the movement of medium and low-skilled service providers between developing and developed countries.

[37] ChAFTA (n 31) Memorandum of Understanding on an Investment Facilitation Agreement.

[38] ibid, Memorandum of Understanding on a Work and Holiday Visa Arrangement.

[39] ibid para 11 Annex 10-A (Specific Commitments on the Movement of Natural Persons, Section A: Australia's Specific Commitments), together with Side Letter on Traditional Chinese Medicine.

included in China's previous FTAs (other than Closer Economic Partnership Arrangements (CEPAs) between Mainland China and Hong Kong and Macau respectively under the framework of 'One Country, Two Systems'; and the Economic Cooperation Framework Agreement (ECFA) between Mainland China and Taiwan).

B. Sectoral Commitments made by China in ChAFTA

ChAFTA provides Chinese services suppliers with the assurance that they are treated equally with Australia's other key FTA partners. Australia already maintains an open and transparent services market, ensuring that Australian companies remain globally competitive and consumers have access to quality services from overseas, which comprises 73 per cent of the Australian economy. In addition to areas covered in all Australia's FTAs, Australia has made specific assurances in ChAFTA concerning areas of interest to China, including Australia's advanced system for protecting the interests of international students studying in Australia, the ability for Chinese financial institutions to participate in the Reserve Bank Information and Transfer System (RITS), among others.

China's services commitments under ChAFTA cover a wide range of sectors such as legal, financial, telecommunications, education, medical services, and construction and engineering services. Some important sectoral commitments are highlighted below.

i. Financial Services

Financial services is one of the primary cooperation sectors of China and Australia. On the one hand, ChAFTA provides new commercial opportunities for Australian banks, insurers and securities firms. Australian financial services providers are allowed to establish joint venture futures companies with up to 49 per cent Australian ownership. Also, Australian insurance providers enjoy more liberal access to China's statutory third-party liability motor vehicle insurance market compared with the commitments made in China's previous FTAs. Furthermore, Australia is the first country whose insurance providers are allowed to engage in limited statutory insurance business in China. Australian banks are also allowed to engage in the credit asset securitisation business and now benefit from significantly relaxed prudential requirements when engaging in RMB business.[40]

[40] ibid Annex 8-B (Financial Services) together with pt 2 (Schedule of the People's Republic of China) Annex III (Investment and Services Schedules of Australia and China).

On the other hand, as required by China, Australia commits to reduce the required liquidity coverage ratio of branches of foreign banks from 100 per cent to 40 per cent, so the capital costs of branches of Chinese banks in Australia could be significantly reduced. For Chinese persons nominated to work as 'responsible managers' of Australian branches or sub-branches of Chinese-funded banks, Australia under ChAFTA facilitates the movement of such managers to Australia to conduct business subject to certain requirements including the obtaining of relevant qualifications and experience in China. On the basis of national treatment, Chinese institutions may provide payment services in Australia in the capacity of a member or an operator of a payment system.[41] These commitments create a better business environment for Chinese financial institutions to operate in Australia. In addition, Australia and China have also committed to greater cooperation and information-sharing regarding regulatory frameworks for financial services—such as for payment systems and securities—in order to manage risks, improve transparency and obtain other mutually beneficial outcomes.

ii. Telecommunications Services

In ChAFTA, China has provided its most extensive telecommunications market access commitments of any of its FTAs thus far, including guaranteeing market access for Australian companies investing in specified value-added telecommunications services in the SFTZ. These commitments provide greater certainty for Australian telecommunications investments. Australian telecommunications services providers now enjoy increased foreign equity limits; and wholly Australian-owned enterprises are allowed to supply domestic multiparty communication (DMPC) services, application store services, store and forward services and call centre services.[42] More significantly, Australia's telecommunications services firms are able to establish wholly owned businesses to engage in several designated types of telecommunications services and to obtain a majority ownership of up to 55 per cent in a joint venture with Chinese firms that undertake online data and transaction processing services in the SFTZ. China also agreed to specific commitments addressing behind-the-border issues—such as licensing and transparency—affecting telecommunications providers, as well as commitments to consult with Australian industry participants in China.[43] The Trade in Services Committee, established under ChAFTA, provides an avenue for Australian telecommunications companies to have their concerns voiced in China.

[41] ibid Annex 8-B (Financial Services) together with pt 1 (Schedule of Australia) Annex III (Investment and Services Schedules of Australia and China).

[42] ibid pt 2 (Schedule of the People's Republic of China) Annex III (Investment and Services Schedules of Australia and China).

[43] ibid.

iii. Education Services

Australia is a major supplier of education services. China was already Australia's largest education services export market by 2014–15.[44] Under ChAFTA, China and Australia agree to expand and deepen cooperation in respect of education services. As specified in the Agreement, Australian private higher education providers will gain an improved profile with prospective Chinese students and employers and hence greater access to China's higher education market. Within one year of entry into force, China will list an additional 77 Australian private higher education institutions, registered with the Commonwealth Register of Institutions and Courses for Overseas Students (CRICOS), on a key Ministry of Education overseas study website, which adds to the existing 105 Australian institutions on the website. The website is intended to provide Chinese students and employers with guidance on quality and fraud assurance issues in selecting educational institutions. In fact, the vast majority of Chinese higher education students studying in Australia choose to study at institutions listed on the website.[45] In the meantime, Australia provides China with detailed information on the relevant regulatory decisions applicable to the Australian higher education institutions registered with the CRICOS, further enhancing the transparency of the conditions of these institutions and protecting rights and interests of Chinese students in Australia.

Australia likewise permits Chinese education institutions to establish Chinese international schools in Australia. China's participation in the Australian government's New Colombo Plan from 2015 is strengthening university links and supporting a greater two-way flow of students.[46] In sum, ChAFTA has, to some extent, deepened the cooperation of both parties in the education sector and created favourable conditions for exchange of teachers and students from the two countries.

iv. Legal Services

ChAFTA is unique in securing China's first ever treaty commitments on commercial association between law firms. In addition to guaranteeing

[44] ICEF Monitor, 'Australian Education Exports Reach AUS$18 Billion in 2014/15' (12 August 2015), monitor.icef.com/2015/08/australian-education-exports-reach-aus18-billion-in-201415/.

[45] 'China–Australia Free Trade Agreement—Fact Sheet: Trade in Services', dfat.gov.au/trade/agreements/chafta/fact-sheets/Documents/fact-sheet-trade-in-services.pdf.

[46] The New Colombo Plan is a signature initiative of the Australian Government which aims to lift knowledge of the Indo-Pacific in Australia by supporting Australian undergraduates to study and undertake internships in the region. Under the programme, Australian undergraduates are being encouraged to undertake study and internships in China and other countries. China has been a highly sought after destination by Australian universities and students. For more information, visit the website, dfat.gov.au/people-to-people/new-colombo-plan/pages/new-colombo-plan.aspx.

existing access for Australian law firms in China, it ensures that Australian law firms are able to establish commercial associations with Chinese law firms in the SFTZ. There is something different in having the rights enshrined in a treaty versus a simple domestic liberalisation arrangement, such as the SFTZ. These commercial associations are able to offer Australian, Chinese and international legal services, without restrictions on where clients are located. Within such commercial associations, Australian qualified lawyers are able to practise Australian and international law. Legal practitioners qualified to practise law in other foreign countries are also able to practise in the laws of those countries. Chinese qualified lawyers are able to practise Chinese and international law without suspension of their Chinese practising certificates.[47] China and Australia have also agreed to promote increased mobility for Australian and Chinese lawyers, including the facilitation of professional secondments between law firms in Australia and China, and through cooperation between the top legal professional bodies in each country.

v. Tourism and Travel-Related Services

Under ChAFTA, China guarantees that Australian services suppliers are able to construct, renovate and operate wholly Australian-owned hotels and restaurants in China. Australian travel agencies/tour operators are also able to establish wholly Australian-owned subsidiaries in China, providing travel, hotel accommodation and tours for domestic and foreign tourists, and travellers' check cashing services.[48]

vi. Pension Services

China has been in the process of establishing an effective pension services system in recent years. In September 2013, the State Council of China issued the 'Several Opinions on Accelerating the Development of the Pension Service Industry', under which it is proposed to establish a comprehensive pension service system, with improved functions and a proper scale and covering urban and rural areas by 2020. The Opinions clearly stipulated that the creation of pension institutions will be vigorously strengthened, and foreign investments in the pension service industry are encouraged.[49] Developed countries including Australia have rich experience in the development of the pension service industry and a relatively sound pension system. As the providers of pension services, governments, non-profit institutions and

[47] 'China–Australia Free Trade Agreement—Fact Sheet: Trade in Services' (n 45).

[48] ibid.

[49] 《国务院关于加快发展养老服务业的若干意见》 [Several Opinions from the State Council on Accelerating the Development of Pension Services], State Council, Guo Fa [2013] No 35.

commercial enterprises in Australia have advanced service philosophies and management experience.

Against this background, it is not surprising that ChAFTA provides that Australian services providers are allowed to establish foreign-invested or sole for-profit pension institutions in China.[50] The permission for the establishment of pension institutions in China by Australian providers may not only meet the demands of some domestic consumers for high-end pension services, but also help promote the steady development of the domestic pension industry to better satisfy the massive demands for pension services.

vii. Hospital Services and Aged Care Services

Perhaps the most critical of the commitments contained in ChAFTA, Australian medical services suppliers are able to establish wholly Australian-owned hospitals in China, including in Beijing, Tianjin and Shanghai, as well as in the provinces of Jiangsu, Fujian, Guangdong and Hainan. China has also made commitments on aged care services for the first time, allowing Australian medical services suppliers to establish wholly Australian-owned profit-making aged care institutions in China with no geographical restrictions.[51] These will greatly expand the Australian private health sector's offering of medical services. In the fast growing Chinese healthcare sector, Australian hospitals and aged care institutions are the first to be allowed to establish wholly owned businesses in China.

viii. Traditional Chinese Medicine (TCM) Services

Traditional Chinese medicine services have secured remarkable market access under ChAFTA. TCM is an important component of Chinese culture. After hard negotiations, Australia agreed to make legally binding commitments concerning the trade in TCM services in the form of articles of agreement. Through the Side Letter on TCM, both parties are committed to promoting cooperation in the research and development of TCM and information exchanges with respect to policies, regulations and measures about TCM·.[52]

Towards this end, as some have correctly observed:

> The above does not cover all service commitments under the ChAFTA. As pointed out, given the inclusiveness of the ChAFTA, similar exclusive or preferential market access is also available to other service sectors, such as Australia's transport services, manufacturing services, architecture and urban planning services and

[50] 'China–Australia Free Trade Agreement—Fact Sheet: Trade in Services' (n 45).

[51] ibid.

[52] More about the cooperation arrangement with respect to TCM is found in ChAFTA (n 31) Side Letter on Traditional Chinese Medicine.

> mining-related services. Also unprecedentedly, Australia's construction and engineering services firms will be allowed to undertake joint construction projects with Chinese companies in the SFTZ without any restrictions on business scope.[53]
>
> In the meanwhile, it is also noted that despite the depth and breadth of services liberalization under the ChAFTA, most of the commitments are somewhat limited either to some selected types of services or to the SFTZ. In some sectors, China's limitations on the types of commercial presence still apply although higher foreign equity is granted. This is viewed as an incremental approach that China has taken in opening up its services sectors, which are underdeveloped compared to those in countries like Australia. This approach is in line with China's overall opening-up and reform policy, where greater trade liberalization helps develop China's services sectors, but not at the expense of exposing Chinese firms to too much foreign competition.[54]

Along with the gradual development of China's services economy, there certainly will be ample room, as discussed below, for China to further liberalise its services market.

IV. SERVICES SCHEDULING IN CHAFTA: FROM SOLO TO DUET OF 'NEGATIVE LIST APPROACH'

Seemingly minor rules may make big differences in outcomes depending on how negotiating parties agree to make their trade and investment commitments. While debates over trade negotiation and scheduling strategies may seem arcane, they are indeed important in shaping the ultimate form of an agreement. The so-called 'positive list' and 'negative list' approaches are, broadly speaking, the two methods for negotiating modalities of trade agreements and scheduling commitments. This section studies the hybrid method adopted by ChAFTA for services scheduling and its future upgrading arrangement.

A. The Basics: Negative List Versus Positive List

Under the negative list approach, negotiators begin by agreeing to liberalise all forms of trade protection between the parties. All services sectors and measures are included in the scope of the Agreement, and usually all the disciplines apply to these sectors and measures without limitation—unless otherwise specified. Recognising some sectors as 'too sensitive' to be fully liberalised, a list of sectors for exclusion is negotiated by the parties. In other words, the negative list approach presumes everything is on the table, with

[53] 'China–Australia Free Trade Agreement—Fact Sheet: Trade in Services' (n 45).
[54] Lumsden, Knight and Zhou (n 10).

negotiation and scheduling focused on identifying *what will be left out* of an agreement. Such an approach obliges trade negotiators to review the entire range of regulatory measures and restrictions in the services sector and to identify which measure or sector and mode of delivery should be placed in a list of exceptions when the measure or sector cannot meet the obligation of nondiscriminatory treatment for the core disciplines.[55] In general, the negative list lends itself to broader and deeper trade liberalisation, as it places the onus on governments to justify why a sector should be excluded.

Conversely, positive list negotiation presumes nothing is on the table initially, and gradually adds content as negotiators decide which sectors are most important to them. This approach focuses on *what will be included*. Negotiators start by presenting a list of requests and then offers and counter-offers until an agreeable balance is struck. Positive schedules, adopted by GATS, require a Member to affirmatively commit to market access and national treatment with respect to each of the four modes of supply. Moreover, the affirmative commitments typically contain limitations on national treatment and market access. In general, positive lists often lead to shallower and narrower agreements, though it is a useful strategy in cases where trade liberalisation is politically contentious or difficult and governments feel uncomfortable with deep reform in certain areas.

These two approaches tend to produce different outcomes. With respect to the negative list approach, one question would be what will happen to emerging services sectors not presently on the list, especially services associated with emerging technologies. Thus, the negative list approach tends to discriminate against new products and services, which are not protected under past commitments. Many of the modern RTAs have shifted away from the architecture of GATS to adopt the negative list negotiating modality, which seems to be a more liberalised approach than the positive list approach. Yet another approach can be seen with respect to the Trade in Services Agreement (TiSA) which is currently in negotiation and has adopted a hybrid scheduling method, ie, positive list for market access commitments and negative list for national treatment commitments.[56] This means that while negotiating parties retain autonomy regarding whether to open a services sector or subsector, once a sector is open, any exceptions to national treatment need to be set out in a transparent list of non-conforming measures, ie, a negative list architecture.

[55] Hufbauer, Jensen and Stephenson (n 9) 2.

[56] The TiSA (Trade in Services Agreement) is being negotiated by 23 WTO Member countries, but represents 70% of global trade in services, with the ultimate objective of multilateralisation within the framework of the WTO. The novelty compared with GATS is that TiSA incorporates a horizontal national treatment approach. This is the reason why the TiSA scheduling is called the 'hybrid' approach. For more explanation, see, eg, European Union, 'How to Read the TiSA Initial Offer of the European Union?' (July 2014), trade.ec.europa.eu/doclib/docs/2014/july/tradoc_152691.pdf.

B. The Mixed ChAFTA Approach

The creativity of ChAFTA lies in its departure from a pure GATS positive list approach and the adoption of a mixed method (albeit different from the hybrid approach adopted by the TiSA), allowing China and Australia to undertake services commitments by different approaches, ie, the positive list approach for China and the negative list approach for Australia.[57] This mixed approach takes into account the different development levels of the two countries' services sectors. In order to tune the solo of 'negative list approach' into a duet, ie, a more balanced scheduling method, pre-arrangements have been made for upgrading the services commitments in ChAFTA. Both parties agreed that, after the implementation of ChAFTA, they would carry out negotiations on trade in services using the negative list approach within the time frame as agreed to achieve a higher level of openness.[58] Given Australia's apparent comparative advantage in services trade and the importance of services as intermediate inputs to many economic activities, the upgrading negotiation mainly aims to further open China's services market through the negative list approach.

The same upgrading arrangement also exists in the China–South Korea FTA. This reflects China's gradual acceptance of a negative list approach in its recent FTA negotiations. In fact, the initial acceptance of a negative list approach took place on 1 July 2013, in the negotiation of the China–US BIT.[59] Subsequently, the concept of the negative list was introduced into China and implemented on a trial basis in the SFTZ.[60]

[57] Chapter 8 (Trade in Services) contains two sections: Section A: Positive Listing Approach; and Section B: Negative Listing Approach.

[58] ChAFTA (n 31) para 3, Art 8.24 (Review). It reads: 'After the entry into force of this agreement, at a time to be mutually agreed by the Parties, the Parties shall initiate next round of the negotiation on trade in services in the form of negative listing approach, and conclude such negotiation as soon as they could'.

[59] On 1 July 2013, China for the first time agreed to negotiate a BIT with the US on the basis of a negative list approach plus pre-entry national treatment. The subsequently launched BIT negotiations between China and the EU follows the same pattern. This indicates China's acceptance of a negative list approach and pre-entry national treatment in its economic and trade negotiation.

[60] The concept of a negative list was first introduced and implemented on a trial basis when the China (Shanghai) Pilot Free Trade Zone was launched in 2013 (the FTZ Negative List). The FTZ Negative List divides industries into 50 items across 15 categories which are subject to special administrative measures (eg, foreign shareholding restrictions or regulatory approvals). In general, whilst foreign investments into industries expressly referred to on the FTZ Negative List must satisfy the requirements stipulated therein and/or fulfil the specified regulatory approval procedures, foreign investment into industries outside the FTZ Negative List may only make filings with the competent authorities. Similar regimes have been implemented in the other three free trade zones in Guangdong, Fujian and Tianjin. With the success of the trial in the free trade zones, the State Council is now in the process of finalising a Negative List to be applicable nationwide (National Negative List) to work in conjunction with the Filing Regime. This National Negative List is expected to be published soon and take effect from 1 October 2016.

The coverage of a negative list approach is comprehensive rather than piecemeal. The architecture for upgrading ChAFTA should strive to cover all services sectors, as required by the essence of the negative list approach. This would contribute to a higher level of liberalisation of China's services industry, adapting to the new trend of economic globalisation, promoting the orderly and free flows of international and domestic factors, efficient resource allocations and deep market integration, and providing more market opportunities for foreign service providers.

Despite these positive effects, the negative list architecture may pose challenges for China. On the one hand, China has not followed such an approach in any of its previous FTAs and therefore lacks experience in this regard. On the other hand, this approach obliges China to review the entire range of regulatory measures and restrictions in place in the services sector and to identify which measure or sector and mode of delivery should be placed in a list of exceptions if the measure or sector cannot meet the obligation of nondiscriminatory treatment for the core disciplines such as market access, national treatment, no local presence[61] and unconditional MFN status.

During the transitional stage of the Chinese economy, services exports are likely to become more prominent while primary commodities less so, giving ample room for China to develop its services industry and trade. For China, in negotiating further liberalisation through a negative list approach, it is imperative to bear China's practical needs in mind and incorporate the necessary disciplines of the recent FTAs as well as new developments that reflect current realities in services trade. With these in mind, in the upgrading negotiation, a variety of elements might be considered by China. First, a commitment not to impose new restrictions on trade in services is required. This commitment should be combined with an explicit commitment by the two countries to bind existing levels of openness in services trade. Second, a commitment to eliminate barriers to FDI, either immediately or in a phased manner, is needed. Third, transparency is important and will be very much enhanced under the negative list approach since every exception must be listed. Whatever measure or sector is not listed must be liberalised according to the common standards of the Agreement.

V. CONCLUSION

This chapter shows that ChAFTA is an excellent instrument both for China and Australia, providing for significant services liberalisation. It includes some provisions in GATS but considerably strengthens them. However,

[61] 'No local presence' refers to the requirement that the benefits of market access should not be conditional on maintaining a local establishment or entering into a joint venture with a local firm. Hufbauer, Jensen and Stephenson (n 9) 5.

ChAFTA is not a perfect Agreement in terms of services liberalisation. Some sectors are in, and others are out, partly due to the mixed scheduling methods.

Along with the rapid development of China's services industry, and gradually shaped services-led economy, now is the right time to bring those international trade regimes to which China is a signatory into the twenty-first century. As further talks begin on how to modernise ChAFTA on trade in services, China should commit to implementing a negative list approach so that the services commitments of two parties are moving towards a more balanced direction.

7

Culture-Oriented Mode 4 under ChAFTA: Policy Considerations

SHIN-YI PENG, HAN-WEI LIU AND CHING-FU LIN

I. INTRODUCTION: DEFINING CULTURE-ORIENTED 'MODE 4'[1]

MUCH HAS BEEN written about cultural goods and services.[2] Commentators have been focusing on questions as to whether the distinctive features of different cultures will, through the economic globalisation process, become blunted or replaced by a universal set of cultural symbols.[3] However, the 'trade and culture' debate has so far centred on the food/dress or film/television industries, and to some extent the term 'culture' has become synonymous with the word 'audiovisual'.[4] The existing literature seems to miss an arguably more significant component of culture—embodied in 'people'. In particular, cultural professionals/labour have surprisingly received little attention among trade lawyers, despite the attention paid to other trade and mobility issues.

[1] 'Mode 4', the presence of natural persons, refers to movement of labour to deliver services in the territory of another WTO Member. See section II.A of this chapter for a more detailed discussion.

[2] See generally, T Voon, *Cultural Products and the World Trade Organization* (Cambridge, Cambridge University Press, 2007); see also ME Footer, 'Trade Liberalization and Cultural Policy' (2000) 3 *Journal of International Economic Law* 115; M Hahn, 'A Clash of Cultures? The UNESCO Diversity Convention and International Trade Law' (2006) 9 *Journal of International Economic Law* 515; R Neuwirth, 'The Future of the 'Culture and Trade Debate: A Legal Outlook' (2013) 47 *Journal of World Trade* 391.

[3] D Throsby, *Economics and Culture* (Cambridge, Cambridge University Press, 2001) 156.

[4] See, eg, T Voon, 'UNESCO and the WTO: A Clash of Cultures?' (2006) 55 *ICLQ* 635; C Beat Graber, 'The New UNESCO Convention on Cultural Diversity: A Counterbalance to the WTO' (2006) 9 *Journal of International Economic Law* 553; CM Bruner, 'Culture, Sovereignty, and Hollywood: UNESCO and the Future of Trade in Cultural Products' (2008) 40 *New York Journal University of International Law & Politics* 35; Shin-yi Peng, 'Liberalization of Trade in Television Services: The Negotiation Dilemma and Challenges for the Future' (2009) 43 *Journal of World Trade* 657; Jingxia Shi et al, 'The "Specificity" of Cultural Products versus the "Generality" of Trade Obligations: Reflecting on "China—Publications and Audiovisual Products"' (2011) 45 *Journal of World Trade* 159; R Weber et al, *Classification of Services in the Digital Economy* (Heidelberg, Springer, 2013).

To this extent, this chapter is intended to fill the gap in the literature. Mobility is not just about travelling across borders. Rather, it should also concern the implications of mobility, especially on culture.[5] Mobility promotes the dissemination of fresh ideas and skills, and the understanding of other cultures and traditions.[6] Taking a long view, globalisation and mobility are twin subjects,[7] and that is particularly true if the 'labour' brings the 'cultural' skills.

Culture, which covers a wide spectrum of human concerns,[8] is a word employed in a variety of senses in everyday use but without a generally agreed meaning.[9] The term in this modern society has been used in a broader sense to describe the intellectual and spiritual development of civilisation as a whole.[10] How, then, to define 'culture' in a manner that is analytically and operationally useful? In this chapter we do not intend to offer an explicit definition of the term 'culture' in a theoretical sense, as it lies beyond the scope of this study.[11] To this end, Throsby instructively indicates two principal ways to defining culture—one supports an 'anthropological framework to describe a set of attitudes, beliefs, morals, customs, values and practices which are common to or shared by any group,' and the other favours a 'functional orientation, denoting certain activities that are undertaken by people, and the products of those activities, which have to do with the intellectual, moral and artistic aspects of human life'.[12] Nevertheless, there has not been a well-settled approach to defining culture. In the trade context, the UNESCO Convention on the Protection and Promotion of the Diversity of Cultural Expressions (UNESCO Convention) refers to 'cultural goods and services' as goods, services and other activities that embody or yield 'cultural expressions'.[13] This chapter follows a similar conceptual approach

[5] T Sowell, *Migrations and Cultures 2* (New York, BasicBooks, 1996); see also J Gordon, 'People Are Not Bananas: How Immigration Differs from Trade' (2010) 104 *Northwestern University Law Review* 1109, 1130.

[6] Sowell (n 5) 2–3; see also European Union, *Report on Building a Strong framework for Artists' Mobility: Five Key Principles* (2012), www.ec.europa.eu/culture/library/reports/artist-mobility-report_en.pdf, 5, 11, 13.

[7] J Tomlinson, *Globalization and Culture* (Chicago, University of Chicago Press, 1999); J Nederveen Pieterse, *Globalization & Culture: Global Melange* (Lanham, MD, Rowman & Littlefield Publishers, 2004).

[8] Sowell (n 5) 379.

[9] D Throsby, *Economics and Culture*, 1st edn (Cambridge, Cambridge University Press, 2001).

[10] ibid 5.

[11] The focus on Chinese chefs, Wushu martial arts coaches, Mandarin language tutors and Traditional Chinese Medicine practitioners suggests a clarification of what we actually mean when we talk about cultural-oriented Mode 4 in the context of trade. Viewed in this light, a precise definition of 'culture' would appear to be less crucial in this chapter.

[12] Throsby (n 9) 4.

[13] United Nations Educational, Scientific and Cultural Organization (UNESCO), *International Flows of Selected Cultural Goods and Services* (29 August 2016), www.portal.unesco.org/culture/en/.

by defining cultural-oriented Mode 4 as labour/professionals who embody 'cultural expressions', or have technical or professional skills and experiences that reflect the totality of traditional production of a given cultural group.[14]

That being said, the China–Australia Free Trade Agreement (ChAFTA) provides an interesting case study on cultural-oriented Mode 4. In Annex 10-A, Australia explicitly sets a quota limit on Chinese chefs, Wushu martial arts coaches, Mandarin language tutors and Traditional Chinese Medicine (TCM) practitioners, permitting only a combined total of 1,800 per year to enter Australia. Mode 4, indeed, is an area where China stands to make clear gains, as greater concessions under Mode 4 can contribute a needed element of balance to trade in services by allowing China to achieve its natural comparative advantages under ChAFTA.[15] However, even in such a liberal trade package, culture-oriented Mode 4 seems to remain a major concern for the Australian government,[16] as opposed to all other service sectors. This chapter will explain the underlying rationales for these differentiated treatments by identifying economic and social policy considerations. The first section will analyse the scheduling patterns of Mode 4 at the multilateral, plurilateral and bilateral levels, with a particular emphasis on the fact that Mode 4 remains significantly less extensive than those found in the other three Modes. The second section will start by asking a basic question of whether and to what extent cultural-oriented Mode 4 can provide a pathway towards breakthrough developments in the liberalisation of Mode 4 trade. The main body of this chapter will then explore the issues that lie ahead to further liberalise the cultural-oriented Mode 4. In the final section of this chapter, we will close with concrete suggestions on the question of what steps should be taken to promote the mobility of cultural labour under ChAFTA. Using ChAFTA as a case study, this chapter seeks to go beyond traditional discourse by exploring a key component inherently embedded in culture-oriented professionals, Mode 4 commitments, and their implications for future trade negotiations in the age of mega-regionals.

[14] See J Gibson, *Community Resources: Intellectual Property, International Trade and Protection of Traditional Knowledge* (Oxford, Routledge, 2005) 28.

[15] See generally, Hidetaka Yoshimatsu, *Comparing Institution-Building in East Asia: Power Politics, Governance, and Critical Junctures* (Basingstoke, Palgrave Macmillan, 2014) 35–63; S Hoadley et al, 'China's Free Trade Negotiations: Economics, Security, and Diplomacy' in S Katada et al (eds), *Cross Regional Trade Agreements: Understanding Permeated Regionalism in East Asia* (Berlin, Springer, 2010).

[16] See, eg, M Brown, 'Workers Rally in Sydney Against Abbott Government's Free Trade Agreement with China' *ABC News* (31 July 2015), www.abc.net.au/news/2015-07-31/unions-take-to-martin-place-to-protest-china-fta/6662530.

II. STOCKTAKING OF MODE 4 COMMITMENTS: GATS-PLUS?

A. GATS at 20: Mode 4 Trade

In many industrialised countries, the services sector has grown dramatically since the Second World War.[17] While services were once considered as non-tradeable, they were thought to be produced and consumed simultaneously and hence could hardly be tradeable as a technical matter, advances in the information and communication technology industries have changed this perception by enabling data to be stored and transmitted for later use via electronic media.[18] The inclusion of 'trade in services' under the multilateral framework thus emerged on the agenda of the Uruguay Round negotiations which, in turn, gave rise to the General Agreement on Trade in Services (GATS) that brought services into the world trading regime.[19] GATS sets out four possible ways in which services can be traded between countries: (1) Mode 1 (cross-border supply), which is more analogous to trade in goods; (2) Mode 2 (consumption abroad) refers to the movement of consumers to the territory of service suppliers; (3) Mode 3, or known as 'commercial presence' involves foreign investment for the purpose of supplying services; and (4) the presence of natural persons, best known as Mode 4, refers to movement of labour to deliver services in the territory of another World Trade Organization (WTO) Member.[20]

GATS adopts a 'progressive liberalisation' approach by removing obstacles to trade in services through successive rounds of negotiations. Under this model, GATS consists of two parts: general provisions (eg, 'Most-Favoured Nation' or 'MFN' treatment) and obligations that apply to commitments only for specific sectors undertaken by a WTO Member.[21] In the Uruguay Round, countries liberalised trade in services through horizontal and sector-specific commitments in relation to market access and national treatments. However, these commitments were unevenly distributed among different sectors and modes of supply. This is particularly true in the case of Mode 4.

[17] See JH Jackson et al, *Legal Problems of International Economic Relations: Cases, Materials, and Text*, 6th edn (St Paul, MN, West Group, 2013) 1035.

[18] RJ Self and BK Zutshi, 'Mode 4: Negotiating Challenges and Opportunities' in A Mattoo and A Carzaniga (eds), *Moving People to Deliver Services* (Washington DC, World Bank, 2003) 27.

[19] For a recount of the pre-Uruguay Round arrangements in relation to trade in services see, eg, G Feketekuty 'Trade in Professional Services: An Overview' (1986) 1 *University of Chicago Legal Forum* 1.

[20] General Agreement on Trade in Services (GATS) Marrakech Agreement Establishing the World Trade Organization (15 April 1994) Annex 1B, 33 ILM 1167, Art I.2. (GATS).

[21] For an understanding see, eg, M Trebilcock et al, *The Regulation of International Trade*, 4th edn (Oxford, Routledge, 2012) 480–89.

Quantitatively, as the WTO reports, Mode 4 remains the smallest among these four Modes of supply, accounting for less than five per cent of the overall trade in services.[22] Qualitatively, Mode 4-related commitments made by all Members, be they horizontal or sectoral, have been the most limited.[23] A cursory look at the structure of Mode 4 commitments reveals such restrictiveness: countries have typically inscribed their concessions on a horizontal basis by leaving market access and national treatment entries 'unbound' in sectoral schedules.[24] These Mode 4 horizontal commitments are subject to an array of restrictions, such as the length of stay, economic needs or labour market test, wage parity, or requirements for technology and skill transfer.[25] Moreover, such unbound schedules often come with a positive undertaking to grant access to certain types of person based upon hierarchal and/or functional criteria;[26] these categories are confined to: intra-corporate transferees (ICT), executives, managers, specialists (EMS)[27] and business visitors (BV).[28]

The overall pattern marks a systematic bias towards liberalising the movement of natural persons with higher skills and those linked with commercial presence.[29] Such scheduling exercise fails to, on one hand, realise potential gains by liberalising Mode 4,[30] and on the other, reflects actual practice in admitting service suppliers from abroad.[31] Having been frustrated with the limited commitments in areas where they have comparative advantage—that is, human capital—developing countries thus called for greater openness by delinking Mode 4 from Mode 3 in the GATS 2000 negotiations.

[22] J Magdeleine and A Maurer, 'Measuring GATS Mode 4 Trade Flows' (2008) The World Trade Organization Staff Working Paper ERSD-2008-05, 18.

[23] A Carzaniga, 'The GATS, Mode 4, and Pattern of Commitments' in A Mattoo and A Carzaniga (eds), *Moving People to Deliver Services* (Washington DC, World Bank, 2003) 25. See also R Chanda, 'Movement of Natural Persons and the GATS' (2001) 24 *The World Economy* 631, 641 (noting that higher income countries have liberalised around 50% of service sectors while developing countries have opened only 11% of overall service sectors).

[24] Council for Trade in Services, *Presence of Natural Persons: Background Note by the Secretariat*, S/C/W/301 (15 September 2009) 20; Self and Zutshi (n 18) 24.

[25] Chanda, 'Movement of Natural Persons' (n 23) 641–42.

[26] *Background Note on Mode 4* (n 24) 20.

[27] While many have included executives, managers and specialists under the category of ICT, others have included these persons based on their respective functions. Thus, the EMS is often broad enough to cover the ICT. The lack of an agreed definition is a recurring problem in Mode 4 negotiations. *Background Note on Mode 4* (n 24) 22–23.

[28] ibid.

[29] ibid. See also Shin-yi Peng, 'Towards Greater Mobility: Movement of Service Suppliers in East Asia' (2006) 1 *Asian Journal of WTO & International Health Law and Policy* 105.

[30] See, eg, A Winters, 'The Temporary Movement of Workers to Provide Services (GATS Mode 4)' in A Mattoo et al (eds), *A Handbook of International Trade in Services* (Oxford, Oxford University Press, 2008) 480 (suggesting that an increase in developed countries' quotas in inwards movement of skilled and non-skilled temporary workers equivalent to 3% of their workforce would approximately generate an increase in world welfare of US$150 billion).

[31] Carzaniga, 'Pattern of Mode 4 Commitments' (n 23) 24.

India, for instance, sought to liberalise independent professionals (IP) and contractual services suppliers (CSS) while urging the elimination of cumbersome procedures for visas and work permits, economic needs tests (ENTs) and residency/citizenship requirements, among others.[32]

In the developed world, the desire of multinational firms for greater mobility of personnel, as well as looming demographic crises and skills shortages, too, have prompted high-income countries to reflect upon their conservative stances towards Mode 4.[33] In this regard, the European Union (EU) was at the forefront by tabling the initial offers in 2003, as revised in 2005, against the context of the Doha Round Agenda (DDA).[34] The EU, for instance, offered greater coverage under the CSS and IP, expanded the ICT to include graduate trainees in its horizontal commitments, and liberalised its sectoral commitments in areas like professional services, computer services, business services and financial services.[35] Similarly, other developed countries such as Australia,[36] Canada,[37] Japan[38] and New Zealand[39] offered to improve their commitments.[40] Be that as it may, these seemingly promising offers, nevertheless, remain constrained by various restrictions, and in most cases, are related to the ICTs and BVs.[41]

[32] Among other developing countries, India was the most active; see, eg, Council for Trade in Services, Communication from India: Proposed Liberalisation of Movement of Professionals under General Agreement on Trade in Services (GATS) (24 November 2000) S/CSS/W/12.

[33] Mattoo and Carzaniga (n 18) 1.

[34] Roughly, the Mode 4 negotiations can be divided into two phases. The first phase took place from January 2000 to the Doha Ministerial in late 2001. During this period, the WTO Members focused more on an effective way to improve the Mode 4 commitments. In the second phase, countries submitted their requests and offers. For a background on Mode 4 negotiations in the post-Uruguay Round era see, eg, J Neilson and D Taglioni, 'A Quick Guide to the GATS and Mode 4' (6 April 2016), www.iom.int/jahia/webdav/site/myjahiasite/shared/shared/mainsite/microsites/IDM/workshops/Trade_2004_04051004/related%20docs/quick_guide.pdf.

[35] See Council for Trade in Services, *Communication from the European Communities and its Member States: Conditional Revised Offer* (29 June 2005) TN/S/O/EEC/Rev.1.

[36] Council for Trade in Services, *Australia: Revised Services Offer* (31 May 2005) TN/S/O/AUS/Rev.1.

[37] Council for Trade in Services, *Canada: Revised Conditional Offer on Services* (23 May 2005) TN/S/O/CAN/Rev.1.

[38] Council for Trade in Services, *Japan: Revised Offer* (24 June 2005) TN/S/O/JPN/Rev.1.

[39] Council for Trade in Services, *New Zealand: Revised Conditional Offer* (17 June 2005) TN/S/O/NZL/Rev. 1.

[40] As Carzaniga reports, as of January 2008, only about half of 71 offers (with the EC counted as one) offered to upgrade their horizontal commitments. Such improvements, however, are still limited in terms of the quality. A Carzaniga, 'A Warmer Welcome? Access for Natural Persons under PTAs' in JA Marchetti and M Roy (eds), *Opening Markets for Trade in Services: Countries and Sectors in Bilateral and WTO Negotiations* (Cambridge, Cambridge University Press, 2009) 482.

[41] ibid. See also R Leal-Arcas, 'The GATS and Temporary Migration Policy' in M Kolsky Lewis and S Frankel (eds), *International Economic Law and National Autonomy* (Cambridge, Cambridge University Press, 2010) 208–11.

The chaos of the Doha Round negotiations has resulted in a move for WTO Members to focus their efforts instead on preferential trade agreements (PTAs), bilaterally or plurilaterally. Trade in services, and of course, movement of natural persons, are an integral part of such economic integration. Yet, Mode 4 remains controversial in the context of PTAs. Without delving into the details of Mode 4 concessions undertaken outside the scope of the WTO, the section that follows offers a skeleton of major developments through bilateral and mega-regional initiatives.

B. Mode 4 in the Bilateral Context: What has been done in the PTAs?

Mode 4 commitments in the context of bilateral PTAs present a mixed picture. Developed countries like the US, EU, Japan and Australia have, though of limited scale, upgraded Mode 4 concessions. While the US, for instance, once adopted the positive list approach by reproducing what it has undertaken under the GATS framework in the US–Jordan PTA,[42] it began to, albeit still modestly, liberalise Mode 4 in its PTAs with Singapore and Chile, both signed in 2003. Three improvements are noteworthy: first, both PTAs have a separate chapter on temporary entry for business persons.[43] Second, Mode 4 categories include investors, traders, ICTs and professionals. Third, on professionals, the US granted, annually, access up to 1,400 and 5,400 persons from Chile and Singapore respectively.[44] However, mindful of the constitutional limits of the power over immigration,[45] the US trade policymakers have since then fallen back by avoiding a chapter on the temporary entry of business persons in the subsequent bilateral PTAs and reserving the right to safeguard its immigration policies, thereby ruling out significantly improved commitments on Mode 4.[46]

On the other side of the Atlantic, the EU has largely followed the GATS-type model by scheduling concessions through a positive list; categories of

[42] See Agreement Between the United States of America and the Hashemite Kingdom of Jordan on the Establishment of a Free Trade Area (24 October 2000) Annex, ustr.gov/trade-agreements/free-trade-agreements/jordan-fta/final-text [hereinafter US-Jordan FTA].

[43] See Free Agreement US–Singapore (6 May 2003), www.ustr.gov/trade-agreements/free-trade-agreements/singapore-fta/final-text; Free Trade Agreement, US–Chile (6 June 2003), www.ustr.gov/trade-agreements/free-trade-agreements/chile-fta/final-text.

[44] These professionals are, however, subject to the H1-B1 visa programme, and thus the overall cap of the H1-B. Office of the United States Trade Representative, Chile and Singapore FTAs: Temporary Entry of Professionals, www.ustr.gov/about-us/policy-offices/press-office/fact-sheets/archives/2003/july/chile-and-singapore-ftas-temporary-entry-profes.

[45] See, eg, A Umberger, 'Free Trade Visas Exploring the Constitutional Boundaries of Trade Promotion Authority' (2008) 22 *Georgetown Immigration Law Journal* 319.

[46] Carzaniga, 'A Warmer Welcome?' (n 40) 488–89; S Stephenson and G Hufbauer, 'Increasing Labor Mobility: Options for Developing Countries' in O Cattaneo et al (eds), *International Trade in Services: New Trends and Opportunities for Developing* (The International Bank for Reconstruction and Development/World Bank, Washington DC, 2010) 39.

Mode 4 include traders, investors, BVs, ICTs and to a lesser extent, IPs.[47] However, as revealed by certain PTAs recently concluded by the EU and its developing countries' partners, the EU appears more liberal towards labour mobility. In the EU–CARIFORUM Economic Partnership Agreement, for instance, the EU expands, horizontally, the scope of Mode 4 to include, on top of the types of personnel illustrated above, CSSs and graduate trainees, while making sectoral-specific commitments in 29 sub-sectors.[48]

Negotiations on Mode 4 are in progress elsewhere in developed[49] and developing worlds.[50] These PTAs, in general, indicate several trends. First, traditional limitations in the GATS schedules are nevertheless retained in many of these PTAs. To date, most upgrades are still linked to commercial presence by focusing on BVs and ICTs.[51] Second, professional service providers emerge as another new focal point in the PTAs concluded between developed and developing countries: many have gone beyond GATS by expanding the covered types of professional services.[52] Third, the 'GATS-minus' issue has become a growing concern that can cut back on the quality of Mode 4 concessions. According to Rudolf and Miroudot, as of 2012, there are 49 out of 66 PTAs under survey that introduce new restrictions on horizontal commitments; 43 per cent impose new disciplines inconsistent with national treatment clauses, like new residency and land ownership constraints; 18 per cent of these PTAs place additional market access limitations on Mode 4.[53] Overall, however, Mode 4 has witnessed some, albeit limited, progress in the context of PTAs.

C. Recent Development of Mode 4 in the Context of Mega-PTAs

In addition to bilateral efforts, plurilateral or thematic mega-PTAs have emerged as the popular route for industrialised countries. In this regard, the

[47] While, for instance, the EU–Korea FTA refers to IPs, no commitments have been made. See Free Trade Agreement Between the European Union and its Member States and the Republic of Korea, EU–S Korea, Art 7.17, www.eur-lex.europa.eu/legal-content/EN/TXT/PDF/?uri=OJ:L:2011:127:FULL&from; see also, Stephenson and Hufbauer (n 46) 44.

[48] Economic Partnership Agreement Between the CARIFORUM States, of the One Part, and the European Community and its Member States, of the Other Part, CARIFORUM-EU (30 October 2008) [2008[OJ L289/1, Art 83 EU–CARIFORUM EPA.

[49] Japan generally offers basic concessions it had already made under the GATS framework, together with certain partner-specific additional commitments. Carzaniga, 'A Warmer Welcome?' (n 40) 490–91.

[50] Among others, Mercosur countries are reported to have made the most significant progresses in Mode 4. See ibid.

[51] ibid 499.

[52] Stephenson and Hufbauer (n 46) 55.

[53] On the 'GATS-minus' problem in the context of PTA, see generally R Adlung and S Miroudot, 'Poison in the Wine? Tracing GATS-Minus Commitments in Regional Trade Agreements' (2012) 46 *Journal of World Trade* 1045.

development of the Trade in Services Agreement (TiSA) and the Trans-Pacific Partnership (TPP) Agreement bears particular relevance to services negotiations. Originally emerging from the US, the TiSA was launched in 2012 by a group of like-minded countries called 'Really Good Friends of Services' (RGFs).[54] Since then, negotiations on the TiSA have been intensive, touching upon not only new ground rules for emerging issues like e-commerce, data flow and the liberalisation modalities, but the possible expansion of Mode 4.[55] However, despite this progress, it is far from clear how TiSA can push towards greater labour mobility. As the limited available data reveals, for instance, while the EU in its initial offer removes certain restrictions such as an economic needs test, Mode 4 commitments in the horizontal schedule are, still, intertwined with Mode 3 by extending to only the following categories of personnel: Business Visitors for Establishment Purposes (BVEP), Service Sellers (SeSe) and ICT.[56] Other commentators also remark that the Mode 4 offers tabled by the TiSA participants seem to involve those who 'look for investment opportunities or are providing highly-specialized, time-bound services'.[57]

While the TiSA negotiations are in progress, recent developments that were the result of the TPP negotiations may shed light on the future of Mode 4 in the mega-regional context. It should be noted that despite Trump's withdrawal from the TPP, the Mode 4-related commitments made in this context can nevertheless feature the latest development of cross-border movement of service providers in the age of mega-regionals. First, structurally, the TPP includes, on top of Chapter 10 on 'Cross-Border Trade in Services', a set of separate disciplines on 'Temporary Entry for Business

[54] At the time of writing, there are 23 WTO Members taking part in the TiSA negotiations, including Australia, Canada, Chile, Taiwan, Colombia, Costa Rica, the EU, Hong Kong, Iceland, Israel, Japan, Korea, Liechtenstein, Mauritius, Mexico, New Zealand, Norway, Pakistan, Panama, Peru, Switzerland, Turkey and the US; see European Commission, 'TiSA in A Nutshell', www.ec.europa.eu/trade/policy/in-focus/tisa/. Currently, the TiSA negotiations are conducted through a plurilateral approach with a view to, eventually, multilateralising the results under the aegis of the WTO; see European Commission, 'A Modular Approach to the Architecture of a Plurilateral Agreement on Services', www.trade.ec.europa.eu/doclib/docs/2014/july/tradoc_152686.pdf. On this, see also S Peng, 'Is the Trade in Services Agreement (TiSA) A Stepping Stone for the Next Version of GATS?' (2013) 43 *Hong Kong Law Journal* 611, 614–16.

[55] As of February 2016, 16 rounds of negotiations had been taken place. No formal deadline, however, has been fixed for ending the negotiations; see Report of the Sixteenth TiSA Negotiation Round: 31 January–5 February 2016, www.trade.ec.europa.eu/doclib/docs/2016/february/tradoc_154306.doc.pdf. JA Marchetti and M Roy, 'TiSA Initiative: An Overview of Market Access Issues' WTO Staff Working Papers ERSD-2013-11, www.wto.org/english/res_e/reser_e/ersd201311_e.pdf.

[56] Trade in Services Agreement: European Union Schedule of Specific Commitments and List of MFN Exemptions (November 2013), www.trade.ec.europa.eu/doclib/docs/2014/july/tradoc_152689.

[57] Notes on 'Trade in Services Agreement (TiSA) Annex on Movement of Natural Persons' (8 April 2015), wikileaks.org/tisa/natural-persons/04-2015/analysis/Analysis-TiSA-Movement-of-Natural-Persons-Annex.pdf.

Persons' under Chapter 12. By 'business persons', the TPP refers to those who are 'engaged in trade in goods, the supply of services or the conduct of investment activities'.[58] In this light, the scope of Mode 4 under the TPP seems to go beyond GATS. Second, all TPP parties except the US have made Mode 4 concessions. These commitments, as summarised in Table 1 below, are related to BV, CSS/Installer & Servicer, ICT, Investor/Independent Executive, and IP.[59] Also, temporary entry and work permits are extended, subject to applicable laws in relevant TPP parties, to family dependants of certain categories of personnel.[60] Third, the oft-criticised ENTs or requirements of similar contents, and numerical restrictions are somewhat moderated.[61] Last, Chapter 10 of the TPP also includes an annex to facilitate the recognition of professional qualifications, licensing or registration in the sector of professional services.[62]

Table 1: An Overview of Mode 4 Commitments by TPP Parties

Category Country	BV	CSS/Installer & Servicers	ICT	Independent Professionals	Investors/ Independent Executives
Australia	X	X	X	X*	X
Brunei Darussalam	X	X	X	X*	X
Canada	X	X*	X	X*	X

(continued)

[58] The full text of the TPP Agreement is now available on the websites of relevant TPP parties. The deal is, however, subject to the final approval in various national legislatures. Trans-Pacific Partnership Agreement, Ch 12, www.mfat.govt.nz/en/about-us/who-we-are/treaties/trans-pacific-partnership-agreement-tpp/text-of-the-trans-pacific-partnership (TPP Agreement).

[59] Note, however, that the TPP seemingly fails to have an agreed definition of different categories of Mode 4. While Australia, for instance, scheduled IP as part of the CSS, Chile, Japan and Malaysia have inscribed IP as a stand-alone category. For the present purpose, we focus on and thus calculate the commitments by looking into the substance of each schedule.

[60] For instance, Australia in the category of CSS, grants 'the right of temporary entry, movement and work to the accompanying spouse or dependent so far a business person that is granted temporary entry or an extension of temporary stay under these commitments'. Similar concessions can also be found in Mode 4 commitments by Brunei Darussalam, Canada, Chile, Japan, Malaysia, Mexico, Peru and Vietnam; see TPP Agreement (n 43) Annex 12-A.

[61] See ibid. Mexico, for instance, undertakes not to apply a labour certification test or the like as a condition of temporary entry, nor does it impose quotas relating to temporary entry.

[62] Annex 10-B of the TPP addresses, in particular, the professional qualifications for two sub-sectors: (1) engineering and architectural; and (2) legal services. For the former, the TPP directs its participants to the work in APEC to promote recognition of professional competence; for the latter, the TPP calls for more flexibility for foreign lawyers and transnational legal practice. TPP Agreement (n 58).

Table 1: *(Continued)*

Category Country	BV	CSS/Installer & Servicers	ICT	Independent Professionals	Investors/ Independent Executives
Chile	X	X	X	X	X
Japan	X	X	X	X	X
Malaysia	X	X	X	X	X
Mexico	X	X	X	X*	X
New Zealand	X	X	X	X	X
Peru	X	X	X	X	X
Singapore	X	–	–	–	X
Vietnam	X	X	X	–	X
US	–	–	–	–	–

Note: * Relevant schedules can be read as covering the categories of IP or CSS/Installers & Servicers.

Still, despite these welcome changes, regulatory concerns over Mode 4 continue to manifest themselves in these concessions. For the most part, these commitments are linked to Mode 3. Worse, these offers are typically conditional upon the principle of reciprocity, rather than MFN.[63] The conservatism of two major trading partners in the TPP can make the already bumpy path towards greater mobility of Mode 4 even more difficult: the US does not make any Mode 4 commitments while Singapore grants market access only to the BV and Investors.

Overall, as revealed by reference to many different scheduling patterns—be they multilateral, pluralteral, or bilateral, Mode 4 remains a 'politically sensitive and highly emotive' issue that touches upon complicated labour and immigration policies for every receiving country.[64] These hurdles lead us to reflect upon a way to avoid zero-sum games and identify common interests to improve Mode 4. By using ChAFTA as a case study, we examine whether and the extent to which cultural-oriented Mode 4 can provide a pathway to diminish misunderstandings and defensive positions among different policy communities.[65]

[63] ibid. New Zealand, for instance, extends its commitments under the category of IP to any TPP Member that has made commitments in the category of IP, CSS, Installers and Servicers, Professionals or Technicians.

[64] See also P Henry, 'Mode 4: Through A Canadian Immigration Policy Lens' in A Mattoo and A Carzaniga (eds), *Moving People to Deliver Services* (Washington DC, World Bank, 2003).

[65] Above (n 64).

III. CULTURE-ORIENTED MODE 4 UNDER CHAFTA: MORE RESTRICTIONS?

A. Mode 4 under ChAFTA: An Overview

ChAFTA, after years of negotiation, was concluded between the two countries in November 2014 and entered into force in December 2015.[66] Marking a historic development of the bilateral cooperation in trade and investment matters, ChAFTA includes 17 chapters, 11 related annexes, two memorandums of understanding (MoUs), and a few side letters.[67]

Similar to the structural arrangement of the TPP, ChAFTA includes a set of separate disciplines on 'Movement of Natural Persons' under Chapter 10, besides its Chapter 8 on 'Trade in Services'. By 'natural persons', ChAFTA refers to those who are Australian citizens, permanent residents of Australia, or nationals of China under Chinese law,[68] rendering it a rather broad coverage. Chapter 10 stipulates specific rights and obligations regarding Mode 4, such as expeditious application procedures,[69] grants of temporary entry,[70] transparency,[71] dispute settlement,[72] and the establishment of the Committee on Movement of Natural Persons.[73] Nevertheless, despite such structural arrangement, both parties' schedules of commitments on the movement of natural persons rest separately in ChAFTA. Australia's Mode 4 commitments are provided in Annex 10-A, while China's commitments are listed under Annex III (Chapter 8).

China's Mode 4 commitments are provided in a horizontal manner under Part 2, Annex III, and all other sectors are unbound except as indicated in the horizontal commitments. In terms of market access under Mode 4, China agrees to open its services market to the entry and temporary stay of natural persons who fall into any of the specified categories, including BV, EMS temporarily moving as ICT, CSS,[74] installer

[66] Free Trade Agreement between the Government of Australia and the Government of the People's Republic of China (signed 17 June 2015, entered into force 20 December 2015) [2015] ATS 15 (ChAFTA). The full text of ChAFTA can be found on the website of the Australia Government, Department of Foreign Affairs and Trade, www.dfat.gov.au/trade/agreements/chafta/official-documents/Pages/official-documents.aspx.

[67] ibid. The two Memorandums of Understanding (MoU) and the Side Letter on Traditional Chinese Medicine are part of the overall ChAFTA package, yet they are not part of the Agreement.

[68] ChAFTA (n 66) Art 10.2(c).

[69] ibid Art 10.3.

[70] ibid Art10.4.

[71] ibid Art10.5.

[72] ibid Art 10.7.

[73] ibid Art 10.6.

[74] According to the schedule of commitments, the services provided by CSS are further limited to specific sectors, including medical and dental services, architectural services, engineering services, urban planning services, integrated engineering services, computer and related services, construction and related engineering services, education services, tourism services, and accounting services.

and maintainer.[75] China extends its commitments to the accompanying spouses and dependants of such natural persons, who are also granted working rights, subject to relevant Chinese laws, regulations and rules.[76]

Australia does not specify its Mode 4 commitments in Annex III, but leaves a general reference to Chapter 10 where it reserves its right to 'adopt or maintain any measure with respect to the supply of a service by the presence of natural persons, or other movement of natural persons, including entry or temporary stay, subject to the provisions of Chapter 10'.[77] Under Annex 10-A, Australia agrees to open its services market to the entry and temporary stay of BV, ICT, independent executives, CSS, and installers and servicers from China.[78] Australia further divides CSS into two categories—those who are employees of an enterprise of China and those who are independent service suppliers (the latter can be understood as independent professionals, IP, so we hereinafter use CSS *and* IP for better clarity) executing a contract for the supply of a service in Australia.[79] Similarly, Australia grants the accompanying spouses or dependants of the covered natural persons 'the right of entry and temporary stay, movement and work for an equal period' given therein.[80]

B. The Mobility of Cultural Labour/Professionals under ChAFTA

ChAFTA's level of liberalisation with regard to the movement of natural persons goes beyond that of GATS and even the TPP. Both China and Australia agree to generally open up their services markets to a broad range of service suppliers, granting general entry and temporary stay not only to BV, EMS and ICT, but also to CSS and IP without explicit specific restrictions. Under ChAFTA, Australia significantly liberalises the Mode 4 market access beyond the traditionally innocent and uncontroversial categories such as BV and ICT, stretching to CSS and IP. Indeed, Australia commits to allow the entry and temporary stay—for a period of up to four years—of all sectors of CSS and IP, covering any natural person who has 'trade, technical or professional skills and experience and who is assessed as having the necessary qualifications, skills and work experience accepted as meeting Australia's

[75] ChAFTA (n 66) Annex III, pt 2, sch of the People's Republic of China.

[76] ibid.

[77] ibid ChAFTA (n 66) 9, Annex III, sch of Australia, s B.

[78] ibid, Annex 10-A, Specific Commitments on the Movement of Natural Persons, Australia's Specific Commitments.

[79] Since the GATS era, Australia has used the term 'CSS' to incorporate these two categories—employee CSS and independent CSS (usually referred to as IP by other WTO Members). ChAFTA follows the same practice.

[80] ChAFTA (n 66) Annex 10-A, Specific Commitments on the Movement of Natural Persons, Australia's Specific Commitments, para 14.

standards for their nominated occupation'.[81] Moreover, the Australian government agrees to 'remove the requirement for mandatory skills assessment for ... ten occupations on the date of entry into force of the Agreement', such as those for automotive electrician, cabinetmaker, carpenter and joiner, and diesel motor mechanic.[82] The two parties are to further cooperate in streamlining the skills assessment processes for other occupations, with the aim of reducing or even eliminating such requirements in five years.[83] However, there seems to be a special category of CSS and IP singled out to receive a differentiated treatment, arguably due to its *culture-oriented* nature, which this chapter now turns to discuss.

i. Numerical Quotas

With regard to culture-oriented Mode 4, Australia seems rather vigilant as it specifies certain restrictions on Chinese chefs, Wushu martial arts coaches, Mandarin language tutors and TCM practitioners. More specifically, with regard to the entry and temporary stay of the above culture-oriented CSS and IP of a Chinese origin, Australia explicitly sets a quota limit, permitting only a combined total of 1,800 per year to enter Australia.[84]

An ideal Mode 4 policy would take into account the ever-changing state of the economy and the domestic labour market in determining the appropriate number of immigrants to admit.[85] However, one of the ingredients of immigration policies in developed countries is numerical quota systems that restrict the number of immigrants that will be accepted each year in each category.[86] For Australia, placing upper limits on the degree of mobility permitted in its sensitive Mode 4 concessions seems to be the easiest way for administration,[87] as the mobility will cease once the quota is full.

Numerical quotas on cultural-oriented Mode 4, however, have many of the same adverse effects on economic welfare in the host countries as import quotas in international trade in goods.[88] Once the quota has been exhausted, such restrictions will unduly hamper the flow of would-be

[81] ibid para. 10.

[82] ChAFTA (n 66) Side Letter on Skills Assessment and Licensing (17 June 2015).

[83] ibid.

[84] ibid para 11. Interestingly, the New Zealand–China Free Trade Agreement (NZ–China FTA) signed in 2008 also contains similar but stricter quotas to Traditional Chinese Medicine practitioners, including nurses (up to 200), Chinese chefs (up to 200), Mandarin teaching aides (up to 150), martial arts coaches (up to 150), and tour guides (up to 100). NZ–China FTA, Annex 11, Australia's Commitments on Temporary Employment Entry by Natural Persons.

[85] M Trebilcock et al, 'The Political Economy of Emigration and Immigration' (2006) 81 *New York University Law Review* 234, 281.

[86] ibid 281.

[87] A Winters et al, *Liberalising Labour Mobility Under the GATS* (Commonwealth Secretariat, 2002) 53.

[88] Trebilcock et al, 'The Political Economy of Emigration and Immigration' (n 85) 281–82.

cultural labour/professionals who can demonstrate that they will not be a 'burden' in Australia. In addition, as quotas have been set in advance, predicting the needs of the labour market may be misdirected because it substitutes the bureaucrats' values for the consumers' preferences.[89]

ii. Qualification Assessment

Another restriction concerns qualification assessment. Article 10 of Annex 10-A explicitly requires that

> [a] contractual service supplier of China means a natural person of China who has trade, technical or professional skills and experience and who is assessed as having the necessary qualifications, skills and work experience accepted as meeting Australia's standards for their nominated occupation.

Furthermore, one of the side letters to ChAFTA confirms that Australia will uphold its own assessment and regulation with regard to TCM in accordance with those applied to other healthcare services.[90]

Domestic regulation and practices regarding technical and professional qualifications, which generally require careful case-by-case work to define levels of skills and experience, can severely restrict the ability of natural persons to move across borders to deliver services.[91] At the core of the issue is the 'recognition' of 'equivalence', which is based on the concept that a professional who already met certain conditions in his or her home country should not be asked to meet the same conditions again.[92] That said, such a concept of equivalence works much better among countries with similar regulatory regimes, which obviously is not the case between China and Australia. Moreover, in the area of cultural industry, 'equivalence' between on-the-job experience and academic qualifications is extremely difficult to establish.[93] In addition, it is the incumbents who manage the equivalency process and who are possibly the only people who can assess if the professional skills of the Chinese cultural labour meet 'Australia's standards'.[94] The discretion of the incumbent professional bodies in Australia may be

[89] R Van Harpen, 'Reconciling Trade and Cultural Independence' (1995) 4 *Minnesota Journal of Global Trade* 165.

[90] ChAFTA (n 66) Side Letter on Traditional Chinese Medicine (17 June 2015).

[91] Winters et al, *Liberalising Labour Mobility* (n 87) 61.

[92] Winters, 'The Temporary Movement of Workers to Provide Services' (n 30) 523.

[93] M Krajewski, *National Regulation and Trade Liberalization in Services* (The Hague, Kluwer Law International, 2003) 147–48; T Cottier et al, *Regulatory Barriers and the Principle of Non-Discrimination in World Trade Law* (Ann Arbor, MI, University of Michigan Press, 2002) 13; J Pauwelyn, 'Rien ne Va Plus? Distinguishing Domestic Regulation from Market Access in GATT and GATS' (2005) 4 *World Trade Review* 131; K Nicolaïdis et al, 'From Policed Regulation to Managed Recognition in GATS' in P Sauvé et al (eds), *GATS 2000: New Directions in Services Trade Liberalization* (Washington DC, Brookings Institution, 2000).

[94] See Winters et al, *Liberalising Labour Mobility* (n 87) 62.

abused by prohibiting the use of recognition as a means of discrimination,[95] which would reduce the transparency and credibility of commitments in Annex 10-A.

It seems clear that even in such a liberal trade package, culture-oriented CSS and IP remain a concern for the Australian government, as opposed to all other service sectors. This chapter tries to unpack and explain below the underlying rationales for these differentiated treatments particularly to culture-oriented Mode 4, by identifying economic and social policy considerations.

C. Policy Considerations: Why More Restrictions?

i. Economic Impact

The heart of Mode 4 trade lies in differences. The larger the differences, the larger the potential gains from opening up international trade.[96] Potentially large returns would be feasible if those cultural-oriented workers, ie, Chinese chefs, Wushu martial arts coaches, Mandarin language tutors and TCM practitioners, who are relatively abundant in China but scarce in Australia, were allowed to move and provide their services in Australia.

At the crux of the issue is the economic impact on those who compete directly with Chinese service suppliers for jobs. Will Chinese displace Australian nationals working in the same industry? We argue that in the sector of cultural-oriented Mode 4, there will be more a supplement to, than a substitute for, local labour.[97] First, the greater the cultural difference between foreign and local suppliers, the less likely the competition there is in a market.[98] The historical role of migration in spreading skills from where they are abundant to where they are scarcer has been important in this consequence.[99] Among other stories, skills in clockmaking among the Huguenots who migrated to Geneva in the sixteenth century made the city a leading clockmaking centre of the world.[100] In this context, we argue that,

[95] The authors thank Henry Gao for sharing his insights and providing this viewpoint at the conference on ChAFTA: One Year after its signing, at the University of New South Wales, 17–18 June 2016.

[96] HF Chang, 'Liberalized Immigration as Free Trade: Economic Welfare and the Optimal Immigration Policy' (1997) 145 *University of Pennsylvania Law Review* 1147; see also RM Stern, 'Conflict and Cooperation in International Economic Policy and Law' (1996) 17 *University of Pennsylvania Journal of International Economic Law* 539.

[97] OECD, *Trade and Migration: Building Bridge for Global Labour Mobility* (2004) 86.

[98] Winters et al, *Liberalising Labour Mobility* (n 87) 64, 86.

[99] Sowell (n 5) 388.

[100] ibid 2. Similarly, skills in beer brewing among Germans have led to German domination of the beer industry in various countries around the world.

with some exceptions (ie, Sydney and Melbourne, where there are significant numbers of Australians or permanent residents of Chinese cultural background), there exist arguably few local substitutes for Chinese chefs, Wushu martial arts coaches, Mandarin language tutors and TCM practitioners in Australia mostly due to considerable cultural divergences between China and Australia. In other words, Chinese workers will be brought in to fill a labour need.[101] The increased supply of the cultural-oriented Mode 4 labour/professionals does not necessarily harm native workers.[102] In addition, at higher skill levels, there may be some positions for which the native labour force might not yet be qualified. Hiring competent Chinese labour/professionals is a reasonable short-term solution because they can complement the work of native workers. Skilled Mode 4 can foster economic development directly by creating new jobs as well as indirectly providing the linguistic and cultural know-how.[103]

On the other hand, although the negative effects of 'brain drain' in some cases are undeniable,[104] China seems much less concerned about losing the human capital of highly-skilled cultural-oriented labour/professionals. For most sectors,[105] higher education is heavily subsidised in China and skilled migrants carry away human capital built with public investment.[106] However, the cultural sector is a prominent example that brain drain is not an issue and the emigration of highly-skilled workers will not lead to skill shortages.

To conclude, Mode 4 is an area where China stands to make clear gains. Greater concessions under Mode 4 can contribute a needed element of balance to trade in services by allowing China to exploit its natural comparative advantages in bilateral trade.[107] At the same time, opening up cultural-oriented Mode 4 can address skill gaps in the Australian local market. Nevertheless, the question remains: is cultural-oriented Mode 4 socially desirable and politically popular?

[101] Winters, 'The Temporary Movement of Workers to Provide Services' (n 30) 493.

[102] OECD (n 97) 86.

[103] Sowell (n 5) 389. See also NSW Government, *The Economic Advantages of Cultural Diversity in Australia* (2011), www.nsw.gov.au,15. See, eg, Government of Western Australia, *The Economic and Social Contribution of Migrants to Western Australia* (2012), www.www.omi.wa.gov.au/resources/publications/localgovernment/Economic_Social_Contributions_MigrantsWA_Full_Report.pdf, 30–31.

[104] B Ghosh, 'Managing Migration: Whither the Missing Regime? How Relevant is Trade Law to Such a Regime?' (2007) 101 *American Society of International Law Proceedings* 303, 304.

[105] OECD (n 97) 89.

[106] ibid.

[107] ibid 28.

ii. Social Concerns

In light of the issue of illegal immigrants Australia has faced, taking a more prudent step towards culture-oriented Mode 4 makes regulatory sense. While under certain conditions, liberalising temporary movement of workers might 'lead to a decrease in illegal migration',[108] many WTO Members have been reluctant to increase their Mode 4 commitments due to the '[f]ears of Mode 4 being a conduit for illegal migration'.[109] According to the Department of Immigration and Border Protection's recent report on *Australia's Migration Trend 2013–14*, the unlawful stay of non-citizens from China topped the list in the past couple of years, accounting for more than 7,000 visa over-stayers (out of about 60,000).[110] As culture-oriented CSS and IP face less market friction and may thus translate into a stronger flow of natural persons, setting an extra safety valve to one of the potential channels of illegal migration seems rational.

Moreover, there are genuine safety and public interest concerns under some circumstances, justifying regulatory cautiousness. Contrary to Australia's lift of regulatory assessments for 10 covered occupations, it holds TCM subject to more stringent scrutiny. According to ChAFTA's Side Letter on Traditional Chinese Medicine, '[a]ll suppliers of [Traditional Chinese Medicine] services in Australia must comply with relevant public health and safety measures'.[111] Indeed, Australia has a stake in ensuring that foreign natural persons delivering medical services are as equally qualified as their domestic counterparts to fulfil their professional tasks. Rather than allowing TCM practitioners to supply services straightaway, Australia will work together with China in a piecemeal manner, such as in exchanging information and discussing relevant policies and regulations 'in order to find opportunities for further cooperation', encouraging and supporting engagement between professional bodies and registration agencies in both jurisdictions, and clarifying and providing advice on the qualifications of such practitioners.[112] Similarly, Australia has not waived the assessment requirements for other culture-oriented CSS or IP. Assessment procedures as such will certainly take a considerable amount of time to develop.

It should also be noted that, although we consider that the quota system will unduly hamper the flow of would-be cultural labour, we recognise that a number of social concerns need to be addressed. Completely open borders

[108] See, eg, Mohamed Hedi Bchir, 'Effect of Mode 4 Liberalization on Illegal Immigration' (2007) Africa Trade Policy Centre (Economic Commission for Africa) ATPC Work in Progress No 55, www.uneca.org/Portals/atpc/CrossArticle/1/WorkinProgress/55.pdf.

[109] J Kategekwa, *Opening Markets for Foreign Skills: How Can the WTO Help? Lessons from the EU and Uganda's Regional Services Deals* (2014) 73.

[110] See Department of Immigration and Border Protection, *Australia's Migration Trend 2013–14*, www.border.gov.au/ReportsandPublications/Documents/statistics/migration-trends 13-14.pdf.

[111] ChAFTA (n 66) Side Letter on Traditional Chinese Medicine (17 June 2015).

[112] ibid.

would be problematic because of the safety and public interest considerations. We also share the viewpoints that other most frequent use of entry criteria such as ENTs cannot provide a sufficient safeguard in the case of cultural oriented Mode 4.[113] When there are sufficient local substitutes, the market itself may well pose certain limits, and the government can rely on ENTs to allow entry to workers only if there is a need for them. Conversely, when there are few local substitutes and therefore less market competition, additional restrictions to cap the total number of temporary workers who enter and stay seems logical.

After all, the flow of 'people' has political and social effects that differ from the flow of goods.[114] Mode 4 is a sensitive area due to its social issues as well as it security concerns.[115] As a result, Mode 4 generates a more complex set of anxieties and political reactions in immigrant-destination countries than do inflows of capital or goods or capital. As demonstrated by the policy considerations discussed above, it seems that Australia's special treatment of culture-oriented Mode 4 has come less from worries about adverse economic impact, and more from social and safety concerns. It is evident that the economic gains do not appear to be large or certain enough to overcome the reluctance caused by the political obstacles.[116] To conclude, greater liberalisation in Mode 4 will no doubt have to be rationalised in terms of policy interests. It is also important to be reminded of the fact that the mission of most immigration and labour authorities is not to facilitate Mode 4 trade. In the context of trade negotiations, their functions are largely defensive in nature.[117] The regulators responsible for considering new Mode 4 commitments under PTAs have generally remained cautious, if not hostile, to the incorporation of additional trade obligations.[118]

IV. CONCLUDING REMARKS: FROM KUNG FU PANDA TO KUNG FU KOALA

It should be remembered that the task we set ourselves was to interpret the Mode 4 commitments from cultural perspectives. While scholars and practitioners of international economic law have worked extensively on the 'trade versus culture' issues, there has been relatively little work in the legal studies that has explicitly examined Mode 4 commitments from cultural perspectives.

Turning now to the cultural implications of Annex 10-A. Arguably, the mobility of cultural professionals/labour—as agents of the forces of global

113 See generally OECD (n 97) 25.
114 Gordon (n 5) 1112–17.
115 OECD (n 97) 11–17.
116 Gordon (n 5) 1131–33.
117 Peng, 'Towards Greater Mobility' (n 29) 136–38.
118 ibid.

cultural change—is a significant way to promote culture diversity.[119] For example, Chinese Wushu, which has its theoretical foundation in Chinese classical culture, emphasises the 'unification of internal and external'.[120] The mobility of Wushu martial arts coaches, therefore, is indeed about cultural expression, dialogue and exchange. Under ChAFTA, Mode 4 Wushu coaches will interact with local people, invest in activities promoting assimilation, stimulate curiosity and eventually develop a bridge to the recognition of shared cultures and values.[121] In this context, the mobility of Kung Fu Masters has much more cultural impact than the production of 'Kung Fu Panda' movies. From Kung Fu Panda to Kung Fu Koala, cultural labour/professionals who bring unique cultural talent and specialised skills should be at the centre of the 'trade and culture' debate.

This chapter concludes that the cultural, economic and social consequences of rising tides of temporary movements between Australia and China is a fertile field for the future. The case of ChAFTA demonstrates the high level of sensitivity found in Mode 4 liberalisations. It lies at the centre of labour, migration and security policy,[122] and both the numerical quotas and qualification assessment on cultural-oriented Mode 4 reflect immigration policy, not economic protectionism. China, which is interested in the further development of services supply through Mode 4, should strive for a full implementation of concessions under Annex 10-A. In particular, the Australian market access obligations need to be sustained through disciplines on domestic regulations, eg, a mechanism for the verification of competences which allows the Australian authorities to satisfy themselves that the Chinese cultural labour/professional demonstrates an equivalent level of competence to that of a 'like supplier' originating in Australia. In particular, consensus is needed on how and when to accord 'equivalence' between cultural professionals' on-the-job experiences. To conclude, after using ChAFTA as a case study to examine whether cultural-oriented Mode 4 can provide a pathway to diminish misunderstandings and defensive positions among different policy communities, we find that while the economic gains from liberalisation of cultural-oriented Mode 4 might be potentially substantial, regulatory interference with the market motivated by the need for accomplishing non-economic social goals may seriously prevent foreign cultural labour/professionals from competing on a level playing field.

[119] Van Harpen (n 89) 187–88; see also T Broude, 'Taking "Trade and Culture" Seriously: Geographical Indications and Cultural Protection in WTO Law' (2005) 26 *University of Pennsylvania Journal of International Economic Law* 623, 636–38.

[120] See Kung Fu Dragon, 'Wushu Concept, Theories, Principles and Philosophies', www.www.kungfudragonusa.com/wushu-concept-theories-principles-and-philosophies.

[121] See generally, I Wallerstein, 'The National and the Universal: Can There Be Such a Thing as World Culture?' in A King (ed), *Culture, Globalization and the World-System* (Minneapolis, MN, University of Minnesota Press, 1997).

[122] See OECD (n 97) 11–17.

8

Breakthrough or Standstill? China's Liberalisation of Legal Services under ChAFTA†

WEIHUAN ZHOU AND JUNFANG XI

I. INTRODUCTION

THE LANDMARK ChAFTA, which entered into force on 20 December 2015, has been commonly observed in Australia as having created widespread and in many areas unprecedented market access for Australian businesses in the country's largest export market.[1] This chapter examines China's commitments to liberalising the legal services sector under ChAFTA, exploring the market access Australian legal services providers may actually gain and the challenges they are likely to face.

Global expansion of law firms for market opportunities, profits and clients is one of the most remarkable and continuing trends of globalisation.[2] Given the potential of the Chinese market, international law firms have long strived to expand businesses into China over the past decades.[3] By the end of 2014, a total of 170 foreign law firms, including 39 of the world's top 50, had established 225 foreign representative offices (FROs) in China.[4]

† This chapter is based on W Zhou and J Xi, 'China's Liberalisation of Legal Services under the ChAFTA: Market Access or Lack of Market Access for Australian Legal Practices' (2017) 51 *Journal of World Trade* 233, 233–64.

[1] See, eg, Department of Foreign Affairs and Trade (DFAT), 'Historic China–Australia FTA Enters into Force' (Media Release, 20 December 2015), trademinister.gov.au/releases/Pages/2015/ar_mr_151220a.aspx.

[2] See Jomati Consultants LLP, 'The Next Wave: Globalisation after the Crisis' (March 2010), www.altmanweil.com/dir_docs/resource/b1834c69-8653-4fc8-961e-fee62e308ab8_document.pdf.

[3] See generally, RE Stern and S Li, 'The Outpost Office: How International Law Firms Approach the China Market' (2015) *Law & Social Inquiry* 1.

[4] 《司法部公告第147号——关于232家外国律师事务所驻华代表机构通过 2013 年度检验获准在中国境内执业的公告 [Announcement No 147 of the Ministry of Justice—Announcement on China Offices of 232 Foreign-based Law Firms Passing Inspection in 2013 to Obtain the Approval to Operate in China] (People's Republic of China) Ministry of Justice (MOJ), Announcement No 147, 13 August 2014; see also, ZW, '法律大数据之：外资律所驻华代表机构大揭秘 [INTELLIGEAST, Representative Offices of Foreign Law Firms in China] (2 August 2015), zhihedongfang.com/article-12342/ (in Chinese).

The expansion of foreign law firms in China has mirrored the development and reforms of China's legal services sector, even as it has encountered considerable regulatory barriers. While Western countries managed to open the Chinese market following the admission of China to the World Trade Organization (WTO), China's WTO commitments on legal services have been proven insufficient to allow foreign law firms to expand presence and legal practice in China, hence the ongoing call for further liberalisation of the market.[5]

While such liberalisation may not be forthcoming within the WTO context, regional trade agreements provide another potential avenue for such liberalisation. Indeed, since its WTO membership, China has been active in regional cooperation and integration. By April 2017, China had 13 FTAs, and was negotiating eight FTAs, reviewing and upgrading three existing FTAs and conducting feasibility studies for nine further FTAs.[6] Among the existing FTAs including ChAFTA, China has made specific commitments on legal services in all but one FTA, that is, the China–ASEAN FTA. However, other than the arrangements between China and the Hong Kong and Macau Special Administrative Regions (SAR), China's FTA commitments have yet to lead to any fundamental changes in its domestic regulatory regime on legal services. China's approaches to opening the market for HK and Macau legal service providers, therefore, provide a model for its future liberalisation of legal services to all foreign legal services suppliers.

Separately, as part of its economic reforms, China has also made efforts to unilaterally liberalise its legal services market; however, progress has been very slow due to the cautious approach China took to avoid any undue impacts of foreign competition on its own legal profession.[7] Nonetheless, the recent launch of the Shanghai Free Trade Zone (SHFTZ) in 2013 was significant as it creates enhanced market access for foreign law firms and provides a testing ground for further liberalisation across the nation.

All the aspects above are relevant to our assessment of the implications for Australian access to the legal services market in China under ChAFTA. This chapter is organised as follows. Section II provides an overview of China's economic environment for foreign services providers, and in particular China's legal profession market and the position of foreign legal practice in that market. Section III conducts a comparison between China's ChAFTA commitments on legal services and those under the WTO and its

[5] See generally, MA Cohen, 'International Law Firms in China: Market Access and Ethical Risks' (2012) 8 *Fordham Law Review* 2569; LY Huang, 'The Legal Service Market in China: Implementation of China's GATS Commitments and Foreign Legal Services in China' (2012) 5 *Tsinghua China Law Review* 29.

[6] China FTA Network, fta.mofcom.gov.cn/english/index.shtml.

[7] J Heller, 'China's New Foreign Law Firm Regulations: A Step in the Wrong Direction' (2003) 12 *Pacific Rim Law & Policy Journal* 751, 753–60.

other FTAs. Section IV explores China's regulatory regime on legal services with a focus on the major regulatory constraints on the provision of legal services by foreign suppliers. As part of the analysis, this section examines the liberalisation of legal services within the SHFTZ. Section V offers observations on China's approach to liberalising legal services and the implications of its ChAFTA commitments for Australia's legal services suppliers. Section VI concludes.

II. THE LEGAL SERVICES MARKET IN CHINA

China's development model based on government-driven investment and exports over the decades since the 'Open Door' policy has largely run its course and is not sustainable in the long term. The Chinese government, therefore, has launched a series of economic reforms to optimise its economic structure. The ongoing reforms, as recently affirmed in China's Thirteenth Five-Year Plan (2016–20), aim to encourage investment in the services sector and, as shown in Figure 1, have led to steady growth of the tertiary industry.

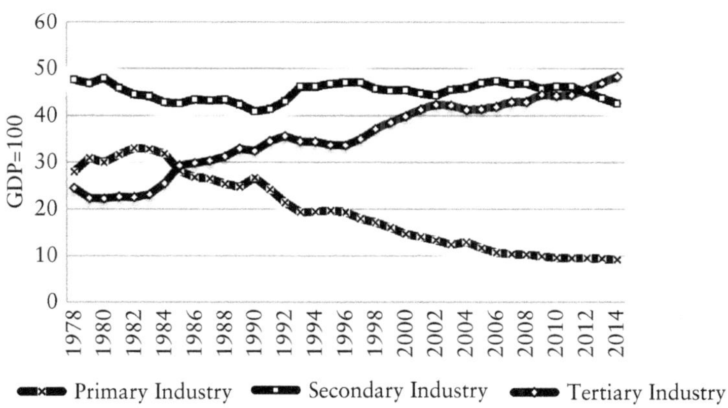

Figure 1: China's Industry Structure Distribution, Share of GDP (1978–2014)[8]

Consistent with the policy directive, the launch of the SHFTZ in 2013 and another 10 free trade zones since then serves to create a regulatory and

[8] The data is collected from the National Bureau of Statistics of China, China Statistical Yearbook 2015, Table 3-7: Share of Contributions of the Three Strata of Industry and Main Sectors to the Increase of the GDP. National Bureau of Statistics of China, 'China Statistical Yearbook 2015' (China Statistics Press, 2016), www.stats.gov.cn/tjsj/ndsj/2015/indexeh.htm.

operating environment for testing new initiatives and market reforms, particularly in the services sector.[9] As a result, China's services imports have continued to grow in recent years, and in 2015 accounted for 20.2 per cent of China's total imports.[10]

China's new model of development, in furtherance of the development of a strong service- and innovation-based economy, unleashes massive growth potential for foreign service providers in the Chinese market. Australia's economic growth relies predominantly on services. For example, in 2014–15, Australia's services sector represented approximately 60 per cent of its GDP, worth around AUD$970 billion.[11] In the same period, Australia's direct service exports amounted to AUD$62 billion, accounting for approximately 20 per cent of Australia's total value of exports.[12] China is the largest importer of services from Australia, with an average annual growth of 12 per cent (by value) over the 10 years up to 2014: see Figure 2.[13] Accordingly, ChAFTA would contribute to both China's continuous economic reforms by attracting Australian services investors and the needs of Australian services providers to enter and grow in the Chinese market.

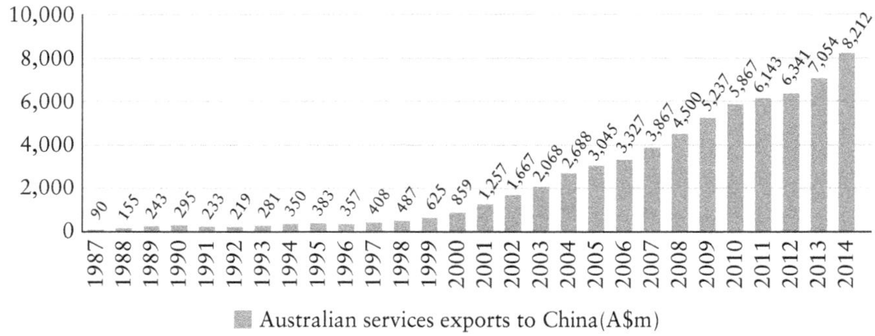

Figure 2: Australia's Services Exports to China (1987–2014)[14]

[9] See eg, H Wong, 'China's Free Trade Zones Will Accelerate Reform' *The Australian* (3 April 2015), www.theaustralian.com.au/business/business-spectator/chinas-free-trade-zones-will-accelerate-reform/news-story/ef5e52067b99bd3ec10dc2098425f59b.

[10] 商务部综合司[Comprehensive Department, Ministry of Commerce], '中国服务贸易状况' ['Current Status of China's Services Trade'] (10 May 2016), zhs.mofcom.gov.cn/article/Nocategory/201605/20160501314855.shtml (in Chinese).

[11] Department of Industry, Innovation and Science, 'Australian Industry Report 2015' (2015), www.industry.gov.au/Office-of-the-Chief-Economist/Publications/Documents/AIR2015.pdf, 3.

[12] Productivity Commission, 'Barriers to Growth in Service Exports' (November 2015), www.pc.gov.au/inquiries/completed/service-exports/report/service-exports.pdf, 2.

[13] ibid 9.

[14] DFAT, 'Trade Statistics: Australia's Direction of Goods & Services Trade', dfat.gov.au/trade/resources/trade-statistics/Pages/trade-time-series-data.aspx.

The legal profession in China has developed rapidly over the last few decades. By the end of 2015, the number of Chinese law firms had soared to almost 24,000 from approximately 70 in 1979, and the number of lawyers to 297,000 from approximately 200.[15] To enter the Chinese market, foreign law firms must take the form of FROs which was not permitted until 1992. Between 1992 and 2013, an average of 12 new international law firms per year have set up FROs in China's major cities (see Figure 3), particularly in Beijing, Shanghai and Guangdong. In 2014, the number of FROs dropped slightly, partially due to the global mergers between law firms and the collapse of certain international law firms. For example, Australian firms Allens, and Mallesons Stephen Jaques, both closed their China offices as a result of, respectively, an alliance with Linklaters and a merger with the Chinese firm King & Wood. In contrast, 2015 saw a slight increase in the number of FROs from 225 to 229.[16]

Figure 3: Number of International Law Firms in China (1992–2014)[17]

Despite the growing presence of foreign law firms in China, they face considerable challenges in the market. Besides stringent Chinese regulations of FROs (which will be discussed in section IV), foreign law firms must compete not only with themselves but also with the huge number of Chinese law firms which generally enjoy a price advantage as they operate at

[15] News reports on Ninth National Lawyer Representatives Conference held on 30 March 2016: 全国律师事务所已达2.4万家，律师发展到29.7万 （新浪网[Sina.com.cn], 30 March 2016), news.sina.com.cn/c/2016-03-30/doc-ifxqxcnp8227504.shtml (in Chinese).

[16] 《司法部公告第166号——关于229家外国律师事务所驻华代表机构通过2015年度检验获准在中国境内执业的公告》 [Announcement No 166 of the Ministry of Justice—Announcement on China Offices of 229 Foreign-based Law Firms Passing Inspection in 2015 to Obtain the Approval to Operate in China] MOJ, Announcement No 166, 12 September 2016.

[17] The data is compiled by the authors from the annual list published by the MOJ between 1992 and 2014.

significantly lower costs due to, for example, labour and compliance costs. Consequently, 70 per cent of foreign law firms in China are reportedly not covering operating costs.[18] However, foreign law firms treat China as a marginal source of revenue of their global businesses but a market too strategically important to abandon. Given the constrained Chinese market, foreign law firms have focused on pursuing high-end, non-litigation services related to foreign capital, such as cross-border mergers and acquisitions, overseas IPOs, technology transfer and IP protection etc. Thanks to the surge in China's outbound foreign direct investment in the past decade (with an average growth of 35 per cent annually), foreign law firms have managed to grow their businesses in cross-border transactions. Also, China's continuing liberalisation via both domestic initiatives and FTAs will continue to create increasingly more business opportunities for foreign legal services providers. As China's first comprehensive FTA with a developed economy and its latest efforts at trade liberalisation, ChAFTA has great potential to create opportunities for Australian services suppliers in the Chinese market. Australia's law firms, while smaller in both number and scale than US and UK law firms in China, are among the most innovative and experienced providers of legal and business services in the world. With the gradual liberalisation of other types of services and the regulatory barriers to foreign investment between China and Australia, Australian law firms are well positioned to succeed in the Chinese market. Yet, the degree of success Australian legal services providers would achieve largely depends on whether ChAFTA has lifted the major regulatory hurdles in China and hence provided them with a competitive advantage over other foreign legal services providers.

III. CHINA'S LIBERALISATION OF LEGAL SERVICES

A. China's WTO Commitments

China's WTO commitments on legal services are specified in its Schedule of Specific Commitments attached to the General Agreement on Trade in Services (GATS Schedule).[19] China committed to not imposing restrictions on the provision of legal services by foreign suppliers by way of Cross-Border Supply or Consumption Abroad. However, various types of restriction are maintained in relation to services supplied via Commercial Presence.

[18] R Lewis, 'Ranking the Top Domestic and Foreign Firms in China–A Snapshot of the Present as a Basis for a Projection of Future Market Trends' (July–August 2013), www.zhonglun.com/UpFile/File/201309261413278376.pdf, 17.

[19] Report of the Working Party on the Accession of China, Addendum—Schedule CLII—The People's Republic of China, Part II—Schedule of Specific Commitments on Services & List of Article II MFN Exemptions (1 October 2001) WT/ACC/CHN/49/Add.2, docsonline.wto.org.

First, foreign law firms must use representative offices to supply legal services in China.

Second, the scope of legal services of FROs is confined to the following:

a. To provide clients with consultancy on the legislation of the country/region where the lawyers of the law firm are permitted to engage in lawyers' professional work, and on international conventions and practices.
b. To handle, when entrusted by clients or Chinese law firms, legal affairs of the country/region where the lawyers of the law firm are permitted to engage in lawyers' professional work.
c. To entrust, on behalf of foreign clients, Chinese law firms to deal with Chinese legal affairs.
d. To enter into contracts to maintain long-term entrustment relations with Chinese law firms for legal affairs.
e. To provide information on the impact of the Chinese legal environment.

Entrustment allows the foreign representative office to directly instruct lawyers in the entrusted Chinese law firm, as agreed between both parties.

Essentially, FROs cannot provide legal services in relation to Chinese law but are only allowed to advise on laws of foreign jurisdictions where they are qualified and on international laws. To avoid any ambiguities, China explicitly excludes 'Chinese law practice' from its specific commitments on legal services. This restriction on scope of services is further confirmed by clauses (c) and (d) above which require FROs to engage Chinese law firms for services relating to Chinese law via matter-based or long-term 'Entrustment'. Under an Entrustment arrangement, FROs are permitted to 'directly instruct lawyers in the entrusted Chinese law firm'. The only practice that FROs are allowed to undertake in relation to Chinese law is set out in clause (e), ie, to 'provide information on the impact of the Chinese legal environment' (Legal Environment Services). Accordingly, it is generally understood that China's WTO commitments on legal services are intended to draw a clear line between legal services on matters relating to Chinese law and those on foreign and international laws and to restrict the practice of FROs to the latter.[20] A deviation from this general understanding arises from the controversies over the exact scope of the Legal Environment Services. While it was the expectation of some Western countries that China's commitment on Legal Environment Services would allow foreign law firms to provide services on Chinese law,[21] the expectation conflicts with the intention of the Chinese government which was not prepared to open the market. The entrenched position of the Chinese government is to isolate the domestic

[20] See, eg, Huang (n 5) 37; Stern and Li (n 3) 6–7.

[21] A Godwin, 'The Professional "Tug of War": The Regulation of Foreign Lawyers in China, Business Scope Issues and Some Suggestions for Reform' (2009) 33 *Melbourne University Law Review* 132, 136–37.

legal profession from foreign competition in relation to 'Chinese law practice'. This position is clarified in the domestic regulations issued to implement the WTO commitments, which will be discussed in section IV.

Third, FROs are not allowed to employ Chinese national registered lawyers. As will be discussed in section IV, this restriction is elaborated on and strengthened in the relevant Chinese regulations to reinforce the efforts to prevent FROs from engaging in 'Chinese law practice'. In addition, all representatives of an FRO must be resident in China for at least six months a year (Residency Requirement).

Fourth, apart from some limited horizontal commitments applicable to all the services sectors listed in China's GATS Schedule, China has made no specific commitments and hence can impose restrictions on the supply of legal services by the temporary presence of foreign lawyers. The horizontal commitments allow senior employees of foreign law firms (ie, managers, executives and specialists), as intra-corporate transferees (ICTs), to enter and temporarily stay for up to three years in China. Furthermore, service salespersons are allowed to enter and temporarily stay in China for up to 90 days subject to certain conditions. These commitments, however, do not affect China's ability to use other measures such as visa policies to restrict the entry and stay of foreign lawyers.

The restrictions contemplated in China's GATS Schedule do not exhaust the regulatory barriers foreign law firms may face in providing legal services in China. Other restrictions such as qualification requirements also limit the market access and business opportunities of foreign legal services providers. However, the restrictions China maintains on foreign legal services providers are not uncommon. As noted by the WTO Secretariat, similar types of regulatory barrier also exist in many other jurisdictions, particularly restrictions on the type of legal entity, partnership with local professionals, the hiring of local professionals, and the movement of professional, managerial and technical personnel, as well as qualification/licensing requirements, and residency and nationality requirements.[22] Therefore, China's committed level of liberalisation of legal services does not seem to fall short of the standard among WTO Members.

B. China's Commitments under FTAs

As of 31 December 2016, China has made commitments on legal services in 12 FTAs. Like its WTO commitments, China agreed to not impose any restrictions on the supply of legal services by foreign providers via

[22] Council for Trade in Services, Legal Services: Background Note by the Secretariat (6 July 1998) S/C/W/43 8–11, docsonline.wto.org; Council for Trade in Services, Legal Services: Background Note by the Secretariat (14 July 2010) S/C/W/318 16–18, docsonline.wto.org.

Cross-Border Supply or Consumption Abroad under the FTAs. Therefore, our discussions below focus on China's commitments in relation to the other two modes of services, especially Commercial Presence.

i. FTAs Reproducing GATS-Specific Commitments

Eight FTAs essentially reproduce China's GATS specific commitments on the supply of legal services via Commercial Presence, including the FTAs with New Zealand (2008),[23] Singapore (2009),[24] Pakistan (2009),[25] Peru (2010),[26] Chile (2010),[27] Costa Rica (2011),[28] Iceland (2014)[29] and Switzerland (2014).[30] The commitments and restrictions on legal services under these FTAs, therefore, remain the same as those under the WTO.

However, four of the eight FTAs (New Zealand,[31] Singapore,[32] Peru[33] and Switzerland) extend the period of temporary stay for services salespersons

[23] Free Trade Agreement between the Government of the People's Republic of China and the Government of New Zealand (signed 7 April 2008, entered into force 1 October 2008) (China–New Zealand FTA) Annex 8-A (China's Schedule of Specific Commitments on Services).

[24] Free Trade Agreement between the Government of the People's Republic of China and the Government of the Republic of Singapore (signed 23 October 2008, entered into force 1 January 2009) (China–Singapore FTA) Annex 5A (China's Schedule of Specific Commitments on Services).

[25] Agreement on Trade in Services between the Government of the People's Republic of China and the Government of the Islamic Republic of Pakistan (signed 21 February 2009, entered into force 10 October 2009) (China–Pakistan FTA) (China's Schedule of Specific Commitments).

[26] Free Trade Agreement between the Government of the People's Republic of China and the Government of the Republic of Peru (signed 28 April 2009, entered into force 1 March 2010) (China–Peru FTA) Annex 6-A (China's Schedule of Specific Commitments).

[27] Supplementary Agreement on Trade in Services of the Free Trade Agreement between the Government of the People's Republic of China and the Government of the Republic of Chile (signed 13 April 2008, entered into force 1 August 2010) (China–Chile FTA) Annex II-I (Schedule of Specific Commitments—Schedule of China).

[28] Free Trade Agreement between the Government of the People's Republic of China and the Government of the Republic of Costa Rica (signed 7 April 2011, entered into force 1 August 2011) (China–Costa Rica FTA) Annex 7-1 (Schedule of Specific Commitments—Schedule of China).

[29] Free Trade Agreement between the Government of the People's Republic of China and the Government of Iceland FTA (signed 15 April 2013, entered into force 1 July 2014) (China–Iceland FTA) Annex VII-1 (China's Schedule of Specific Commitments).

[30] See Annex 6 on General Provision and Definitions and Annex 7 on Specific Commitments. Free Trade Agreement between the Government of the People's Republic of China and the Government of the Swiss Confederation (signed 6 July 2013, entered into force 1 July 2014) (China–Switzerland FTA) Annexes 6, 7 (China's Schedule of Specific Commitments).

[31] China–New Zealand FTA (n 23) Annex 10-A (China's Commitments on Temporary Entry by Natural Persons).

[32] China–Singapore FTA (n 24) Annex 6 (Commitments on Temporary Entry of Natural Persons). China's Commitments on Temporary Entry of Natural Persons, available at: fta.mofcom.gov.cn/topic/ensingapore.shtml. For definitions of Business Visitors and ICTs, see Ch 9 (Movement of Natural Persons).

[33] China–Peru FTA (n 26) Annex 7 (China's Commitments for Temporary Entry for Business Persons). For definitions of Business Visitors and ICTs, see ibid Ch 9 (Temporary Entry for Business Persons).

(which are also referred to as a type of 'Business Visitor') from 90 days to six months. Business Visitors also include an investor or an authorised representative of the investor seeking to 'establish, expand, monitor, or dispose of an investment of that investor' in China. Such investors or representatives are also entitled to a temporary stay of up to six months.

In addition, China's FTAs with Pakistan, Chile, New Zealand, Peru, Costa Rica and Switzerland do not include the following language which appears in China's horizontal commitments under GATS:

> The conditions of ownership, operation and scope of activities, as set out in the respective contractual or shareholder agreement or in a licence establishing or authorizing the operation or supply of services by an existing foreign service supplier, will not be made more restrictive than they exist as of the date of China's accession to the WTO.

The impact of the absence of the language in the above-mentioned FTAs would be negligible. To the extent that the language applies to legal services, it requires China to at least maintain certain conditions of market access for FROs already established in China before its WTO accession. However, the language does not alter the various restrictions set out in China's specific commitments on legal services. In other words, restrictions on the form of legal entity, scope of activities etc, remain applicable to the supply of legal services by foreigners in China regardless of the language. Furthermore, all these FTA parties (Pakistan, Chile, New Zealand, Peru, Costa Rica and Switzerland) were already Members of the WTO before the FTAs took effect. Therefore, it appeared unnecessary to include the language in the FTAs as China had assumed the obligations embedded in the language as part of its GATS commitments under the WTO. Where the language is explicitly included in China's FTAs with Singapore, Iceland and South Korea (2015),[34] the following qualification is added: 'Any new sector and sub-sector scheduled after China's accession to the WTO shall not be subject to the preceding sentence'.

As discussed above, the inclusion of the language does not seem to alter China's specific commitments on legal services. Nor does the qualification seem to be applicable to the legal services sector which was scheduled at the time of China's entry into the WTO and hence was not a new sector.

ii. China–South Korea FTA and ChAFTA

The China–South Korea FTA and ChAFTA entered into force on the same day. Under both the FTAs, China made additional/WTO-plus specific

[34] Free Trade Agreement between the Government of the People's Republic of China and the Government of South Korea (signed 1 June 2015, entered into force 20 December 2015) (China–South Korea FTA) Annex 8-A-2 (China's Schedule of Specific Commitments). For China's commitments on Mode 4, see ibid Annex 11-A s A (China's Specific Commitments on Movement of Natural Persons).

commitments on legal services. While these commitments used slightly different language, they are essentially the same in effect. The commitments are set out in Table 1 below.

Table 1: China's Commitments on Legal Services under the China–South Korea FTA and ChAFTA

China–South Korea FTA	ChAFTA[35]
Korean law firms which has [sic] representative offices in China can provide legal services with Chinese law firms in the form of joint operation in [the] Shanghai Pilot Free Trade Zone. During the period of joint operation, both parties' legal status, names and financial status are independent, each of the said parties bears its own civil liabilities. The clients of the joint operation are not limited to Shanghai. Korean lawyers in the joint operation are not allowed to deal with the Chinese legal affairs. Korean law firms which has [sic] representative offices in Shanghai Pilot Free Trade Zone and Chinese law firms can send lawyers to each other as legal consultants.	(1) In accordance with Chinese laws, regulations and rules, Australian law firms which have established their representative offices in the China (Shanghai) Pilot Free Trade Zone ('FTZ') may enter into contracts with Chinese law firms in the FTZ. Based on such contracts, these Australian and Chinese law firms may dispatch their lawyers to each other to act as legal counsels. This means Chinese law firms may dispatch their lawyers to the Australian law firms to act as legal counsels on Chinese law and international law, and Australian law firms may dispatch their lawyers to the Chinese law firms to act as legal counsels on foreign law and international law. The two sides shall cooperate within their respective business scope. (2) In accordance with Chinese laws, regulations and rules, Australian law firms which have established their representative offices in the China (Shanghai) Pilot Free Trade Zone ('FTZ') are permitted to form a commercial association with Chinese law firms in the Shanghai FTZ. Within validity of this commercial association, the two law firms of each side respectively have independent legal status, name, financial operation, and bear civil liabilities independently. Clients of the commercial association are not limited within the Shanghai FTZ. Australian lawyers in this type of commercial association are not permitted to practise Chinese law.

[35] Free Trade Agreement between the Government of Australia and the Government of the People's Republic of China (ChAFTA) (signed 17 June 2015, entered into force 20 December 2015) [2015] ATS 15, Annex III pt 2 (China's Schedule of Specific Commitments).

The additional commitments go beyond China's specific commitments under GATS and all the other FTAs discussed above by allowing Korean/Australian law firms to: (1) form joint operations, and (2) exchange lawyers as legal consultants with Chinese law firms in the SHFTZ.

Under the first commitment, 'joint operation' or 'commercial association' is simply different translations of the same Chinese legal term which is defined under Chinese law. Under the General Principles of Civil Law 1986, a 'joint operation' or 'commercial association' may be undertaken by forming an incorporated or unincorporated entity.[36] Evidently, the commitment only allows unincorporated entities given the condition that the cooperating parties must remain independent with regard to legal status, names, financial status and civil liabilities. Subject to the condition, the rights and obligations of the cooperating parties are negotiated and specified in their 'joint operation' or 'commercial association' agreement. Furthermore, there are no restrictions on the duration of 'joint operation' or 'commercial association'; hence, both long-term and ad hoc/matter-based cooperation are permissible. Finally, 'joint operation' or 'commercial association' can only be formed by Korean/Australian law firms that have already established an FRO in the SHFTZ and must be undertaken within the SHFTZ. However, the clients that a 'joint operation' or 'commercial association' can serve are not subject to any geographical restrictions. In addition, the restriction on scope of activity still applies so that Korean/Australian lawyers in a 'joint operation' or 'commercial association' must not provide legal services in relation to Chinese law.

The second commitment permits FROs of Korean/Australian law firms established in the SHFTZ to enter into contracts with Chinese law firms for the exchange of lawyers to act as legal consultants. Such consultancy arrangements should not be considered as the employment of Chinese lawyers by FROs of Korean/Australian law firms. Rather, it seems to be merely intended to allow secondment of Chinese qualified lawyers to these FROs to provide advice on matters relating to Chinese law. Such secondment arrangements can be undertaken within the SHFTZ only. ChAFTA further clarifies that this commitment is intended to facilitate cooperation between Chinese and Australian law firms subject to the restriction that the lawyers dispatched under consultancy arrangements (ie, secondees) can only provide the legal services they are qualified to provide.

As with China's horizontal commitments under some of the other FTAs discussed above, ChAFTA allows a period of stay of up to three years for ICTs (ie, senior employees) and six months for Business Visitors. However,

[36] 《中华人民共和国民法通则 [General Principles of Civil Law of the People's Republic of China] (General Principles of Civil Law 1986) (People's Republic of China) National People's Congress (12 April 1986) Arts 51–53.

ChAFTA provides a slightly higher level of liberalisation by granting spouses and dependants of ICTs the same period of stay in China subject to the condition that the ICTs stay in China for more than 12 months.

iii. The Closer Economic and Partnership Arrangements

China signed a Closer Economic and Partnership Arrangement (CEPA) with Hong Kong[37] and Macau[38] respectively in 2003. Given the unique position of the SARs in China's political structure, they are often used as 'a testing ground for foreign policy by the Mainland Chinese authority'.[39] Consequently, the overall level of liberalisation under the CEPAs extends beyond what is under the WTO and the other FTAs.[40] Since the conclusion of the CEPAs in 2003, 10 supplementary agreements have been entered into between the Mainland and each of the SARs between 2004 and 2013.[41] The level of liberalisation of legal services under the CEPAs is mainly reflected in the following commitments which permit (using HK as an example):

— HK law firms which have established representative offices in the Mainland to form a 'joint operation' or 'commercial association' with Mainland law firms without geographic restrictions. However, HK lawyers in a 'joint operation' must not practise Mainland law.
— Mainland law firms to employ HK qualified lawyers. However, the employed HK lawyers must not practise Chinese law.
— HK legal practitioners to practise as lawyers in the Mainland provided that they have had at least five years' experience in legal practice and have passed the National Judicial Examination (NJE) as well as training and assessment offered by lawyers' associations in the Mainland. However, such HK legal practitioners are allowed to work at only one Mainland's law firm and must not at the same time be employed by FROs of any foreign law firms in the Mainland.

[37] 《内地与香港关于建立更紧密经贸关系的安排 [Mainland and Hong Kong Closer Economic and Partnership Arrangement] (Mainland and Hong Kong CEPA) (signed 29 June 2003, entered into force 29 June 2003).

[38] 《内地与澳门关于建立更紧密经贸关系的安排》 [Mainland and Macau Closer Economic and Partnership Arrangement] (signed 17 October 2003, entered into force 17 October 2003) Annex 4 (Mainland—Schedule of Specific Commitments) (in Chinese).

[39] See Huang (n 5) 46–47.

[40] See, eg, H Gao, 'The Closer Economic Partnership Arrangement (CEPA) between Mainland China and Hong Kong–Legal and Economic Analyses' in PJ Davidson (ed) *Trading Arrangements in the Pacific Rim: ASEAN and APEC* (New York, Oceana Publications, 2004).

[41] See 'Mainland and Hong Kong Closer Economic Partnership Arrangement (CEPA)' (Trade and Industry Department, 30 December 2016), www.tid.gov.hk/english/cepa/tradeservices/leg_liberalization.html; '内地与澳门关于建立更紧密经贸关系的安排 [Mainland and Macau Closer Economic and Partnership Arrangement]' (27 January 2017), www.cepa.gov.mo/cepaweb/front/eng/itemI_2.htm.

On 27 and 28 November 2015, the Mainland entered into a 'CEPA Trade in Services Agreement' with Hong Kong and Macau respectively, which took effect on 1 June 2016.[42] The Agreements provide a negative list of restrictions on national treatment, meaning that the Mainland is not to maintain any restrictions on national treatment on HK or Macau services providers except for those listed. On legal services, the national treatment restrictions to be maintained include (using HK as an example):

— FROs of HK law firms must not practise Mainland law or employ Mainland practising lawyers.
— Cooperation between Mainland law firms and FROs of HK law firms is limited to the following ways: (1) secondment of lawyers as legal consultants to advise on the laws of their respective jurisdictions; (2) 'joint operation' or 'commercial association' based on contractual arrangements and their own authorised scope of practice; and (3) partnership in Guangzhou, Shenzhen and Zhuhai in accordance with the specific rules approved by the judicial administrative authority.

Accordingly, HK/Macau legal services providers are treated more favourably than those from other countries in several aspects. Essentially, HK/Macau law firms are subject to fewer geographical restrictions in cooperating with Mainland law firms and are entitled to form partnerships with Mainland firms in the designated cities. HK/Macau legal practitioners are allowed to work for Mainland law firms as employees and to attend the required tests and training to become qualified to practise in the Mainland. The CEPAs and subsequent arrangements between the Mainland and the SARs represent the direction of China's future liberalisation of legal services. However, the fact that it took over a decade for the Mainland to commit to the above market-opening to HK/Macau suggests that China has been very cautious and is likely to continue to move slowly in liberalising its legal services market.

C. An Appraisal of China's ChAFTA Commitments on Legal Services

China's ChAFTA commitments on legal services reflect its latest approaches to the liberalisation of legal services. As the major areas of liberalisation, the

[42] See 'Mainland and Hong Kong Closer Economic Partnership Arrangement (CEPA)–Agreement on Trade in Services' (Trade and Industry Department, 29 May 2017), www.tid.gov.hk/english/cepa/legaltext/cepa13.html; 商务部新闻办 [Information Office, Ministry of Commerce], '《内地与澳门CEPA服务贸易协议》在澳门签署 (中国自由贸易区服务网[China FTA Network], 30 November 2015), fta.mofcom.gov.cn/article/zhengwugk/201511/29558_1.html (in Chinese).

commitments relating to 'commercial associations' and exchange of lawyers extend beyond China's commitments under the WTO and the other FTAs (excluding the CEPAs). However, as will be elaborated in section V, the practical effects of the commitments may be very limited. As correctly observed by the Law Council of Australia, there are a number of market access commitments that Australia has failed to obtain for its legal services providers in China. These mainly include:[43]

- The right to enter into different forms of commercial associations (including partnership or incorporated legal practice) with Chinese law firms without geographical restrictions.
- The right to undertake Chinese law practice or employ Chinese legal practitioners to do so.
- The removal of the Residency Requirement for ICTs.
- The removal of the citizenship restrictions for Australians to gain legal practice admission in China.
- Mutual recognition of legal qualifications between Australia and China.

While some of the commitments above have been made available to HK/Macau legal services providers, others have not been offered by China in any existing FTAs. It is, therefore, not a surprise that Australia was unable to obtain these commitments. In this connection, ChAFTA mandates that the parties continue to work together with a view to develop measures to enhance mobility for Australian and Chinese lawyers and promote closer cooperation between Australian and Chinese law firms.[44] This provides a framework for negotiation of further liberalisation of legal services as legal services play an increasingly significant role in the growing economic activities between China and Australia. However, the mandate seems to be limited to the areas of liberalisation to which China has committed under ChAFTA, ie, cooperation between Chinese and Australian law firms and their lawyers, and movement of legal professionals. This suggests that China has not been prepared to allow foreigners including Australian citizens to gain admission in China or to recognise Australian legal qualifications. On the latter point, ChAFTA merely mandates the parties 'to explore possibilities for mutual recognition of respective professional and vocational qualifications'.[45] Last but not least, the ban of foreign law firms from providing services

[43] Law Council of Australia, 'Discussion Paper: The Proposed China–Australia Free Trade Agreement: Key Issues Regarding Legal Practice in China for Australian Lawyers' (16 October 2013) 21–30, www.researchgate.net/publication/282355582_October_2013_Discussion_Paper_The_proposed_China-Australia_Free-Trade_Agreement_Key_Issues_Regarding_Legal_Practice_in_China_for_Australian_Lawyers.

[44] ChAFTA (n 35) Side Letter on Legal Services.

[45] ChAFTA (n 35) Art 8.15.

on Chinese legal matters including through the employment of Chinese lawyers to do so will not be lifted. In any event, China's further liberalisation of legal services to Australian legal services providers is unlikely to extend beyond China's commitments to HK and Macau but may follow the model of arrangements between the Mainland and the SARs. This suggests that further negotiations under the ChAFTA framework are likely to progress slowly such that significant market access for Australian legal services providers may not be achievable in the near future.

IV. CHINA'S REGULATION OF FOREIGN LEGAL PRACTICES

This section reviews the major regulatory barriers to foreign legal services providers in China that ChAFTA has failed to remove.

A. The Major Regulatory Barriers

The *Catalogue of Industries for Guiding Foreign Investment*, which was first issued in 1995 and subsequently amended many times,[46] has consistently restricted foreign investment in legal consultation services. In the current 2015 *Catalogue*, foreign legal services providers in China are prohibited from the provision of legal services in Chinese legal matters except for Legal Environment Services. This is consistent with China's commitments under the WTO and the FTAs. As a general list, the *Catalogue* does not provide for specific regulations of foreign legal services providers. Such regulations are developed by the State Council: the main ones are the Regulations on Representative Offices of Foreign Law Firms in China 2001[47] (FRO Regulation) and its implementing rules.[48]

The major restrictions on foreign legal services providers, as set out in the FRO Regulation and the implementing rules, are summarised below:

(1) **Form of investment:** Foreign law firms are required to establish a representative office to conduct business in China. The creation of FROs must be approved by China's Ministry of Justice (MOJ) in accordance with certain qualification requirements on FROs and their representatives and an 'actual

[46] Issued by the State Planning Commission, State Economic and Trade Commission and the MOFTEC, effective on 20 June 1995, as amended in 1997, 2004, 2007, 2011 and 2015.

[47] 《外国律师事务所驻华代表机构管理条例 [Regulations on Representative Offices of Foreign Law Firms in China] (FRO Regulation) (People's Republic of China) State Council, Decree No 338, 22 December 2001.

[48] 《司法部关于执行<外国律师事务所驻华代表机构管理条例>的规定 [Rules on the Implementation of the Regulations on Representative Offices of Foreign Law Firms in China] (Implementation Rules) MOJ, Order No 92, 2 September 2004, Art 4.

need' test which involves consideration of, amongst others, the social and economic conditions and the needs for development of legal services in the area where an FRO is proposed to be established. The broad drafting of the test is essentially intended to allow Chinese authorities the discretion to determine the number and location of FROs. Furthermore, the establishment of an additional FRO is not allowed until the most recently established FRO has operated for three consecutive years.[49] In practice, these conditions may be abused by Chinese authorities to impose both geographic and quantitative restrictions on FROs and to delay the establishment of multiple offices by foreign law firms.[50]

(2) **Scope of activities:** The scope of activities of FROs is confined to legal services on laws of foreign jurisdictions in which their lawyers are qualified and on international laws and practice.[51] For all services on Chinese legal matters, FROs must engage a Chinese law firm to provide via Entrustment and are not allowed to make profits out of the Entrustment. While FROs are permitted to provide Legal Environment Services, they must not provide any specific opinions or judgements on the application of Chinese law and must not make profit from such services.[52] According to observers with local experience, Legal Environment Services are limited to 'preparing client newsletters and reporting generally on the impact of the Chinese legal environment for marketing purposes' and should in no case be considered to include services on any matter that is subject to, or governed by, Chinese law.[53] In practice, however, foreign law firms have been accused of undertaking extensive practice prohibited under the legislation, taking advantage of the regulatory ambiguity and more importantly the lax enforcement of the rules by Chinese authorities.[54] While the ambit of Legal Environment Services remains debatable, it is subject to the interpretation of the MOJ. This means the permitted scope of activities of FROs may well be restricted as the MOJ considers necessary to strictly interpret and enforce the laws. Finally, the prohibition of foreign law firms from making profit out of Entrustment and Legal Environment Services confirms the intent of Chinese regulators to exclude FROs from Chinese legal practice and to preserve the market share and profits from such practice for the Chinese legal profession.[55] Collectively, the Chinese laws at least have the potential to constitute a complete denial of access to foreign law firms to the Chinese

[49] ibid Art 10(1).
[50] See Heller (n 7) 771–72.
[51] See FRO Regulation (n 47) Art 15.
[52] See Implementation Rules (n 48) Arts 32, 33.
[53] See Godwin (n 21) 140–41; Huang (n 5) 40–41.
[54] See Godwin (n 21) 141–43; Huang (n 5) 45–46.
[55] See Huang (n 5) 41–42.

legal services market. Such restrictions are likely to considerably restrain the profitability of foreign law firms in China.[56] In addition, foreign law firms and their FROs are not allowed to invest directly or indirectly or hold an equity interest in Chinese law firms.[57] These restrictions are to ensure that the operations of Chinese law firms remain 'independent from the influence of foreign law firms'.[58]

(3) **Employment of Chinese lawyers:** FROs are prohibited from employing Chinese lawyers via formal employment agreements or de facto employment relationships.[59] Chinese citizens including Chinese lawyers may be employed by FROs as non-legal supporting staff provided they suspend their practising certificate and do not provide legal services to clients during the employment. This prohibition not only creates a disincentive for Chinese qualified lawyers to become employees of FROs, but also eliminates the capacity of Chinese qualified lawyers to advise on Chinese law if they choose to work at foreign law firms. Accordingly, the prohibition reinforces the ban on foreign law firms from engaging in Chinese law practice.

(4) **Qualification restrictions:** Foreign lawyers are unable to satisfy the requirements for admission in China as they are not allowed to attend the NJE which is available for Chinese citizens (including HK, Macau and Taiwan residents) only.[60] This citizenship requirement makes it impossible for foreign lawyers to become Chinese legal practitioners and hence for them to undertake Chinese law practice. While Australia takes the position that qualification requirements should be based on knowledge, ability and professional fitness and not on nationality,[61] China is unlikely to remove the nationality requirement in the foreseeable future.

B. Shanghai Free Trade Zone

On 29 September 2013, China launched its first free trade zone—the SHFTZ. As a testing ground for institutional reforms and market liberalisation, the SHFTZ reduces regulatory barriers for businesses. Amongst others,

[56] See Stern and Li (n 3) 12–13.

[57] See Implementation Rules (n 48) Art 39.

[58] See Huang (n 5) 44.

[59] See FRO Regulation (n 47) Art 16; Implementation Rules (n 48) Art 40.

[60] 《国家司法考试实施办法》 [Measures for the Implementation of National Judicial Examination] MOJ, Order No 11, 14 August 2008, arts 15, 24; 《香港特别行政区和澳门特别行政区居民参加国家司法考试若干规定》 [Provisions on the Participation of Residents of the Hong Kong Special Administrative Region and the Macao Special Administrative Region in the National Judicial Examination] MOJ, Order No 94, 24 May 2005.

[61] See Law Council of Australia (n 43) 29.

it adopts a 'negative list' approach to further the opening up of services sectors and level the playing field for foreign service suppliers as opposed to domestic ones.[62] On legal services, it is mandated that the possible mode of cooperation between Chinese and foreign law firms needs to be explored.[63] To implement this mandate, the Shanghai Municipal Bureau of Justice published two pilot programmes or measures on 18 November 2014 which allow (1) exchange/secondment of lawyers between Chinese law firms and FROs of foreign law firms,[64] and (2) establishment of 'joint operation' or 'commercial associations' between Chinese and foreign law firms.[65] While these two areas of liberalisation are exactly the same as those China committed under ChAFTA, the two measures have provided significant clarity on the scope of the liberalisation.

In relation to exchange of lawyers, while it is confirmed that Chinese and foreign law consultants can only provide legal services that they are qualified to provide, it is clarified that Chinese law secondees in FROs are allowed to provide legal services on Chinese legal matters in the capacity of a Chinese legal practitioner, including advising on Chinese law and representing clients in civil and commercial litigation and non-litigation matters. More importantly, various requirements apply to the Chinese and foreign law firms wishing to enter into such an arrangement. These include:

- The Chinese law firm must have been established for at least three years with more than 20 lawyers and its head office or a branch in Shanghai (including the SHFTZ).
- The FRO must have been established for at least three years in Shanghai or other cities. In the latter case, an additional FRO must have already been established in Shanghai (including the SHFTZ).
- The secondees must have five or more years of full-time practising experience in their respective jurisdictions and cannot be managing partners of the law firms or the chief representative of the FRO.

[62] 《中国（上海）自由贸易试验区条例 [Regulations of China (Shanghai) Pilot Free Trade Zone] Standing Committee of the Shanghai Municipal People's Congress, Decree No 14, 25 July 2014.

[63] 《国务院关于印发中国（上海）自由贸易试验区总体方案的通知》 [Notice on Printing and Distributing the Overall Plan for the China (Shanghai) Pilot Free Trade Zone] (People's Republic of China) State Council, Notice No 38, 18 September 2013.

[64] 《中国（上海）自由贸易试验区中外律师事务所互派律师担任法律顾问的实施办法》 [Implementing Measures of the China (Shanghai) Pilot Free Trade Zone for the Secondment of Lawyers as Legal Consultants by Chinese and Foreign Law Firms] General Office of the Shanghai Municipal People's Government, Hu Fu Ban Fa [2014] No 63, 18 November 2014.

[65] 中国（上海）自由贸易试验区中外律师事务所联营的实施办法》 [Implementing Measures of the China (Shanghai) Pilot Free Trade Zone for the Establishment of Association between Chinese and Foreign Law Firms] General Office of the Shanghai Municipal People's Government, Hu Fu Ban Fa [2014] No 63, 18 November 2014.

Other major restrictions include:

— Only one foreign law firm is allowed to enter into such a secondment arrangement with one Chinese law firm.
— The Chinese and foreign law firm already in such an arrangement must not create an association with other law firms.
— The number of secondees is limited to three.

A secondment arrangement must be based on a contract which must set out matters such as fee arrangements, distribution of incomes and debts arising from the cooperation, and the term which shall in principle not be shorter than two years.

The second measure allows Chinese and foreign law firms to create a 'commercial association' within the SHFTZ and to provide legal services in the name of the association. The parties may charge clients as an association or separately. In the former case, the parties will distribute incomes based on their association agreement. Most of the requirements and restrictions applicable to the secondment arrangement also apply to the association arrangement, such as the requirements on Chinese and foreign law firms, the restriction that only one Chinese law firm can enter into an association with one foreign law firm and that the term of an association must generally not be less than two years. Major additional requirements include:

— The applicants for the creation of an association must be the head office of a Chinese law firm (ie, not its branches) and a foreign law firm (ie, not its representative offices).
— During the term of the association, the parties must remain independent in relation to legal status, name, financial status and liabilities. However, the parties *must* share office space and equipment and may also share non-legal supporting staff. The office space must be chosen between the Chinese law firm (including branch) or the FRO established in the SHFTZ.

The pilot programmes are aimed at promoting cooperation between Chinese and foreign law firms. In a press interview on the programmes, Ma Yi, an official in charge of lawyer administration at the Shanghai Bureau of Justice clarified that the promotion of the cooperation seeks to address the increasing demand for cross-jurisdiction legal services such that Chinese and foreign law firms work together to provide one-stop shop services to clients in cross-border transactions.[66] However, the existence of various restrictions and limitations suggests that the programmes are not intended to bring

[66] SM Hu and SM Ji, 'Official of Shanghai Bureau of Justice on the Liberalisation of Legal Services in the SHFTZ' *FTZ Post*, (17 March 2014), www.ftzsino.com/cn/interpretation/20140317/MTM5NTAZMJY2OTC.html.

radical changes to the market but merely gradual and experimental ones. As Ma stressed, the programmes do not alter the fundamental rules on foreign legal services providers such as the prohibition of foreign law firms from advising on Chinese legal matters or employing Chinese legal practitioners to do so. On the latter point, Chinese lawyers dispatched to foreign law firms are not employees of the foreign firms and must provide services in Chinese law under the name of their Chinese employers.

V. OBSERVATIONS AND IMPLICATIONS

China, like many other countries, has long taken a highly cautious approach to the liberalisation of the legal services sector.[67] This approach was a result of weighing and balancing the benefits and costs of opening up the sector. On the one hand, the liberalisation of the sector would attract foreign capital, expertise and know-how necessary for the development of the local legal profession; while on the other hand, the Chinese government was concerned about the impact of liberalisation on national security and on the business of domestic law firms which were unlikely to be able to compete with their foreign counterparts.[68] These conflicting values have continued to influence the policy directive of the Chinese government on the liberalisation of the sector post-China's WTO accession; hence, liberalisation has been taking place incrementally with considerable caution.[69]

The liberalisation of legal services under ChAFTA and within the SHFTZ falls within the policy directive contemplated in the Twelfth Five-Year Plan (2011–15).[70] The policy directive was carefully drafted with an emphasis on

[67] See Huang (n 5) 38–39; Heller (n 7) 754–60. For example, Japan has adopted similar approaches to the liberalisation of legal services as China. Japan's GATS schedule contains detailed restrictions on the mode of service supply, the types of legal entities, the scope of activities, qualification requirements etc. in relation to legal services. Thanks to the growing global M&A market and hence the need for foreign lawyers with the relevant expertise, Japan reformed and liberalised its legal services market by relaxing various restrictions in 2005 and 2010. While the liberalisation was designed to serve the interests of Japanese businesses, it has provided enhanced market access and opportunities to foreign legal services providers. Japan's GATS Schedule can be found here: www.wto.org/english/thewto_e/countries_e/japan_e.htm. For discussions of Japan's legal services market and recent reforms, see Japan External Trade Organization (JETRO), 'Analysis of the Liberalisation of Japan's Legal System–Implications & New Opportunities in Japan for FLFs' (11 August 2011), www.jetro.go.jp/australia/topics/20110811539-topics.html; L Ciano and D Martin, 'The Foreign Lawyer Law of Japan: Legitimate Complaints or Red Herrings?' (2002) 76 *Journal of Inquiry and Research* 121, 121–36.

[68] See Huang (n 5) 33–35.

[69] See Godwin (n 21) 149–50.

[70] 《服务贸易发展"十二五"规划纲要》 [Outline of the 12th Five-Year Plan for the Development of Trade in Services] (People's Republic of China) Ministry of Commerce et al, Shang Fu Mao Fa [2011] No 340, 27 September 2011.

the goals to promote the internationalisation and competitiveness of domestic law firms and to enhance their expertise and experience in cross-border transactions. While cooperation between Chinese and foreign law firms was regarded as one of the key approaches in the pursuit of the policy goals, it was also recognised that such cooperation must be undertaken in a way that minimises the negative impacts on the development of the domestic legal profession. Thus, concerns such as the loss of market share, profit and talented professionals to foreign law firms, national security etc, have caused the reluctance of the Chinese government to open quickly the market for foreign legal services suppliers.[71]

China's cautious approach to the liberalisation of legal services determined that the market access granted to Australian legal services providers under ChAFTA would not be as significant as expected. Essentially, China's commitments are designed to promote cooperation between Chinese and Australian law firms to the benefit of China's own legal profession. For Australian legal services providers, these commitments remain within the boundaries of China's regulatory framework on legal services and confer limited benefits.

Thus, China's ChAFTA commitment on 'joint operation' or 'commercial association' merely allows a loose form of cooperation based on contractual arrangement which must not involve merger or partnership or any other stronger cooperation. The commitment would allow Australian and Chinese law firms to share profits, clients, workplace, supporting staff, etc, and their lawyers to work together in an established office so as to provide one-stop shop services to clients. The commitment meets the needs of clients in cross-border transactions and the needs of Chinese lawyers to acquire expertise and experience from working side by side with their foreign colleagues. However, given the forms of cooperation already undertaken by foreign and Chinese law firms in practice, the commitment is unlikely to provide additional market access for Australian law firms. It is the authors' understanding that many foreign and Chinese law firms have entered into certain Strategic or Friendship Arrangements under which they undertake cross-referrals of matters and clients, marketing activities, secondment of lawyers etc, and work together (although often remotely) for clients in cross-border transactions. Such arrangements may not achieve the level of cooperation allowed under 'commercial associations' to the extent that they are often non-exclusive and do not create a separate entity which allows foreign and Chinese lawyers to physically work together and which may provide legal services in its own name. A more sophisticated form of cooperation between Chinese and foreign law firms has been the so-called Swiss

[71] See Huang (n 5) 33–34; Godwin (n 21) 149–50.

Verein structure[72] used, for example, in the merger between China's King & Wood and Australia's Mallesons Stephen Jaques to form King & Wood Mallesons in March 2012 and lately in the merger between Chinese firm Dacheng and international firm Dentons in January 2015. These structures include similar features to the 'commercial association' approach. Under both the structures, foreign and Chinese law firms may share branding, clients, strategy and other functions as agreed and act for clients as a single entity, while they remain independent in terms of financial operation and civil liabilities. Furthermore, it is common that under Swiss Vereins Chinese and foreign lawyers work together in one workplace with shared administrative and supporting staff, as would be the case under 'commercial associations'. In addition, as shown above, China allowed 'commercial associations' generally within the SHFTZ on 18 November 2014, only one day after the conclusion of ChAFTA negotiations. As ChAFTA limits the area of operation of an association within the SHFTZ, it does not appear to grant any additional market access to Australian law firms compared with other foreign law firms.

As far as the commitment on the exchange of lawyers is concerned, the most significant benefit for Australian law firms would be the capacity to use Chinese secondee lawyers to provide legal services to clients and to make profit from such services via secondment arrangements. However, in practice, such an exchange of lawyers has frequently taken place under Friendship or Swiss Verein cooperation agreements whereby fee arrangements between foreign and Chinese law firms have also been common. Moreover, to build China practice and human resources, most foreign law firms in China have employed Chinese legal practitioners as professional staff.[73] As required by Chinese law, these employees must suspend their practising certificates and must not provide legal services during their employment with the FROs. However, FROs have often used the local professional staff as 'Chinese legal consultants' to provide legal services to clients; and due to various considerations and difficulties in enforcement, the Chinese authorities have given some flexibility to such practice.[74] Finally, to avoid hiring Chinese lawyers as employees, an alternative practice has been for foreign law firms to engage a Chinese law firm to provide services in Chinese law via matter-based or long-term Entrustment.[75] Given the existing practice above, the ChAFTA commitment on the exchange of lawyers does not seem

[72] 'Swiss Verein', a formal legal structure recognised under Swiss law, is akin to a voluntary association and has been frequently used in mergers between multinational law firms in the past decade. A more comprehensive introduction of Swiss Verein can be found at: en.wikipedia.org/wiki/Swiss_association.

[73] See Godwin (n 21) 143.

[74] ibid 143–47.

[75] ibid 143–44; see also, Stern and Li (n 3) 17–18.

to create any new market opportunities for Australian law firms. Rather, it is better seen as gradual recognition of the existing practice. More significantly, this form of cooperation was also introduced in the SHFTZ immediately after the ChAFTA negotiations were concluded. Therefore, the market access ChAFTA granted to Australian law firms does not extend beyond what other foreign law firms would also enjoy within the SHFTZ.

In short, China's major commitments on legal services under ChAFTA may turn out to be of little practical importance and commercial benefit. What Australian law firms are allowed to do under the commitments is largely similar to the existing practice in the market and has been granted to all foreign law firms. Consequently, Australian law firms will continue to compete with other foreign law firms under the same market conditions. The regulatory barriers erected by the Chinese laws will continue to constrain the ability of Australian law firms to expand businesses and market share and increase profitability.

Despite the above, the impacts of ChAFTA on the practice of Australian law firms in the Chinese market are not yet discernible as ChAFTA has not been in operation very long. At the time of writing, there have been no 'commercial associations' formed between Australian and Chinese law firms. However, it is observed that in the future Australian law firms may enter the Chinese market through such associations as it would be the most effective way to compete in the market. This observation finds support in the practice of other foreign law firms after the launch of the pilot programmes in the SHFTZ. For example, Baker & McKenzie entered into a formal association with FenXun Partners in April 2015, the very first such association in the SHFTZ.[76] This was followed by an association established by international firm Holman Fenwick Willan and Shanghai-based Wintell & Co in April 2016.[77] It is therefore reasonable to predict that Australian law firms may soon take similar steps to secure first-mover advantages for the purpose of either entering the Chinese market or strengthening their existing presence in the market through cooperation or a closer cooperation with Chinese law firms.

VI. CONCLUSION

ChAFTA is undoubtedly a landmark achievement in the development of the China–Australia economic relationship. While it is still too early to assess

[76] SJ Li, 'Bakers First Intl Law Firm in Shanghai FTZ "Joint Operation"' *Asian Legal Business* (16 April 2015), www.legalbusinessonline.com/news/bakers-first-intl-law-firm-shanghai-ftz-%E2%80%98joint-operation%E2%80%99/68578.

[77] SJ Li, 'HFW in Shanghai FTZ Tie-up with Wintell & Co' *Asian Legal Business* (6 April 2016), www.legalbusinessonline.com/news/hfw-shanghai-ftz-tie-wintell-co/72023.

the actual degrees of liberalisation and benefits to businesses in specific areas of trade, in general ChAFTA is expected to have the effect of promoting trade and investment and of opening up new prospects of economic cooperation between the two countries. As far as legal services are concerned, the level of liberalisation under China's ChAFTA commitments is apparently overstated. ChAFTA does not provide Australian legal services providers any competitive advantage over other foreign legal services providers. Australian law firms will continue to compete with other foreign law firms in the same regulatory environment in which major restrictions on all foreign legal services providers will continue to apply. However, as ChAFTA liberalises many other areas of trade and investment, it has the potential to create massive opportunities for Australian law firms to grow their businesses in cross-border transactions between the two countries. Furthermore, as with other FTAs ChAFTA creates intangible benefits for businesses in both countries including Australian law firms by bolstering incentives and confidence in doing business in the markets of the trading partners. Finally, while China has been cautious in its approach to the liberalisation of legal services, it has taken steps to unilaterally open up this sector via the free trade zones. This unilateral liberalisation demonstrates China's willingness to allow more market access to foreign legal services providers and is in alignment with China's policy goals to strengthen the competitiveness and global outlook of domestic law firms. As China creates and extends the liberalisation applied in SHFTZ to more FTZs, it is likely that ChAFTA will also be expanded to these FTZs during the reviews scheduled to commence in 2017. Nevertheless, any further liberalisation of this kind is unlikely to lead to significant market-opening in a short period of time, and is likely to be made available to all foreign legal services providers across the board.

9

Trade in Education Services under ChAFTA: What does it Mean for Australia?†

EVA CHYE

I. OVERVIEW

THE CHINA–AUSTRALIA FREE Trade Agreement (ChAFTA) entered into force promising 'significant opportunities for Australia in China'.[1] This chapter examines how this free trade agreement (FTA) affects trade in education services,[2] Australia's largest service export.

According to the Organisation for Economic Co-operation and Development's (OECD's) trade restrictive index, China has one of the world's highest service barriers.[3] This makes the inclusion of education services under ChAFTA particularly momentous. Trade in education services contributed AUD$21.8 billion to the economy in 2016, after iron ore and coal exports.[4] Globally, it puts Australia at the forefront of international education, behind only the United States (US) and the United Kingdom (UK). Given the significance of this sector and the fact that China is by far Australia's largest

† This chapter was written as part of a Masters in International Commercial Law degree at UWA and drew upon 16 years of managerial experience at the university overseeing collaboration with Chinese government and higher education institutions. The present chapter and some of its topics were previously presented at the 2016 Sino–Australia Law Deans Conference and 2016 Australian International Education Conference.

[1] ChAFTA was signed in Canberra on 17 June 2015 by Australian Minister for Trade and Investment Andrew Robb and Chinese Commerce Minister Gao Hucheng. It entered into force on 20 December after the completion of domestic legal and parliamentary processes in China and Australia. Department of Foreign Affairs and Trade (DFAT), 'China–Australia Free Trade Agreement' (20 December 2015), dfat.gov.au/trade/agreements/chafta/Pages/australia-china-fta.aspx.

[2] Ch 8 of ChAFTA covers Trade in Services including education services.

[3] Sean Miner, 'At Long Last, A China–Australia FTA' (*Peterson Institute for International Economics*, 5 December 2014), piie.com/blogs/china-economic-watch/long-last-china-australia-fta.

[4] Universities Australia, 'Australia's Education Exports at Record High' (3 February 2017), link.universitiesaustralia.edu.au/m/1/67805778/02-b17033-83cd9700e12447e6b09b68ae8789a01e/1/393/e8ddd382-2c77-40d2-b906-95aa5b9226d7.

importer of education services,[5] analysing the regulatory framework and impact on Australia's trade in education services has practical relevance.

Whilst early attention has been given to aspects of ChAFTA such as investment and trade in merchandise, there has been much less analysis in relation to trade in services and almost none regarding education services. This chapter will contribute to filling a gap in current literature. It will examine how ChAFTA addresses the key areas of liberalisation—transparency, harmonisation and market access—and answer these questions:

— How does ChAFTA improve market access to trade in education services?
— What is good for Australia, what is not, and what is unclear under ChAFTA?
— What else affects Australia's trade in education services with China?

Given the downturn in the resource industry and the relative strength of education services, might ChAFTA buoy up Australia's economy? Will ChAFTA propel Australia into the world's largest provider of international education, given that neither the US nor the UK has an FTA with China? The following section will analyse these issues.

II. HOW DOES CHAFTA IMPROVE MARKET ACCESS TO EDUCATION SERVICES?

Trade in education services under ChAFTA is modelled on the World Trade Organization's General Agreement on Trade in Services (GATS). First, ChAFTA has adopted GATS 'Most-Favoured-Nation' (MFN) principle.[6] This requires Australia and China to afford each other the same benefits granted to other trading partners, with the exception of Hong Kong, Macau and Taiwan under the 'one country, two systems' policy. MFN is distinct from 'national treatment', which would bind Australia and China to affording each other the same privileges it provides its own citizens and institutions, such as public funding for education and research. This is something neither country is prepared to do. After all, education is intertwined with a society's values and culture, and trade in education services sits on the cusp of free market and government intervention. As Altbach pointed out

[5] China accounts for 26.7% of total market share, far exceeding India, the second largest market at 9.0%. Department of Education and Training, 'Education Brief—China' (December 2015), internationaleducation.gov.au/International-network/china/publications/Documents/Country%20Brief%20China%20December%202015.pdf.

[6] Free Trade Agreement between the Government of Australia and the Government of the People's Republic of China (ChAFTA) (signed 17 June 2015, entered into force 20 December 2015) [2015] ATS 15, Art 8.7 (Most-Favoured-Nation Treatment).

metaphorically, it is 'simply not on the same level as free trade in automobiles or equal access to markets for soybeans'.[7]

Like GATS, ChAFTA categorises education services into four modes of supply based on the location of the supplier and consumer:

1. Mode 1: Cross-border supply—The service, rather than the supplier (institution) or consumer (student), crosses borders. Examples include the provision of e-learning and distance education. Typical barriers include restrictions on the importation or electronic transmission of learning materials, and non-recognition of studies through distance mode.

   China's Schedule of Specific Commitments on Services provides 'unbound'[8] access to Mode 1.[9] In comparison, the Trans-Pacific Partnership (TPP) Agreement, should it go ahead, gives Australian universities guaranteed access to deliver online education services to most TPP markets.[10] It is a shame that ChAFTA has stopped short of providing similar market entry for Australia. One reason could be online learning is at the early stages of development in China. Beijing does not yet have the regulations for cross-border supply and may prefer to take a cautious approach by leaving Mode 1 unbound.
2. Mode 2: Consumption abroad—Overseas fee-paying students travelling between China and Australia form the most common mode of supply. This market mode is already open with few barriers.

   ChAFTA states explicitly that there will be no limitation on market access under Mode 2.[11] Furthermore, Australia's Simplified Student Visa Framework, which came into effect in July 2016, makes it easier for Australian providers to recruit international students.
3. Mode 3: Commercial presence—This refers to education services supplied through a branch campus or joint venture in another country. Barriers to Mode 3 are typically investment barriers such as financing rules, repatriation of profits, and the host country's insistence on a local partner.[12]

[7] PG Altbach, 'Knowledge and Education as International Commodities: The Collapse of the Common Good' (2015) 28 *International Higher Education* 2, 2.

[8] The right to maintain existing limitations or make them more severe.

[9] Schedule of Non-Conforming Measures (Annex III) referred to in Ch 8 (Trade in Services) and Ch 9 (Investment). ChAFTA (n 6) Annex III.

[10] DFAT, 'Trans-Pacific Partnership' (12 October 2015), dfat.gov.au/trade/agreements/tpp/outcomes-documents/Pages/outcomes-education-services.aspx.

[11] Other than Australia, TPP Members include Brunei, Canada, Chile, Japan, Malaysia, Mexico, Peru, New Zealand, Singapore, the United States and Vietnam. ibid.

[12] Pt 2: Schedule of Specific Commitments on Services, Schedule of the People's Republic of China. ChAFTA (n 6) Annex III.

Under ChAFTA, a branch campus or joint school may be established with majority foreign ownership.[13] This is a significant improvement on market access as China's *Regulations for Sino-Foreign Cooperation in Joint Schools 2003* requires at least 50 per cent Chinese control in a joint venture.[14] This should lead to greater interests by Australian institutions interested in establishing a presence in China.

4. Mode 4: Presence of natural persons—This is when natural persons such as academics and researchers move temporarily to another country to provide their service. Systematic barriers typically include visa and entry restrictions, and nationality or residency requirements.

   Under ChAFTA, China will grant stays of up to 180 days for business visitors, and up to three years for intra-corporate transferees to Australian citizens and permanent residents. Moreover, China will guarantee equivalent stays for spouses and dependants of intra-corporate transferees, a first in its history of any FTA.[15] As collaborative activities between Australian and Chinese universities are on the rise, this measure makes it easier for Australian academics and researchers to spend some time in China teaching into joint programmes or conducting joint research.

Having looked at the systematic barriers to trade in education services, this section examines the seven specific measures ChAFTA is implementing to open market access:[16]

1. Recognition of Australia's Commonwealth Register of Institutions and Courses for Overseas Students (CRICOS): The Ministry of Education (MOE) in China will add 77 CRICOS-registered higher education institutions to its Study Abroad website within a year of entry into force.[17] Since 88 per cent of Chinese students who plan to go overseas check the website and Chinese employers use it as a measure of quality and to prevent against fraudulent degrees,[18] being listed opens up the market

[13] ibid.

[14] Art 21: 'A Chinese–foreign cooperatively-run school with the legal person status shall set up a board of trustees or a board of directors, and a Chinese-foreign cooperatively-run school without the legal person status shall set up a joint managerial committee. Chinese members on the board of trustees, the board of directors or of the joint managerial committee shall not be less than half of the total number'. 《中华人民共和国中外合作办学条例》 [Regulations of the People's Republic of China on Chinese-Foreign Corporation in Running Schools] (People's Republic of China) Executive Meeting of the State Council, Decree No 372, 1 March 2003, Art 21.

[15] DFAT, 'Factsheet: Movement of Natural Persons' (5 January 2016), www.google.com.au/#q=chafta+%2B+working+holiday+visa&gws_rd=cr.

[16] ibid.

[17] This increases the number of Australian institutions on the Study Abroad website from 105 to 182.

[18] Department of Education and Training, 'China–Australia Free Trade Agreement', internationaleducation.gov.au/News/Latest-News/Pages/Article-China-Australia-Free-Trade-Agreement%202015.aspx.

for Australian institutions. It gives them credibility and assures Chinese students and employers that the institutions they are dealing with have been endorsed by both Australian and Chinese authorities.

2. Mutual recognition of higher education qualifications:[19] Accreditation and recognition of studies are de facto obstacles to trade in education services. ChAFTA has taken a step in the right direction by recognising a need to address these issues. Unfortunately, it stopped short of offering details, just a lofty goal. Its adoption of GATS 'measures relating to qualification requirements and procedures … not more burdensome than necessary to ensure the quality of the service'[20] provides little clarification. In fact, the GATS only goes as far as to invite members to collaborate with professional accrediting bodies.[21]

   A comparison of China's FTAs with other countries shows that it has taken the issue of quality assurance one step further with New Zealand. Out of the 14 FTAs it has signed to date, New Zealand is the only country with which it has agreed to evaluate quality assurance standards, including that for distance education.[22] This may be because New Zealand was the first country to conclude an FTA with China,[23] and the New Zealand institutions recognised by China's MOE include a wholly distance education provider.[24] After the China–New Zealand FTA was signed in 2008, China became more involved with international assessment standards,[25] and has not entered into similar provisions in any of its FTAs.

3. Exploring ways Australian education providers can increase marketing and recruitment opportunities in China: Both countries have agreed to hold discussions which include processing of applications, issuing of

[19] Concerning qualifications recognition cooperation, ChAFTA 'encourage[s], where possible, the relevant bodies in their respective territories responsible for the issuance and recognition of professional and vocational qualifications to strengthen cooperation and to explore possibilities for mutual recognition of respective professional and vocational qualifications'. ChAFTA (n 6) Art 8.15.

[20] ibid Art 8.13(4)(b).

[21] General Agreement on Trade in Services (GATS) (15 April 1994) LT/UR/A-1B/S/1 Art VII.5, docsonline.wto.org.

[22] 中华人民共和国商务部[Ministry of Commerce of the People's Republic of China (MOFCOM)], '中国自由贸易区服务网' ['China Free Trade Zone Service Network'], fta.mofcom.gov.cn.

[23] New Zealand Ministry of Foreign Affairs and Trade, 'China', www.mfat.govt.nz/en/countries-and-regions/north-asia/china.

[24] New Zealand Ministry of Foreign Affairs and Trade, 'New Zealand–China Free Trade Agreement and Associated Instruments: National Interest Analysis', webcache.googleusercontent.com/search?q=cache:XzlP6uKQS3YJ, www.mfat.govt.nz/assets/_securedfiles/FTAs-agreements-in-force/China-FTA/National-interest-analysis.pdf+&cd=1&hl=en&ct=clnk&gl=au&client=firefox-b-ab.

[25] Such as the Asia-Pacific Regional Convention on the Recognition of Qualifications in Higher Education mentioned earlier.

offers, and provision of visa assistance.[26] However, the ensuing details have not been released at the time of writing.

4. ChAFTA's Side Letter on Education stated that China will welcome more Australian students through Australian government funded programmes such as the New Colombo Plan (NCP), a Department of Foreign Affairs and Trade (DFAT) initiative which encourages Australian undergraduates to study and take up internships in the Indo-Pacific region.[27] To this end, the MOE pledged to create better conditions, including internship opportunities, to support the NCP.[28] The past year has seen more businesses such as the National Australia Bank, Huawei, and Dalia Neusoft partnering with Australian universities to provide work-based experiences in China. More than 1,200 students from 33 universities will go to China under the NCP in 2017.[29]
5. Increasing student and teacher exchanges: This includes providing Australians with the language and cultural skills to engage more meaningfully with China. The Chinese government already funds 14 Confucius Institutes and five Confucius Classrooms in Australia to promote Chinese language teaching and cultural training.[30] This may not be enough. As bilateral links grow, as they are expected to under ChAFTA, it is important to have citizens who understand each other. To this end, Australia is allocating a combined total of 1,800 visas per year, valid for stays of up to four years, to four specific occupations: Chinese language teachers, martial arts coaches, traditional Chinese medicine practitioners, and Chinese chefs.[31] Whilst some of these professions are not directly linked to education services, their presence strengthens Australia's engagement with Chinese language and cultures.
6. Ensuring the legal rights and interests of students from the other country in accordance with their respective laws and regulations:[32] This measure helps to protect the consumers (students). For instance, Australia's Education Services for Overseas Students framework offers financial protection to Chinese students in the event they are not delivered what was promised to them by their education institution.[33]

[26] ChAFTA Side Letter on Education (17 June 2015), dfat.gov.au/trade/agreements/chafta/.../chafta-side-letter-on-education.docx.

[27] ibid.

[28] 中华人民共和国商务部 [MOFCOM], '中澳自贸协定解读' ['Commentary on the China Australia Free Trade Agreement'] (18 June 2015), www.mofcom.gov.cn/article/zhengcejd/bq/201506/20150601019585.shtml.

[29] Department of Education and Training, 'China—Most Popular Destination for 2017 New Colombo Plan Mobility Grants' (October 2016), us3.campaign-archive2.com/?u=d424590d5b561cb5f29b4240e&id=ec3aec6134&e=b55064b108.

[30] Confucius Institute Headquarters (Hanban), english.hanban.org.

[31] DFAT, 'Fact Sheet: Trade in Services' (12 December 2016), dfat.gov.au/trade/agreements/chafta/fact-sheets/Pages/fact-sheet-movement-of-natural-persons.aspx.

[32] ChAFTA Side Letter on Education (n 26).

[33] Education Services for Overseas Students Act 2000, pt 5 (Tuition Protection Service).

7. Establishing Chinese international schools in Australia:[34] This market liberalisation measure aligns with China's *National Development Plan 2010–2020* and *Plans for a New Era* which encourages Chinese education institutions to set up a presence overseas,[35] taking into account strategies that align with private investment. This is because under Chinese laws, public education funding cannot be used overseas so an institution can only invest abroad through private funds.[36] The aforementioned visas for up to 1,800 Mandarin language tutors, Chinese medicine practitioners and other professions with 'Chinese characteristics' should go some way in assisting with the human capital required for international schools. At the same time, it should be noted that rules governing international schools in Australia come under the jurisdiction of state and territory governments. Chinese providers planning to set up a presence in Australia will need to investigate these in more detail.

Last but not least, both countries have agreed to a future work programme to review liberalisation measures and further improve market access two years after ChAFTA's entry into force.[37]

Even though Australia's National Interest Analysis 2015 stated in no uncertain terms that ChAFTA 'delivers China's best ever service commitments, including the provision of new or significantly improved access not included in any of China's previous Free Trade Agreements',[38] it is important for Australian institutions to be better informed of the practicalities of ChAFTA and understand how it can be applied for a competitive edge.

III. WHAT IS GOOD FOR AUSTRALIA, WHAT IS NOT, AND WHAT IS UNCLEAR?

Ultimately, an FTA's effectiveness depends upon what the existing barriers are and the potential for market penetration. Since ChAFTA aims to 'ensure a predictable, transparent and consistent commercial framework for

[34] ChAFTA Side Letter on Education (n 26).

[35] 'High-quality Chinese educational institutions shall be encouraged to run branches overseas, undertake international exchanges, cooperation and education service extensively'. 国务院[State Council of the People's Republic of China], '国家中长期教育改革和发展规划纲要' (2010–2020年) ['National Plan for Medium and Long Term Education Reform and Development (2010–2020)'] (National Development Plan 2010–20) (1 March 2010), www.china.com.cn/policy/txt/2010-03/01/content_19492625_3.htm, s 50.

[36] ibid.

[37] China Scholarship Council, 'Plan for Study in China' (25 March 2012), www.csc.edu.cn/studyinchina/newsdetailen.aspx?cid=192&id=1348.

[38] Other than its agreements with Hong Kong and Macau. DFAT, 'National Interest Analysis 2015 ATNIA 7 with Attachments: Free Trade Agreement between the Government of Australia and the Government of the People's Republic of China' (15 June 2015).

business operations', to protect 'Australia's competitive position into the future', and to provide 'new or significantly improved market access',[39] this section will assess ChAFTA's measures for transparency, harmonisation and market access.

A. Transparency

As mentioned earlier, the inclusion of all CRICOS-registered education providers on the MOE's website enables more Australian institutions to gain recognition in China. During this process, Australia is obliged to provide details of its regulatory decisions, including the Tertiary Education Quality and Standards Agency's (TEQSA) rules around risk assessments, re-registration, and accreditation. This is both about transparency and China's desire to learn from Australia's experiences in these areas.[40]

Australian universities often attribute price sensitivity to tuition fees and a high Australian dollar as barriers to attracting international students. In fact, an OECD study shows that students do not mind paying more 'as long as the quality of education provided and its likely returns make the investment worthwhile'.[41]

Since a federal government review in 2008 showed that a superior education system is the key to sustainable trade in education services, the government has taken on the task of assessing and auditing a range of performances from student services to financial management.[42]

In contrast, China's quality control for international education, primarily transnational education (TNE)[43] programmes in China, is based on

[39] DFAT, 'China–Australia Free Trade Agreement Outcomes at a Glance' (2015) i, dfat.gov.au/trade/agreements/chafta/fact-sheets/Pages/key-outcomes.aspx.

[40] 李晓述[X Li], '关于完善中外合作办学法律体系的思考' ['Thoughts on the Improvement of the Legal System of the Sino-Foreign Cooperative Education'] (2010) 4 河北法学 *Journal of Hebei Legal Studies* 24.

[41] Organisation for Economic Co-operation and Development (OECD), 'Education at Glance 2008: OECD Indicators' (2008), www.oecd.org/education/skills-beyond-school/41284038.pdf, 357.

[42] 吴婷 、刘利[T Wu and L Liu], '探索多元合作方式开展更有效的教育一访澳大利亚驻上海总领事馆商务处教育领事徐佩仪' ['Exploring Multifaceted Cooperation and Developing More Effective Education—An Interview with Eliza Chui, Australian Education Counsellor Based in Shanghai'] (2015) (12)世界教育信息 *Journal of World Education* 52, 55.

[43] TNE is defined as: '[a]ll types of higher education study programmes, or sets of courses of study, or educational services(including those of distance education) in which the learners are located in a country different from the one where the awarding institution is based. Such programmes may belong to the education system of a State different from the State in which it operates, or may operate independently of any national education system'. Council of Europe and UNESCO, 'Code of Good Practice in the Provision of Transnational Education' (2014), www.coe.int/t/dg4/highereducation/recognition/Code%20of%20good%20practice_EN.asp.

self-evaluation with random inspections by the relevant authorities.[44] This may be due to the disjointed regulatory structure around international education. To address this issue, the MOE has set up a website called 'Supervisory and Information Platform for Sino-Foreign Education Collaboration'.[45] This initiative is in the early stages of development and the plan is for it to evolve into an independent and comprehensive source of information covering all aspects of TNE administration, from approval through to quality assessment and certification.[46]

Meanwhile, key issues such as financing and repatriation of profits under Mode 3 (commercial presence) have not been clarified. For instance, even though China now allows private investment in higher education and ChAFTA enables Australian providers to have majority ownership, Article 25 of its Education Act prevents the establishment of educational institutions for profit.[47] This goes against commercial interests and may hamper Australia's investment in education services in China.

As Ian Gow, founding Provost of the first MOE-approved Sino-foreign university in China pointed out,[48] 'China frequently reinterprets what it means'.[49] Beijing allows investors to recover a 'reasonable return'[50] on investment when profits are viewed in light of costs recovery.[51] However, when this option is chosen, institutions are unable to qualify for government

[44] 童彦成、陈立波、林爱华 [Y Tong, L Chen and A Lin, '协同:中澳合作办学项目政府质量审计与社会认证评价' ['Synergy Between the Governmental Quality Audit and the Societal Quality Authentication in the Sino-Australia Cooperation Educational Programs'] (2016) 2 价值工程 *Value Engineering* 244, 244.

[45] '中外合作办学监管工作信息平台' ['Official Database on Sino-Foreign Joint Schools and Education'], www.crs.jsj.edu.cn/index.php/default/index (in Chinese).

[46] Ka Ho Mok and Xiaozhu Xu, 'When China Opens to the World: A Study of Transnational Higher Education in Zhejiang, China' (2008) 9(4) *Asia Pacific Education Review* 393, 404–05.

[47] 'No school may charge any fee in violation of the provisions of the State or seek profits by selling goods or services to students or by doing so in any disguised form'. 中华人民共和国教育法[Education Law of the People's Republic of China (People's Republic of China) National People's Congress, Order No 45, Art 25.

[48] Professor Ian Gow OBE is Pro Vice-Chancellor of the University of the West of England. He was the founding Provost of the University of Nottingham Ningbo, China between 2004 and 2006.

[49] 李欣亮等[X Li et al], '国际法视野下我国高等教育服务贸易存在的问题及对策' ['The Problems with and Remedies for China's Trade in Higher Education Services from an International Law Perspective'] (2010) 10 科技信息基础理论研讨 *Science & Technology Information* 49, 49.

[50] In Chinese: 合理回报.

[51] For calculation of 'reasonable return' and withdrawal procedures, refer to the Law on the Promotion of Non-Public Schools of the People's Republic of China. 《中华人民共和国民办教育促进法》[Law on the Promotion of Non-Public Schools of the People's Republic of China] (Private Education Promotion Law) (People's Republic of China) Standing Committee of the National People's Congress, Order No 80, 28 December 2002, Arts 37–47.

assistance such as tax exemptions.[52] Some private providers have sought to work around this barrier by structuring the venture whereby partners to the joint venture provide a service contract to the institution in return for fees for service.

B. Harmonisation

As countries with different constitutions, different positions on trade and education and at different stages of economic development, the legal frameworks and policies in Australia and China need to respond to each other and to ChAFTA in different ways. These differences create de facto barriers. However, there are some common grounds.

A substantial amount of work has already been done between some Australian and Chinese universities to track, cross-credit and recognise academic qualifications. According to the MOE's 'Supervisory and Information Platform for Sino-Foreign Education Collaboration' website, 155 Sino-Australia TNE programmes have already been approved.[53] This means the groundwork and hard work have already begun between key stakeholders.

In addition, both countries have adopted most of the United Nations Educational Scientific and Cultural Organization (UNESCO)'s guidelines on national policies for TNE programmes and certification,[54] and are signatories to the Asia-Pacific Regional Convention on the Recognition of Qualifications in Higher Education. These initiatives seek to ensure that tertiary education studies are recognised as widely as possible regardless of the economic backgrounds and educational diversity.

A harmonised framework for mutual recognition of professional qualifications is a possibility. For example, the Singapore–Australia FTA saw the number of Australian law degrees recognised in Singapore double from four to nine.[55] More recently, Singapore and Australia agreed to work on mutual recognition of professional engineers and accountants.[56] These are positive examples for ChAFTA. If more attention can be paid to the protocol

[52] ibid Art 38.

[53] Official Database on Sino-Foreign Joint Schools and Education (n 45).

[54] Wu and Liu (n 42) 54.

[55] Recognition is limited to individuals who are Singapore citizens or permanent residents, and additional qualifications in Singapore law are required. C Fink and M Molinuevo, 'East Asian Free Trade Agreements in Services: Key Architectural Elements' (2008) 11(2) *Journal of International Economic Law* 263, 303–05.

[56] The University of Western Australia's Juris Doctor degree was also recognised in Singapore in May 2016, in addition to the eight cited on DFAT's website. DFAT, 'Singapore–Australia FTA', dfat.gov.au/trade/agreements/safta/pages/singapore-australia-fta.aspx.

for quality assurance and professional recognition, there will no doubt be greater workforce mobility, business confidence and stronger ties between both countries.

C. Market Access

The market is already open with few barriers in the way of students travelling between China and Australia. Unfortunately, an unbound Mode 1 (cross-border supply) represents missed opportunities. A number of Australian universities are already delivering e-learning, or Massive Open Online Courses (MOOCs). For example, the University of Tasmania's MOOCs on 'Understanding Dementia' registered 9,300 students from more than 60 countries when it was launched; and Deakin University's MOOCs can be credited towards a degree.[57] These are lucrative markets for prospective students. A liberalised market access would have been tremendously helpful to Australian providers.

On the whole, ChAFTA provides some improved market access for trade in education services. For a start, the recognition of all CRICOS-registered institutions helps Australian providers to increase both profile and market share in China. Making long-term business visits more accessible also helps academics and researchers to engage in more collaborative activities. ChAFTA's plans to mutually recognise higher education qualifications is also a step in the right direction. The fact that the FTA encourages more student and teacher exchanges will also go a long way towards shared understanding. Last but not least, the fact that an Australian branch campus or joint school may be established with majority foreign ownership, and Chinese international schools are allowed to set up in Australia, serves to encourage trade in education services. Nevertheless, a lot more work is required to 'ensure a predictable, transparent and consistent commercial framework', and to protect 'Australia's competitive position into the future'.[58]

IV. WHAT ELSE AFFECTS AUSTRALIA'S TRADE IN INTERNATIONAL EDUCATION WITH CHINA?

There is more than meets the eye. Having examined the effects of ChAFTA, this section looks at other factors impacting trade in education services.

[57] M Gardner and J Wells, 'Regulation and Markets' (2007) 49 (1) and (2) *Australian Universities Review* 22 23.

[58] New Zealand Ministry of Foreign Affairs and Trade, 'China' (n 23).

The Ministry of Commerce stated in no uncertain terms that '[t]he Chinese Government deems [FTAs] as a new platform to further opening up to the outside and speeding up domestic reforms'.[59] ChAFTA is only a means to an end for China. Its national agenda contains real, major implications for Australia.

In order to delve deeper into the drivers and factors affecting market penetration, trade in education services can be broken down into the following market movements:

— Chinese students remaining in China
— International students going to China
— Chinese universities going overseas

A. Chinese Students Remaining in China

In 2015, 523,700 Chinese students went overseas, an increase of 13.9 per cent from the previous year.[60] Currently, China sends more students overseas than it receives. However, it is not so much a loss of income or trade deficit that concerns China. Chinese students remaining overseas represent a loss of human capital and something needs to be done to stop the brain drain.[61] China also needs to up-skill its workforce and to do so on a large scale. TNE is the ideal platform.

From the government's perspective, TNE enables Chinese universities to import academic knowledge and management know-how by collaborating with 'renowned schools, education institutions, research institutions and companies', 'world-class experts and scholars', 'high-level professionals and academic teams'.[62] It also helps to address the country's shortage of professional resources.

From the students' perspective, TNE enables them to receive a coveted foreign degree without having to leave China. Moreover, the tuition fees are only a fraction of what it would cost overseas even before travel and living expenses are taken into consideration.

In 2015, 550,000 students enrolled in TNE programmes. Of these, 450,000 (1.4 per cent of all university students in China) were in a higher

[59] MOFCOM, 'China FTA Network' (15 January 2016), fta.mofcom.gov.cn/english.
[60] 新华网 [Xinhua Net], '教育部发布2015年度中国出国留学人员情况' ['Ministry of Education Releases Overview of Chinese Students Abroad in 2015'] (18 March 2016), www.mnw.cn/news/china/1128221.html.
[61] R Choudaha, 'How China Plans to Become a Global Force in Higher Education" *The Guardian* (13 October 2015), www.theguardian.com/higher-education-network/2015/oct/12/how-china-plans-to-become-a-global-force-in-higher-education.
[62] National Development Plan 2010–20 (n 35) Art 49.

degree programme. Employment prospects for TNE graduates have proven positive: 88.32 percent secured a job immediately after graduation. Of the remaining, 95.61 per cent were employed within six months.[63]

All these reasons indicate that TNE will continue to grow in China. However, its growth will be calibrated for quality control. For a start, the MOE has slowed down the approvals for TNE in order to assess admission standards, university performance and funding expenditure. For example, there is now a mandate for providers to make their enrolment plans known to the MOE prior to recruitment. Once this is approved, they are unable to lower entry scores to meet recruitment targets should enrolments fall short of expectations.

B. International Students Going to China

Not only has TNE led to Chinese students remaining in-country, it has even brought foreign students into China. The English language teaching environment of TNE programmes and much lower tuition fees have motivated international students to go to China.[64]

When students take into consideration the cost of obtaining a degree overseas both in terms of tuition fees and living expenses, China is much cheaper than the US, the UK, Australia and even when compared with Asian suppliers such as Singapore and Malaysia. China even offers international students the added benefit of learning Mandarin (in addition to academic courses in English), and immersion in one of the world's most influential trading nations.

Meanwhile, China's higher education sector is on a rising trajectory in world rankings. According to the *2016 QS World University Rankings*, four Chinese universities were in the top 100.[65] In a further effort to climb up the ladder, Beijing launched 'World Class 2.0',[66] an initiative aimed specifically at propelling six Chinese universities into the world's top 100 by 2020, and

[63] 中国教育国际交流协会 [China Education Association for International Exchange], '中外合作办学和境外办学的最新发展及政策导向' ['Latest Development and Policies in Transnational Education Between China and Other Countries'] (24 February 2016), mp.weixin.qq.com/s?__biz=MzAwMzA3MjQwMw==&mid=402122585&idx=1&sn=32f3bd14363f8af5cb448aa5483554c2&scene=5&srcid=0224yn33imt9TH5txcqmliPR#rd.

[64] '中外合作大学办学成果显著愈发受考生青睐' ['Sino-Foreign Universities Increasingly Favoured by Students'] (15 June 2016), education.news.cn/2016-06/15/c_129064950.htm?from=timeline&isappinstalled=0.

[65] Tsinghua University ranked at 24th, Peking University at 39th, Fudan University at 43rd, and Shanghai Jiao Tong University at 61st.

[66] Introduced at the end of 2015 and formally known as the Notification by the State Council on Promotion of World-Class Universities and Academic Disciplines.

some into the top 15 by 2030. It also wants to see China's higher education system recognised overall as one of the world's best by 2050.[67]

Trade in education services is not just about economic growth for China. It is the currency to soft power and public diplomacy. As President Xi Jinping pointed out, international education is the 'people-to-people bond that provides public support'.[68]

To this end, the *Plan for Study in China* was put in place in 2010 to attract 500,000 international students by 2020, 30 per cent of which should be full degree students.[69] The *Plan* offers scholarships to developing countries and introduces courses that maximise China's capabilities such as Chinese Law and traditional Chinese medicine. By 2015, almost 400,000 students from 203 countries had studied in China, 46 per cent of whom were enrolled in a degree programme.[70]

In an effort to attract even more international students and foreign talents to China, the government piloted changes to its visa framework. Since 2016, Shanghai and Beijing, followed by Guangdong, have allowed international students to work part-time, take on internships and even own their own businesses in designated free trade and innovation zones.[71] These are significant policy changes. Previously, international students were not allowed to take on part-time jobs, and companies were forbidden from hiring foreigners with less than two years of relevant work experience. It is now even possible for holders of Personnel Affairs Resident Permits to apply for permanent residency if they work in specified sectors of priority.[72]

By engaging actively in education services, China is cultivating alumni and allies who possess an understanding of Chinese cultures and values.

C. Chinese Universities Going Overseas

China's ambition to host international students extends beyond the boundaries of its shores. As far back as 2004, the first Confucius Institute was

[67] Ministry of Education of the People's Republic of China, '关于做好新时期教育对外开放工作的若干意见' ['Views on Opening Up International Education in a New Era'] (30 April 2016).

[68] X Zhang, X Hu and Z Qu, *China's Education Development and Policy, 1978–2008* (Leiden, Koninklijke Brill NV, 2011) 42.

[69] China Scholarships Council, 'Plan for Study in China' (25 March 2012), www.csc.edu.cn/studyinchina/newsdetailen.aspx?cid=192&id=1348.

[70] L Career, 'China Opens the Labor Market to International Students' (21 March 2016), www.mandarin.cafe/blog/china-opens-the-labor-market-to-international-students.

[71] 'China Focus: China to Boost import, Export in Ambitious Education Plan' *Xihua News* (29 April 2016), news.xinhuanet.com/english/2016-04/29/c_135323984.htm.

[72] R Qian, 'Beijing Opens Paths for International Students' *China Daily* (13 January 2016), www.ecns.cn/2016/01-13/195670.shtml.

established in South Korea. Since then, more than 500 Confucius Institutes and 1,000 Confucius Classrooms have been established around the world.[73]

The MOE is encouraging Chinese institutions to establish a presence overseas through policy reforms and funding initiatives. In 2015, it abolished the *2003 Interim Measures for the Administration of Universities and Colleges Engaged in Overseas Education*,[74] so that Chinese institutions can set up offshore programmes and campuses without MOE approval, as long as they maintain the same level of teaching quality and standard as China.[75]

For example, Global Innovation Exchange (GIX), a partnership between Tsinghua University and the University of Washington funded by Microsoft, will be launching a joint master's programme in technology innovation in Seattle in the 2017–18 academic year.[76] Meanwhile, Wenzhou University established a campus in Italy in November 2016,[77] and Global Business College of Australia (GBCA), a wholly owned Chinese higher education institution, received its first cohort of students in Melbourne in 2016.

Other than GBCA, another Chinese-owned provider, Top Education Institute, became the first private provider in Australia to teach a bachelor of laws programme accredited by the NSW Legal Practice Admissions Board.[78] It appears there is an emerging trend towards Chinese education providers setting up a commercial presence in Australia. Another example is an AUD$20 billion project in Victoria called Australian Education City which aims to provide pathways for 40,000 students from high school through to vocational training and higher education, half of whom will be international students, plus housing for 80,000 residents.[79]

It is a common view that an increase in the number of education providers in Australia will dilute the market and result in fewer students for existing institutions. However, the other side of the coin is that Chinese providers are better able to reach out to a wider pool of prospective students through

[73] Confucius Institute Headquarters (Hanban) (n 30).

[74] In Chinese: 《高等学校境外办学暂行管理办法2003》.

[75] Department of Education and Training, 'Chinese Universities Establishing Programs and Campuses in Foreign Countries' (September 2016), internationaleducation.gov.au/News/Latest-News/Pages/Chinese-universities-establishing.aspx.

[76] State Council of the People's Republic of China, 'China to Deliver Five-Year Plan on Education' (9 March 2016), english.gov.cn/news/top_news/2016/03/09/content_281475304305670.htm.

[77] Department of Education of Zhejiang Province, '对接"一带一路"教育行动计划，蔚蓝的地中海畔将出现浙江高校的分校' ['Zhejiang University Branch Campus Appears in the Mediterranean as One Belt One Road Education Plan Gets into Action'] (28 November 2016), mp.weixin.qq.com/s?__biz=MzAxMDAwMzU1Nw==&mid=2651174433&idx=2&sn=e7023da3152ce40623d4f9efa5124b04&chksm=80a7e32bb7d06a3d17cddc584b0a81cf68fe0d0a8394a80b1a699027feb160f473dc690acaa2&mpshare=1&scene=5&srcid=1128KKSHCsPZMBBlXz0YHjZn#rd.

[78] Top Education Institute, 'Program Overview Bachelor of Laws (LLB)' (2015), www.top.edu.au/school-of-law/program-overview.

[79] Australian Education City (australianeducationcity.com).

their networks and contacts. This strengthens the profile of Australia as a study destination, and depending on the business model of establishment, may well provide an additional source of student recruitment.

The international education landscape is changing. Both Australian education providers and Australian government need to be aware of the bigger picture and rethink strategies for trade in education services.

V. WHAT DOES IT ALL MEAN FOR AUSTRALIA?

So far, it has been shown that ChAFTA provides some improved market access for trade in education services, but a lot more work is needed to 'ensure a predictable, transparent and consistent commercial framework', and to protect 'Australia's competitive position into the future'.[80]

The Australian government admitted that it had to leave some things out of ChAFTA in order to move forward with the Agreement.[81] It is unclear what went on behind closed doors and what had to be left out. What is clear is that the final outcomes from China's point of view will be based on its best interests, rather than what suits an open market.

Frances Adamson, the immediate past Australian Ambassador to China who was involved in the conclusion of ChAFTA negotiations pointed out, 'don't mistake the market's more decisive role for a decline in the influence of the state, or its close involvement in setting economic policy'.[82]

An FTA can only do so much. China is going through a series of major education reforms and these have much more impact on Australia than ChAFTA alone. Beijing's agenda will not always be obvious. As Chinese participants at a recent TNE workshop explained, 'there's a degree of judgment being exercised by the ministry, and so there is a purpose to not having very explicit rules'.[83]

One way to understand the legal approach in China is to recognise that for a very long time, China has relied on 'executive orders',[84] rather than laws and regulations, to implement its policies. This is both a legacy of its society as well as a system designed to allow for flexibility. This feature is

[80] DFAT, 'China–Australia Free Trade Agreement' (n 1) i.

[81] G Hutchens, '10 Questions about the China–Australia Free Trade Agreement' (18 November 2014), www.smh.com.au/federal-politics/political-news/10-questions-about-the-chinaaustralia-free-trade-agreement-20141118-11p6b5.html.

[82] 岑建君[J Cen], '完善教育涉外法律法规 推进教育有序开放' ['The Improvement of International Education Regulations and Systematic Opening Up of Education'] (教育部 [Ministry of Education], 5 January 2015), www.moe.edu.cn/jyb_xwfb/moe_2082/s7866/s8444/201501/t20150105_182736.html.

[83] E Bothwell, 'UK Universities Want More "Transparency" from China on TNE Laws' *Times Higher Education*, (28 March 2016), www.timeshighereducation.com/news/uk-universities-want-more-transparency-from-china-on-transnational-education-tne-laws.

[84] In Chinese: 行政命令.

particularly useful when the economy is developing rapidly. It allows the government to balance its roles as market creator and lawmaker, although this also means Chinese laws lack the openness and transparency its Western counterparts are accustomed to.

It does not mean legal structures are unimportant. In fact, it is a first line of defence for anyone doing business with China and proof of compliance with the law is necessary in case of a dispute. ChAFTA has provided some regulatory assurance for Australia. The MOE also acknowledges that engaging in international education according to the letter of the law concerns China's 'international image'.[85] Section 20 of the *National Development Plan 2010–2020* also specifies improving legislations and administering enforcement as matters of priority.[86]

From Australia's point of view, international education is a AUD$21.8 billion market. Whilst there will be better market access under ChAFTA, there is also greater competition. Australia is just one of a number of countries Chinese students can choose from. The US and the UK are Australia's main competitors. In recent years, American universities ramped up their recruitment drives in China following an economic downturn and reduced funding from state governments. As a result, the number of students going to the US has almost doubled from 560,000 to 970,000 over the last decade.[87] In another move to attract more students, the US is issuing three-year work visas to Science, Technology, Engineering and Mathematics (STEM) graduates under an 'Optional Practical Training' (OPT) programme.[88] Graduates can even enter a visa lottery during OPT to win one of 65,000 permanent residency places.[89]

The UK is also highly sought after by Chinese students. At the British Council's UK–China Education Policy Week last year, both countries issued a Beijing Statement to enhance collaboration including TNE.[90] Whilst not

[85] 万可佳[K Wan], '教育服务贸易相关法律问题浅探' ['A Probe into Legal Issues Surrounding Trade in Education Services'] (中国民商法律网 [China Civil and Commercial Law Network], 26 December 2003), old.civillaw.com.cn/article/default.asp?id=13830.

[86] Article 62: Improving educational legislations—'A relatively complete system of socialist education legislations with Chinese characteristics' and article 64: Vigorously advance on-campus rule of law— China will 'launch publicity campaigns to promote legal knowledge among public'. National Development Plan 2010–20 (n 35) Arts 62, 64.

[87] 旷群、戚业国[Q Kuang and Y Qi], '赴澳留学热探源—基于推拉因素理论的分析' ['An Analysis of the Pull-Push Factor in Australia's Popularity as a Study Destination'] (2016) 1 高教探索 *Higher Education Exploration* 20, 22.

[88] Most international students are eligible for one-year work visas after graduation. STEM students make up 40% of international students in the US.

[89] J Ross, 'US Campuses Enlist Agents to Boost Student Numbers' *The Australian* (10 February 2016) 30.

[90] The parties to this Statement are the British Council, the Quality Assurance Agency, and the UK Higher Education International Unit on the English side, and the Chinese Education Association for International Exchange, and China Academic Degrees and Graduate Education Development Centre from the Chinese side.

legally binding like ChAFTA, the Statement pledged to strengthen regular exchange of information, inter-agency cooperation and best practice.[91] Such efforts tend to lead to an increase in the number of TNE programmes and institutions, and as a result, more Chinese students turning to the UK.

These examples bear testament to how deeper relationships can be developed without an FTA. In fact, as far as international education is concerned, Australia is not only competing with other countries but gradually with China.

There are more and more opportunities for Chinese students to gain overseas experiences either through TNE, or study tours and student exchange programmes. Foreign degrees are also gradually losing prestige as Chinese universities climb up international rankings and the pay gap between overseas and Chinese degrees narrows. And when one takes into consideration the financial costs associated with going overseas, the return on investment is no longer as attractive.[92]

Australia needs to look at trade in education services through different lenses. It needs to work with China as an equal trade partner, rather than see it as a supplier of international students.

For example, both countries can develop TNE programmes that helps China to recruit international students from developing countries. This, in turn, translates into students for Australia in later years when the students move into senior undergraduate studies or postgraduate degrees in Australia.

Australian institutions can also band together, just like airlines do with codeshare, to establish a stronger presence in China. Not only does this achieve economies of scale for the consortium, it also allows each institution to focus on delivering courses where it has comparative advantage. In addition, a collaborative effort enables Australia to have stronger brand recognition in China, and greater engagement with both Chinese institutions and students.

Australia also needs to better understand China through more in-depth, mutual exchange of information. For instance, Australia is obliged to provide details of its regulatory decisions for the MOE to list CRICOS-registered institutions on its website. It is unclear how much transparency Australia requires of China in return. Candid information exchanges need to go both ways in a win–win partnership.

Last but not least, just because Mode 1, which includes online learning, is unbound under ChAFTA it does not mean that both countries cannot

[91] Ross, 'US Campuses Enlist Agents to Boost Student Numbers' (n 89) 30.

[92] J Ross, 'Glut of Overseas Students to Fall as China Rises' *The Australian* (23 September 2016), www.theaustralian.com.au/higher-education/glut-of-overseas-students-to-fall-as-china-rises/news-story/e1789e497b58268f87482a60fc1d406f.

start working together on joint delivery and even regulatory consultation. China is actively in MOOCs, albeit largely within the domestic market at this stage. There are more than 500 MOOCs platforms delivering at least 3,000 courses in China.[93] The example of the Harbin Institute of Technology's (HIT) MOOCs experience provides food for thought. Between 2014 and 2015, 20,000 students undertook its courses, 40 per cent of which were credit bearing. Ninety per cent of the courses offered were in liberal arts and social sciences.[94] For a university that is renowned for engineering, MOOCs has allowed Harbin to expand its disciplinary focus. Australian universities wishing to expand their presence in China would do well to partner with Chinese universities. E-learning is an area of exponential growth and foresight should be given to its impact on trade in education services in the forthcoming work programme to review liberalisation measures.

VI. CONCLUSION

ChAFTA came into force at a time when trade in education services is vastly different from what it was when the GATS entered into force in 1995, or when ChAFTA negotiations began more than a decade ago. Whilst ChAFTA includes additional commitments compared with the GATS,[95] market conditions, market composition and domestic regulations in China are not what they once were.

An FTA's effectiveness depends upon what the existing barriers are and the potential for market penetration. At the same time, the landscape for international education is changing. The real impact on Australia's trade in education services needs to take into account Beijing's key drivers and evolving domestic regulations.

Regardless of what ChAFTA says, domestic reforms in China, as well as growing competition from the US, UK and even China itself, have the potential to direct demand and interests away from Australia. Both Australian education providers and the Australian government need to be aware of the bigger picture and rethink strategies for trade in education services.

When the *National Strategy for International Education 2025* was released in 2016, Richard Colbeck, then Minister for International Education

[93] 江志斌 [Z Jiang], 'MOOCs Better Education: The Case of Shanghai Jiao Tong University and Its CnMOOC' (April 2016), www.austrade.gov.au/ArticleDocuments/1418/AWIC2016_MOOCsBetterEducation_SHJiaotongUniMOOCInstitute_JIANGZhibin_EDU.pdf.aspx.

[94] China Online Education Research Institute, 'Wireless Learning: Development of China's Online Education' (April 2016), www.prnewswire.com/news-releases/china-online-education-industry-report-2016-300219521.html.

[95] DFAT, 'ChAFTA—Summary of Chapters and Annexes' (26 August 2015), dfat.gov.au/trade/agreements/chafta/fact-sheets/Pages/chafta-summary-of-chapters-and-annexes.aspx, 3.

said trade in education services is a 'super growth' sector.[96] Unfortunately, the strategy for such a critically acclaimed industry is one with a 'lack of vision' and 'dearth of program initiatives'.[97] The 1980s notion that education can be treated as a commodity to boost export earnings is no longer appropriate. In fact, overt commercialisation has been shown to damage Australia's reputation,[98] especially in a culture where education is revered, such as China.

China's education system is not there to provide foreign universities with external sources of funding or profits. ChAFTA does not oblige China to supply Australia with students. It has provided a degree of transparency, harmonisation and market access to trade in education services. But this is not enough to 'ensure Australia remains a leader in the provision of education services to overseas students'.[99]

Australia needs a step change in performance. It needs to look at trade in education services through different lenses, and work with China more as an equal trade partner, rather than just a supplier of international students.

[96] Australian Government, 'National Strategy for International Education 2025' (April 2016), nsie.education.gov.au/sites/nsie/files/docs/national_strategy_for_international_education_2025.pdf, v.

[97] D Murray, 'International Strategy Sticks to the Mantras' *The Australian* (4 May 2016) 34.

[98] Federal Education Minister Simon Birmingham has confirmed that the Australian government will cut university funding in the next budget. L Yaxley, 'University Deregulation: Government Still Committed to Higher Education Reforms' (*ABC News*, 5 April 2016), www.abc.net.au/news/2016-04-05/government-committed-to-university-funding-cuts/7299508.

[99] Australian Government (n 96) v.

Part IV

Insights and Lessons for the Regulation of Investment

10

Substantive Provisions in ChAFTA's Investment Chapter

VIVIENNE BATH

IT IS AN interesting feature of the China–Australia Free Trade Agreement (ChAFTA) that, after 10 years of negotiation, completion of most of the substantive provisions of the investment chapter has been deferred for later negotiations. Thus, with the exception of the provisions on Most-Favoured-Nation (MFN) treatment and national treatment, and the very comprehensive section on investor–state dispute settlement (ISDS), the 1988 Agreement between the Government of Australia and the Government of the People's Republic of China on the Reciprocal Encouragement and Protection of Investments (the Australia–China Bilateral Investment Treaty (BIT)) continues—for the moment—to contain the main commitments between the two states in relation to the protection of investment. This chapter looks at the current substantive provisions of the investment chapter and considers the options for the work programme foreshadowed in the investment chapter in the context of Chinese and Australian investment commitments and policies.

I. BACKGROUND: CHINA–AUSTRALIA INVESTMENT AND INVESTMENT POLICIES

Chinese investment in Australia, as well as Australian investment in China, has undergone a rapid increase over the last five to ten years. By 2015, China was the seventh largest source of investment into Australia, with AUD$74.9 billion of investment (2.5 per cent of total investment in Australia).[1] China accounted for AUD$70.2 billion of Australian outbound investment (3.4 per cent of the total), putting it in fifth place, but well behind the

[1] Department of Foreign Affairs and Trade (DFAT), 'Australia and Foreign Investment: Which Countries Invest in Australia?', dfat.gov.au/trade/topics/investment/Pages/which-countries-invest-in-australia.aspx. This does not include investment from (or through) Hong Kong (AUD$85.4 billion).

US (28.6 per cent), the UK (17 per cent), New Zealand and Japan.[2] A study by KPMG and the University of Sydney[3] estimates that total Chinese investment into Australia in 2015 alone was AUD$15.09 billion, a 32.9 per cent increase over the previous year.

The investment chapter of ChAFTA constitutes the first attempt since the Australia–China BIT was signed to formulate an agreement between the two countries on investment protection.[4] The Australia–China BIT is a succinct document, although it provides protection and benefits in a range of areas. It does not, however, contain a national treatment provision, and its MFN provision (Article 3(c)) relates only to post-admission activities. The limited scope of this Agreement no longer corresponds to the pattern of China's international investment agreements[5] or to Australia's more comprehensive commitments in its free trade agreements (FTAs), commencing with Chapter 11 of the Australia–US Free Trade Agreement in 2004.[6]

For both Australia and China, which maintain carefully regulated systems relating to the inflow of foreign investment, a challenge in negotiating investment agreements is the need to accommodate domestic policies while also taking steps to protect and encourage foreign investment.

A foreign company which proposes to make an acquisition of land or assets in Australia may be subject to the notification and review process established pursuant to the federal Foreign Acquisitions and Takeovers Act 1975 (FATA). This applies based on the nature of the investor (whether private, or foreign government-owned), the sector in which the investment is made and the size of the investment.[7] Once the investment is effected, often through the establishment or acquisition of an Australian incorporated subsidiary, the ownership of shares or the acquisition of assets, the foreign-owned operational entity is subject to the same legal regime as all other companies or entities operating in Australia. Increasingly, however, the foreign acquirer may be subject to ongoing conditions related to ownership, management and operations as part of the screening process.[8]

[2] DFAT, 'Australia and Foreign Investment: Where Does Australia Invest?', dfat.gov.au/trade/topics/investment/Pages/where-does-australia-invest.aspx. Note that investments in Hong Kong were eighth, although it can be assumed that a large amount of those funds ultimately flowed into China.

[3] KPMG and the University of Sydney, *Demystifying Chinese Investment in Australia, The New Normal: Health, Happiness, Lifestyle and Services* (April 2016), demystifyingchina.com.au/reports/demystifying-chinese-investment-in-australia-april-2016.pdf.

[4] See Free Trade Agreement between the Government of Australia and the Government of the People's Republic of China (signed 17 June 2015, entered into force 20 December 2015) [2015] ATS 15, Ch 9 (ChAFTA).

[5] See, eg, N Gallagher and W Shan, *Chinese Investment Treaties: Policies and Practice* (Oxford, Oxford University Press, 2009) 35–43.

[6] Australia–US Free Trade Agreement (signed 4 May 2004, entered into force 1 January 2005) [2005] ATS 1.

[7] See Foreign Investment Review Board (FIRB), 'Australia's Foreign Investment Policy' (most recent version issued 1 July 2017), firb.gov.au/resources/policy-documents/.

[8] Foreign Acquisitions and Takeovers Act 1975, s 74.

China has traditionally pursued foreign investment, but subject to a comprehensive system of regulation. From 1979, when foreign investment was first permitted by the Sino-Foreign Equity Joint Venture Law,[9] a foreign investor was obliged, with some limited exceptions, to invest in China through the establishment of a foreign investment enterprise or entity. The establishment of a foreign investment entity was subject to government review and approval. The regulatory regime determined the sector in which a foreign investor could invest, the limits (if any) on the equity interest which the foreign investor could hold and the level of the Chinese government empowered to approve the investment.

The Chinese government is, however, in the process of effecting fundamental changes to its regulation of investment, both domestic and foreign, pursuant to the policies outlined in 2015 in the Several Opinions of the Communist Party of China (CPC) Central Committee and the State Council on Developing a New System of Open Economy[10] and further elaborated in the Opinions of the State Council on Implementing the Market Access Negative List System.[11] The stated aim of these policies is the liberalisation of investment and the opening up of the Chinese economy to foreign and domestic business. Pursuant to this policy, both investment and business operations in China are to be subject to a 'market access negative list' regime under which foreign investors will receive national treatment for their investments in China (ie, the same treatment as Chinese investors), subject to a registration requirement or, in the case of investments on the negative list, prior government approval.

ChAFTA came into effect at a time when these policies were contemplated but had not yet been implemented, although steps had been taken to implement a negative list in China's Free Trade Zones.[12]

However, effective on 1 October 2016, the Standing Committee of the National People's Congress resolved to amend China's foreign investment laws to implement the negative list system.[13] Thus there is now no universal requirement for specific prior approval for foreign investment, unless the project is in an industry or of a type set out on the negative list. It should be

[9] 'Law on Sino-Foreign Equity Joint Ventures' (2nd Session of the Fifth National People's Congress, Beijing, 1 July 1979).

[10] Issued 5 May 2015.

[11] *Guo Fa* [2015] No 55 (2 November 2015).

[12] See, eg, Notice of the General Office of the State Council on Printing and Distributing the Special Management Measures for the Market Entry of Foreign Investment in Pilot Free Trade Zones (Negative List) (2017 Version) (5 June 2017); see also, National Development and Reform Commission (NDRC) and Ministry of Commerce (MOFCOM), Catalogue of Industries for Guiding Foreign Investment (2017 Revision), *Order No 4 of the NDRC and MOFCOM* (28 June 2017).

[13] Standing Committee of the National People's Congress, Decision on Revising the Law of the People's Republic of China on the Four Laws on Foreign-Investment Enterprises (issued 3 September 2016, effective 1 October 2016) and accompanying implementing regulations.

noted that the introduction of a negative list market access approach does not change the underlying dichotomy in the Chinese legal system, which distinguishes between state-owned, foreign and Chinese invested entities.[14] What is being changed is the cumbersome process whereby every foreign investment (other than most investments in free-trade zones) is subject to a government approval process.

The anticipated introduction of this system was foreshadowed in China's Agreement with the US in 2013 to negotiate a BIT on the basis of a negative list,[15] and is reflected in the two-stage negotiation process which underlies the investment chapter of ChAFTA. As discussed in more detail below, it has also had an impact on the content of the 2015 China–Korea FTA.[16]

II. THE TWO-STAGE PROCESS OF NEGOTIATING INVESTMENT COMMITMENTS IN ChAFTA AND THE WORK PROGRAMME

Chapter 9 of ChAFTA contains 25 provisions and two annexes. Annex III sets out the Investment and Services Schedules of Australia and China (although China's schedule is limited to its commitments in relation to services under Chapters 8 and 10).

Articles 9.10 to 9.25 deal with dispute resolution, particularly investor–state dispute settlement (ISDS).[17] The substantive provisions are contained in Articles 9.1 to 9.9. These Articles include definitions, provisions for the grant of national treatment and MFN treatment, non-conforming measures (which set out exceptions to general agreements), denial of benefits, and the plan for a work programme which will flesh out the commitments in the investment chapter.

The work programme is set out in Article 9.9. It provides that, unless otherwise agreed, the parties will conduct a review of the investment legal framework no later than three years after the date of entry into force of the Agreement (ie, 20 December 2018).[18] The review will cover both Chapter 9 and the Australia–China BIT and is to be followed by negotiations between

[14] See, eg, Notice of the Ministry of Commerce on Soliciting Public Opinions on the 'Foreign Investment Law of the People's Republic of China (Draft for Comments)' (19 January 2015).

[15] Office of the US Trade Representative, 'Fact Sheet: 2014 National Trade Estimate Report Major Developments' (March 2014), ustr.gov/about-us/policy-offices/press-office/fact-sheets/2014/March/2014-National-Trade-Estimate-Report-Major-Developments.

[16] Free Trade Agreement between the Government of the People's Republic of China and the Government of the Republic of Korea (China–Korea FTA) (signed 1 June 2015, entered into force 20 December 2015).

[17] See, eg, ChAFTA (n 4) Chs 13, 16 and 17.

[18] Pursuant to an agreement signed in March 2017 during Premier Li Ke Qiang's visit to Australia; however, the parties agreed to bring the review of the services and investment chapters forward by one year. See also, S Ciobo, 'New agreement with China to drive economic co-operation' (24 March 2017), trademinister.gov.au/releases/Pages/2017/sc_mr_170324a.aspx.

the parties on a comprehensive investment chapter reflecting the outcomes of the review. Matters to be covered will include—but are not limited to—amendments to the provisions of the chapter; the inclusion of additional provisions and the scheduling of commitments by China on a negative list basis. The additional provisions will include provisions on minimum standards of treatment; expropriation; transfers; performance requirements; senior management and board of directors; investment-specific state to state dispute settlement; and the application of investment protections and ISDS to services supplied through commercial presence. (Pursuant to Article 9.12, an investor may currently institute investor–state arbitration only in respect of a breach of Article 9.3 (national treatment)).

The reasons for this unusual two-stage negotiation process are to some extent explained in a document prepared by the Department of Foreign Affairs and Trade (DFAT), entitled 'ChAFTA: Summary of Chapters and Annexes',[19] which 'recites the historical basis, bilateral context and broad aims of the China–Australia Free Trade Agreement'. In relation to Chapter 9, the summary explains that the Agreement takes a 'two-stage approach to investment'. The first stage comprises commitments effective on the entry of the Agreement into force and the second stage is the work programme. As the summary explains, Australia has already made its market access commitments to China, including higher screening thresholds, in stage one. The non-reciprocal nature of China's commitments in Article 9.3 in relation to national treatment and the very limited scope ('short-form') of the chapter is apparently due to this two-stage approach. China's commitments under Article 9.4 (MFN treatment) will apply subject to any non-conforming measures scheduled by China in an agreement entered into on a negative list basis with a non-party or, if more than one such agreement, the terms most favourable to Australian investors and investments.[20] The national treatment commitments will continue to be non-reciprocal unless and until they are renegotiated.

In contrast, the China–Korea FTA, which came into effect on the same day as ChAFTA, also provides for the renegotiation of the investment chapter in a work programme,[21] but contains substantive provisions relating not only to national treatment and MFN treatment, but also to a minimum standard of treatment, access to courts, prohibition of performance requirements, transparency, expropriation and compensation, transfers, subrogation, denial of benefits and environmental measures. Thus, although China's negative list reforms and negotiations with the US were expected to have

[19] DFAT, 'ChAFTA Summary of Chapters and Annexes' (26 August 2016), dfat.gov.au/trade/agreements/ChAFTA/fact-sheets/Pages/ChAFTA-summary-of-chapters-and-annexes.aspx.

[20] ChAFTA (n 4) Ch 14, Art 9.5.

[21] China–Korea FTA (n 16) Annex 22-A.

a significant effect on both of these FTAs, the China–Korea FTA has a functioning high-quality investment chapter (which is, in many respects, very similar to the Australia–Korea FTA),[22] while the two-stage approach adopted in ChAFTA means that enforceable investment protection is available only in limited circumstances.

Australia does seem to be quite relaxed about agreements which leave much of the substantive negotiation of the investment chapter to a later work programme. The investment chapter (Chapter 11) of the ASEAN–Australia–New Zealand FTA (AANZ FTA), which came into effect in 2010, also contains a work programme, pursuant to which the parties agreed to discuss schedules of reservations to the national treatment clause (which will not come into effect until these are finalised), treatment of investment in services which does not qualify as commercial presence, and the potential application of MFN treatment to the chapter.[23] Given the lengthy duration of the ChAFTA negotiations and China's general willingness to negotiate and sign investment agreements, the agreement to grant non-reciprocal concessions while deferring negotiations on the investment chapter certainly suggests that trade liberalisation was prioritised over investment protection. The recent agreement between the parties to move the review of the services and investment chapters forward is potentially a positive step in filling in the lacunae in the chapter.[24]

III. SUBSTANTIVE PROVISIONS OF THE INVESTMENT CHAPTER

A. Definitions: Article 9.1

The *World Trade Investment Review 2016*[25] comments that a feature of investment agreements signed in 2015 was the tightening of the definition of investment, for example, by requiring that an investment have 'the characteristics' of an investment and excluding portfolio investment and commercial contracts. The definitions in ChAFTA illustrate this trend. Pursuant to

[22] Free Trade Agreement between the Government of Australia and the Government of the Republic of Korea [2014] ATS 43 (signed 8 April 2014, entered into force 12 December 2014) (Korea–Australia FTA) [2014] ATS 43.

[23] Agreement Establishing the ASEAN–Australia–New Zealand Free Trade Area [2010] ATS 1, Ch 11, Art 16. The work programme was to be completed within five years from the date of entry into force of the Agreement, unless otherwise agreed, but it appears that the schedules of reservations are still under discussion. See summary of the Eighth Meeting of the FTA Joint Committee (14–18 March 2016), dfat.gov.au/trade/agreements/aanzfta/Documents/summary-of-outcomes-aanzfta-8th-fjc.PDF.

[24] See above (n 18).

[25] United Nations Commission on Trade and Development (UNCTAD), *World Investment Report 2016: Investor Nationality: Policy Challenges*, unctad.org/en/PublicationsLibrary/wir2016_en.pdf, 113.

Article 9.1, an investment 'means every kind of asset that an investor owns or controls, directly or indirectly, which has the characteristics of an investment, such as the commitment of capital or other resources, the expectation of gain or profit, or the assumption of risk'. This wording also reflects the provisions in the recent treaties signed by Australia and China, including the China–Korea FTA, the Australia–Korea FTA, the Australia–Japan Economic Partnership Agreement (JAEPA) and the Trans-Pacific Partnership Agreement (TPP).[26] The comprehensive list of forms of investment included in the definition in ChAFTA generally reflects the provisions of these four treaties quite closely.

A 'covered investment' (ie, an investment which is entitled to receive investment protection under ChAFTA) is an investment 'which, where applicable, has been admitted by the host Party, subject to its relevant laws, regulations and policies'. This reflects Australian and Chinese governmental policy in relation to the admission of investment and the ongoing investment regimes of both countries and makes clear that investors must comply with domestic government procedures in relation to the admission and establishment of investments in order to enjoy investment protection.

The definition of 'enterprise' specifically includes entities that are governmentally owned or controlled, making clear that foreign government-owned enterprises are entitled to the benefits set out in the chapter. The definition of 'investor of a Party' in the Australia–Korea FTA also specifically includes a state-owned enterprise. The TPP, in contrast, includes an entire chapter on state-owned enterprises and their responsibilities.[27] ChAFTA does not contain such a provision or chapter, but the Agreement is so drafted that Australia's policy of reviewing all investments by entities which are owned by a foreign government (which has had an impact on Chinese investment)[28] is not subject to restriction or review. Australia's policy of screening all investments by a foreign government-owned entity prior to admission is also specifically protected in Annex III.[29]

[26] See, eg, Korea–Australia FTA (n 22) Art 11.28; China–Korea FTA (n 16) Art 12.1; Agreement between Australia and Japan for an Economic Partnership (signed 8 July 2014, entered into force 15 January 2015) (JAEPA) Ch 14 ('Australia-Japan EPA') Art 14.2; Trans-Pacific Partnership Agreement between the Government of Australia and the Governments of: Brunei Darussalam, Canada, Chile, Japan, Malaysia, Mexico, New Zealand, Peru, Singapore, United States of America and Vietnam (TPP Agreement) (signed 4 February 2016, not in force) [2016] (ATNIF 2) Ch 9, Art 9.1.

[27] Ch 17: State-Owned Enterprises and Designated Monopolies.

[28] See, eg, KPMG and The University of Sydney, *Demystifying SOE Investment in Australia* (29 August 2014), hhome.kpmg.com/au/en/home/insights/2014/08/demystifying-soe-investment-in-australia-august-2014.html.

[29] Sch of Non-conforming Measures, sch of Australia, s A. Section B preserves the right of the Australian government to adopt or maintain any measure in relation to investment by a foreign government investor in urban land or in any assets in order to protect Australia's 'essential security interests'.

B. Scope: Article 9.2

This Article provides that the investment chapter applies to measures relating to investors and covered investments only. It does not extend to measures of a party relating to trade in services or movement of natural persons *to the extent* that they are covered in Chapters 8 and 10. It also does not apply to government procurement or subsidies or grants provided by a party, including government-supported loans, guarantees or insurance. Article 16.8, however, provides that upon China's accession to the Agreement on Government Procurement, the parties should commence negotiations on government procurement with a view to concluding reciprocal commitments.[30]

C. National Treatment: Article 9.3

As noted above, the provisions relating to national treatment in ChAFTA are not reciprocal. Article 9.3 commits Australia to provide to investors of China and to covered investments treatment not less favourable than it accords to its own investors, in like circumstances (national treatment) with respect to the 'establishment, acquisition, expansion, management, conduct, operation and sale or other disposition of investments in its territory'. China's commitments do not include establishment or acquisition of investments and a footnote makes clear that 'expansion' does not include establishment or acquisition of a new, separate investment. Notwithstanding the two-step process of negotiating this chapter, it is not completely clear why Australia made concessions in relation to national treatment for the establishment and admission of Chinese investment. China has traditionally not been prepared to concede this point,[31] and there does not seem to be a good reason for Australia to concede it unilaterally,[32] particularly since Article 9.12 limits ISDS to disputes 'between a Party and an investor of the other Party relating to a covered investment made in accordance with the Party's laws, regulations and investment policies'. This accords with Australia's approach when it does agree to reciprocal national treatment clauses in relation to the establishment or admission of investment.[33] In all

[30] Australia is also not a party to the Article on Government Procurement, although it is in the process of acceding. See WTO, 'Agreement on Government Procurement, Parties, Observers and Accessions', www.wto.org/English/tratop_e/gproc_e/memobs_e_.htm; See also DFAT, 'Government Procurement, Agreement on Government Procurement', www.wto.org/english/tratop_e/gproc_e/gp_gpa_e.htm.

[31] A Berger, 'Hesitant Embrace: China's Recent Approach to International Investment Rule-Making' (2015) 16 *Journal of World Investment & Trade* 843, 853–54; see also China–Korea FTA (n 16) Art 12.3.

[32] See, eg, K Tienhaara and G Van Harten, 'Half-baked China–Australia Free Trade Agreement is lopsided' *Sydney Morning Herald* (19 June 2015).

[33] See, eg, Korea–Australia FTA (n 22) Annex 11-G; JAEPA (no ISDS provision) (n 26); TPP Agreement, Annex 9-H (n 26).

cases, Australia's commitments to the admission of foreign investment are qualified to protect Australia's screening process from external review.

Although the work programme does not specifically refer to the non-reciprocal national treatment provision, presumably the move to the scheduling of commitments by China on a negative list basis will allow China to grant national treatment on the same terms as Australia—ie, on a pre-establishment basis. This possibility is referred to specifically in the China–Korea FTA, the work programme for which requires the conduct of negotiations 'based on a negative list approach covering pre-establishing phase of investment and trade in services in mode 3'.[34]

D. Most-Favoured-Nation Treatment: Article 9.4

In contrast to Article 9.3, the terms of Article 9.4, pursuant to which Australia and China agree to extend to investors and covered investments 'treatment no less favourable than it accords, in like circumstances, to investors and investors in its territory of any non-Party' are reciprocal and extend to the establishment and acquisition of investments. However, the ISDS provision does not currently extend to this provision. The extension of ISDS under any other treaty or agreement is specifically excluded.

A party may adopt or maintain a measure giving more favourable treatment to a non-party pursuant to any bilateral or multilateral agreement in force prior to the effective date of ChAFTA, as well as pursuant to any subsequent agreement to modify such an agreement.

This provision grandfathers Australia's existing agreements, as well as China's numerous bilateral investment treaties and free trade agreements. Benefits such as higher screening thresholds for acquisition of agricultural land accorded to the US and other partners pursuant to free trade agreements in effect prior to the change of government policy in 2014 are not accorded to China under this Agreement. Australia's different agreements in relation to the screening thresholds have resulted in the increasing inconsistency and complexity of Australia's investment policies in relation to investments made under different FTAs.[35]

Measures in bilateral or multilateral international agreements, in force or signed after the date of entry of force of ChAFTA, granting more favourable treatment to investors of non-parties involving aviation, fisheries or maritime matters, including salvage, are also excluded.[36]

[34] See, eg, China–Korea FTA (n 16) Annex 22-A, A.3.

[35] Above (n 7).

[36] In contrast: Art 12.4 of the China–Korea FTA excludes obligations for a party to give preferential treatment pursuant to membership of the Customs Unions, free trade areas and monetary unions; international agreements for the facilitation of small-scale trade and aviation, fisheries and maritime matters including salvage.

For China, granting MFN treatment is not problematic given its longstanding unilateral implementation of foreign investment policy, although its willingness to agree to pre-establishment MFN provisions is a recent development.[37] A relatively unqualified provision occurs in the China–New Zealand FTA (Article 142).[38] In the China–Korea FTA, however, Article 12.4 is carefully phrased to apply to 'investment activities', which do not include establishment and admission of investments, and highly qualified obligations in relation to the admission of investment (Article 12.2).[39]

E. Non-Conforming Measures: Article 9.5

Article 9.5 deals with existing and potential measures which will continue to be in effect, or which may be adopted, as exceptions to Articles 9.3 and 9.4. In the case of Australia, these are limited to existing non-conforming measures as set out in Section A of Annex III[40] and continuations or limited amendments to those measures. Section B of Annex III sets out a list of sectors and activities in relation to which Australia reserves the right to adopt or maintain non-conforming measures. These measures essentially reflect Australia's existing investment regime. China's commitments in paragraph 2 are less extensive and relate only to existing non-conforming measures, which are not spelt out, although China's commitments on services pursuant to Chapters 8 and 10 may have an effect on investment where services are provided through presence in China.[41] This accords with the practice of both states. Australia customarily includes a negative list, while China refers generally to non-conforming measures (as in Article 12.3(2) of the China–Korea FTA).

Paragraph 4 of Article 9.5 commits the parties to 'endeavour to progressively remove the non-conforming measures'. If taken literally, this would oblige Australia to reduce its list and processes for review of foreign investment, as well as requiring China systematically to cut back the list of sectors in which foreign investment in China is prohibited or restricted. In practice, it does not seem likely that Australia intends to reduce the sectors in which foreign investment may be regarded as sensitive or to cut back on the process

[37] Berger (n 31) 853–54.

[38] Free Trade Agreement between the Government of New Zealand and the Government of the People's Republic of China (signed 7 April 2008, entered into force 1 October 2008).

[39] This replicates Art 4.1 of the 2014 Agreement among the Government of Japan, the Government of the Republic of Korea and the Government of the People's Republic of China for the Promotion, Facilitation and Protection of Investment (Japan–Korea–China Trilateral Investment Agreement) (signed 13 May 2012, entered into force 17 May 2014).

[40] With some reservations. For example, Australia may add any non-conforming measure at a regional level of government that existed as at 1 January 2005 (Section A, Introductory Note 3).

[41] See, eg, discussion in Part II on service commitments.

of review. If anything, the trend has been the other way, with the introduction of lower thresholds for the review of investments in agricultural land in 2015[42] and the amendment of the Foreign Acquisitions and Takeovers Regulation (FATR) in 2016 to make clear that federal government approval is required for sales of critical infrastructure by the states and territories.[43]

As noted above, Australia's willingness to agree to negative lists with a ratchet mechanism in its free trade agreements means that different screening thresholds apply in relation to agricultural land for investors from the US, New Zealand, Chile, Singapore and Thailand,[44] countries which signed agreements with Australia before the new lower thresholds agreed with Korea, China and Japan came into effect. This raises the question whether Australia's approach when negotiating negative lists in its agreements is sufficiently flexible to allow subsequent modifications when the government considers they are in Australia's interests.

Although there is no Annex attached to Article 9.5 in relation to China's commitments in relation to investment, the footnote to this Article states that until the entry into force of renegotiated commitments pursuant to the work programme, China's commitments under Article 9.4 'shall apply subject to any non-conforming measures scheduled by China against the most-favoured-nation (MFN) obligation in any negative list investment agreement with a non-party'. If there is more than one such agreement, Australia will enjoy the benefits of the most favourable agreement. The DFAT 'Summary of Chapter Outcomes' states that 'China's market access commitments will be based on the schedules it develops for the US–China BIT'.[45] In practice, China's domestic reforms have now moved ahead of the negotiations with the US. It also appears that compiling and agreeing on a form of negative list acceptable both to the Chinese government and to the US has proved difficult.[46] At the Chinese domestic level, although there have been three versions of negative lists for investment in the free-trade zones, as well as a revision of the *Foreign Investment Catalogue* on a negative list basis which opens up more sectors for foreign investment, these lists are still lengthy and have arguably not resulted in substantial liberalisation of the sectors

[42] Joe Hockey, 'Government tightens rules on foreign purchases of agricultural land' (11 February 2015), jbh.ministers.treasury.gov.au/media-release/005-2015/.

[43] Foreign Acquisitions and Takeovers (Government Infrastructure) Regulation 2016 (Cth).

[44] See, eg, Foreign Acquisitions and Takeovers Regulation 2015 (Cth), definition of 'relevant agreement country', and ss 40, 52 and 53.

[45] 'ChAFTA: Summary of Chapter Outcomes', www.austlii.edu.au/au/other/dfat/treaties/ATS/2015/15.html (Attachment III to the National Interest Analysis [2015] ATNIA 7).

[46] See, eg, discussion in L Gloudeman and N Salidjanova, 'Policy Considerations for Negotiating a US–China Bilateral Investment Treaty' US–China Economic and Security Review Commission Staff Research Report (1 August 2016), origin.www.uscc.gov/sites/default/files/Research/Staff%20Report_Policy%20Considerations%20for%20Negotiating%20a%20U.S.-China%20Bilateral%20Investment%20Treaty080116.pdf.

in which foreign investment is permitted.[47] Indeed, there is a strongly held view by some foreign businesses that in practice China has not taken the necessary steps to establish a truly reciprocal investment climate.[48]

The 2017 *Foreign Investment Catalogue* reduces the number of sectors in which foreign investment is restricted or prohibited.[49] However, the restricted list (which covers projects for which government approval is required and includes requirements in many cases for Chinese participation or control) still contains 63 negative list entries (reduced from 93) (35 restricted industry sectors, and 28 prohibited list items).[50] A notice from the State Council, however, reiterated China's commitment to further opening the Chinese market to foreign investment, which may result in further liberalisation in the future.[51]

For the purposes of ChAFTA, the footnote to Article 9.5 makes clear that there will be no item by item commitments until China negotiates a negative list agreement with another state, or in the course of the work programme. In practice, ChAFTA reflects the reality that the US negotiations—should they continue—will place much stronger pressure on China to reduce the negative list than Australia could apply on its own.

F. Denial of Benefits: Article 9.6

Article 9.6 allows a party to deny the benefits of the chapter to an investor of the other party that is owned or controlled by persons of a non-party or of the denying party that has no substantive operations in the territory of the other party. Alternatively, benefits may be denied to an investor of the other party if the investor is owned or controlled by persons of a non-party and the denying party adopts or maintains measures with respect to the non-party or its persons that prohibit transactions with the enterprise, or that would be violated or circumvented if the enterprise or its investments received the benefits of the chapter.

The first provision (set out in Article 9.6.1) appears in the China–Korea FTA (Article 12.15(2)) and the Australia–Korea FTA (Article 11.11(2)). The second provision deals with the situation of an investor ultimately controlled

[47] A Koty and Z Qian, 'China's 2017 Foreign Investment Catalogue Opens Access to New Industries' (28 July 2017), www.china-briefing.com/news/2017/07/11/china-releases-2017-foreign-investment-catalogue-opening-access-new-industries.html.

[48] The European Union Chamber of Commerce in China, 'Position Paper 2016/2017' 25 *et seq*.

[49] Above (n 12).

[50] Above (n 12). Note that the negative list items do not include sectors such as gambling where investment by both domestic and foreign investors is prohibited.

[51] Notice of the State Council on Several Measures for Expanding Opening to Outside and Making Active use of Foreign Investment, *Guo fa* [2017] No 5 (12 January 2017).

in a state which is subject to sanctions or other forms of embargo. It appears in a very similar form in the Australia-Korea FTA (Article 11.11(1)) and in the China–Korea FTA (Article 12.15 (1)), with the addition of the further provision that benefits may be denied if the denying party does not maintain 'normal economic relations" with the non-party state. A variation of this provision in JAEPA provides for denial of benefits if the denying state does not maintain diplomatic relations with the non-party state (Article 14.17).[52]

G. Committee on Investment: Article 9.7

Article 9.7 provides for the creation of a Committee on Investment, the functions of which are to review the implementation of the chapter, identify and recommend measures to promote and increase investment flows and, unless the parties otherwise agree, conduct the review referred to in Article 9.9 on the operation of the chapter. The Committee must also establish and maintain a list of arbitrators for the purpose of ISDS and may adopt a joint decision of the parties interpreting a provision of the chapter and Annex 9-A (which sets out the code of conduct for arbitrators) and propose amendments to section B (ISDS) 'in the light of experience of its operation'.

Interestingly, despite the significance of its functions, Article 9.7 does not specify the number of members, the method of appointment of members or its procedures, meetings or operations. This contrasts with the provisions of Chapter 14, which formally establishes the FTA Joint Commission, and the provisions setting up the other committees which report to the FTA Joint Commission, such as the Committee on Trade in Goods established pursuant to Article 2.15 (which must comprise representatives of each party). The Committee has apparently been established, although details of membership are not provided on the DFAT website. It appears that no meetings have been held, nor are any meetings scheduled at the time of writing.[53]

H. General Exceptions: Article 9.8

Despite the restricted nature of the substantive commitments in Chapter 9, Article 9.8 provides for general exceptions, which clarify the ability of each party to regulate in certain respects. Article 9.8 provides that, subject to the usual exception that the measures not be applied in a discriminatory manner

[52] See, eg, L Gastrell and P-J Le Cannu, 'Procedural Requirements or 'Denial-of-Benefits' Clauses in Investment Treaties: A Review of Arbitral Decisions' (2015) 30(1) *ICSID Review* 78, 79; see also *World Investment Report* (n 25) ch IV, 'Investment Nationality: Policy Challenges'.

[53] DFAT, 'China–Australia Free Trade Agreement, Implementation', dfat.gov.au/trade/agreements/chafta/implementation/Pages/implementation.aspx.

or as a disguised restriction on international trade or investment, nothing in the Agreement prevents a party from adopting or enforcing measures:

a. necessary to protect human, animal or plant life or health;
b. necessary to ensure compliance with laws and regulations that are not inconsistent with this Agreement;
c. imposed for the protection of national treasures of artistic, historic or archaeological value; or
d. relating to the conservation of living or non-living inexhaustible natural resources.

Paragraph 2 clarifies that the measures include environmental measures in relation to paragraphs (a) and (d). The DFAT summary links these provisions with public welfare exceptions from ISDS (Article 9.11(4)), and reservations in Annex III relating to sensitive areas. It describes them as 'explicit safeguards to protect legitimate government regulation'.[54] In Annex III, Section B(5), Australia also specifically reserves the right to adopt or maintain measures that it considers necessary to protect its 'essential security interests" in relation to a proposed investment. Security exceptions under ChAFTA are set out in Article 16.3, and refer to the incorporation into the Agreement of Article XXI of the General Agreement on Tariffs and Trade (GATT) 1994 and Article XIV *bis* of the General Agreement on Trade in Services (GATS) (which generally provide that a state need not disclose information nor is it prevented from taking steps it considers necessary for the protection of its 'essential security interests').[55] The China–Korea FTA, by way of contrast, does not include a general exceptions clause. However, in addition to a provision on Essential Security which replicates Article 16.3 of ChAFTA (Article 21.2), the investment chapter contains a Security Exceptions clause (Article 12.14) roughly based on Article XXI of GATT 1994 and an exception in the expropriation clause for 'non-discriminatory regulatory actions adopted … for the purpose of legitimate public welfare' (Annex 12-B).

Australia's Foreign Investment Policy[56] lists factors relevant to the national interest test, in which it includes 'national security', a concept tied to protection of Australia's strategic and security interests. However, national security has recently become more significant in Australia's investment policy, with recent amendments to the FATR referring to investment in certain types of

[54] DFAT, 'China–Australia Free Trade Agreement, Fact Sheet: Investment and Investor–State Dispute Settlement', dfat.gov.au/trade/agreements/chafta/fact-sheets/Pages/fact-sheet-investment.aspx; see also TPP, Art 9.16, which allows for measures which a party considers appropriate to ensure investment activity 'is undertaken in a manner sensitive to environmental, health or other regulatory objectives'.

[55] On the self-judging nature of these provisions, see S Schill and R Briese, '"If the State Considers": Self-Judging Clauses in International Dispute Settlement' (2009) 13 *Max Planck Yearbook of United Nations Law* 61.

[56] See above (n 7).

infrastructure as relevant to national security.[57] The decision in 2016 by the Treasurer to reject the bid by a Chinese state-owned enterprise to buy a 99-year lease of Ausgrid, the New South Wales electricity network distribution network, was based on national security issues in the 'crucial power and communications services' provided by Ausgrid.[58] A recent government announcement provides for the creation of a Critical Infrastructure Centre, which will 'provide greater certainty and clarity to investors and industry on the types of assets that will attract national security scrutiny'.[59]

In China, national security is also an integral component of investment decisions following the adoption of a national security review scheme in 2011 in relation to foreign mergers and acquisitions, which places a focus on infrastructure, defence and technology.[60] The draft Foreign Investment Law includes a chapter providing for the extension of national security review to the establishment of new investment projects.[61] Draft Article 73 provides that a national security review decision will not be subject to administrative reconsideration or an administrative lawsuit, which suggests that China is unlikely to agree that such a decision would be subject to ISDS.

The role of national security in trade and investment is generally a matter of increasing interest in both domestic legislation and investor–state relations. The 2016 *World Investment Report*[62] comments on the growth in importance of national security considerations in relation to foreign investment, although states take quite different approaches to regulation and different views on how national security should be defined and determined.[63]

IV. FUTURE STEPS AND THE WORK PROGRAMME

There are a number of possibilities in relation to the next stage of the negotiation process. As noted above, the content of the China–Korea FTA suggests that it should be possible for Australia and China to negotiate a comprehensive agreement on investment. At this stage, however, it is not clear what model the parties could or should follow.

[57] Foreign Acquisitions and Takeovers Regulation (FATR) reg 31, para (2).

[58] S Morrison, 'Foreign Investment Applications for the 99-year Lease of Ausgrid' (11 August 2016), sjm.ministers.treasury.gov.au/media-release/067-2016/.

[59] G Brandis and S Morrison, 'Keeping Australia's Critical Infrastructure Secure' (23 January 2017), www.attorneygeneral.gov.au/Mediareleases/Pages/2017/FirstQuarter/Keeping-australias-critical-infrastructure-secure.aspx.

[60] See, eg, V Bath, 'Foreign Investment, the National Interest and National Security–Foreign Direct Investment in Australia and China' (2012) 34(1) *Sydney Law Review* 5; See also V Bath, 'The "National Interest" in Australian and Chinese Investment Law and Policy' in J Farrar, V Hiscock and J lo Lo (eds), *Australia's Trade, Investment and Security in the Asian Century* (New Jersey, World Scientific Publishing, 2015).

[61] See above (n 14) ch 4.

[62] UNCTAD (n 25) 94 *et seq*.

[63] See also discussion in JK Jackson, 'Foreign Investment and National Security: Economic Considerations' (4 April 2013), Congressional Research Service 7-5700, www.crs.gov.

First, the negotiation of ChAFTA coincided with China's negotiations with the US on a BIT and its agreement to move towards a pre-establishment negative list approach to investment. It also coincided with the negotiation of the detailed and comprehensive TPP. Both of these Agreements could, potentially, have an effect on the content of the Regional Comprehensive Economic Partnership (RCEP), involving China, Japan, Korea, Australia, New Zealand, India and the members of the Association of South-East Asian Nations. Their content could also serve as a basis for the work programmes under both ChAFTA and the China–Korea FTA. However, in view of the decision by President Trump to withdraw the US' signature from the TPP and his statements regarding trade policy,[64] it is not clear whether the TPP model will continue to have an impact on negotiations in Asia. It is also not clear what will happen to the US–China BIT negotiations.

ChAFTA's investment chapter could follow the investment chapter in the RCEP, when this is finalised. Since the parties to the RCEP include Australia and China, as well as countries with which both Australia and China have ongoing agreements, including Korea, Japan, the ASEAN states and New Zealand, there are potential advantages in revised investment chapters in ChAFTA and the China–Korea FTA which track the provisions of the RCEP. The possible downside of this proposal is that, given the number and differing interests and policies of the RCEP parties, the substantive provisions in the RCEP may well be less rigorous in terms of obligations than Australia's most recent Agreements (the Australia–Korea FTA and JAEPA). The working text of the RCEP is not publicly available, but the duration of the negotiations suggests that reaching agreement is not proving to be easy.[65]

Since the RCEP is proceeding on the basis that parties may continue to implement bilateral arrangements,[66] the third possibility is that the RCEP parties will continue to negotiate individual agreements on an ad hoc basis with terms which do not parallel existing treaties, thus adding to the mix of overlapping treaties within the Asia-Pacific region.

The work programme in ChAFTA is clearly intended to result in a more comprehensive investment chapter. Although the parties agreed to wait upon China's move to a negative list approach to investment, as reflected in its Agreement with the US, China has already moved ahead with internal reforms, although it may well be that, without the impetus of US pressure, China will not issue a negative list which is particularly satisfactory to

[64] B Heimand and S Ettinger, 'How US Federal Elections Will Impact US–China Relations' (14 November 2016), www.law360.com/articles/862131/how-us-federal-elections-will-impact-us-china-relations; see also P Baker, 'Trump Abandons Trans-Pacific Partnership, Obama's Signature Trade Deal' *The New York Times* (23 January 2017).

[65] DFAT, 'Guiding Principles and Objectives for Negotiating the Regional Comprehensive Economic Partnership' (20 November 2012), dfat.gov.au/trade/agreements/rcep/Pages/regional-comprehensive-economic-partnership.aspx.

[66] ibid principle 5.

Australia or Korea. China's domestic reforms should, however, be a basis for the negotiation of the reciprocal grant of national treatment in these Agreements.

Article 9.9 refers specifically to a number of provisions to be negotiated which may prove controversial. Discussed below are a number of provisions which have traditionally raised issues in China's treaty negotiations.

A. Customary International Law and Fair and Equitable Treatment

China has in the past been generally reluctant to include a customary international law minimum standard in relation to fair and equitable treatment and the protection of aliens.[67] Australia's FTAs do, however, generally include such a provision, as well as a definition of customary international law. These occur most recently in the Korea–Australia FTA (Article 11.5 and Annex 11-A: 'a general and consistent practice of states that they follow from a sense of obligation') and JAEPA (Article 14.5; no definition). The China–Korea FTA does, however, include both the customary international law minimum standard (Article 12.5) and a definition of the concept (Annex 12-A) in terms which are almost identical to the Korea–Australia FTA.[68] On this basis, it should be possible for Australia to obtain agreement to a similar provision as part of the work programme.

B. Indirect Expropriation: Definitions and Exceptions

Article VIII of the Australia–China BIT simply refers to 'measures of expropriation or nationalisation or other measures having a similar effect' and does not provide any definition of these concepts. However, recent agreements signed by both China and Australia provide a more nuanced definition of the concept of expropriation. In particular, Annex 12-B of the China–Korea FTA is very similar to Annex 11-B of the Australia–Korea FTA, and incorporates both the concept of indirect expropriation and terms describing how an action arguably constituting indirect expropriation should be addressed.

Both Annexes include a reference to distinct and reasonable expectations, and provide an exception for non-discriminatory regulatory actions 'adopted by the Party for the purpose of legitimate public welfare'. The Australia–Korea FTA is more specific in providing examples of legitimate

[67] Berger (n 31) 858–59; see also the Bilateral Agreement Concerning the Promotion and Protection of Investments (Colombia–China) (signed 22 November 2008, entered into force 2 July 2013) Art 2 of which refers to the customary international law standard for the minimum treatment of aliens (but does not define customary international law).

[68] Note, however, that the Minimum Standard of Treatment provision is specifically included in the work programme (Annex-22A, D(15)).

public welfare objectives (pharmaceuticals, in the case of Australia, and real estate price stabilisation, in the case of Korea). In view of the provisions in Article 9.11 of ChAFTA, providing for a 'public welfare notice' in relation to the matters which are not subject to an investor claim which to a large extent replicate the exceptions in the Annex to the Australia–Korea FTA (non-discriminatory and 'for the legitimate public purposes of public health, safety, the environment, public morals or public order'), these limitations should not be controversial in revisions to ChAFTA. Preservation of the ability of the host state to regulate is, after all, an important part of China's policies on investment agreements.[69]

C. Performance Requirements

The work programme in ChAFTA provides for the negotiation of a provision prohibiting the imposition of performance requirements on investors. The potential scope of performance requirements is very wide, and may include such requirements as local content rules, export performance requirements, price controls and equity and capital requirements.[70] Potentially, this is very significant for China, which has generally been reluctant to include provisions on performance requirements in its treaties.[71] The China–NZ FTA (Article 140), the Canada–China BIT (Article 9),[72] the Japan–Korea–China Trilateral Investment Agreement (Article 7) and the China–Korea FTA (Article 12.7) also contain provisions relating to the prohibition of performance requirements. These are, however, generally limited to the incorporation of the provisions of the Agreement on Trade-Related Investment Measures (TRIMS) into the Agreements.[73] The Japan–Korea–China Trilateral Investment Agreement and the China–Korea FTA also incorporate a general prohibition on 'unreasonable or discriminatory measures on covered investment ... concerning performance requirements on export or transfer of technology'.

The Australia–Korea FTA, however, contains a very detailed provision (Article 11.9), which appears, in large part, to be drawn from Article 9.10

[69] See, eg, 'Certain Opinions of the State on Accelerating the Implementation of the Free Trade Area Strategy' *Guo Fa* [2015] No 69 (6 December 2015) Art 3(9).

[70] See, eg, D Collins, *Performance Requirements and Investment Incentives under International Economic Law* (Cheltenham, Edward Elgar, 2015) ch 1, 'Performance Requirements and Investment Incentives: An Overview'.

[71] ibid 122.

[72] Agreement Concerning the Promotion and Reciprocal Protection of Investments (Canada–China) (signed 9 September 2012, entered into force 1 October 2014).

[73] WTO, *Agreement on Trade-Related Investment* Measures WT/ Annex 1(a)/143, www.wto.org/english/docs_e/legal_e/18-trims_e.htm. TRIMS prohibits the imposition of requirements which are inconsistent with the national treatment requirement and the prohibition on quantitative restrictions set out in Arts III and XI of the General Agreement on Tariffs and Trade (GATT).

of the TPP, and sets out requirements related to hidden forms of domestic protectionism in considerable detail, with a focus on domestic content, local production and export requirements. Article 14.9 of JAEPA is very similar.

Chinese rules and activities in this regard have been, and continue to be, the subject of complaints by foreign businesses.[74] It can be anticipated that this provision will present significant issues if Australia wishes to obtain stronger assurances in relation to performance requirements.

V. CONCLUSION

Although the investment chapter in ChAFTA serves a purpose in facilitating the process for Chinese private investors to invest in Australia and in setting out the parameters for investor–state dispute resolution in the future, the two-stage negotiation process has deferred the negotiation of most provisions relating to investment protection while locking Australia in to non-reciprocal obligations in relation to national treatment and to a highly specific negative list without receiving definite investment-related commitments in return. The content of the China–Korea FTA and, potentially, the ongoing RCEP negotiations, do present the possibility that the parties will negotiate a comprehensive and high-standard investment chapter along the lines of Australia's existing FTAs and the Korea–Australia FTA.[75] Since Australia has already made a number of important concessions in relation to screening thresholds, national treatment and its negative list, it is difficult to see what leverage Australia will have in the course of these negotiations to obtain a higher degree of investment liberalisation or protection from China other than the expansion of the scope of ISDS (or possibly, changes to Australia's policies in relation to investment by foreign government-owned entities). There is thus a substantial risk that the two-stage process may result in a less comprehensive investment chapter than Australia has negotiated with its other Asian partners, particularly Korea and Japan.

[74] See, eg, comments on China's compliance with its commitments under TRIMS in United States Trade Representative, '2015 Report to Congress on China's WTO Compliance' (December 2015), ustr.gov/sites/default/files/2015-Report-to-Congress-China-WTO-Compliance.pdf, 93 et seq.

[75] ChAFTA contains a number of provisions requiring regular reviews of the implementation of sections of the Agreement, and Art 16.5 provides for regular general reviews of ChAFTA. However, only a small number of Articles provide for negotiations of the terms of agreement. Art 8.24 provides for negotiations on trade in services on a negative list approach; Art 9.9 provides for negotiation of a detailed investment chapter; Art 9.23 deals with negotiations with a view to establishing an appellate mechanism for investment awards and Art 16.8 provides for negotiating commitments on government procurement when China has acceded to the Agreement on Government Procurement. The wording of Art 9.9 thus suggests that the comprehensive investment chapter will be negotiated separately. The announcement of a review of the services and investment chapters, together with the Investment Facilitation Agreement (n 18), raises the possibility that the negotiations on investment will be linked to the services chapter.

11

Australia, China and the Coexistence of Successive International Investment Agreements[†]

TANIA VOON AND ELIZABETH SHEARGOLD

I. INTRODUCTION

THE BILATERAL INVESTMENT treaty (BIT) between Australia and China was signed on 11 July 1988 and entered into force on the same day.[1] Twenty-seven years later, the parties signed a free trade agreement including an investment chapter (Chapter 9) on 17 June 2015. That Agreement (ChAFTA) entered into force on 20 December 2015.[2] Together, these two Treaties form the international legal framework for investment between China and Australia. The coexistence of these Treaties raises difficult questions of treaty interpretation and application in international law, particularly because of the major differences between their investment provisions. The Australia–China BIT was Australia's first international investment agreement (IIA): a 'first-generation' agreement in terms of its content and the broad scope of its obligations, including a mechanism for investor–state dispute settlement (ISDS). In contrast, ChAFTA constitutes a much more modern style IIA to the extent of its inclusion of explicit safeguards for regulatory autonomy, although it has very limited

† This chapter derives from independent research funded by the Australian Research Council pursuant to the Discovery Project scheme (project ID DP130100838) and by Melbourne Law School pursuant to the Melbourne Collaborative Project Fund. The authors thank Professor Colin Picker and Dr Weihuan Zhou for helpful comments as well as the participants in the ChAFTA conference held on 17–18 June 2016 at the University of New South Wales, Sydney, Australia, at which this research was first discussed. The opinions expressed here are our personal views as academics and are not necessarily shared by any employer or other entity. Any errors or omissions are ours.

1 Agreement between the Government of Australia and the Government of the People's Republic of China on the Reciprocal Encouragement and Protection of Investments (Australia–China BIT) (signed 11 July 1988, entered into force 11 July 1988) [1988] ATS 14.

2 Free Trade Agreement between the Government of Australia and the Government of the People's Republic of China (ChAFTA) (signed 17 June 2015, entered into force 20 December 2015) [2015] ATS 15.

substantive investment obligations, with ISDS currently extending only to disputes concerning the national treatment obligation. These Treaties provide a useful case study for analysing the intersection of investment law and treaty law in the context of successive treaties between the same parties, not only in the context of the Australia–China relationship but also as a basis for understanding the overlapping IIAs around the world.

This chapter begins in section II by comparing the coverage and substance of the Australia–China BIT and ChAFTA in order to understand their relationship and joint significance, including with reference (in section III) to the planned future 'joint work' programme to expand ChAFTA Chapter 9 into a comprehensive investment chapter. These sections reveal an asymmetry under both ChAFTA (with greater substantive obligations imposed on Australia) and the BIT (with greater potential for ISDS claims against Australia, although this discrepancy may not have been the parties' original intention). In sections IV and V we explain respectively how the BIT obligations continue to apply notwithstanding ChAFTA's entry into force (pursuant to Article 1.2 of ChAFTA and Article 30 of the Vienna Convention on the Law of Treaties (VCLT)),[3] and why ChAFTA has only a minimal role in the interpretation of those BIT obligations. We conclude that, despite the parties' modern approach to treaty drafting in ChAFTA with an eye to maintaining policy space, the 'old style' obligations as drafted in the decades-old BIT continue to apply without qualification. In section VI, we point out possibilities for unilateral or joint termination of the BIT to remove the risk of an ISDS claim under the BIT regarding these broad obligations. That risk appears much greater for Australia than China.

II. THE CURRENT AUSTRALIA–CHINA INVESTMENT FRAMEWORK: CHAFTA AND THE BIT

A. Overview: Comparing ChAFTA and the BIT

Table 1: ChAFTA and the BIT—A Comparison of Key Features

	Australia–China BIT (1988)	ChAFTA Chapter 9 (2015)
Key substantive obligations	— Treatment of investments (including fair and equitable treatment and broad MFN obligation) — Expropriation — Transfers — Adherence to written undertakings	— National treatment (NB for Australia applies to both pre- and post-establishment) — MFN treatment (narrow)

(continued)

[3] Vienna Convention on the Law of Treaties (VCLT) (opened for signature 22 May 1969, entered into force 27 January 1980) 1155 UNTS 331.

Table 1: *(Continued)*

	Australia–China BIT (1988)	ChAFTA Chapter 9 (2015)
ISDS	— Only for disputes re compensation payable for expropriation (Annex A) — Also under ICSID Convention for those disputes (against China) and others (against Australia)	— Only for breach of national treatment (with carve-out for review by Australia's Foreign Investment Review Board)
Safeguards for regulatory autonomy	— No explicit safeguards — Limited assistance from text of other provisions	— Non-conforming measures (negative list approach for Australia) — General exceptions — 'Public welfare notice' mechanism for ISDS — Committee can issue joint binding interpretation — Annex 9A Code of Conduct

In this section of the chapter, we set out the current legal framework for investments as between Australia and China pursuant to the BIT and ChAFTA, by examining in turn under the two Agreements: substantive obligations; availability of ISDS; and safeguards for regulatory autonomy. Table 1 above summarises our comparison between the BIT and Chapter 9 of ChAFTA.

From the comparison of the substantive obligations and availability of ISDS we conclude that the negotiators intended the two Treaties to coexist, with little likelihood of inconsistency due to their largely distinct obligations. The only substantive obligation covered by both Treaties is Most-Favoured-Nation (MFN) treatment, and ISDS is available under ChAFTA only for national treatment. Under the BIT, in the absence of consent by the disputing parties, ISDS against China appears to be available only for disputes concerning the amount of compensation for expropriation, whereas for Australia it may be available more generally regarding all the substantive provisions in the BIT. The conclusion that the parties intended the Treaties to coexist is strengthened by Article 9.9 of ChAFTA, which provides for a future work programme on the investment chapter (and mentions the BIT in doing so), as addressed in section III below.

Our comparison also demonstrates a major discrepancy between the high level of safeguards for regulatory autonomy contained in ChAFTA and the low level of such safeguards under the BIT. This discrepancy raises potential concerns regarding the continuing operation of BIT obligations as addressed in sections IV and V below, particularly in relation to the potential for ISDS claims against Australia under the BIT.

B. Substantive Obligations

Before considering the interrelationship of the BIT and ChAFTA, we must first examine the content of the two Agreements, with a particular focus on whether their coverage overlaps and, if so, whether the obligations contained within them are cumulative or inconsistent. The BIT contains a range of substantive obligations that are relatively typical of first-generation IIAs. Its provisions are phrased as protections for investments (not investors) and, like many other agreements of the period, it protects only investments that have been admitted by either Contracting Party. The definition of 'investment' contained in Article I:1 of the BIT is limited to assets 'admitted by the other Contracting Party subject to its law and investment policies applicable from time to time', while Article II—which relates to the encouragement and admission of investments—requires the Contracting Parties to admit investments only in accordance with their law and policy. Thus, the BIT does not provide the sort of 'pre-establishment' protections that have become common in more recent IIAs.

Article III of the BIT contains several of its most important standards of protection, including that each party must ensure fair and equitable treatment and protection and security for investments and 'shall not impair by unreasonable or discriminatory measures the management, maintenance, use, enjoyment or disposal of investments'. Paragraph (c) of Article III imposes an MFN obligation for covered investments. The BIT contains no explicit national treatment obligation, although the requirement under Article III(b) of the BIT that measures not be 'discriminatory' may be broad enough to capture policies or administrative decisions that treat a covered investment less favourably than a domestic counterpart. Importantly, however, the non-discrimination requirement in Article III(b) comes after the qualification that it is 'without prejudice to [the Contracting Party's] law', which significantly limits the impact of Article III(b), particularly since 'law' is defined to include regulations. As a result of this limitation, the BIT cannot be said to include a general national treatment obligation.

The BIT also contains, inter alia: a prohibition on expropriations that are not in the public interest and against reasonable compensation (Article VIII); a requirement to allow transfers of funds related to investments (Article X); and an obligation for Contracting Parties to adhere to any written undertakings given by a competent national authority with regard to an investment (Article XI).

In comparison to the BIT, the substantive obligations contained in Chapter 9 of ChAFTA are very limited, although these obligations do apply in respect of both investments and investors (Article 9.2). A covered investment is defined to include an investment established after the date of entry into force of the treaty 'which, where applicable, has been admitted by the host Party, subject to its relevant laws, regulations and policies' (Article 9.1(a)), while investor is defined to include a person or entity that 'seeks to make, is making or has made a covered investment' (Article 9.1(e)), which provides protection for prospective investors. The two core obligations contained in Chapter 9 are non-discrimination requirements: national treatment (Article 9.3) and MFN treatment (Article 9.4). Unlike the BIT, the ChAFTA MFN obligation applies to the establishment and acquisition of investments (Article 9.4.1), rather than solely to conduct post-establishment. However, the national treatment obligation extends to establishment and acquisition only in respect of Australia (Articles 9.3.1, 9.3.3); for China, the national treatment obligation is explicitly specified not to apply to establishment or acquisition (Articles 9.3.2, 9.3.4, footnote 1).

This asymmetry in obligations is also evident in the approach to existing non-conforming measures, with only Australia adopting a 'negative list' approach (such that the national treatment and MFN obligations apply to existing measures except for non-conforming laws and regulations listed in the relevant Australian schedule) (Article 9.5.1). For future measures, Australia has a scheduled list of sectors and sub-sectors in which it may enact new non-conforming measures. This 'negative list' approach of having obligations broadly apply to investments in all sectors in Australia, with only limited and specified exceptions, is shared with Australia's commitment under ChAFTA to liberalise trade in services (Australia's Schedules A and B in Annex III apply across the disciplines of trade in services and investment).

In relation to trade in services under ChAFTA, China's obligations take a 'positive list' approach, meaning that its obligations apply only in the specified sectors (see China's Schedule of Commitments in Part 2 of Annex III). China has not extended this positive list approach to investment, but it does have a broad carve-out for all existing non-conforming measures, without a requirement that such measures be listed in a schedule (Article 9.5.2). This approach provides China with much more extensive protection for its existing non-conforming measures than Australia, although, as noted below, the future work programme on investment envisages negotiations towards a negative listing of investment obligations for China (Article 9.9.3(c)). Some limit is placed on the extent of the protection this non-conforming measures clause provides to China by a footnote to Article 9.5, which states that, until the more comprehensive investment chapter is concluded under the future work programme, China's MFN obligation is subject only to the non-conforming measures specified in any other IIA to which China is party and that takes a negative list approach. If China concludes more than one other IIA with a negative list approach to non-conforming measures, then the agreement with the schedule most favourable to Australian investors and investment will apply.

The MFN treatment obligation represents the main substantive overlap between the BIT and Chapter 9 of ChAFTA (however, as discussed below, this obligation is notably excluded from the scope of ISDS under ChAFTA). Reflecting a general trend in the drafting of twenty-first century IIAs, Article 9.4.2 of ChAFTA limits the MFN treatment obligation by excluding ISDS mechanisms and procedures from its scope. The MFN treatment obligation in the BIT (Article III(c)) contains no comparable restriction and may thus apply to procedures relevant to foreign investors such as ISDS. Arguably, the unqualified scope of the BIT MFN treatment obligation is inconsistent with the narrower obligation in Article 9.4 of ChAFTA, with ChAFTA (as the subsequent treaty) prevailing to the extent of any inconsistency. However, this reading would appear to lead to a derogation from the BIT, contrary to Article 1.2.2 of ChAFTA (which is discussed further below). In our view, therefore, the better interpretation is that the two MFN obligations are cumulative: the parties are able to comply with both by meeting the higher (BIT) standard.

C. Availability of ISDS

Although both the BIT and ChAFTA provide for ISDS, the two ISDS mechanisms differ significantly in terms of coverage and procedures. An exhaustive discussion of the scope and operation of ISDS under these Agreements is beyond the scope of this chapter and is instead covered by other chapters in this volume. Nevertheless, here we compare this aspect of the two Agreements in order to shed further light on their relationship and coexistence in respect of investment protections.

The scope of consent to ISDS by Australia and China under ChAFTA is relatively straightforward. Article 9.12 grants investors the right to submit a case to arbitration, but only when the dispute concerns an alleged breach of the national treatment obligation. As discussed above in subsection B, national treatment is the main substantive obligation contained in Chapter 9 of ChAFTA, whereas the BIT contains no national treatment obligation. The MFN obligation contained in ChAFTA, a broader version of which is also present in the BIT, is not subject to ISDS.

Unlike other 'first-generation' BITs, the Australia–China BIT does not provide the advance, blanket consent of the Contracting Parties for the resolution of all disputes through ISDS. While both ChAFTA and the BIT restrict ISDS, the BIT does so in a more complicated manner. Before turning to the specific terms of the BIT regarding initiation of an ISDS claim, we note that an additional possibility for ISDS under the BIT would be if an investor sought to use the broad MFN treatment clause under the BIT to import a broader ISDS provision from another BIT. Arbitral tribunals have been divided on whether an investor may invoke a MFN clause to establish jurisdiction,[4] but the controversy surrounding this possibility and notable cases where it has occurred has led to important reforms in treaty drafting.[5] Most contemporary IIAs, including ChAFTA, clearly state that an investor cannot use the MFN clause to seek access to a more favourable dispute resolution mechanism.[6] However, as discussed above, the BIT contains no such limitation. However, the chances of an investor successfully using the MFN clause contained in Article III(c) of the BIT as a basis for arbitral jurisdiction are limited by the fact that that clause is about the treatment of 'investments' rather than investors.[7]

Under the terms of Article XII of the BIT (working from the English language version), an investor could potentially initiate ISDS and submit a claim to an arbitral tribunal: (i) where the parties to the dispute agree to 'submit the dispute to an Arbitral Tribunal constituted in accordance with Annex A' of the BIT (Article XII:2(b)); (ii) 'where the dispute relates to the amount of compensation payable under Article VIII' of the BIT (ie, for expropriation) (Article XII:2(b)); or, (iii) if Australia and China join the Convention on the Settlement of Investment Disputes between States and Nationals of Other States (ICSID Convention),[8] 'in accordance with the terms on which the Contracting Party which has admitted the investment is a party to the [ICSID Convention]' (Article XII:4). The first of these situations—where consent is provided by the host state on an ad hoc basis for arbitration of a particular dispute—is uncontroversial. However, the scope of disputes covered by the other two situations is uncertain. At the time of writing, no arbitral decision has addressed this issue under the BIT.

As noted above, the second basis upon which a dispute could be referred to ISDS under the BIT is where the dispute 'relates to the amount of compensation payable' for an expropriation. On its face, this language is clear. However, arbitral tribunals have interpreted similar provisions in a variety of ways. The Tribunal in *Tza Yap Shum v Peru* held:

> the words 'involving the amount of compensation for expropriation' must be interpreted to include not only the mere determination of the amount but also

[4] See, eg, *Maffezini v Spain (Decision of the Tribunal on Objections to Jurisdiction)*, ICSID Case No ARB/97/7 (25 January 2000) [64]; *H&H Enterprises Investments, Inc v Egypt (Award)*, ICSID Case No ARB/09/15 (6 May 2014) [358].

[5] See, eg, Draft Text of the Central American Free Trade Agreement, Ch 10, fn 1 (28 January 2004), sice.oas.org/TPD/USA_CAFTA/Jan28draft/Chap10_e.pdf.

[6] See, eg, Trans-Pacific Partnership (TPP) (signed 4 February 2016, not yet in force) Art 9.5.3; Korea–Australia Free Trade Agreement (signed 8 April 2014, entered into force 12 December 2014) fn 35 to Art 11.4.

[7] *RosInvest Co UK Ltd v Russian Federation (Award on Jurisdiction)*, Arbitration Institute of the Stockholm Chamber of Commerce, Case No V 079/2005 (October 2007) [128]–[129].

[8] Convention on the Settlement of Investment Disputes between States and Nationals of Other States (opened for signature 18 March 1965, entered into force 14 October 1966).

> other issues that are normally inherent in an expropriation, including whether the property was actually expropriated in accordance with the standards and requirements of the BIT.[9]

In this way, the Tribunal broadened the scope of issues that could be subject to ISDS beyond the amount of compensation payable, to include a consideration of whether or not an expropriation occurred. The Tribunal's finding relied on the fact that the relevant treaty provision referred to disputes 'involving' the amount of compensation, rather than disputes that were limited to or exclusively about the amount of compensation.[10] A similar argument could be made with regard to the Australia–China BIT, given that it refers to a dispute that 'relates to' the amount of compensation payable.[11]

Other cases, however, reflect a different approach to the interpretation of similar provisions. The *RosInvest* Tribunal held that the phrase 'concerning the amount or payment of compensation' payable under the Treaty for expropriation could 'only be understood as a limitation of the jurisdiction conferred by that clause'.[12] The Treaty at issue in *Berschader v Russian Federation*, the Belgium–Luxembourg–Soviet Union BIT, included an arbitration clause covering disputes 'relative au montant ou au mode de paiement des indemnités' (ie, relating to the amount or method of payment of compensation).[13] The Tribunal interpreted this language, which is similar to that used in the Australia–China BIT, as excluding from the scope of arbitration any dispute relating to obligations other than expropriation, as well as disputes concerning whether or not an expropriation occurred.[14]

Thus, the case law to date is unclear. Article XII:2(b) of the Australia–China BIT might allow adjudication of only valuation disputes regarding expropriation, or also broader questions *relating to* compensation for expropriation, such as determining whether or not an expropriation has actually taken place.

[9] See, eg, *Tza Yap Shum v Republic of Peru (Decision on Jurisdiction and Competence)*, ICSID Case No ARB/07/6 (19 June 2009) [188], reproduced in *Tza Yap Shum v Republic of Peru (Decision on Annulment)*, ICSID Case No ARB/07/6 (12 February 2015) [103].

[10] *Tza Yap Shum v Republic of Peru (Decision on Jurisdiction and Competence)* (n 9) [151], reproduced in *Tza Yap Shum v Republic of Peru (Decision on Annulment)* (n 9) [74].

[11] The view taken by the Tribunal in *Tza Yap Shum* has been controversial, and the Respondent state (Peru) requested annulment under the ICSID procedure on the basis of manifest excess of powers (among other grounds for review). The ad hoc committee considering the annulment application held that the Tribunal had been through an interpretive process as required by the VCLT, and that while an appellate body 'might well find fault as a matter of law with some aspects of the Arbitral Tribunal's application of the VCLT', that it did not have such powers and could not 'replace the Arbitral Tribunal's Judgment by its own'. *Tza Yap Shum v Republic of Peru (Decision on Annulment)* (n 9) [99].

[12] *RosInvest Co UK Ltd v Russian Federation (Award on Jurisdiction)* (n 7) [110].

[13] Reproduced in *Vladimir Berschader and Moïse Berschader v Russian Federation (Award)*, Arbitration Institute of the Stockholm Chamber of Commerce, Case No 080/2004 (21 April 2006) 151.

[14] ibid 153.

The third possible basis for ISDS under the BIT is resolution pursuant to the ICSID Convention if both parties become party to that Convention. Since the conclusion of the BIT, Australia and China have both become party to the ICSID Convention, which came into force for Australia on 1 June 1991 and for China on 6 February 1993. Article XII:4 of the BIT allows for submission of disputes in accordance with the terms of the relevant party's accession to the ICSID Convention. Under Article 25(4) of the ICSID Convention, any party may notify a 'class or classes of disputes which it would or would not consider submitting to the jurisdiction of the Centre'. While Australia has made no such notification, on 7 January 1993, China notified International Centre for the Settlement of Investment Disputes (ICSID) that it would 'only consider submitting to the jurisdiction of the [ICSID] disputes over compensation resulting from expropriation and nationalization'.[15] The wording of the notification (in identifying disputes *over* compensation) is arguably narrower than the wording of Article XII:2(b) of the BIT (disputes *relating to* the amount of compensation) and might therefore avoid the potential broader interpretation discussed above, which could possibly extend to expropriation claims.

China's notification under Article 25(4) constitutes not consent to arbitration for disputes relating to compensation for expropriation, but rather a limit on the disputes in which China may consent to ICSID jurisdiction. Article XII:4 of the BIT does not explicitly limit the types of disputes that may be resolved pursuant to the ICSID Convention to those relating to compensation for expropriation (unlike Article XII:2(b)); nor does Article XII:4 incorporate such a limitation by way of a cross-reference to Article XII:2(b). However, by referring to the terms of accession to the ICSID Convention, Article XII:4 must be understood as indirectly incorporating such a limitation by virtue of China's continuing notification under Article 25(4) of the ICSID Convention.[16] As no such notification or limitation applies to Australia's consent to ICSID jurisdiction, the types of dispute that may be subject to ISDS claims against Australia under the BIT are not similarly restricted.

This discrepancy in the scope of potential ICSID claims under the BIT may be surprising given that the BIT (unlike ChAFTA) appears to impose reciprocal obligations in an even-handed manner. At the time of the BIT's

[15] See ICSID, Contracting States and Measures Taken by them for the Purpose of the Convention, Notifications Concerning Classes of Disputes Considered Suitable or Unsuitable for Submission to the Centre List ICSID/8-D, May 2016, Art 25(4) of the Convention, icsid.worldbank.org/apps/ICSIDWEB/icsiddocs/Documents/ICSID%208-Contracting%20States%20and%20Measures%20Taken%20by%20Them%20for%20the%20Purpose%20of%20the%20Convention.pdf.

[16] *cf Sanum v Laos*, where it was found that such declarations are for information purposes only and are not legally binding declarations which narrow or broaden an otherwise existing consent to jurisdiction. *Sanum Investments Limited v Lao Peoples Democratic Republic (Award on Jurisdiction)*, PCA Case No 2013-13 (13 December 2013).

conclusion and entry into force in 1988, neither China nor Australia had joined the ICSID Convention; thus, China had not yet made the notification restricting its potential consent to ICSID jurisdiction. The parties to the BIT did not appear to intend to provide a one-sided approach to investment protection, even if they did in relation to substantive obligations more recently under ChAFTA. Australia could have limited its accession to the ICSID Convention just as China did, but as Australia chose not to do so, in our view the BIT provides a basis for a much wider range of ICSID claims by Chinese investors in Australia than by Australian investors in China.

This discussion of Article XII of the BIT and analogous arbitral decisions shows that the scope of disputes in relation to which an investor may pursue ISDS under the BIT is uncertain. In the absence of agreement by the disputing parties (or the successful invocation of an ISDS provision from another IIA pursuant to the MFN obligation in the BIT), ISDS claims against China may be limited to those relating to the amount of compensation for expropriation (which might possibly include whether an expropriation has occurred). However, ICSID claims that may be brought against Australia could potentially extend to the other substantive obligations in the BIT. This asymmetry in the scope of ICSID jurisdiction pursuant to the BIT compounds the asymmetry in substantive obligations under ChAFTA as noted above, with Australia taking on a greater burden under both Treaties.

D. Safeguards for Regulatory Autonomy

Like many contemporary IIAs, ChAFTA contains a range of provisions designed to safeguard the regulatory autonomy of the parties.[17] Chapter 9 contains a general exceptions clause modelled on Article XX of the General Agreement on Tariffs and Trade 1994 (GATT)[18] (Article 9.8), as well as an allowance for each party to maintain a limited range of non-conforming measures (Article 9.5). In addition, ChAFTA provides some innovative procedural mechanisms that may improve the chances of a respondent host state being able to defend measures taken in the public interest. Article 9.11.4 states: 'Measures of a Party that are non-discriminatory

[17] For a more general discussion of these developments in treaty drafting and their impact on regulatory autonomy, see generally: SA Spears, 'The Quest For Policy Space in a New Generation of International Investment Agreements' (2010) 13(4) *Journal of International Economic Law* 1037; C Henckels, 'Protecting Regulatory Autonomy through Greater Precision in Investment Treaties: The TPP, CETA, and TTIP' (2016) 19(1) *Journal of International Economic Law* 27; BJ Condon, 'Treaty Structure and Public Interest Regulation in International Economic Law' (2014) 17(2) *Journal of International Economic Law* 333.

[18] The original GATT 1947 has now been incorporated in GATT 1994: Marrakesh Agreement Establishing the World Trade Organization (opened for signature 15 April 1994, entered into force 1 January 1995) 1867 UNTS 3, Annex 1A (General Agreement on Tariffs and Trade 1994).

and for the legitimate public welfare objectives of public health, safety, the environment, public morals or public order shall not be the subject of a claim under this Section'. Where a respondent state faced with a claim from an investor feels that this provision applies, it may issue a 'public welfare notice' (Article 9.11.5). The issuance of a public welfare notice triggers a 90-day period of consultations between the respondent state and the other state party to ChAFTA, during which the dispute resolution procedure is suspended (Article 9.11.6). During this consultation period, the states parties have an opportunity to reach an agreement on whether or not the measure at issue falls within the scope of the Article 9.11.4 carve-out, and any such decision is binding on the arbitral tribunal (Article 9.18.3).[19] In addition, under ChAFTA, the Committee on Investment formed by the parties is able to issue binding interpretations of any provision of Chapter 9 (Articles 9.7.3(b) and 9.18.2), and may also determine whether a specific measure falls within the scope of the non-conforming measures provision, if the relevant party asserts this as a defence (Articles 9.7.3(b) and 9.19).

As noted in Table 1, as is typical of first-generation IIAs, the BIT contains no explicit safeguards for regulatory autonomy. No modern safeguards found in more recent IIAs appear, such as general exceptions or clarifications on the scope of broad obligations such as fair and equitable treatment. Nevertheless, two elements of the BIT text are worth noting as possible protections for the regulatory autonomy of the BIT parties. First, Article XI creates a stand-alone obligation for each party to comply with written undertakings it makes to covered investors. While this provision appears intended to operate in a manner analogous to an umbrella clause, allowing breach of other written agreements to be brought within the scope of the BIT, the reference to written undertakings may be helpful as support for a narrow interpretation of other obligations in the BIT where the concept of the legitimate expectations of the investor is relevant, such as fair and equitable treatment. The emphasis on written undertakings in Article XI could be used to suggest that verbal or implied undertakings cannot give rise to legitimate expectations for investors. Second, the limited scope of ISDS under the BIT with respect to China provides a powerful protection for its regulatory autonomy.[20]

[19] For more discussion of this provision, see: The Parliament of the Commonwealth of Australia, Joint Standing Committee on Treaties, *Report 154–Treaty tabled on 17 June 2015: Free Trade Agreement between the Government of Australia and the Government of the People's Republic of China* (Canberra, 15 June 2015) (tabled 19 October 2015) [5.13]; A Roberts and R Braddock, 'Protecting Public Welfare Regulation Through Joint Treaty Party Control: A ChAFTA Innovation' *EJIL: Talk!* (21 June 2016).

[20] In a recent exercise that sought to quantify various drafting reforms in IIAs and their contribution to regulatory autonomy, Broude, Haftel and Thompson suggest that the exclusion of ISDS from an agreement is one of the most significant protections for regulatory autonomy. See, eg, T Broude, YZ Haftel and A Thompson, 'Legitimation through Renegotiation: Do States Seek More Regulatory Space in their BITs?' (2016) Hebrew University of Jerusalem Legal Studies Research Paper Series No 17-1, 14–15, 27.

III. THE FUTURE WORK PROGRAMME ON INVESTMENT: CHAFTA ARTICLE 9.9

Article 9.9.1 of ChAFTA provides for Australia and China to review 'the investment legal framework between them no later than three years after the date of entry into force of this Agreement'. Article 9.9.2 of ChAFTA confirms that the review of 'the investment legal framework' under Article 9.9.1 is to include consideration of both ChAFTA Chapter 9 and the Australia–China BIT. In addition, under Article 9.9.3, Australia and China are to 'commence negotiations on a comprehensive Investment Chapter, reflecting outcomes of the review ... immediately after [it] is completed'. Although not explicitly stated, since the review is to encompass both ChAFTA and the BIT, the comprehensive investment chapter could be expected to consolidate the BIT obligations into ChAFTA. Article 9.9.3 specifies that the negotiations towards a comprehensive investment chapter are to include:

(a) amendments to Articles included in this Chapter;
(b) the inclusion of additional Articles in this Chapter, including Articles addressing:
  (i) Minimum Standard of Treatment;
  (ii) Expropriation;
  (iii) Transfers;
  (iv) Performance Requirements;
  (v) Senior Management and Board of Directors;
  (vi) Investment-specific State to State Dispute Settlement; and
  (vii) The application of investment protections and ISDS to services supplied through commercial presence; and
(c) scheduling of investment commitments by China on a negative list basis.

As ChAFTA entered into force on 20 December 2015, the review of ChAFTA Chapter 9 and the BIT must be carried out by 20 December 2018. However, ChAFTA imposes no time limit for the conclusion of the subsequent negotiations on a comprehensive investment chapter. Moreover, the inclusion of the words '[u]nless the Parties otherwise agree' in both Articles 9.9.1 and 9.9.3 means that Australia and China could agree to cancel or postpone the review and/or the subsequent negotiations. In contrast, if either party unilaterally declined to participate in the review or the negotiations, then that party would be in breach of the Treaty. The other party, however, would have difficulty enforcing the requirement. Even if the latter party raised the matter through ChAFTA's state-to-state dispute settlement mechanism, an arbitral tribunal would have difficulty forcing the other party to participate actively in the review process or subsequent negotiations, notwithstanding the potential threat of suspension of concessions under ChAFTA Article 15.16.

Assuming that Australia and China maintain the timetable envisaged in ChAFTA Article 9.9, the review of the investment framework will be completed by the end of 2018, and the negotiations will take place immediately thereafter and could be more or less protracted depending on the surrounding circumstances. These negotiations can be expected to depend in part on the conclusion of negotiations by China towards IIAs with certain other countries. According to the report on ChAFTA of the Joint Standing Committee on Treaties of the Parliament of the Commonwealth of Australia (referring to evidence by senior officials from Australia's Department of Foreign Affairs and Trade), ChAFTA Chapter 9 is limited and subject to a broad future work programme because China is working out its position on modern IIAs, including through negotiations with other countries[21] such as the United States (US)[22] and the European Union (EU). These extraneous negotiations may impose additional barriers and delays to the conclusion of a comprehensive Australia–China investment chapter under ChAFTA, particularly following the election of US President Donald Trump.

In the meantime, the question arises whether the Australia–China BIT continues to operate notwithstanding the conclusion of ChAFTA and the decision by the ChAFTA negotiators to postpone the agreement of a comprehensive investment chapter. In the following sections, we consider first whether the BIT obligations continue to operate despite the conclusion of ChAFTA, and then whether the BIT obligations can be reinterpreted in the light of ChAFTA's regulatory safeguards.

IV. CONTINUING BIT OBLIGATIONS: VCLT ARTICLE 30 AND CHAFTA ARTICLE 1.2

Both China and Australia are parties to the VCLT, which sets out general rules on treaty interpretation and application. As the BIT and ChAFTA both contain rules on investment, they could be regarded as 'successive treaties relating to the same subject-matter' under Article 30 of the VCLT, which reads in relevant part:[23]

> *Article 30: Application of successive treaties relating to the same subject-matter*
>
> 1. Subject to Article 103 of the Charter of the United Nations, the rights and obligations of States parties to successive treaties relating to the same subject-matter shall be determined in accordance with the following paragraphs.

[21] The Parliament of the Commonwealth of Australia, Joint Standing Committee on Treaties, Report 154 (n 19) [5.7]–[5.8].

[22] See, eg, 'Froman Says China Improved BIT Offer, But Experts Doubt 2016 Deal' (24 June 2016) 34.25 *Inside US Trade* (online).

[23] The later paras of Art 30 relate to the situation where there are differences between the parties to the agreements.

2. When a treaty specifies that it is subject to, or that it is not to be considered as incompatible with, an earlier or later treaty, the provisions of that other treaty prevail.

3. When all the parties to the earlier treaty are parties also to the later treaty but the earlier treaty is not terminated or suspended in operation under article 59, the earlier treaty applies only to the extent that its provisions are compatible with those of the later treaty.

...

Paragraph 2 of Article 30 does not apply to the ChAFTA–BIT relationship, because neither Agreement specifies that it is subject to the other. The BIT is silent on the effect of subsequent treaties, while ChAFTA does not specify that its provisions are subject to or limited by the BIT. Thus, the relevant element of VCLT Article 30 is paragraph 3, which applies when two treaties operate between the same parties. Applying this provision, as the BIT has not been terminated or suspended by ChAFTA, the BIT applies only to the extent that its provisions are compatible with those of ChAFTA. In other words, pursuant to Article 30(3) of the VCLT, ChAFTA prevails over the BIT to the extent of any inconsistency.

However, the text of ChAFTA itself creates some uncertainty about this conclusion. Article 1.2 of ChAFTA provides:

Article 1.2: Relation to Other Agreements

1. The Parties affirm their existing rights and obligations with respect to each other under multilateral and bilateral agreements to which both Parties are party, including the WTO Agreement.

2. Nothing in this Agreement shall derogate from the existing rights and obligations of a Party under the WTO Agreement or any other multilateral or bilateral agreement to which both Parties are party.

3. In the event of any inconsistency between this Agreement and any other multilateral or bilateral agreement to which both Parties are party, the Parties shall immediately consult with a view to finding a mutually satisfactory solution.

Paragraphs 1 and 2 of this Article suggest that, in concluding ChAFTA, the parties intended the BIT to remain in force unaltered. However, Article 1.2.3 provides that, where an inconsistency arises with an earlier treaty, the parties shall consult to resolve it.

In our view, two different approaches could be adopted to resolve an inconsistency between the BIT and ChAFTA on which the parties disagree. The first possibility is that VCLT Article 30(3) applies, as noted above, such that ChAFTA prevails. The second possible approach is that ChAFTA Article 1.2.2 is *lex specialis*, taking precedence over Article 30(3) of the VCLT. Following this approach, ChAFTA cannot derogate from the BIT, which therefore prevails over ChAFTA to the extent of any inconsistency.

Regardless of which approach is adopted, an inconsistency may exist (in other words, identifying the appropriate conflict rule does not make the underlying conflict vanish). In the context of the clear statements in Articles 1.2.1 and 1.2.2, we read Article 1.2.3 as setting out the *process* to be adopted in the event of inconsistency between ChAFTA and the BIT (namely consultation), rather than as identifying which treaty prevails to the extent of such inconsistency. In other words, ChAFTA Article 1.2.3 addresses the process for resolving any inconsistency with the BIT without addressing the substance of the inconsistency in the absence of agreement as to its resolution through consultation. Similarly, the reference in ChAFTA Article 15.9 to the VCLT rules on *interpretation* does not assist in determining which treaty prevails, since VCLT Article 30 is a rule about the application of treaties rather than their interpretation.

On balance, we regard the second approach as correct: the BIT prevails over ChAFTA to the extent of inconsistency. As a treaty, the ChAFTA rules prevail in this specific situation over the more general VCLT rules. States are generally free to contract out of the general rules contained in the VCLT or customary international law. In this instance, Article 1.2.2 of ChAFTA suggests the ChAFTA parties intended that the BIT (and other bilateral agreements) remain in force without being in any way curtailed. Article 1.2.2 does not explicitly state that the parties are contracting out of the VCLT position or that the BIT is intended to prevail over ChAFTA in the case of inconsistency. However, IIAs rarely include 'transparent and intelligible clauses' that directly address issues of possible conflicts with overlapping treaties.[24] Where a subsequent treaty expresses the parties' intentions to extend or complement prior protections for investors, rather than replacing or rewriting them, it follows that narrower standards of protection contained in the subsequent agreement do not override the more general standards in the earlier agreement.[25]

In relation to a similarly worded clause to Article 1.2.2 in the Australia–Malaysia Free Trade Agreement (FTA),[26] Alexander Orakhelashvili has argued that the provision is of little use in resolving conflicts with concurrent treaties, and that instead the rule contained in VCLT Article 30 should be followed.[27] However, Orakhelashvili was examining the impact of the Australia–Malaysia FTA on the earlier FTA between Australia, New Zealand

[24] A Orakhelashvili, 'Article 30 of the 1969 Vienna Convention on the Law of Treaties: Application of the Successive Treaties Relating to the Same Subject-Matter' (2016) 31(2) *ICSID Review–Foreign Investment Law Journal* 344, 345.

[25] M-F Houde and K Yannaca-Small, 'Relationships between International Investment Agreements' (2004) OECD Working Papers on International Investment Number 2004/1, 8–9.

[26] Free Trade Agreement between Australia and Malaysia (signed 22 May 2012, entered into force 1 January 2013) [2013] ATS 4, Art 21.2.

[27] Orakhelashvili (n 24) 345–46.

and the Association of Southeast Asian Nations (ASEAN), concluding that the relevant conflicts provisions in the two Treaties create a situation of 'mutual deference' requiring resort to Article 30 of the VCLT.[28] The situation between ChAFTA and the Australia–China BIT can be distinguished, as only one Treaty (ChAFTA) has any provision regarding the relationship between the two Agreements. Thus, we see no principle of 'mutual deference' or cancelling out of the conflicts provisions of the two Treaties.

Very few arbitral decisions have had to address how successive treaties affecting the rights of investors relate to one another. One relevant decision was *Electrabel v Hungary*, where the Tribunal concluded that EU law prevails between Member States and can override their pre-existing rights under the Energy Charter Treaty,[29] and that even if EU law did not provide for such an outcome, the same conclusion would be reached under Article 30 of the VCLT.[30] On the facts of that case, however, the Tribunal found that the relevant treaty provisions were not inconsistent and therefore the issue did not arise.[31] Again, this case is different from that posed by the Australia–China BIT and ChAFTA. In contrast to the relevant provisions of EU law, ChAFTA states in Article 1.2.2 that it does *not* affect obligations under the BIT. Although ChAFTA could have been more explicit regarding how any inconsistency between the two Treaties should be resolved in the absence of agreement between the parties (beyond Article 1.2.3), The parties do appear to have intended that the BIT continue to operate without alteration.

Arbitral tribunals have resolved most situations of allegedly concurrent treaties relating to investment by finding no conflict between the two treaties, because their subject matter does not directly overlap.[32] The failure of ChAFTA to definitively establish which treaty takes precedence in the event of inconsistency supports our earlier conclusion that China and Australia drafted Chapter 9 of ChAFTA with a view to minimising the overlap in substantive obligations with the BIT, reducing the likelihood of any inconsistency arising in the first place. Perhaps if the negotiators had expected inconsistencies to arise between the two they would have provided more clarity in drafting ChAFTA Article 1.

[28] ibid 345, fn 4.

[29] Energy Charter Treaty (opened for signature 17 December 1994, entered into force 16 April 1998) corrected by the Protocol of Correction 2 August 1996, 2080 UNTS 95.

[30] *Electrabel SA v Hungary (Award)*, ICSID Case No ARB/07/19 (20 November 2015) [4.186]–[4.190].

[31] ibid [4.191].

[32] See, eg, *Eastern Sugar BV (Netherlands) v The Czech Republic (Partial Award)*, Stockholm Chamber of Commerce, Case No 088/2004 (27 March 2007) 159–64, 169; *European American Investment Bank AG (EURAM) v Slovak Republic (Award on Jurisdiction)*, PCA Case No 2010-17 (22 October 2012) 270.

V. THE LIMITED ROLE OF ChAFTA IN INTERPRETING THE BIT: VCLT ARTICLE 31(3)

The expected coexistence of the BIT and ChAFTA for some years to come raises the concern that the extensive BIT obligations and the corresponding ISDS mechanism (particularly for wide-ranging claims against Australia) will continue to operate in the absence of the more modern explicit safeguards for regulatory autonomy found in ChAFTA Chapter 9. One possible way of avoiding that problematic scenario would be if the BIT can be properly interpreted in the light of ChAFTA to reflect such safeguards. In order to determine whether this approach is possible, we need to examine whether ChAFTA relevantly modifies the obligations under the BIT pursuant to the customary rules of interpretation under the VCLT. In particular, does Article 31(3) of the VCLT provide a basis for somehow reading ChAFTA's regulatory safeguards into the Australia-China BIT?

> *Article 31: General rule of interpretation*
>
> 1. A treaty shall be interpreted in good faith in accordance with the ordinary meaning to be given to the terms of the treaty in their context and in the light of its object and purpose.
>
> ...
>
> 3. There shall be taken into account, together with the context:
> (a) any *subsequent agreement* between the parties regarding the interpretation of the treaty or the application of its provisions;
> (b) any *subsequent practice* in the application of the treaty which establishes the agreement of the parties regarding its interpretation;
> (c) any *relevant rules of international law* applicable in the relations between the parties.[33]

ChAFTA does probably constitute a 'subsequent agreement' between Australia and China regarding the interpretation or application of the BIT, within the meaning of VCLT Article 31(3)(a). However, if anything, the ChAFTA provisions (and particularly Article 1.2.2 as discussed above) suggest that ChAFTA Chapter 9 is not intended to alter the interpretation or application of the BIT. Therefore, Article 31(3)(a) of the VCLT is unlikely to prove fruitful in modifying the interpretation of the BIT obligations to enhance policy space.

Pursuant to VCLT Article 31(3)(b), if the acts and practice of Australia and China suggested that they intended the BIT not to apply or to be interpreted in a modified way following the entry into force of ChAFTA, this intention could have some effect as 'subsequent practice' in interpreting the

[33] Emphasis added.

BIT. However, the terms of ChAFTA itself (particularly Article 1.2.2) may mean that especially clear and consistent practice of the parties over an extended period of time would be required to establish the existence of such an intention. Again, at this stage, no provisions of ChAFTA or conduct of the parties with respect to the application of the BIT suggest an agreement or even an intention to modify the interpretation of the BIT.

Finally, pursuant to VCLT Article 31(3)(c), ChAFTA certainly contains 'rules of international law' concerning investment that are applicable between Australia and China and therefore relevant to the BIT. The next step in the interpretative process is therefore to identify the impact of taking those rules into account in interpreting the BIT. On the one hand, the terms of ChAFTA Article 1.2.2 may mean that ChAFTA has no impact on the interpretation of the BIT, even if ChAFTA falls squarely within VCLT Article 31(3)(c). On the other hand, perhaps a treaty interpreter could take ChAFTA Chapter 9 into account in interpreting the BIT without 'derogat[ing]' from the rights and obligations imposed by the BIT. Yet even on that basis, how exactly could the ChAFTA Chapter 9 regulatory safeguards be said to influence the interpretation of the BIT?

To begin with, as noted above, ChAFTA contains no fair and equitable treatment or expropriation provisions and therefore does not contain the clarifications commonly imposed in modern IIAs to restrict the scope of those provisions for the sake of maintaining policy space (as discussed further below). Furthermore, the safeguards that are contained in ChAFTA Chapter 9 do not easily translate into particular interpretations of the broad BIT obligations.

For example, in interpreting the ISDS provisions in Articles XII:2(b) and XII:4 of the Australia–China BIT, no particular treaty terms or phrases seem amenable to incorporating the procedural 'public welfare notice' mechanism from Article 9.11.5 of ChAFTA (which, together with Article 9.18.3, allows the exclusion of certain 'non-discriminatory' measures for certain 'public welfare objectives' from ISDS by agreement between Australia and China). Similarly, ChAFTA Article 9.5 by its terms prevents the application of the national treatment and MFN treatment obligations in ChAFTA Articles 9.3 and 9.4 respectively; Article 9.5 and the corresponding non-conforming measures cannot easily be read as precluding the application to those measures of the non-discrimination and other substantive investment obligations in the Australia–China BIT. The Australia–China BIT also contains no obvious language that would allow such an interpretation by reference to ChAFTA. Finally, the broad 'general exceptions' clause in ChAFTA Article 9.8 provides (specifically 'for the purposes of' ChAFTA Chapter 9) that nothing in 'this Agreement' is to be construed as preventing a party from adopting or enforcing certain measures. The words 'this Agreement' must be understood as referring exclusively to ChAFTA rather than ChAFTA and the BIT, particularly since the parties identified the BIT by name in ChAFTA Article 9.9.2.

The most reasonable conclusion from this analysis is that the Australia–China BIT obligations remain in force, without being explicitly subject to any of the common modern safeguards for regulatory autonomy, despite the parties' agreement on such safeguards in ChAFTA. One way to deal with this rather unsatisfactory situation would be to terminate the BIT, although this would limit the investment protections between the two countries to those contained in ChAFTA Chapter 9 until further obligations are agreed. We now turn to the various possibilities for terminating the BIT.

VI. RESOLUTION THROUGH TERMINATION OF THE BIT

The Australia–China BIT contains fairly standard provisions on termination, allowing either party (after an initial 10-year period ending in 1998)[34] to terminate the Treaty unilaterally by giving one year's written notice, pursuant to Article XIV:3:

> At the end of the first period of ten years referred to in paragraph 1 of this Article and thereafter at any time either Contracting Party may terminate this Agreement by giving one year's written notice to the other Contracting Party.

In addition, the BIT contains a survival clause in Article XIV:4, also common in IIAs, such that the agreement will continue to apply following such unilateral termination:

> Notwithstanding its termination in accordance with paragraph 3 of this Article, this Agreement shall continue to apply, for a further period of ten years from the date of its termination, to investments made or acquired prior to the date of its termination.

If Australia (or China) becomes concerned about the ongoing effect of the BIT, and particularly its absence of regulatory protections, they therefore have several options. First, they could attempt to resolve these matters through the ChAFTA work programme on investment. Second, if that process proves unsatisfactory or does not provide sufficient comfort sufficiently quickly, then either of them could terminate the BIT by providing one year's written notice to the other, subject to the 10-year survival clause. Third, the parties could terminate the BIT by mutual agreement, in which case they could also agree at the same time to extinguish or reduce the survival period. Such a modification of the survival clause is possible as a matter of public international law and has occurred in practice in other instances.[35]

[34] Australia–China BIT, Art XIV:1.

[35] See, eg, T Voon, A Mitchell and J Munro, 'Parting Ways: The Impact of Mutual Termination of Investment Treaties on Investor Rights' (2014) 29(2) *ICSID Review* 451, 465–68; T Voon and A Mitchell, 'Denunciation, Termination and Survival: The Interplay of Treaty Law and International Investment Law' (2016) 31(2) *ICSID Review* 413, 429–32.

These options of unilateral or bilateral termination may take place irrespective of other negotiations between Australia and China. However, recent Australian treaty practice provides examples of how the two countries could use the opportunity of new negotiations to terminate the outdated Australia–China BIT. If the parties eventually agree on a comprehensive investment chapter under ChAFTA, that achievement would provide an obvious occasion to terminate the BIT. Similarly, Australia and Chile agreed to terminate their 1996 BIT[36] upon entry into force of their preferential trade agreement[37] in 2009 (subject to a modified survival period of three years for ISDS claims under the BIT).[38]

Another possibility for termination in conjunction with other negotiations is for Australia and China to agree to terminate the BIT upon conclusion of broader plurilateral negotiations, such as the ongoing negotiations towards the Regional Comprehensive Economic Partnership (RCEP). The RCEP is being negotiated among the 10 Member States of ASEAN[39] and countries with existing preferential trade agreements with ASEAN: Australia, China, India, Japan, the Republic of Korea and New Zealand. Negotiators are aiming to achieve 'a swift and successful conclusion' to the negotiations[40] and have already announced that the Treaty will have an investment chapter including ISDS.[41] A modern, comprehensive investment chapter in the RCEP may obviate the need for continuing investment obligations under the BIT, providing Australia and China with another opportunity to agree to terminate the BIT.

Australia took the opportunity to reach mutual agreements to terminate some of its older BITs in conjunction with the (anticipated) entry into force of the 12-country Trans-Pacific Partnership (TPP).[42] In side letters to the TPP with Mexico,[43] Peru[44] and Viet Nam,[45] Australia agreed to terminate

[36] Agreement between the Government of Australia and the Government of the Republic of Chile on the Reciprocal Promotion and Protection of Investments (Australia–Chile BIT) (signed 9 July 1996, entered into force 18 November 1999).

[37] Australia–Chile Free Trade Agreement (ACIFTA) (signed 30 July 2008, entered into force 6 March 2009) [2009] ATS 6.

[38] ACIFTA (n 37) Annex 10-E; *cf* Australia–Chile BIT (n 36) Art 12(3).

[39] ASEAN Member States are: Brunei Darussalam, Burma, Cambodia, Indonesia, Laos, Malaysia, the Philippines, Singapore, Thailand and Viet Nam.

[40] Joint Statement on the RCEP Negotiations, Tangerang, Indonesia (20 December 2016).

[41] Statement by Australian Chief Negotiator Michael Mugliston, stakeholder event on investment, 12th Round of RCEP Negotiations, Perth, Australia (27 April 2016).

[42] TPP (n 6).

[43] Exchange of letters between Andrew Robb, Minister for Trade and Investment, Australia, and Ildefonso Guajardo Villareal, Minister of Economy, Mexico (4 February 2016).

[44] Exchange of letters between Andrew Robb, Minister for Trade and Investment, Australia, and Ana María Sánchez de Ríos, Minister of Foreign Affairs, Peru (29 January 2016).

[45] Exchange of letters between Andrew Robb, Minister for Trade and Investment, Australia, and Vu Huy Hoang, Minister of Industry and Trade, Socialist Republic of Viet Nam (4 February 2016).

its BITs with those countries[46] upon entry into force of the TPP, subject to a modified three-year survival period.[47]

VII. CONCLUSION

In this chapter we have considered what is likely to be an increasingly important issue in international investment law: how do successive treaties with overlapping subject matter relate to one another, particularly in the absence of a clear indication from the parties as to whether one treaty takes precedence over the other to the extent of any inconsistency? Our analysis of the scope and content of the two Agreements suggests that China and Australia intended the BIT and ChAFTA to operate cumulatively, viewing the possibility of inconsistency between the two Agreements as unlikely. ChAFTA contains very few substantive investment obligations and provides for ISDS only in relation to national treatment. Only the MFN treatment obligation applies under both Agreements. However, important distinctions exist between the two Agreements. Chapter 9 of ChAFTA, like most modern IIAs, contains novel and important safeguards of the states parties' regulatory autonomy. Yet those safeguards do not apply to the broad investment protections in the BIT, under which Australia (but not China) could potentially still face a wide range of ISDS claims.

The ChAFTA parties appear to have seen this discrepancy (between ChAFTA and the BIT, and between the burdens imposed on Australia and China under the two Treaties) as a temporary problem, to be addressed by inserting a comprehensive set of investment rules in ChAFTA after other major powers such as the US had reached agreement on such rules with China. At that time, the parties might also have terminated the BIT or rendered it subject to ChAFTA. Post-ChAFTA developments in US policy risk delaying or negating the conclusion of an IIA between China and the US, leaving ChAFTA with significant gaps in substantive investment protections and the BIT with insufficient safeguards for regulatory autonomy.

[46] Agreement between Australia and the Socialist Republic of Vietnam on the Reciprocal Promotion and Protection of Investments (Australia–Viet Nam BIT) (signed 5 March 1991, entered into force 11 September 1991) [1991] ATS 36; Agreement between Australia and the Government of the Republic of Peru on the Promotion and Protection of Investments (Australia–Peru BIT) (signed 7 December 1995, entered into force 2 February 1997) [1997] ATS 8; Agreement between the Government of Australia and the Government of the United Mexican States on the Promotion and Reciprocal Protection of Investments (Australia–Mexico BIT) (signed 23 August 2005, entered into force 21 July 2007) [2007] 2483 UNTS 247.

[47] *cf* Australia–Viet Nam BIT (n 46) Art 15 (initial 15-year period; 15-year survival period following unilateral termination with one year's notice); Australia–Peru BIT (n 46) Art 16 (initial 15-year period; 15-year survival period following unilateral termination with one year's notice); Australia–Mexico BIT (n 46) Art 24 (initial 10-year period; 10-year survival period following unilateral termination with one year's notice).

The apparent unwillingness of China and Australia to address this issue directly in the ChAFTA text provides an important lesson for the negotiation of future IIAs. Negotiating parties need to think carefully about the relationship of the new treaty to past agreements, taking the opportunity provided by the negotiations to resolve these questions unambiguously. For the bilateral investment framework established between China and Australia, the RCEP negotiations and the future work programme required under ChAFTA both provide avenues through which the parties could provide clarity on the issues raised in this chapter. Unilateral or joint termination of the BIT in conjunction with those processes may also be warranted.

12

A Comparative Review of the Investor–State Arbitration Clause in ChAFTA from China's Perspective: Moving Forwards or Sideways?

SHU ZHANG

I. INTRODUCTION

DESPITE THE CRITICISMS against the nature of investor–state arbitration (ISA),[1] it is now a common feature of bilateral investment treaties (BITs) and other international investment agreements (IIAs).[2] China has become the second largest economy in the world and

[1] See, eg, 11 types of criticism are identified in a European research. See European Federation for Investment Law and Arbitration (EFILA), *A Response to the Criticism against ISDS*, www.efila.org/wp-content/uploads/2015/05/EFILA_in_response_to_the-criticism_of_ISDS_final_draft.pdf Criticisms include that ISA infringes the state's sovereignty and their power to regulate; arbitrators are manipulating the ISA practice and getting benefits by favouring investors; and that ISA is used as a weapon of the investors from Western developed countries against the developing countries who would like to attract FDIs. See, eg, N Bernasconi-Osterwalder, 'Who Wins and Who Loses in Investment Arbitration? Are Investors and Host States on a Level Playing Field? The Lauder/Czech Republic Legacy' (2005) 6(1) *Journal of World Investment & Trade* 69; O Chung, 'The Lopsided International Investment Law Regime and Its Effect on the Future of Investor-State Arbitration' (2007) 47(4) *Virginia Journal of International Law* 953; and I Odumosu, 'The Antinomies of the (Continued) Relevance of ICSID to the Third World' (2007) 8(2) *San Diego International Law Journal* 345; P Eberhardt, C Olivet, T Amos and N Buxton, 'Profiting from Injustice: How Law Firms, Arbitrators and Financiers are Fuelling an Investment Arbitration Boom' (2012) *Corporate Europe Observatory* (CEO), www.corporateeurope.org/sites/default/files/publications/profiting-from-injustice.pdf; G Van Harten, 'Arbitrator Behaviour in Asymmetrical Adjudication: An Empirical Study of Investment Treaty Arbitration' (2012) 50(1) *Osgoode Hall Law Journal* 211. These concerns, however, are to some extent addressed by others. See, eg, CN Brower and S Blanchard, What's in a Meme? The Truth about Investor-State Arbitration: Why it Need Not, and Must Not, Be Repossessed by States (2014) 52 *Columbia Journal of Transnational Law* 689.

[2] See L Reed and J Paulsson et al, *Guide to ICSID Arbitration* (Austin, TX, Kluwer Law International 2010) 6–7, 57; see also J Höffken 'Global Policy, More than Regional Investment Protection—ISDS in the EU–US trade agreement' (8 May 2014), www.globalpolicyjournal.

has a significant number of BITs and IIAs,[3] most of which contain an ISA clause. China's foreign investment and economic cooperation policy has developed and shifted significantly during the last decade. China is now negotiating a BIT with the European Union and the US, respectively,[4] and has created the Asian Infrastructure Investment Bank (AIIB)[5] and the Silk Road Economic Belt and the 21st-Century Maritime Silk Road (the Belt and Road) Initiative.[6]

The China-Australia Free Trade Agreement (ChAFTA), which was signed on 17 June 2015, is another significant step in China's recent treaty-making. It is considered that the new features of this Treaty fit the need for rapid development of the trade and investment relationship between China and Australia.[7] In 2015, China was ranked as the seventh largest foreign investor in Australia with an amount of AUD$74.9 billion, and the fifth preferred destination of Australia's outbound investors, with an amount of AUD$70.2 billion.[8]

Based on the background, this chapter reviews the ISA clause in ChAFTA in the context of China's historical developments in drafting ISA clauses, and examines whether ChAFTA's approach of drafting the ISA clause is a move towards a high level of comprehensiveness in investor–state arbitration, or a move towards a more restricted approach. It also discusses the impact of this ISA clause on the rapidly developing China–Australia trade and investment relationship, and whether it would

com/blog/08/05/2014/more-regionalinvestment-protection-%E2%80%93-isds-eu-us-trade-agreement, which refers to the generally positive understandings on including an ISA clause from both the EU and the US. Doubts on ISA, however, remain in many countries in South America and the Pacific; see a summary provided in L Trakman, 'Choosing Domestic Courts over Investor-State Arbitration: Australia's Repudiation of the Status Quo' (2012) 35(3) *University of New South Wales Law Journal* 979, 979–81.

[3] C Salomon and S Friedrich, 'A Statistical Analysis of Bilateral Investment Treaties, Other International Investment Agreements and Investment Arbitrations in the Region' (2015) 16(5–6) *Journal of World Investment & Trade* 800, 801.

[4] The 9th round of China–EU BIT negotiation took place in Beijing, January 2016, www.english.mofcom.gov.cn/article/newsrelease/significantnews/201601/20160101234801.shtml. The 23rd round of China–US BIT negotiation took place in Washington DC, November 2015, www.mofcom.gov.cn/article/ae/ai/201511/20151101195891.shtml.

[5] For China's role in AIIB, eg, see Sue-Lin Wong, 'China Launches New AIIB Development Bank as Power Balance Shifts', www.reuters.com/article/us-asia-aiib-investment-idUSKCN0UU03Y.

[6] The National Development and Reform Commission, Ministry of Foreign Affairs, and Ministry of Commerce of the People's Republic of China,'Action Plan on the Belt and Road Initiative' www.english.gov.cn/archive/publications/2015/03/30/content_281475080249035.htm.

[7] See, eg, remarks by the Australian Department of Foreign Affairs and Trade, www.dfat.gov.au/trade/agreements/chafta/Pages/australia-china-fta.aspx and www.dfat.gov.au/trade/agreements/chafta/fact-sheets/Documents/chafta-snapshot.pdf.

[8] Australian Department of Foreign Affairs and Trade, www.dfat.gov.au/trade/topics/investment/Pages/where-does-australia-invest.aspx; www.dfat.gov.au/trade/topics/investment/Pages/which-countries-invest-in-australia.aspx.

contribute to a consistent and harmonised pro-investment environment in the Asia-Pacific region.[9]

II. IIA DRAFTING AND ISA EXPERIENCES: AN OVERVIEW

A. China's IIA Negotiations and ISA Experiences

Since 1982 (when China concluded its first BIT with Sweden),[10] China has been active in reaching BITs and other international investment agreements such as Free Trade Agreements (FTAs) with substantial investment chapters, multilateral investment agreements, and the Energy Charter Treaty (ECT).[11] So far China has signed 145 BITs and 111 of them are currently in effect.[12] In addition, China has recently reached a few FTAs and multilateral investment agreements, eight of which include a substantive set of rules on investment.[13] Figure 1 shows China's BITs and other IIAs signed since 1982.[14]

China's actions in concluding BITs and IIAs can be divided into different phases in accordance with different versions of BIT provisions.[15]

[9] This chapter defines the Asia-Pacific region as including East Asia (including China, Hong Kong, Macau and Taiwan, Japan, Mongolia, South and North Korea); South East Asia (the ASEAN countries); South Asia (India, Pakistan, Bangladesh, Sri Lanka, Bhutan, the Maldives, Nepal, etc); and Oceania (Australia, New Zealand, Fiji, New Caledonia, Papua New Guinea, the Solomon Islands, Vanuatu, etc).

[10] China–Sweden BIT (signed and in force on 29 March 1982), www.investmentpolicyhub.unctad.org/IIA/country/42/treaty/976. Years of IIAs and BITs noted in this chapter are given as the date of conclusion, not ratification, which suits the purpose of this chapter of analysing the development of China's approach to drafting and negotiating IIAs (and the ISA clause contained in such IIAs).

[11] eg, China's participation in the ECT, see: www.www.energycharter.org/who-we-are/members-observers/countries/china/. it shows 145 BITs in total and 110 in force.

[12] See www.investmentpolicyhub.unctad.org/IIA/IiasByCountry#iiaInnerMenu; it shows 145 BITs in total and 110 in force. According to MOFCOM, the China–Congo Democratic Republic BIT (2011) is now in force, www.english.mofcom.gov.cn/.

[13] These include the China–Australia Free Trade Agreement (2015); China–Korea FTA (2015); China–Costa Rica FTA (2010); China–Peru FTA (2009); China–New Zealand FTA (2008); China–Japan–Korea Trilateral Investment Agreement (2012); ASEAN–China Investment Agreement (2009); and China–Pakistan FTA (2006).

[14] See a list of China's BITs and other investment-related instruments at: www.investmentpolicyhub.unctad.org/IIA/CountryBits/42#iiaInnerMenu. For a discussion of China's BITs and IIAs from the perspective of China's 'One Belt One Road' Initiative, see Shu Zhang, 'China's Approach in Drafting the Investor–State Arbitration Clause: A Review from the "Belt and Road" Regions' Perspective' (2017) *Chinese Journal of Comparative Law*, academic.oup.com/cjcl/article/doi/10.1093/cjcl/cxx005/3970839/Chinas-Approach-in-Drafting-the-InvestorState?guestAccessKey=46b05ae3-9930-405d-825a-679aa6af4c86.

[15] See, eg, E Dulac, 'The Emerging Third Generation of Chinese Investment Treaties' (2010) 7(4) *Transnational Dispute Management* 1; A Berger, 'Hesitant Embrace: China's Recent Approach to International Investment Rule-Making' (2015) 16 *Journal of World Investment & Trade* 843, 845.

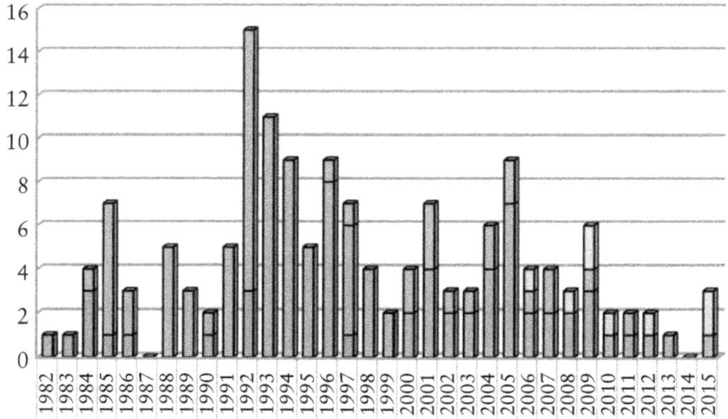

	1982	1983	1984	1985	1986	1987	1988	1989	1990	1991	1992	1993	1994	1995	1996	1997	1998
Other IIAs																	
BIT: Not Ratified	0	0	0	0	0	0	0	0	0	0	0	0	0	0	1	1	0
BIT: In force	0	0	1	6	2	0	5	3	1	5	12	11	9	5	8	5	4
BIT: Terminated	1	1	3	1	1	0	0	0	1	0	3	0	0	0	0	1	0

	1999	2000	2001	2002	2003	2004	2005	2006	2007	2008	2009	2010	2011	2012	2013	2014	2015
Other IIAs								1	0	1	2	1	0	1	0	0	2
BIT: Not Ratified	0	2	3	1	1	2	2	1	2	0	1	1	1	0	0	0	1
BIT: In force	2	2	4	2	2	4	7	2	2	2	3	0	1	1	1	0	0
BIT: Terminated	0	0	0	0	0	0	0	0	0	0	0	0	0	0	0	0	0

Figure 1: BITs and IIAs signed by China

The first phase started with the China-Sweden BIT (1982) and continued until the early 1990s, and during this phase China's treaty-making activities reached their peak, particularly between the late 1980s and early 1990s. During this phase, China reached BITs with most of the Western European countries such as Germany, France and Italy, and then with many other developed and developing countries around Europe, the Asia-Pacific region and South America.[16] The investment agreements concluded in this phase were generally short and abstract without touching upon complicated or sensitive issues such as national treatment; nor did they provide an expansive ISA clause.[17] During this phase, China also joined the New York Convention and the Washington Convention, showing its friendliness towards foreign investors.[18] The second phase started from the conclusion of the China–Barbados BIT (1998), since when an advanced version of investment

[16] Some scholars further divided the first phase into two: first with developed countries (1982–90); and then with developing countries (1991–98). See, eg, Berger, 'Hesitant Embrace' (n 12) 845.

[17] Further discussed in section III.

[18] The Convention on the Recognition and Enforcement of Foreign Arbitral Awards (New York, 1958) (New York Convention); The Convention on the Settlement of Investment Disputes between States and Nationals of Other States (Washington DC, 1965) (Washington Convention). China signed the Agreement to join the Washington Convention on 9 February 1990 and such commitment took effect on 6 February 1993. China's commitment under the New York Convention is further discussed in section VI.

obligations was adopted. During this phase, China concluded BITs with more countries around the world and updated its BITs with several major developed countries in Europe such as Germany, France, Belgium-Luxemburg, Portugal, Spain, Finland and Switzerland. The most recent phase started in the late 2000s, beginning with the China–New Zealand FTA (2008) and the China–Mexico BIT (2008). Several FTAs with comprehensive investment chapters were reached during this phase. Treaties concluded in this phase typically contain comprehensive provisions on investment obligations and dispute resolution, following the US' treaty model, or, as concluded by Berger, a model widely adopted by Member countries of the North America Free Trade Agreement (NAFTA).[19]

The investment chapter of ChAFTA is among the most recent generation of IIAs, and adopts the most recent type of China's ISA clause. The sections below discuss the distinctive features of this ISA clause by comparing it with other China-made ISA clauses, discussing its relationship with the China–Australia BIT and reviewing it in the context of China's achievement in the current global development of ISA schemes, especially in the Asia-Pacific region.

B. ISA Experiences: China, Australia and the Asia-Pacific Region

Compared with the massive numbers of China's BITs and IIAs, China's experience in ISA practice is not extensive. So far, China has only been involved in a handful of ISA cases according to the report of the International Centre for Settlement of Investment Disputes (ICSID), including five claims brought by Chinese parties (including Hong Kong and Macau), three of which were BIT-based,[20] and two cases in which China was the respondent subject to its BITs.[21] In addition, there were two ad hoc arbitration cases brought by

[19] A Berger, 'Investment Rules in Chinese PTIAs—Partial "NAFTA-ization"' in R Hofmann, S Schill, and CJ Tams (eds), *Preferential Trade and Investment Agreements* (Baden-Baden, Nomos Verlagsgesellschaft, 2013). For further discussion of the evolution of China's BITs and IIAs, particularly in Asia, Europe and Africa, see Shu Zhang (n 14).

[20] *Tza Yap Shum v the Republic of Peru*, ICSID Case No ARB/07/6 (relying on China–Peru BIT); *Ping An Life Insurance Company of China Ltd and Ping An Insurance (Group) Company of China Ltd v Kingdom of Belgium*, ICSID Case No ARB/12/29 (relying on China–Belgium and Luxembourg BIT); *Beijing Construction Group Co Ltd v Republic of Yemen*, ICSID Case No ARB/14/30 (relying on the China–Yemen BIT). The other two claims brought by Hong Kong investors relying on investment contracts are not discussed here.

[21] *Ekran Berhad v People's Republic of China*, ICSID Case No ARB/11/15 (relying on China–Malaysia BIT); and *Ansung Housing Co Ltd v People's Republic of China*, ICSID Case No ARB/14/30 (relying on China–Korea BIT).

Chinese investors based on China's BITs.[22] There were no other types of ISA case involving Chinese investors or the Chinese government.[23]

Generally, China's (in)experience in ISA practice is consistent with its neighbours around the Asia-Pacific region. Lack of experience in ISA is a common feature of most jurisdictions in this region. Australia, for example, is not an active user of ISA either; so far, Australian investors have brought eight claims against other host countries under the ICSID Convention, and Australia has only become a respondent once in the *Philip Morris v Australia* case.[24] Inexperience in ISA is partly because of the late inclusion of investment arbitration schemes, especially an expansive ISA clause, by most countries in this region,[25] as well as the cultural reluctance of Asian countries in getting involved in a formal dispute resolution scheme like ISA.[26] Such reluctance is also illustrated by the fact that nine out of the 32 Asia-Pacific countries, including significant economies such as India, are even not members of the ICSID Convention.[27]

It is noteworthy that within the context of ISA practice in the Asia-Pacific region, China's role in ISA is more likely as a respondent than a claimant, as both of the claims against China were brought by Asia-Pacific investors,[28] while most of China's claims targeted countries outside the region (four out of five 5).[29] On the contrary, Australia is more actively a claimant than respondent in ISA in this region: five of the eight claims brought by Australian investors aimed at Asia-Pacific countries, while Australia was a respondent in only one case in this region. Such a difference may reflect the different positions and investment strategies adopted by China and Australia within the Asia-Pacific region: China's role is more likely that of a developing country and a capital importer, while Australia a developed

[22] *China Heilongjiang International Economic & Technical Cooperative Corp, Beijing Shougang Mining Investment Company Ltd and Qinhuangdaoshi Qin Long International Industrial Co Ltd v Mongolia* (relying on China–Mongolia BIT), UNCITRAL, PCA, www.pcacases.com/web/view/48; *Sanum Investments Ltd v Lao People's Democratic Republic* (relying on China–Laos BIT), UNCITRAL, PCA Case No 2013-13.

[23] There are many sources of investor–state arbitration: investment contracts; domestic investment law; BITs and IIAs; regional and international agreements, eg, the Energy Charter Treaty; agreements on a case-by-case basis, etc. There is no case reported in which a Chinese investor, the Chinese government or Chinese state-owned entities are involved in any contract-based ISA case. China is an observer but not yet a member of the International Energy Charter (2015), www.www.energycharter.org/who-we-are/members-observers/countries/china/.

[24] *Philip Morris Asia Ltd (Hong Kong) v The Commonwealth of Australia*, www.pcacases.com/web/view/5.

[25] Salomon and Friedrich (n 3) 840.

[26] L Nottage and JR Weeramantry, 'Investment Arbitration in Asia: Five Perspectives on Law and Practice' (2012) 28(1) *Arbitration International* 19, 31.

[27] These countries are: North Korea, Bhutan, India, the Maldives, Laos, Myanmar, Vietnam, Vanuatu, and New Caledonia.

[28] *Ekran Berhad v People's Republic of China* (n 21); and *Ansung Housing Co Ltd v People's Republic of China* (n 21).

[29] *Sanum Investments Ltd v Lao People's Democratic Republic* (n 22).

country and a capital exporter. However, it is notable that both China and Australia are now moving towards a more balanced position as they both become a capital importer and an exporter.[30] This move may imply a policy shift in investment strategies of both countries, and such a move is to be addressed by instruments like ChAFTA.

III. THE ISA CLAUSE IN CHAFTA: SCOPE OF ARBITRABLE MATTERS

As introduced earlier in section II, alongside the development of China's international investment instrument in general, the ISA clauses in these instruments have also developed. These developments generally reflect the shift in China's position and policymaking in international investment practice. Three generations of ISA clauses have been adopted, and their core features are discussed below.

Most of China's BITs (and their protocols) in the first phase included a simple ISA clause that limited the scope of arbitration to 'dispute in regard to the amount of compensation caused by expropriation'.[31] In some exceptional cases, a few BITs did not include an ISA clause at all.[32] The China–South Africa BIT (1997) for the first time included an expansive ISA clause which was subsequently accepted as a model for the second-generation ISA clause.[33] This type of ISA clause typically provides that 'any dispute' or 'any legal dispute' in connection with a covered investment could be submitted to investor–state arbitration. The ISA clause in the China–Korea BIT (2007) for the first time limited the scope of arbitrable disputes to the breaches of BIT provisions and was regarded as representing the emergence of the third-generation ISA clause. This feature was later adopted by the 2010 China Model BIT Draft,[34] which limited the scope of ISA clauses to certain types of breaches of BIT obligations. A more advanced version of such clauses could also be found in the ASEAN–China IIA (2009).[35]

For the first generation of China's ISA clause, which only provides for disputes of 'amount of compensation for expropriation', a major concern on its practical influence is whether the tribunal could also decide on the existence of expropriation. International practices in this regard were

[30] It means that China and Australia are both an investor party or a host country in cases of ISA. Australia is the respondent in the *Philip Morris* case (above n 24).

[31] See, eg, China–France BIT (1984).

[32] See, eg, China–Romania BIT (1983); and China–Thailand BIT (1985).

[33] See, eg, China–Germany BIT (2003); and China–India BIT (2006).

[34] Wen Xiantao, 'Commentary on China's Model BIT Draft: Part III' (2013) 19(2) *Journal of International Economic Law* (in Chinese) 57, 58–59.

[35] Arts 4, 5 and 7–10 of the ASEAN–China Investment Agreement (signed 15 August 2009, in effect on 1 January 2010).

not consistent. In *European Media Ventures SA v Czech Republic*,[36] the Tribunal adopted an expansive interpretation that allowed the consideration of the preliminary issue, and such decision was subsequently upheld by the English High Court.[37] In contrast, a restrictive approach was adopted by the Tribunals in *RosInvest Co UK v The Russian Federation*[38] and *Berschader v The Russian Federation*,[39] which limits the tribunal's jurisdiction to the amount of compensation only. In the context of China-related ISA and China's BITs, expansive interpretations have been observed in two China-related cases so far: *Tza Yap Shum v The Republic of Peru*[40] and *Sanum Investment Ltd v Government of the Lao People's Republic*.[41] The Sanum Tribunal's approach was finally confirmed by the Court of Appeal of the Singapore Supreme Court,[42] although during the proceedings, the High Court of the Singapore Supreme Court had once expressed a different opinion when dealing with this case as the court of first instance.[43] It is noteworthy, however, that the expansive approach adopted by the Court of Appeal of the Singapore Supreme Court was on the basis of a 'fork-in-the-road' clause in the China–Laos BIT, which might not be adopted on other occasions where such a 'fork-in-the-road' clause does not exist in the applicable IIA.[44]

For China's second-generation ISA clauses, which are expansive and cover all disputes that relate to investment, there are some language issues. Languages used by different BITs vary from 'any disputes in connection with investment' to 'any legal disputes' that reflect the language of the Washington Convention. The broad language raises concerns that it may cause massive arbitration claims against the Chinese government in the future.[45] It is also argued that such an expansive clause may not be

[36] *European Media Ventures SA v Czech Republic*, UNCITRAL Award on Jurisdiction, not published.

[37] The English High Court, Czech Republic v European Media Ventures SA [2007] EWHC 2851.

[38] *RosInvest Co UK v The Russian Federation*, SCC Case No V070/2005, Award of October 2007.

[39] *Berschader v. The Russian Federation*, SCC Case No V080/2004, Award of 21 April 2006.

[40] *Tza Yap Shum v The Republic of Peru*, ICSID Case No ARB/07/6, Award of 7 July 2011.

[41] *Government of the Lao People's Democratic Republic v Sanum Investments Ltd* [2015] SGHC 15; and *Sanum Investment Ltd v Government of the Lao People's Democratic Republic* [2016] SGCA 157 (appeal).

[42] *Sanum Investment Ltd v Government of the Lao People's Democratic Republic* [2016] SGCA 157.

[43] [2015] SGHC 15.

[44] [2016] SGCA 157 (appeal).

[45] See, eg, Wei Yanru, 'On the Impropriety of China's Recent Complete Acceptance of ICSID Jurisdiction' (2006) 13(1) *Chinese Journal of International Economic Law* 109; A Chen, 'Should the Four Great Safeguards in Sino-Foreign BITs Be Hastily Dismantled? Comments on Provisions Concerning Dispute Settlement in Model US and Canada BITs' (2006) 7 *Journal of World Investment & Trade* 899; see Xiantao (n 34).

consistent with China's Article 25(4) Notification under the Washington Convention, which also limits arbitrable disputes to the amount of compensation for expropriation.[46] It is, however, the general opinion that such a restrictive approach in the Notification would not negate the validity of China's liberalised treaty-making after 1998.[47]

The most recent generation of ISA clauses follows the new US Model BIT and limits the scope of claims to the breach of certain treaty obligations. Even within this generation of ISA clauses, the scope of arbitrable disputes varies. Among these documents, ChAFTA is the most restrictive, as it only provides ISA for violations of national treatment obligations.[48] In contrast, other IIAs provided arbitrability for most of the treaty obligations. These treaties took two different approaches: While the ISA clauses in the China–Korea BIT (2007), the China–Japan–Korea Trilateral Agreement (TIA) (2012), and the China–Korea FTA (2015) generally refer to breaches of any obligations under the treaties, with or without certain exceptions,[49] the ISA clauses in the ASEAN–China IIA (2009), the China–Chad BIT (2010), the China–Uzbekistan BIT (2011), and the China–Canada BIT (2012), on the other hand, list all relevant provisions, the breaches of which are arbitrable.[50]

While general acceptance of the arbitrability of most treaty breaches is found in most of China's third-generation ISA clauses, ChAFTA provides an extreme example on how restrictive the scope of arbitrable disputes could be defined in the third-generation ISA clauses. Such a narrow approach is not identical to any other third-generation ISA clauses reached by China or the broadly defined second-generation ISA clauses reached in the last two decades.

Thus, ChAFTA's narrow approach and its departure from China's other third-generation ISA clauses raise doubts as to whether China's flexible approach reflects a deliberate shift from a capital importer's perspective towards a capital exporter's perspective,[51] or simply a compromise towards

[46] It limits its consent to arbitrate in disputes over compensation for expropriation. Notification of 7 January 1993.

[47] N Gallagher and W Shan, *Chinese Investment Treaties: Policies and Practice* (Oxford, Oxford University Press, 2009) 331.

[48] China–Australia FTA, Art 9.12. It is notable that the Australian investor's right is more restricted than the Chinese investor's, as provided in the National Treatment clause in Art 9.3.

[49] See China–Korea BIT (2007) Arts 9(1) and 9(5); China–Japan-Korea TIA, Arts. 15(1) and 15(2)(b); China–Korea FTA (2015) Art 12.12. Only the China–Japan–Korea TIA referred to two exceptions in Arts 9(1)(b) and 20 (matters in relation to establishment and maintenance of a transparent intellectual property regime, and matters in relation to prudential measures taken in regulating financial services).

[50] China–Chad BIT (2010) Art 12.2; China–Uzbekistan BIT (2011) Art 12.2; ASEAN–China Investment Agreement (2009) Art 14.1; China–Canada BIT (2012) Art 20.1.

[51] See, eg, N Gallagher, 'Role of China in Investment: BITs, SOEs, Private Enterprises, and Evolution of Policy' (2016) 31(1) *ICSID Review* 88, 90–91.

the preference of the counterparty. The narrow approach in fact largely reflects Australia's hesitation and reluctance to include any ISA clause since 2011, when the Gillard government denounced its consent to any ISA clause negotiation.[52] The China–Korea FTA (2015), on the other hand, might be an extreme case at the other end showing how broad an ISA clause could be, as the ISA clause covers all treaty breaches. It is doubtful, therefore, whether the flexible approach would satisfy the need of China's foreign investment policy shift or contribute to a more comprehensive regional legal framework governing ISA practice.

IV. INVESTOR–STATE ARBITRATION CLAUSE IN CHAFTA: CONCURRENT TREATIES AND TRANSITION CLAUSES

One further issue in relation to the scope of ISA clause is that ChAFTA is not the first international instrument governing investment-related matters and providing an ISA clause between China and Australia. In 1988, China and Australia signed the China–Australia BIT, which included a first-generation ISA clause that allowed arbitration for a 'dispute [that] relates to the amount of compensation payable' under any relevant expropriation and/or nationalisation. The concurrence of this ISA clause and the ISA clause provided by ChAFTA would affect whether and when the parties could select from these two ISA clauses.

Whether a party could select from these two ISA clauses depends on whether its dispute is excluded by the most recent treaty. China has concurrent international investment agreements with 16 countries, and has signed new ones to replace old with 15 countries, and the numbers are still growing along with China's active treaty negotiation activities.[53] A transition clause, which defines the time effect of the ISA clause, therefore, becomes a common feature of many of the recent BITs and IIAs. Such a clause is particularly crucial because the old ISA clauses and new ones often belong to different generations of China's IIAs, and provide totally different scopes of arbitrable disputes.

[52] It was announced that Australia would no longer agree to any ISA clause in its bilateral and regional trade agreement. See Department of Foreign Affairs and Trade, Australian Government, 'Trading Our Way to More Jobs and Prosperity' (Gillard government Trade Policy Statement, April 2011). A positive but hesitatan step towards ISA after the denouncement can be found in the Australia–Korea BIT (2013), which provided the possibility of ISA on a case-by-case basis. See, eg, L Trakman, 'Investor-State Arbitration: Evaluating Australia's Evolving Position' (2014) 15 *Journal of World Investment & Trade* 152.

[53] Concurrent: Ten countries of ASEAN, Japan, Korea, Pakistan, Australia, New Zealand, Peru. Replaced BITs: Belgium-Luxembourg, the Democratic Republic of Congo, the Czech Republic, Finland, France, Germany, Korea, the Netherlands, Nigeria, Portugal, Romania, Russia, Spain, Switzerland, Uzbekistan.

The following table illustrates several categories of transition clauses adopted in China's BITs and IIAs.

Table 1: Modes of Languages used in Excluding Certain Disputes

Mode 1	The IIA shall not apply to any dispute which 'has arisen' before its entry into force.
Mode 2	The IIA shall not be applicable to claims or disputes arising out of events which occurred prior to its entry into force.
Mode 3	The IIA shall not apply to any dispute or any claim concerning an investment which was already under judicial or arbitral process before its entry into force.
ChAFTA Model	The IIA shall not bind either Party in relation to any act or fact that took place or any situation that ceased to exist before the date of its entry into force.

Modes 1, 2 and 3 are clearly different categories of transition clause and are distinguished from each other regarding the time of the occurrence of the disputes (Mode 1); the time of the occurrence of the events that cause disputes (Mode 2); and the time when the dispute is subject to judicial or arbitral process (Mode 3). Among all IIAs reached by China, 24 adopted Mode 1; three adopted Mode 2; and six adopted Mode 3.[54] The ASEAN–China IIA adopted a combination of Modes 2 and 3.

ChAFTA, however, adopted another mode. Article 9.2.4 of ChAFTA provides that the investment chapter 'shall not bind either Party in relation to any act or fact that took place or any situation that ceased to exist before' the date of its entry into force, which seems to be a variation of Mode 2; such language is also found in the China–New Zealand FTA and China–Peru FTA. For disputes arising in China–Australia investment relationship, the parties would not have the option to choose from the China–Australia BIT and ChAFTA if the involved 'act or fact' took place, or the 'situation' ceased to exist before the commencement of ChAFTA.

Even though the different wording used in these clauses illustrates the treaty drafter's intention in distinguishing the different periods of time

[54] Mode 1: China–Sweden BIT (1982); China–Mongolia BIT(1991); China–Romania BIT (1994); China–Serbia BIT (1995); China–Lebanon BIT (1996); China–South Africa BIT (1997); China–Jordan BIT (2001); China–Myanmar BIT (2001); China-Bosnia and Herzegovina BIT (2002), China-Latvia BIT (2004), China-Tunisia BIT (2004), China–Uganda BIT (2004); China–Equatorial Guinea BIT (2005); China–Madagascar BIT (2005); China–Namibia BIT (2005); China–Portugal BIT (2005); China–Russia BIT (2006); China–Korea BIT (2007); China–Seychelles BIT (2007); China–Mali BIT (2009); China–Malta BIT(2009); China–Chad BIT (2010); China–Libya BIT (2010); China–Uzbekistan BIT (2011). Mode 2: China–Ethiopia BIT (1998); China–Czech BIT (2005); China–Japan–Korea TIA (2012).

covered by an ISA clause, the general ambiguity of a transition clause may provide enormous discretion for the tribunal in applying these ISA clauses, and sometimes may create risks for parties attempting to structure their claims on the basis of an intentional selection of BITs/IIAs. This kind of risk, as illustrated by *Ping An v Belgium*,[55] would arise when the tribunal's interpretation of the BIT arguably departed from the literal meaning of the transition clause in the IIA (in that case, the China–Belgium and Luxembourg BIT (2005), which followed the Mode 3).

In *Ping An v Belgium*, the investor–state dispute had arisen in 2007–08, which was before the new China–Belgium and Luxemburg BIT came into effect on 1 December 2009 replacing the old BIT reached in 1984. Ping An brought its claims before ICSID in 2012 and based its claims on the ISA clause in the new BIT. The ICSID Tribunal, however, decided that the dispute was not covered by the new BIT based on the fact that Ping An had sent letters of complaint to the Belgian government firstly based on the old BIT (on 14 October 2009), and that both parties agreed that the dispute had arisen before the new BIT came into effect. The Tribunal concluded that the wording of the new BIT did not provide that the broad ISA clause under the new BIT should apply to this dispute. Rather than relying on the specific transition clause following Mode 3, the Tribunal emphasised Article 8.1 of the new BIT,[56] focusing on the point that the new BIT did not intend to include any dispute arising prior to its commencement date. This interpretation has been heavily criticised as it is a departure from the literal meaning of the Mode 3 type of transition clause, and the true intention of the treaty-maker to distinguish between the three modes.[57]

Bearing in mind the risks illustrated by the *Ping An* case in drafting and applying a transition clause, an examination of Article 9.2.4 of ChAFTA would suggest that it also gives rise to the uncertainty and discretionary interpretation of the tribunals by using general terms such as 'any act or fact that took place' or 'any situation that ceased to exist'. It is particularly notable that the language used by ChAFTA is different from the transition clauses adopted in most of China's IIAs as shown in Table 1. Therefore, in applying this transition clause, it is unlikely to refer to a consistent pattern in China's treaty-making as an indicator of the true intention of the

Mode 3: China–Netherlands BIT (2001); China–Germany BIT (2003); China–Finland BIT (2004); China–Belgium–Luxembourg BIT (2005); China–Spain BIT (2005); China–France BIT (2007).

[55] *Ping An Life Insurance Company of China Ltd and Ping An Insurance (Group) Company of China Ltd v Kingdom of Belgium* (n 20).

[56] Art 8.1 China–Belgium–Luxembourg BIT (2005): 'When a legal dispute arises between an investor of one Contracting Party and the other Contracting Party, either party to the dispute shall notify the other party to the dispute in writing'.

[57] Q Ren, 'Case Comment on Ping An v Belgium: Temporal Jurisdiction of Successive' BITs (2016) *ICSID Review* 1.

treaty-makers.[58] Given the significantly different ISA clauses provided by the China–Australia BIT (1988) and ChAFTA, the parties may be at risk if they need to choose between these two clauses in dealing with a dispute to which both instruments are arguably applicable.

V. INVESTOR–STATE ARBITRATION CLAUSE IN CHAFTA: CONTRACTING PARTIES' JOINT DECISION IN TREATY INTERPRETATION

It is not only the transition clause but also many other provisions in an IIA that may raise concern about discretionary interpretations by the tribunals. Although the general practice of ISA respects the principles of treaty interpretation provided by instruments such as the Vienna Convention on the Law of Treaties,[59] the outcome of the tribunal's interpretation may sometimes depart from the expectations of the contracting parties. In *Sanum*, China and Laos attempted to clarify their joint intention to exclude Macau from the coverage of the China–Laos BIT (1993). This declaration of their joint intention, however, was denied by the Tribunal, as well as the Court of Appeal of the Singapore Supreme Court.[60] As the Court of Appeal pointed out, the contracting parties never made their intentions clear to exclude Macau from the BIT before the dispute arose. Therefore, the expectation of the investors that Macau should be covered, which could be presumed on the basis of the Moving Treaty Frontier (MTF) principle,[61] should not be frustrated by the diplomatic letters issued later than the commencement or even the conclusion of the arbitration proceedings.[62] The position of the Court of Appeal of the Singapore Supreme Court was strongly criticised by the Chinese Minister of Foreign Affairs as it wrongfully applied the MTF principle and disrespected the true intention of the Chinese government as well as the Laos government.[63]

Confirming the binding effect of the states' joint interpretation in advance, then, seems to be a solution to avoid the Tribunal's discretionary interpretation. The China–Canada BIT, following the NAFTA model, provides that

[58] Regarding the consistent approach and its possible contribution to identify the intention of the drafting parties, see ibid.

[59] Vienna Convention on the Law of Treaties (concluded 23 May 1969, entered into force 27 January 1980) 1155 UNTS 331.

[60] *Sanum Investment Ltd v Government of the Lao People's Democratic Republic* (n 42).

[61] The principle is backed up by the Vienna Convention on the Law of Treaties and the Vienna Convention on Succession of States in respect of Treaties (concluded on 23 August 1978, entered into force on 6 November 1996) 1946 UNTS 3.

[62] *Sanum Investment Ltd v Government of Lao People's Democratic Republic* (n 42).

[63] *China Daily* (21 October 2016), www.chinadaily.com.cn/interface/yidian/1138561/2016-10-21/cd_27134676.html.

the states may take actions including 'issuing binding interpretations of this Agreement'.[64] ChAFTA takes one step further and provides more detailed guidance in this regard. Article 9.18.2 provides that a tribunal of any ongoing or subsequent dispute should follow the joint interpretation of the two contracting parties issued via the Committee on Investment. Article 9.18.3 further provides that a decision between the contracting parties, in the case of an ongoing ISA case, on whether a measure is non-discriminatory and for the legitimate public welfare objectives, shall bind the tribunal's decision. If a measure is decided by the contracting parties as such, it will be excluded from ISA.[65] These provisions, therefore, provide the states with enormous power to issue joint interpretations on treaty clauses and to exclude any dispute regarding 'non-discriminatory measures for legislative public welfare objectives' even after such a dispute arises.

A predominant reason for inserting these provisions may be that the states would like to have the final say on treaty interpretation matters and to maintain consistent interpretations on similar issues. However, while a consistent interpretation would contribute to the predictability of ISA practices, the risk, as illustrated by the *Sanum* case, is that these interpretations made after the commencement of a dispute may frustrate investors who rely on generally accepted treaty interpretation principles. Also, the scope of measures regarding 'public health, safety, the environment, public morals or public order' is broad and ambiguous.[66] The enormous discretionary power for the states to interpret this concept would give rise to concerns that the states would abuse their discretionary power to make amendments rather than interpretations to avoid claims against them.[67]

In the meantime, whether a confirmation of the binding effect of state joint interpretation in treaties could solve this problem would be doubtful. In practice, tribunals may not fulfil the obligations imposed by treaties following the states' joint interpretation. In *Pope & Talbot v Canada*, the Tribunal was once again reluctant to apply the NAFTA Free Trade Commission's interpretation despite the fact that NAFTA clarified its

[64] Art 18, China–Canada BIT (2012).

[65] Art 9.11.4 of ChAFTA provides: 'Measures of a Party that are non-discriminatory and for the legitimate public welfare objectives of public health, safety, the environment, public morals or public order shall not be the subject of a claim under this Section'.

[66] This concept is similar to the 'public policy' ground in international commercial arbitration which gives rise to a concern of its abusive use as an 'unruly horse'.

[67] The distinctions between amendments and interpretations are not clear in practice. However, as ChAFTA clarifies the binding effect of an interpretation, the distinction is meaningful. See J Arato, 'Subsequent Practice and Evolutive Interpretation: Techniques of Treaty Interpretation over Time and their Diverse Consequences' (2010) 9 *The Law & Practice of International Courts and Tribunals* 443, 450, 456–57, 461–64; A Roberts, 'Power and Persuasion in Investment Treaty Interpretation: The Dual Role of States' (2010) 104 *American Journal of International Law* 179, 200–01.

binding effect.[68] They commented that Canada's participation in the deliberations of the Free Trade Commission was a significant breach of the 'rule of international law that no one shall be judge in his own case'.[69] Although the Tribunal's comments did not eventually influence the outcome of this case, the Tribunal's intention to ignore or even negate the binding effect of the states' joint interpretation raised significant concerns. Harten criticised the Tribunal's comments as a misconception of the nature of ISA and the state's dual roles in it, as the state would be both the treaty drafter (the legislator) and a disputed party subject to the treaty.[70] Practices and discussions in this regard have not yet unified, leaving uncertainties for the implementation of ChAFTA.

VI. ENFORCEMENT OF ISA AWARDS AND THE APPEAL SYSTEM

Like most of China's BITs and IIAs which recognise the finality of the award and provide the states' obligations to enforce the award,[71] Article 9.22.8 of ChAFTA also provides that the states shall provide for enforcement of an ISA award. However, the enforcement of an ISA award in China is still problematic because of the absence of a systematic legal framework regulating this matter.

Most of China's recent investment treaties, like ChAFTA, provide various types of ISA schemes including ICSID arbitration and non-ICSID arbitration.[72] For ICSID awards, the enforcement scheme provided by the Washington Convention could be relied upon in enforcement because China has been a member since 1993.[73] However, even under the Washington Convention, the enforcement towards property still largely relies on the domestic law and the national courts, which are still absent in China's current legal system.[74]

[68] For the involved interpretation, see NAFTA Free Trade Commission, *Notes of Interpretation of Certain Chapter 11 Provisions* (31 July 2001).

[69] *Pope & Talbot Inc v Government of Canada (Damages)* (31 May 2012) para 13.

[70] G Van Harten, *Investment Treaty Arbitration and Public Law* (Oxford, Oxford University Press, 2007) 127.

[71] See, eg, China–Hungary BIT (1991) Art 10.5, 'Both Contracting States shall commit themselves to the enforcement of the decision in accordance with their respective domestic law'. China–Uzbekistan BIT (2011) Art 12.8: 'Both Contracting Parties shall commit themselves to the enforcement of the award'.

[72] Art 9.12.4 of ChAFTA provides arbitration under ICSID Rules, ICSID Additional Facility Rules, UNCITRAL Rules or arbitration to any other arbitration institution or under any other arbitration rules subject to the consent of the disputed parties.

[73] See www.icsid.worldbank.org/apps/ICSIDWEB/about/Pages/MembershipStateDetails.aspx?state=ST30.

[74] See Art 54(3) of the ICSID Convention. See also E Baldwin, M Kantor and M Nolan, 'Limits to Enforcement of ICSID Awards' (2006) 23 *Journal of International Arbitration* 1, 5.

Compared with the enforcement of ICSID awards, situations in the enforcement of non-ICSID awards seem more difficult. On the one hand, the BITs and IIAs do not provide detailed enforcement schemes that connect to the specific judicial system of a Member party. On the other, no domestic law in China sets out the mechanism for the enforcement of ISA awards. In addition, China has made it clear that the enforcement scheme of commercial arbitral awards under the New York Convention would not apply to ISA awards.[75] The only applicable scheme seems to be the principle of reciprocity provided by China's Civil Procedure Law.[76] That scheme, however, only refers to an award made by a 'foreign arbitration institution' and says nothing about an award made by ad hoc tribunals, while most non-ICSID ISA cases are structured on an ad hoc basis.[77] It is also not certain whether the application of the principle of reciprocity in this context would require the recognition and enforcement in the other state of a Chinese award in commercial disputes, or of an ISA award. The latter of which would be extremely rare.

The enforceability and enforcing scheme of an ISA award made under ChAFTA (either ad hoc or based on ICSID), therefore, would be unpredictable in China. For both ICSID and ad hoc awards under ISA, it is suggested that the status and applicability of the Washington Convention and the IIAs regarding the enforcement of ISA awards should be further clarified in China, and detailed judicial review proceedings, as well as standard of judicial review, should be provided either in legislation or in judicial interpretations.[78]

In addition, it is noteworthy that ChAFTA's reference to a possible appellate system imposes additional limitations to the finality and enforceability of an ISA award. Generally, an ISA award should be final and only subject to limited review provided either by institutions (such as the annulment scheme provided by ICSID)[79] or by general arbitration legislation, including domestic arbitration law or the New York Convention. All these mechanisms only allow a re-examination of procedural issues arising from arbitration proceedings, such as the establishment of the tribunal, whether there is

[75] See China's 'commercial reservation' under the New York Convention; See also the SPC's Notice in Relation to the Implementation of the Convention on the Recognition and Enforcement of Foreign Arbitral Awards, of which China Becomes a Party, *Fa Jing Fa* [1987] No 5 (10 April 1987).

[76] It is provided by Art 283 of the Chinese Civil Procedure Law.

[77] Although in the practices in relation to international commercial arbitration, China now recognises the enforceability of a foreign award made by an ad hoc tribunal (see, eg, the SPC's Notice in Relation to the Enforcement of Hong Kong Arbitration Award in Mainland China, *Fa* [2009] No 45); it is doubtful whether such practice would extend to the recognition and enforcement of an ISA award.

[78] X Fang, 'Recognition and Enforcement of the International Investment Arbitration Award in China' (2011) 6 *The Jurist* 94, 100 (in Chinese).

[79] Art 52 of the Washington Convention.

a manifestly excessive use of power, corruption or serious departure from procedural justice etc.[80] The possible appellate system provided by Article 9.23 of ChAFTA, however, goes beyond the review of procedural issues and allows appeals on 'questions of law'.

It has long been an issue whether an appellate system should be established in ISA practice. Academic and governmental policy discussions on the pros and cons of an appellate system in ISA are comprehensive.[81] Generally, proponents for an appellate system believe that the system may cure some disadvantages of the current ISA scheme.[82] While it is doubtful whether it is practically possible to establish a unified appellate system applicable to all ICSID cases, a regional and treaty-based appellate system may be the starting point of testing its effectiveness.[83] ICSID has also considered whether it should include an appeal system in its own rules.[84] Despite the heated discussions, only a few treaties have included this option,[85] and a few others have included similar language to that used in ChAFTA that allows the possibility of negotiating on an appellate system in the future.[86]

From China's perspective, an option for an appellate system in ISA has not been seen in any previous China-made IIAs. The 2010 China Model BIT Draft only provides for options of amending, annulling or setting aside an ISA award.[87] ChAFTA, thus, is a significant departure from China's general treaty-making practice and most of China's third-generation ISA clauses. The practical effect of this clause would not be significant given the narrow scope of the ISA clause in ChAFTA, but it is worthwhile to note that an appellate system would take a crucial role in implementing the binding

[80] ibid; see also Art V of the New York Convention, which also provides that an arbitral award may be refused enforcement only if there is no valid arbitration agreement, or breach of agreed arbitration procedure or due process, etc.

[81] See, eg, EU–Canada Free Trade Agreement considered the establishment of an appellate system. See Arts 8.27-8.29, CETA, discussed in www.trade.ec.europa.eu/doclib/docs/2013/november/tradoc_151918.pdf. See also UNCTAD IIA Issues Note, Reform of Investor–State Dispute Settlement: In Search of a Roadmap (29–30 May 2013), www.unctad.org/en/PublicationsLibrary/webdiaepcb2013d4_en.pdf, which also list the establishment of an appellate system as a path of reforming ISDS schemes.

[82] See, eg, it can solve the inconsistencies between different tribunals' decisions. See EY Park, 'Appellate Review in Investor-State Arbitration' in JE Kalicki and A Joubin-Bret (eds), *Reshaping the Investor-State Dispute Settlement System* (Leiden, Brill Nijhoff, 2015).

[83] B Legum, 'Appellate Mechanisms for Investment Arbitration: Worth a Second Look for the Trans-Pacific Partnership and the Proposed EU–US FTA?' in JE Kalicki and A Joubin-Bret (eds), *Reshaping the Investor-State Dispute Settlement System* (Leiden, Brill Nijhoff, 2015).

[84] See ICSID, 'Possible Improvements of the Framework for ICSID Arbitration' (22 October 2004).

[85] ibid. According to an ICSID report, about 20 countries have provided this option in their investment treaties.

[86] See, eg, 2004 US Model BIT, Annex D, www.state.gov/documents/organization/38710.pdf. It is also adopted in the US–Chile, US–Singapore, US–Morocco FTAs. Also, the option provided in CETA, as mentioned above (n 81).

[87] Xiantao (n 34); Art 13 of the Model BIT Draft.

effect of the states' joint interpretation, as discussed in section V. A combination of both schemes, therefore, is a strong indicator of state intervention in ISA under ChAFTA, illustrating ChAFTA's reluctance to utilise ISA as a method of dispute resolution.

VII. AN EVALUATION OF THE ISA CLAUSE IN CHAFTA

In the light of the discussions above, the ISA clause in ChAFTA seems to be a departure from China's general treaty-making practice and the recent IIAs in many major aspects. ChAFTA's ISA clause provides for an extremely narrow scope of arbitrable issues, a transition clause to exclude disputes arising before the commencement of ChAFTA, states' power of issuing joint interpretations on specific issues, and the possibility of a unique appellate system that allows substantive review of ISA awards. Many of these provisions are distinct from other China-made IIAs and even the most recent ones, showing strong caution in committing to ISA, an intention to limit the ISA practice, and a higher degree of state intervention in conducting ISA practice.

The above departure from most of China's 'mainstream' BITs and IIAs may be for many reasons. First, the Chinese treaty negotiators may have adopted a flexible approach in drafting ChAFTA to respect to the caution of the Australian government on the ISA clause. It is not the first Chinese investment treaty that follows the needs or traditions of its counterparties; for example, the China–Canada BIT (2012) and China–Mexico BIT (2008) are considered as following NAFTA and the Canada Model BIT (2003).[88] The China–Korea BIT (2007), China–Japan-Korea TIA (2012) and China–Korea FTA (2015) also adopt similar features in ISA.[89] The limitations of ChAFTA, therefore, could be understood as a compromise to Australia's reluctance to commit to ISA.[90]

Alternatively, it could be understood as a signal that China's attitude towards ISA, as influenced by international practice, has become more conservative than it was in the last two decades. In recent years, the practice of ISA has been severely criticised as lacking neutrality, transparency and consistency, as well as an understanding of standard of review from a

[88] N Gallagher, 'China's BITs and Arbitration Practice: Progresses and Problems' in W Shan and J Su (eds), *China and International Investment Law: Twenty Years of ICSID Membership* (Leiden, Brill Nijhoff, 2015) 203.

[89] See, eg, they provide similar clauses in defining the scope of arbitrable disputes, and such clauses are not observed in any other China-made IIAs. Discussed in section III.

[90] Australia's reluctance in adopting ISA is discussed in section III. See also Trakman, 'Choosing Domestic Courts over Investor-State Arbitration' (n 2); Trakman, 'Investor-State Arbitration' (n 52).

public law perspective.[91] In dealing with these deficiencies, many options are considered, including enhancing the transparency of arbitration proceedings, limiting the parties' access to ISA, establishing supervisory mechanisms (such as the appellate system) or considering alternatives (mediation, or a supernational investment court) etc.[92] Australia's reluctance is just one example of the global movement towards a more carefully tailored and limited scheme of ISA. From China's perspective, the ISA schemes adopted in the most recent generation of IIAs, although they vary from one another, are tailored with limitations to the investors' access to ISA. ChAFTA might be the most conservative one among them, but similar features are at least occasionally seen in other treaties.

It is difficult to conclude whether ChAFTA would signal that China is moving towards a more conservative position in committing to ISA, or merely one extreme example of China's flexible attitude towards ISA, because China's investment treaty-making has been slowing down during these years.[93] China, as the world's second largest economy, is still exploring its position as both a capital importer and a capital exporter and practising to make its voice heard in a broader forum. Its position on commitment to ISA in the future remains to be seen. It is also too early, at this stage, to conclude whether the intention to limit the use and effect of ISA, as illustrated by ChAFTA, would practically impact on China's ISA-related practice given the lack of sufficient ISA cases in which China has been involved.

A more practical impact of the ISA clause in ChAFTA, however, is that it lacks sufficient support at the domestic law level and the ISA practice level in the sense of implementation. The ambiguous language of the ISA clause leaves open many issues, such as the meaning of the transition clause. The strong authority of government-level joint interpretation also lacks sufficient practical instruction and its effects remain to be seen. The risks of these ambiguities have already been illustrated by China-related ISA cases, such as the *Ping An* case and the *Sanum* case. Moreover, the interpretation of ISA clauses in ChAFTA would not benefit from the existing case law that dealt with ISA clauses in Chinese IIAs that are distinct from ChAFTA. Finally, the enforcement of ISA awards remains mysterious in China. These risks and

[91] For criticisms on ISDS and responses, see, eg, European Federation for Investment Law and Arbitration (EFILA), 'A response to the criticism against ISDS', www.efila.org/wp-content/uploads/2015/05/EFILA_in_response_to_the-criticism_of_ISDS_final_draft.pdf. See also Brower and Blanchard (n 1). For the pro-investor concerns, see, eg, Eberhardt, Olivet, Amos and Buxton (n 1); Van Harten, 'Arbitrator Behaviour in Asymmetrical Adjudication' (n 1). For the standard of review concerns, see W Burke-White and A von Staden, 'Private Litigation in a Public Law Sphere: The Standard of Review in Investor-State Arbitrations' (2010) 35 *Yale Journal of International Law* 283.

[92] See, eg, UNCTAD (n 81).

[93] As discussed in section II.

uncertainties must be considered before an investor decides to utilise the ISA mechanism provided by ChAFTA.

VIII. CONCLUSION

The investment chapter of ChAFTA is considered to be one of the most important instruments of China's recent treaty-making practice. However, a thorough study of the ISA clauses adopted in ChAFTA reveals a reluctance of the negotiators to utilise ISA as a method of resolving international investment disputes between China and Australia. Such reluctance is illustrated by the narrow scope of its application, its tendency to emphasise state control in restricting the applicable law and providing a possibility of an appellate system, its failure to address problems such as coexisting ISA clauses in different instruments, and the uncertainty caused by the lack of a functional enforcement mechanism. ISA clauses in ChAFTA seem to be an example of a new restrictive approach in drafting ISA, different from China's first-generation restrictive ISA clauses.

Reviewing ChAFTA's ISA clause drafting in the context of the development of IIAs, particularly the movement towards multilateral investment instruments in recent years,[94] we may conclude that it is not following the general trend of adopting a comprehensive and high-standard ISA clause in international or even regional practice in the last decade, or a departure from the general trend towards investment liberalisation. ChAFTA's distinctive features might be adopted as a compromise to the domestic concerns and needs of China's negotiating partners, illustrating China's flexibility in reaching investment agreements. Alternatively, it might be an indicator of China's new (arguably, more conservative) international investment policy which tends to balance the interest between attracting foreign investment and protecting its own investors abroad. It may also reflect concerns over the use of the ISA clause itself, which is not just limited to China or

[94] Regional movements can be observed in, eg, in the success of NAFTA, ASEAN, and possibly the Lisbon Treaty for the EU; sector-based convergence is represented by the ECT. See Salomon and Friedrich (n 3); W Shan and S Zhang, 'The Treaty of Lisbon: Half Way toward a Common Investment Policy' (2010) 21 (4) *European Journal of International Law* 1049. For progress at the international level, see the proposed TPPA between the NAFTA countries and the broad Asia-Pacific, CETA and proposed TTIP between the two sides of the Atlantic, and emerging investment cooperation around ASEAN represented by RECP. See the EU–Canada Comprehensive Economic and Trade Agreement, www.ec.europa.eu/trade/policy/in-focus/ceta/; Transatlantic Trade and Investment Partnership, www.ec.europa.eu/trade/policy/in-focus; /ttip/; ASEAN's framework of and progress in cooperation under the Region Comprehensive Economic Partnership, www.asean.org/?static_post=asean-framework-for-regional-comprehensive-economic-partnership and www.asean.org/storage/2016/09/56-RCEP_Joint-Leaders-Statement_8-September-2016.pdf, which affirms the possibility of a potential regional agreement in this regard.

Australia, but is raised by some practitioners and scholars, and might affect the next generation of ISA clauses.[95] These factors would create uncertainty in China's treaty-making approach, particularly in a rapidly changing international economic climate.

As both China and Australia are active participants in international investment treaty negotiations, they might benefit from participation at regional and multilateral levels and eliminate these uncertainties in different ways. In the subsequent ChAFTA negotiations on upgrading and modifying the ISA clause, the parties might follow the generally accepted practice at regional or international levels and address the uncertainties by reference to formalised model rules and case law. Alternatively, the parties could develop their unique rules to address common concerns, for example, the impartiality concern, and promote such consent at regional or multilateral platforms such as the Regional Comprehensive Economic Partnership (RCEP).[96] At least in the Asia-Pacific region, both China and Australia would have the ability to be not only the rule takers but also the rule makers. Further developments in ChAFTA's ISA clause would be an opportunity for both parties to make the first step towards a new set of rules that fit their own needs. From that perspective, the current and future ISA clause in ChAFTA may move towards the next generation of international investment order.

[95] See above section I.
[96] See above (n 94).

13

Investor–State Dispute Settlement and the Australian Constitutional Framework

LISA BURTON CRAWFORD, PATRICK EMERTON AND EMMANUEL LARYEA

I. INTRODUCTION

INVESTOR–STATE DISPUTE SETTLEMENT (ISDS) provisions are a common feature of International Investment Agreements (IIAs), including in the investment chapter in the China–Australia Free Trade Agreement (ChAFTA). Yet, as the Chief Justice of the Australian High Court has observed, they are not free from controversy: they can pose significant rule of law concerns, and seem to sit in tension with some features of the Australian constitutional framework.[1] This chapter considers the constitutional issues raised by ISDS provisions in IIAs, in the context of Australia's engagement with international investment law generally, and ChAFTA more specifically, and whether these translate into questions of constitutional validity. In particular, this chapter examines the source and scope of the Australian executive government's power to enter into IIAs that contain ISDS provisions, and the compatibility of such provisions with Chapter III of the Australian Constitution (the Constitution).

Section 61 of the Constitution empowers the federal executive to enter into international agreements, such as ChAFTA, on Australia's behalf. But the executive must act in conformity with the Constitution. In recent years, the High Court has emphasised that, in certain cases, the executive cannot act without parliamentary approval.[2] Furthermore, Chapter III of

[1] R French CJ, 'Investor–State Dispute Settlement—A Cut Above the Courts?' (Supreme and Federal Courts Judges' Conference, 9 July 2014), www.hcourt.gov.au/assets/publications/speeches/current-justices/frenchcj/frenchcj09jul14.pdf.

[2] The most important of these cases is *Williams v Commonwealth* (*Williams*) [2012] HCA 23, (2012) 248 CLR 156, discussed in detail in section IV.C below. See also *Pape v Commissioner of Taxation* [2009] HCA 23, (2009) 238 CLR 1 (*Pape*); *Williams v Commonwealth [No 2]* [2014] HCA 23, (2014) 252 CLR 416 (*Williams [No 2]*).

the Constitution establishes a federal judiciary, which is strictly independent from the other branches of government. As the Chief Justice explained, the courts established by Chapter III of the Constitution are said to have final authority to determine the legality of government action.[3] Yet, by agreeing to an IIA that contains an ISDS provision, the federal executive effectively subjects government action to the external scrutiny of an arbitral body that may lack the independence and other procedural trappings of a Chapter III court. This chapter explores these potential concerns, and investigates whether there is a basis on which the validity of an IIA containing an ISDS provision could be challenged under Australian constitutional law.

We begin in section II with an overview of ISDS, briefly describing what it is, its history and use, and criticisms that have been made of the ISDS system. Section III outlines the Australian constitutional framework and the constitutional questions raised by ISDS provisions. Section IV analyses the interaction between executive, judicial and parliamentary powers under the Constitution, and its ramifications for Australia's ability to enter IIAs that contain ISDS provisions, and makes some recommendations from an Australian constitutional perspective. Section V then briefly overviews the constitutionality of the recognition, under Australian law, of ISDS arbitral awards. This overview reinforces the importance of the conclusions of the previous section.

II. OVERVIEW OF ISDS

A. Development of ISDS

ISDS is a system that allows an investor (often a corporation or a private individual) to use dispute settlement proceedings against a foreign government. Broadly defined, this encompasses any method of settling disputes, including litigation in domestic or foreign courts, domestic or international arbitration, mediation, conciliation and negotiation. However, the term ISDS has become synonymous with investor–state arbitration. Typically, it is a means by which foreign investors challenge a law, regulation, judicial or administrative ruling or other government decision before a panel of private arbitrators who have the power to make decisions in cases and make awards that are binding and enforceable. The discussions in this chapter focus on investor–state arbitration.

The concept of ISDS was created by the International Convention for the Settlement of Investment Disputes of 1965 (ICSID Convention).[4] The ICSID

[3] French, 'Investor–State Dispute Settlement' (n 1).

[4] G Van Harten and M Loughlin, 'Investment Treaty Arbitration as a Species of Global Administrative Law' (2006) 17(1) *European Journal of International Law* 121, 129.

Convention provides a procedural framework for dispute settlement between host states and foreign investors through conciliation or arbitration. It established a centre, the International Centre for Settlement of Investment Disputes, that acts as an arbitral forum for the settlement of international investment disputes between investors of one contracting state (the home state) and the government of another contracting state (the host state).

Up until the promulgation of the ICSID Convention, developing countries asserted that jurisdiction in international investment disputes lies with the host state.[5] Beyond that, foreign investors had to resort to customary international law (CIL) for the settlement of disputes between them and foreign (host state) governments.[6] However, under CIL, sovereigns are immune to suits by private entities for actions taken by a government in pursuance of its administrative functions.[7] Thus, if the actions of a host government injured a foreign national, the injured party would have to rely on its home government to seek redress on its behalf: that home government may exercise diplomatic protection rights on behalf of its injured national abroad.

Developed (capital exporting) countries had concerns about the quality and independence of the laws, governments and judiciaries of developing countries. Capital exporters also saw obvious limitations to the effectiveness of using CIL. For instance, the home government might not be keen to antagonise the foreign government; the decision by the home government to intervene might require a lot of politicking; the remedies that may be sought, or accepted, by the home government might not be what the injured party wants; and the process might take unduly long.[8] Thus capital exporters preferred some form of independent forum under international law.[9]

At the time, the opposing positions between developing (capital importing) countries and developed (capital exporting) countries on forums for settling investment disputes (as well as on the substantive law regarding standard of protection for foreign investments and compensation for injury to foreign investors) were considered to discourage capital exporters from investing in developing economies.[10]

[5] E Laryea, 'Evolution of International Investment Law and Implications for Africa' in FN Botchway (ed), *Natural Resource Investment and Africa's Development* (Cheltenham, Edward Elgar, 2011) 298–300; G Van, 'Investment Treaty Arbitration and Public Law—A Return to the Gay Nineties?' (2007) 4(5) *Transnational Dispute Management* 12, 16–17.

[6] R Dolzer and C Schreuer, *Principles of International Investment Law*, 2nd edn (Oxford, Oxford University Press, 2012) 232.

[7] This stems from the principle of state sovereignty. In its basic form, state sovereignty is the right to exercise, within a territory, the functions of a state exclusive to any other state or kingdom, and subject to no other authority. In practice, such exclusive authority may be limited by obligations under international law.

[8] Dolzer and Schreuer (n 6) 232.

[9] M Brandon, 'Recent Measures to Improve the International Investment Climate' (1960) 9 *Journal of Public Law* 125, 126–31.

[10] See, eg, Laryea (n 5) 298–300.

ICSID was conceived as an independent international forum that would assuage the concerns of capital exporters, and encourage them to invest in developing countries with (perceived) weak judicial systems and governance. Ratification of the ICSID Convention by developing countries was to serve as a kind of insurance to potential investors that they (the investors) would have recourse to the ICSID Centre's independent dispute resolution mechanism if the host state government undermined the property rights of the investor. As observed in *Gas Natural SDS v Argentine Republic* (2005),[11] the independent international dispute resolution mechanisms such as ICSID's 'offered to foreign investors assurances that disputes that might flow from their investments would not be subject to the perceived hazards of delays and political pressures of adjudication in national courts'.[12] The Tribunal felt 'that assurances of independent international arbitration is an important—perhaps the most important—element in investor protections'.[13]

ISDS practice has now developed beyond ICSID. Most IIAs provide for investor–state arbitration, at ICSID or elsewhere, as a mechanism for settling disputes between foreign investors and host governments. And many investor–state arbitrations take place under the auspices of international arbitral tribunals governed by non-ICSID rules and/or institutions, such as the Permanent Court of Arbitration, the London Court of International Arbitration, and the International Chamber of Commerce.

There are currently over 700 publicly known ISDS cases, including one brought (ultimately, unsuccessfully) by Phillip Morris against Australia. By the end of 2015, 444 of those cases had been concluded.[14] Of those, 36 per cent were decided in favour of the state, 26 per cent in favour of the investor and 26 per cent settled.[15] A record high of 70 cases were filed in 2015. Importantly, about 40 per cent of the cases filed in 2015 were against developed countries, many of them by European investors against European countries. Most of these countries have established democracies with a sound rule of law, good governance and independent judiciaries. The record number of ISDS cases against developed countries is a far cry from the underlying concept of ISDS.

B. Criticism of ISDS

The increasing use of ISDS by investors, and the way the system operates, have raised concerns among many policymakers, scholars and

[11] Gas Natural SDG, SA v Argentina (Jurisdiction) (2005) 14 ICSID Rep 282.

[12] ibid [31] M.

[13] ibid [29], [49].

[14] United Nations Conference on Trade and Development, 'IIA Issues Note: Investor–State Dispute Settlement: Review of Developments in 2015' (June 2016), unctad.org/en/PublicationsLibrary/webdiaepcb2016d4_en.pdf, 1.

[15] ibid.

judicial officers.[16] Among the criticisms that have been made are that the ISDS system enhances the power of multinational corporations at the expense of national sovereignty and interests;[17] that the substantive treaty provisions of IIAs are pro-investor, and/or are interpreted in favour of investors by tribunals to the disadvantage of sovereign states;[18] that there is inconsistency and unpredictability in arbitral decisions;[19] that the system and processes lack transparency;[20] that there is a lack of independence and impartiality of arbitrators;[21] and that the ISDS system leads to 'regulatory chill', as host state governments refrain from implementing legitimate policies that may trigger ISDS claims.[22] Indeed, the ISDS system, as it operates currently, has been said to challenge 'core constitutional law values, such as the principle of democracy, the concept of the rule of law, and the protection of fundamental or human rights'.[23] Our particular focus is on whether these broad and general constitutional criticisms translate into concrete problems in Australian law. Before turning to that issue, however, it is necessary to explain the ISDS provision in ChAFTA.

C. ISDS Provisions in ChAFTA

ChAFTA's provisions on investment are contained in Chapter 9. Article 9.12 provides for the submission, by an investor (claimant), of a claim to arbitration under ICSID or under the UNCITRAL Arbitration Rules ('as modified by the Transparency Rules Applicable to ISDS'), or to any other arbitration institution or under any other arbitration rules, if the claimant and the respondent host state agree.

A claimant must first seek consultation with the host government.[24] The claimant and respondent (host state) are to seek to resolve the dispute

[16] See, eg, French, 'Investor–State Dispute Settlement' (n 1); SW Schill, 'Reforming Investor–State Dispute Settlement (ISDS): Conceptual Framework and Options for the Way Forward' (The E15 Initiative, July 2015), e15initiative.org/publications/reforming-investor-state-dispute-settlement-isds-conceptual-framework-and-options-for-the-way-forward/; R Abbott, F Erixon and MF Ferracane, 'Demystifying Investor–State Dispute Settlement (ISDS)' (2014) European Centre for International Political Economy Occasional Paper 5/2014, www.ecipe.org/app/uploads/2014/12/OCC52014__1.pdf; R Dolzer, 'Perspectives for Investment Arbitration: Consistency as a Policy Goal?' (2012) 9(3) *Transnational Dispute Management* 403.

[17] See, eg, Greens/EFA Group in the European Parliament, 'EU–US Trade Negotiations (TTIP): Investor Dispute Mechanism Trojan Horse Must Be Excluded from TTIP' (21 January 2014), www.greens-efa.eu/eu-us-trade-negotiations-ttip-11492.html.

[18] European Federation for Investment Law and Arbitration, 'A Response to Criticisms Against ISDS' (17 May 2015), efila.org/wp-content/uploads/2015/05/EFILA_in_response_to_the-criticism_of_ISDS_final_draft.pdf.

[19] ibid.

[20] ibid.

[21] ibid.

[22] ibid.

[23] Schill (n 16).

[24] Free Trade Agreement between the Government of Australia and the Government of the People's Republic of China (ChAFTA) (signed 17 June 2015, entered into force 20 December 2015) [2015] ATS 15, Art 9.11.

through those consultations.[25] Submission can be made to arbitration only if the dispute has not been resolved after 120 days.[26] Article 9.11.4 provides that measures of a state party that are non-discriminatory, and which are for the legitimate public welfare objectives of public health, safety, the environment, public morals or public order shall not be the subject of a claim. Where a host state considers that a measure that is alleged to be in breach of its obligation under the investment chapter is of the kind described in Article 9.11.4, it may deliver to the claimant and to the non-disputing party (ie, the home state of the claimant) a notice (a 'public welfare notice') specifying the basis for its position within 30 days.[27] The issuance of a public welfare notice shall trigger a 90-day period during which the respondent and the non-disputing party shall consult, and during which the dispute resolution procedure between the claimant and the respondent shall be automatically suspended.

Further, Article 9.8 provides for some general exceptions. It states that, subject to the requirement that measures are not applied in a manner which would constitute arbitrary or unjustifiable discrimination between investments or investors, or a disguised restriction on international trade or investment, nothing in the agreement shall be construed as preventing a host state from adopting or enforcing measures: (a) necessary to protect human, animal or plant life or health; (b) necessary to ensure compliance with laws and regulations that are not inconsistent with the agreement; (c) imposed for the protection of national treasures of artistic, historic or archaeological value; or (d) relating to the conservation of living or non-living exhaustible natural resources.

The above limitations are an attempt to address some of the criticisms of ISDS. They are aimed at empowering the states to decide on legitimate policy, and to enable the states to pursue legitimate policy objectives without being hauled before an ISDS tribunal. However, the stated limitations, and carved-out regulatory space, do not eliminate the constitutional issues raised by ISDS that are the focus of this chapter. More specifically, these limitations do not necessarily ensure that the executive government of Australia is capable of entering into an agreement that contains an ISDS clause (such as ChAFTA), at least not without parliamentary approval.

Besides, Australia is a party to another investment treaty with China, the Australia–China BIT,[28] which does not contain many of the limitations found in ChAFTA. That Treaty, arguably, remains in force and coexists with the investment chapter in ChAFTA.[29] It provides, in Article XII(1),

[25] ibid Art 9.12.2.

[26] ibid.

[27] ibid Art 9.11.5.

[28] Agreement between the Government of Australia and the Government of the People's Republic of China on the Reciprocal Encouragement and Protection of Investments (Australia–China BIT) (signed 11 July 1988, entered into force 11 July 1988) [1988] ATS 14.

[29] T Voon and E Sheargold, 'Australia, China and the Co-Existence of Successive International Investment Agreements', ch 11 of this book.

that 'in the event of a dispute between a Contracting party and a national of the other Contracting party', the disputing parties 'shall initially seek to resolve the dispute by consultations and negotiations'.[30] Article XII(2) then provides that, if the dispute is not settled within three months, either party may initiate proceedings before a court; and where the parties agree or the dispute relates to amount of compensation payable in respect of expropriation, submit to an arbitral tribunal, which may be an ad hoc tribunal or an ICSID tribunal. There is no public policy space carved out for the state parties, as is the case under ChAFTA Article 9. Thus, the broader significance of the discussion in this chapter remains.

We now turn to consider the constitutional questions raised by Australia's entry to IIAs (such as ChAFTA) that contain ISDS provisions. We begin with an overview of the Australian constitutional framework.

III. THE AUSTRALIAN CONSTITUTIONAL FRAMEWORK

Australia is governed by a written, rigid Constitution, which establishes the three branches of the federal government—legislative, executive and judicial—and confers and delineates their powers. The Constitution is interpreted and enforced by the High Court of Australia, the highest and final court in the Australian judicial system.[31] Thus the High Court can review government action to ensure that it conforms to the Constitution, and declare it invalid if it does not (as well as issuing other, appropriate remedies).

When Australia came into existence in 1901,[32] the country was a British dependency with no independent foreign policy or sovereignty. Over the years from the end of the First World War to the end of the Second World War, a combination of legal and political changes led to Australian independence.[33] However, the Australian constitutional framework for

[30] Australia–China BIT (n 28) Art XII(1).

[31] Prior to 1986, the Privy Council played a role in Australian constitutional adjudication, and under s 74 of the Constitution it continues to exist as a formally available, although in fact unused, avenue of appeal: Privy Council (Limitation of Appeals) Act 1968 (Cth); Privy Council (Appeals from the High Court) Act 1975 (Cth); *Kirmani v Captain Cook Cruises Pty Ltd [No 2]* (1985) 159 CLR 461, especially 465; Australia Act 1986 (Cth) s 11; Australia Act 1986 (UK) s 11.

[32] On 1 January 1901, following enactment by the United Kingdom Parliament of the Commonwealth of Australia Constitution Act 1900 (Imp) (63 & 64 Vict c 12) (the Constitution).

[33] The most important of these was the Statute of Westminster 1931 (Imp) (22 & 23 Geo 5 c 4), enacted by the Parliament of the United Kingdom to give legal effect to the agreement reached at the 1926 and 1930 Imperial Conferences, which agreed that the settler-colonies of the United Kingdom (the so-called 'dominions') would be co-equal with the United Kingdom within the 'British Commonwealth of Nations'. The Statute of Westminster became law for Australia by virtue of the Australian Parliament's enactment of the Statute of Westminster Adoption Act 1942 (Cth), which operated retrospectively so as to establish Australia's independence from the United Kingdom from 3 September 1939 (ie, from the commencement of the Second World War).

engaging in international relations and for incorporating international law into the domestic legal framework remains very similar to that of the United Kingdom. Thus, Australia has a dualist system: it is the role of the executive government to engage in foreign relations and, more specifically, to enter into international agreements on Australia's behalf. Executive ratification of, or accession to, a treaty binds Australia at international law. Because Australia has a system of parliamentary, responsible government, in which the executive government holds office only while it enjoys the confidence of the Parliament, the Parliament is able to exercise the same oversight of the treaty-making process as it is of any other governmental action.[34] Nevertheless, it is the role of the executive to enter agreements on Australia's behalf.

The flipside of these arrangements is that international agreements, and international law more generally, have no 'self-executing' domestic legal effect. They do not fetter the legislative power of the Australian Parliament, or the powers of the federal executive,[35] and they are not binding on Australian courts.[36] International agreements and international law will have domestic legal effect only if an Australian parliament enacts legislation that gives expression to the relevant international legal norm. There is no uniform practice in Australia as to how this is done: in some instances, Australian legislation may incorporate international norms into domestic law by direct reference;[37] on other occasions, Australian legislation may impose duties that have the same legal content as, or that ensure compliance with, Australia's international legal obligations.[38]

As a general rule, Australia's national Parliament enjoys the constitutional power to enact legislation giving effect to Australia's international

[34] Since 1996, this oversight has been formalised through the existence of a parliamentary Joint Standing Committee on Treaties: Parliament of Australia, 'Role of the Committee' www.aph.gov.au/Parliamentary_Business/Committees/Joint/Treaties/Role_of_the_Committee.

[35] The mere fact that Australia is a party to an international agreement does not necessarily generate any requirement that the government considers those obligations in exercising a power conferred by statute; this will depend upon the construction of the statute in question: *Minister for Aboriginal Affairs v Peko-Wallsend Ltd* (1986) 162 CLR 24, 39–40 (Mason J); *Re Minister for Immigration and Multicultural and Indigenous Affairs; Ex parte Lam* [2003] HCA 6, (2003) 214 CLR 1, 33–34 [101]–[102] (McHugh and Gummow JJ) (Lam); and World Heritage Properties Conservation Act 1983 (Cth). The prior suggestion (in *Minister for Immigration and Ethnic Affairs v Teoh* (1995) 183 CLR 273) that, as a general matter, international agreements give rise to legitimate expectations that executive officers will act in accordance with them, has been rejected: Lam 1. In any event, the concept of legitimate expectation no longer plays a significant role in Australian administrative law: *Minister for Border and Protection v WZARH* [2015] HCA 40, (2015) 256 CLR 326.

[36] Australia's courts will generally strive to interpret legislation in a way that is compatible with international legal norms, insofar as it is possible to do so, but Parliament remains free to enact legislation that is contrary to those norms.

[37] See, eg, International Tax Agreements Act 1953 (Cth) s 5, which gives certain double taxation agreements to which Australia is a party the force of law within Australia; International Arbitration Act 1974 (Cth) s 16(1) which gives the UNCITRAL Model Law on International Commercial Arbitration (Model Law) the force of law in Australia.

[38] See, eg, World Heritage Properties Conservation Act 1983 (Cth).

legal obligations.[39] Parliament has enacted legislation that gives effect to certain ChAFTA obligations, but not all of them (as we discuss below). However, Parliament's power is itself 'subject to the Constitution',[40] which means that in giving effect to international law by way of domestic legislation, Australian parliaments must respect other constraints and requirements imposed by the Constitution.[41] The executive power of the Australian government is not expressly subject to the Constitution, but it is quite clear that the power is not unlimited, and (as will also be discussed below) there are certain functions that the executive lacks the constitutional capacity to perform.

In light of the constitutional framework just described, Australia's entry into IIAs containing ISDS provisions raises a series of important constitutional questions. The first is the source of authority to enter into such an agreement. This requires consideration of the scope of executive power to enter into such agreements, as well as the application of two constitutional doctrines that may constrain the Australian government's capacity to enter into agreements containing ISDS provisions: the rules that flow from Chapter III of the Constitution, and those that constrain the executive's power to contract and to spend public moneys without legislative authorisation.

The second is the source of authority to make arbitral awards enforceable in Australian courts. Following Australia's entry into the Convention on the Recognition and Enforcement of Foreign Arbitral Award 1958 (New York Convention) and the ICSID Convention, the federal Parliament has enacted legislation that is relevant in this regard: the International Arbitration Act 1974 (Cth).[42] This Act makes foreign arbitral awards binding and enforceable in Australian courts (whether federal, state or territory courts) as if the award were a judgment or order of the Australian court in which it is enforced.[43] Section 3(1) defines 'foreign award' as 'an arbitral award made, in pursuance of an arbitration agreement, in a country other than Australia, being an arbitral award in relation to which the [New York] Convention

[39] Principally by way of the 'external affairs' head of legislative power: the Constitution (n 32) s 51(xxix).

[40] ibid s 51. State (sub-federal) parliaments are similarly constrained: ss 106, 107.

[41] For instance, all laws of the Commonwealth must demonstrate a connection to a head of power found in the Constitution. There are also rules that prevent Parliament from enacting statutes that deal with both taxation and other matters. These constraints are potentially relevant to ChAFTA and are explored further below.

[42] The Act states its objects to include giving 'effect to Australia's obligations under the Convention on the Recognition and Enforcement of Foreign Arbitral Awards adopted in 1958 by the United Nations Conference on International Commercial Arbitration at its twenty-fourth meeting' (s 2D(d)) and giving 'effect to the Convention on the Settlement of Investment Disputes between States and Nationals of Other States signed by Australia on 24 March 1975' (s 2D(f)).

[43] International Arbitration Act 1974 (Cth) ss 8(1)–(3). Where an international commercial arbitral award would not be covered by the New York Convention, the International Arbitration Act 1974 (Cth) renders it enforceable in Australia (pursuant to Arts 35 and 36 of the Model Law, as amended in 2006): ss 16(1), 20.

applies'. Similarly, awards of ICSID tribunals are binding and enforceable in Australian courts.[44] Assessing the constitutional validity of the International Arbitration Act, particularly in relation to awards issued pursuant to an ISDS provision (ISDS awards), requires a consideration of the scope of the legislative power of the Commonwealth, and particularly of the limitations imposed by Chapter III.

Analysis of these two issues may reveal that there is no constitutional hurdle to Australia entering into an international agreement that contains an ISDS provision, and legislating so as to make ISDS awards enforceable in Australian courts. However, without undertaking the enquiry the legal answer is not self-evident,[45] and the constitutional questions are therefore worth exploring. The following two sections address these issues in turn. We begin by examining whether Chapter III of the Constitution constrains the executive's ability to enter IIAs that contain ISDS provisions.

IV. AUTHORITY TO ENTER INTO IIAS CONTAINING ISDS PROVISIONS

A. ISDS Provisions and the Constitutional Exercise of Judicial Power

Chapter III of the Constitution establishes the federal judicature, and vests it with certain power and jurisdiction. Being constitutionally conferred, these provisions are constitutionally entrenched. Further, Chapter III has long been interpreted as an exhaustive statement of the manner in which the judicial power of the Commonwealth can be exercised. That is, Chapter III implies a strict separation of the judicial power of the Commonwealth from the other branches of the federal government and other kinds of governmental power.

This separation is effected by two interlocking rules: first, the 'judicial power of the Commonwealth' can only be exercise by Chapter III courts; second, the federal Parliament cannot vest Chapter III courts with any powers that are not 'judicial'.[46] Though the concept of judicial power defies precise definition,[47] it is tolerably clear that certain functions fall within its scope. These include the power to interpret the Constitution, and to decide whether legislative or executive action is within power; in the case of

[44] International Arbitration Act 1974 (Cth) ss 31–35.

[45] As is shown by the recent flurry of writing expressing doubt about the consistency of ISDS clauses with Australian constitutional principles: see, eg, French, 'Investor–State Dispute Settlement' (n 1); J Allsop CJ, 'International Commercial Arbitration—The Courts and the Rule of Law in the Asia Pacific Region' (Second Annual Global Arbitration Review, 11 November 2014), www.ciarb.net.au/wp-content/uploads/resources/international_commercial_arbitration_._the_courts_and_the_rule_of_law_in_the_asia_pacific_region.pdf; A Matveev, 'Investor–State Dispute Settlement: The Evolving Balance Between Investor Protection and State Sovereignty' (2015) 40(1) *University of Western Australia Law Review* 348.

[46] *R v Kirby; Ex parte Boilermakers' Society of Australia* (1956) 94 CLR 254.

[47] *TCL Air Conditioner (Zhongshan) Co Ltd v Judges of the Federal Court of Australia* [2013] HCA 5, (2013) 251 CLR 533, 553 [27] (French CJ and Gageler J) (*TCL Air Conditioner*).

legislation, this will require scrutiny of whether Parliament has conformed to the Constitution; in the case of executive action, this will require scrutiny of whether the relevant executive actor has conformed to the Constitution and (if relevant) the statute that confers or delimits the actor's power.[48] As these functions are characterised as part of the 'judicial power of the Commonwealth', they can only be exercised by a Chapter III court: they could not be exercised by the legislative or executive branch.

On the other hand, it is accepted that certain functions are so antithetical to established judicial functions, or required to be performed in a manner that is so contrary to ordinary judicial power, that they *cannot* be vested in a Chapter III court. This might be the case if, for example, a statute purportedly required a Chapter III court to decide a certain matter as directed by the executive.

In recent decades, the High Court has also emphasised its constitutional function as the apex of the Australian judicial system.[49] This system includes state and territory, as well as federal, courts, meaning that all Australian courts are constitutionally required to have the degree of institutional integrity appropriate to being part of a national judicial framework with the High Court at its apex.[50]

As noted in section II, ISDS provisions have been criticised on the basis that they transfer significant authority to arbitral bodies—and more particularly, power to make a binding award of damages against a state, as a consequence of state action that has been found to be legally valid in accordance with that state's domestic laws. Consider, for example, the (ultimately, unsuccessful) arbitral action brought by Philip Morris Asia, with respect to the Tobacco Plain Packaging Act 2011 (Cth). The validity of that legislation had by this stage already been adjudicated by the Australian High Court. The Court found that the legislation was valid: it was within the legislative power of the Commonwealth, and did not amount to an unconstitutional acquisition of property.[51] It seems correct to say that the decisions of an arbitral tribunal set up to decide an ISDS dispute may have a significant effect on the Australian economy, or its regulatory framework.[52] The prospect of an ISDS arbitration might therefore deter the Australian government from implementing certain policies that lie within its constitutional power, and in this way have a chilling effect on government. It is also clear that actions of

[48] *Australian Communist Party v Commonwealth* (1951) 83 CLR 1. We explain the distinction between executive power that derives from statute and that which does not in the next section.

[49] See, eg, *Kirk v Industrial Relations Court of New South Wales* [2010] HCA 1, (2010) 239 CLR 531.

[50] *Kable v Director of Public Prosecutions (NSW)* (1996) 89 CLR 51, 138–39, 141–43 (Gummow J).

[51] *JT International SA v Commonwealth of Australia* [2012] HCA 43, (2012) 86 ALJR 1297.

[52] As remarked by French, 'Investor–State Dispute Settlement' (n 1); and see above section II,C.

a state court can provide the trigger for an ISDS arbitration.[53] Thus French CJ has asked: are ISDS tribunals 'a cut above the courts'?[54]

Whatever criticisms might be made of this state of affairs, it is quite clear that arbitral tribunals that adjudicate ISDS provisions are not 'courts' for the purposes of Chapter III. They do not fall within any of the categories of courts referred to in that Chapter.[55] Nor do they necessarily possess the procedural trappings or institutional qualities of a Chapter III court. As French CJ observed:

> Arbitral tribunals set up under ISDS provisions are not courts. Nor are they required to act like courts ... Questions have been raised about the consistency, openness and impartiality of decisions made in ISDS arbitrations.[56]

It may therefore at first appear that ISDS provisions strain the first of the two Chapter III rules. That is, by signing an IIA that contains an ISDS provision, it may seem that the Commonwealth executive purports to authorise a usurpation of the exclusively judicial power of the Commonwealth, by binding the Australian State to the decisions of an international arbitrator not qualified to exercise that power. However, the better view is that such tribunals do not exercise 'the judicial power of the Commonwealth'; hence it is unlikely that they raise any Chapter III concern.

The concept of the 'judicial power of the Commonwealth' is closely connected to the law of the Commonwealth, as found in the Constitution itself, or federal legislation validly enacted thereunder. As explained above, it is undeniably an exercise of judicial power for a court to ascertain whether Parliament has complied with the Constitution, and whether an executive actor has complied with the Constitution and relevant statute law. But international legal norms do not necessarily inform the answer to these questions. As was also explained above, international law does not have domestic legal effect unless it is implemented by legislation. When interpreting a statute that confers executive power, the courts will presume that it should be read in a manner that is consistent with international law, but that presumption can be rebutted.[57] In short, Parliament can authorise the executive to act in a manner that is inconsistent with international law. Even if Parliament has enacted legislation that gives domestic effect to international legal norms, the role of the courts is to decide whether the executive has acted in conformity with that legislation, not the international norm. International

[53] R French CJ, 'ISDS: Litigating the Judiciary' (2015) 26 *Public Law Review* 155, 156.
[54] Fench, 'Investor–State Dispute Settlement' (n 1).
[55] Constitution (n 32) ss 71, 73, 77.
[56] French, 'Investor–State Dispute Settlement' (n 1).
[57] See, eg, International Tax Agreements Act 1953 (Cth). See also, World Heritage Properties Conservation Act 1983 (Cth), which explained that international agreements do not necessarily impose legal limitations on executive power, nor a 'legitimate expectation' that the executive will comply with them.

law will have little influence on a court's assessment of whether a statute is within the scope of the legislative power conferred by the Constitution, for the weight of authority states that international law should not inform the courts' interpretation of the Constitution.[58]

When an arbitral tribunal set up under an ISDS provision considers whether an IIA has been breached, it assesses the relevant state action against an entirely different set of criteria from those which a Chapter III court would apply in assessing the validity of government action. The tribunal applies those legal norms derived from the relevant IIA; the court applies the legal norms that are recognised as authoritative in Australian law, and especially those found in the Constitution or federal legislation. Moreover, the decision of the tribunal does not affect the domestic legal validity of the state action. It may make a binding award against the state, but it does not deprive the act in question of its domestic, legal effect. For example, even if Australia's Tobacco Plain Packaging Act had been found to breach the relevant IIA, it would nonetheless have remained a valid law of the Commonwealth, which could be executed by the Australian executive and enforced by its courts.

The suggestion that ISDS tribunals are 'a cut above the court' must be viewed in this light: such tribunals may well have the opportunity to consider state actions that have already been ruled valid or invalid by Australia's highest court, and their presence may have a chilling effect on government action, but they do not operate as another tier of the judiciary, or have the power to undo the decisions of the High Court.

B. Parliamentary Control of Contracting and Expenditure of Public Moneys

ISDS provisions have been criticised on the basis that they expose states to substantial arbitral awards, in a manner that may fall short of procedural best practice, or otherwise diminishes their sovereignty. In Australia, the prospect of awards being made pursuant to an ISDS clause raises more specific constitutional concerns—revealed by the relatively recent, and unexpected, decision of the High Court in *Williams*.[59] Before explaining that decision, and its potential ramifications for the executive's power to enter into IIAs that contain ISDS provisions (such as ChAFTA), it is necessary to explain the general scope of federal executive power.

The executive power of the Australian government—described in constitutional terms as *the Commonwealth*—derives from section 61 of

[58] This view, and the reasons for rejecting the contrary view, are discussed in *Al-Kateb v Godwin* (2004) 219 CLR 562 at [62]–[73] (McHugh J).

[59] *Williams* (n 2).

the Constitution. This (relevantly) provides that: '[t]he executive power of the Commonwealth ... extends to the execution and maintenance of this Constitution, and of the laws of the Commonwealth.' Thus, it does relatively little to clarify the content of 'executive power'. It has been said that 'the polity which the Constitution established and maintains is an independent nation state with a federal system of government',[60] but the details of the executive power thereby conferred are to be ascertained by reference to the surrounding text and structure of the Constitution and the context in which it was drafted.

One of the most important distinctions is between those executive powers that are 'statutory', and those which are 'non-statutory'. Logically enough, a statutory power is one that has been conferred on the executive by federal statute law. The limits of such power lie in the statute by which it is conferred—and ultimately, the limits of the legislative power of the Commonwealth: for all laws must conform to the Constitution, and the federal Parliament cannot confer any kind of power greater than that which the Constitution allows. For example, the Parliament could not confer executive power by a (purported) law that lacks connection to a head of power in section 51 or 52 of the Constitution, or violates Chapter III of the Constitution (which is explained below).

A non-statutory power is one conferred directly by section 61 of the Constitution. Hence, it can be exercised without statutory authorisation. It is generally accepted that the constitutional phrase 'executive power' encompasses many of the powers that were enjoyed by the British Crown at the time of federation, and which do not require parliamentary authorisation for their exercise. Of particular relevance to the current discussion, these 'prerogative powers' of the British Crown include those to conduct foreign affairs and to enter into treaties and other international agreements. Hence (and as was mentioned in section III), the government of the Commonwealth enjoys the power, under section 61 of the Constitution, to carry out Australia's international relations and to bind Australia at international law.

Somewhat opaquely, the government of the Commonwealth is said to also enjoy 'a capacity to engage in enterprises and activities peculiarly adapted to the government of a nation and which cannot otherwise be carried on for the benefit of the nation'.[61] This reinforces the conclusion that the non-statutory 'executive power of the Commonwealth' extends to the making of international agreements, and that this is a power that can be exercised without statutory authorisation. Indeed, the executive routinely does this, and it is generally assumed that such actions are legally valid. However, it

[60] *Pape* (n 2) 84 [217] (Gummow, Crennan and Bell JJ). On the background to Australian independence from the United Kingdom, see generally, above (n 33).

[61] *Victoria v Commonwealth* (1975) 134 CLR 338, 397 (Mason J) (*AAP Case*); see also *Pape* (n 2) 60–62 [128]–[132] (French CJ); 83–85 [215]–[228] (Gummow, Crennan and Bell JJ).

is not necessarily clear that the executive power extends to entering into an international agreement that contains an ISDS clause.

The executive is also said to enjoy certain non-statutory powers by virtue of the fact that it is a legal person. For example, it is accepted that the Commonwealth can bring an action in tort; conversely, an action may be brought against it. For many years, it was assumed that this included a power to enter into contracts, including agreements to pay out public moneys, without any need for statutory authorisation. However, *Williams* revealed that that assumption was largely mistaken, as we explain below.

It is within this framework of executive power that the constitutionality of entering into agreements containing ISDS provisions must be analysed. At the time of federation, the Crown's prerogative would probably have been accepted to include the power to subject the Crown to international arbitration involving other sovereigns. Arbitration involving the Crown and private persons was unknown at this time, but the more general power to enter into international agreements may well extend to the making of agreements that include ISDS provisions. However, because the scope of the executive power of the Commonwealth is determined by, and constrained by, the Constitution, it is not necessarily coextensive with the powers enjoyed by the British Crown—as the High Court emphasised in *Williams*.

Prior to this decision, it was generally assumed that the federal executive had non-statutory power to enter into contracts, and hence commit itself to pay out public moneys. This was thought to differ little from the contractual powers individuals enjoy as legal persons. This power was either thought to be unlimited (in the sense that the executive could enter into any contract it thought fit), or else coextensive with the range of legislative subject matters listed in sections 51 and 52 of the Constitution (in the sense that if the power to enter into the particular contract *could* have been conferred by the Commonwealth Parliament, then the executive enjoyed the power to enter into such a contract even in the absence of such legislation).[62]

In *Williams*, the High Court found that neither thought was correct. Rather, the Court found that the executive's non-statutory power to contract and spend is substantially constrained. Though the executive enjoys certain legal capacities, it is no ordinary person. Rather, the Commonwealth executive cannot generally enter into contracts, or commit to pay out public moneys, without valid statutory authorisation. The exception to this general rule is that the executive can pay out moneys in the ordinary course of government, without statutory authorisation.

The ultimate constitutional basis for this finding is the federal nature of Australian government, which informs the proper understanding of executive

[62] However, it was long understood that this power was subject to certain 'procedural' constraints; eg, public moneys had to be appropriated from the Consolidated Revenue Fund by a valid appropriation Act before they could be spent.

power in two ways. First, the Commonwealth executive has responsibility for distinctively national matters, but—in the absence of valid legislation—not for matters which fall within the remit of state executive governments.[63] Second, the Commonwealth Parliament is bicameral, with the upper house—the Senate—itself being elected on a federal franchise (similar to the Senate of the United States) rather than a national one.[64] The fundamental constitutional principle that executive expenditure be subject to parliamentary control in Australia therefore has a federalist dimension to it, providing a further reason to require that Commonwealth expenditure typically be sourced in a statute that has (ipso facto) passed both houses of Parliament.[65]

The Court offered little explanation of the kinds of functions that would fall within the exception to the general rule, but it found that the expenditure in question in the *Williams* case—namely, contracts for the provision of 'chaplaincy services' in public schools administered by a state (ie, sub-federal) government, with no statute authorising this contract or expenditure—did not. Hence, the contracts and payments under them were held to be invalid.[66]

It is not clear whether the principles articulated in *Williams* constrain the scope of the power to enter into international agreements. If they do, however, then they may constrain the executive's power to enter into an agreement containing an ISDS clause, because this may be seen as a species of promise to pay, analogous to a contract.

In entering into an IIA, the executive agrees that Australia will abide by the obligations contained therein. If the IIA contains an ISDS provision, the executive further agrees that Australia will pay out any moneys that may be awarded by an arbitral tribunal, if those obligations are breached. Thus, the act of signing an IIA that contains an ISDS provision amounts to a commitment to pay out public moneys, at least in certain circumstances. That commitment is binding, in the sense that the decisions of arbitral tribunals established under ISDS provisions are automatically enforceable in

[63] *Williams* (n 2) 179–80 [4], 192 [36], 193 [38], 216–17 [83] (French CJ); 235 [146] (Gummow and Bell JJ); 346–47 [499], 348 [503] (Crennan J). See also 250–51 [196], 252 [198], 281 [288] (Hayne J, also making the federalist point but declining to decide the larger issue as to the limits of Commonwealth executive power).

[64] See further B Galligan, *A Federal Republic: Australia's Constitutional System of Government* (Cambridge, Cambridge University Press, 1995).

[65] *Williams* (n 2) 205–06 [60]–[61] (French CJ); 232–33 [136], 235 [145] (Gummow and Bell JJ); 351–52 [516], 354–55 [532], 358 [544] (Crennan J). The mere fact of a valid appropriation was not sufficient to answer these concerns, because—consistent with Westminster tradition in relation to upper houses—the power of the Senate in relation to appropriation laws is limited by ss 53 and 56 of the Constitution (n 32).

[66] The plaintiff in the case had sought to contest the expenditure primarily on the ground that it infringed the constitutional prohibition on the establishment of any religion by the Commonwealth: the Constitution (n 32) s 116. The Court's treatment of that argument confirmed the established, and narrow, limits of Australian non-establishment doctrine; but, as discussed in the text, the Court revealed a new and unanticipated constraint on executive power.

the many foreign jurisdictions that are parties to the New York Convention and/or the ICSID Convention, and also (subject to the discussion in section V) in Australian courts.

It must be emphasised that the application of the *Williams* principle in the context of international agreements remains uncertain for several reasons. The first is that that case concerned the scope of so-called legal person-type powers. It did not concern the scope of prerogative-type powers, and the power to enter into an international agreement is often described as a power of the latter type. Although one cannot treat these labels as denoting rigid categories of executive power—as was stated earlier, in every case, the scope of executive power is determined by section 61 of the Constitution—it is nevertheless reasonable to wonder whether the scope of the executive power to enter into treaties may be subject to different limitations than the executive power to enter into contracts. This is especially so, because *Williams* was primarily premised upon federalist concerns. The importance of Senate oversight of public expenditure was noted above. Furthermore, the High Court concluded that the scheme at issue in *Williams* was not supported by the 'nationhood' aspect of executive power, because rather than being an enterprise 'peculiarly adapted to the government of a nation',[67] it would have been within the powers of the Australian states to implement the school chaplain's scheme.[68] Therefore, the Court did not comment on whether the principles articulated constrained the use of non-statutory power to expend money in the settlement of international claims. Other cases do not provide clear answers either.[69]

On the other hand, one may well argue that the principles in *Williams* are of broader application. Those principles reflect not only the federal structure of the Constitution, but the fundamental importance, in the Westminster constitutional tradition, of parliamentary supervision of the expenditure of public moneys. Though it is generally accepted that the states have no authority to enter into international agreements, that does not mean that the Senate, which represents the Australian people by way of a distinct federal franchise, should have no say as to whether Australia should commit itself to the payment of substantial arbitral awards that may result from entering into an agreement that contains an ISDS provision. Because this argument rests on the proper interpretation of a constitutional conferral of 'executive power' in the context of a particular constitutional tradition, it is no answer to it to point out that neither House of Parliament has any say over international legal obligations in general: the very same constitutional principles that establish the creation of international legal obligations as within the

[67] The test enunciated in *AAP Case* (n 61) 397 (Mason J).

[68] *Williams* (n 2) (Gummow and Bell JJ); 250–51 [196] (Hayne J); 348 [503] (Crennan J).

[69] Other recent cases that have dealt with similar issues to *Williams*, but which leave the questions identified in the text unanswered, include *Pape* (n 2) and *Williams [No 2]* (n 2).

remit of the executive also establish the special role of the Parliament (which is to say, an absence of unlimited executive power) in relation to spending, or promising to spend, public moneys.

Furthermore, under the principle of attribution, decisions of an Australia sub-federal government may be the subject of an ISDS claim and, possibly, of an award of damages, under an IIA concluded by the national government. This adds further weight to the argument that the Commonwealth executive cannot use non-statutory executive power to enter into an IIA that contains an ISDS provision, and that the Commonwealth Parliament—including, thereby, the Senate—should be required to confer the relevant power upon the executive by way of statute.[70]

If the Commonwealth executive cannot sign IIAs containing ISDS provisions without statutory power to do so, what would be the result? The first and most obvious consequence would be that the executive would have no legal authority to sign such an agreement unless and until such power was granted by way of legislation: any agreement entered into in the absence of such a conferral of power would be invalid as a matter of domestic Australian law. However, this may not undermine Australia's international legal obligations under the ISDS provision, as Australia in unlikely to be able to rely on its own domestic invalidity to avoid its international obligation.[71]

This has immediate significance for ChAFTA. ChAFTA came into force in December 2015 upon an exchange of notes between Australia and China. As foreshadowed above, Parliament has enacted legislation implementing some of the obligations imposed by ChAFTA, but not all of them. Most importantly, there is no apparent legislative authorisation for the ISDS provision. The Customs Amendment (China–Australia Free Trade Agreement Implementation) Act 2015 (Cth) and the Customs Tariff Amendment

[70] The exception noted in *Williams*, that expenditure undertaken in the ordinary course of government, would not seem to apply to this case. Much of the High Court's discussion of this exception emphasised that such expenditure is itself constitutionally authorised in virtue of s 64 of the Constitution (n 32), which allows the establishment of the Commonwealth ministry and government departments: (n 2), [4], [34], [65], [74], [79], [83] (French CJ); [139] (Gummow and Bell JJ). Crennan J did not draw this particular link, but did say that, in the first year of contracting for chaplaincy services, such services could not be considered a recognised part of government administration: *Williams* (n 2) [532]. In the context of ISDS arbitral awards, this would suggest that if a settlement were reached whereby payments were to be made on a periodic basis, payments subsequent to the first might constitute expenditure in the ordinary course of government; but the first such payment would not.

[71] See, eg, *Balkan Energy Limited (Ghana) v The Republic of Ghana*, UNCITRAL, PCA Case No 2010-7, Award on the Merits (1 April 2014); *Bankswitch Ghana Ltd (Ghana) v The Republic of Ghana*, PCA 118294, UNCITRAL, Award Save as to Costs (11 April 2014). In both cases, Ghanaian courts had ruled that the contracts relied on by the claimants were invalid because the executive had not obtained the necessary parliamentary approvals. Yet, the arbitral tribunals held Ghana liable. See also Arts 27 and 46 of the Vienna Convention of the Law of Treaties (23 May 1969), to which Australia is a party, which provide that a party may not rely on its internal law as justification for not performing its treaty or for invalidating its consent to the treaty.

(China–Australia Free Trade Agreement Implementation) Act 2015 impose tariffs on imported goods originating in China, and make certain other changes to Australian customs procedures, in accordance with Chapters 2 to 4. The Treasury Legislation Amendment (China–Australia Free Trade Agreement) Regulation 2015 (Cth) brings the Australian law governing foreign investment in a range of sectors into conformity with the Schedule of Non-Conforming Measures set out in Part 1 of Annex III, but the other obligations found in Chapter 9 have not been implemented. There is no Australian legislation that incorporates ChAFTA obligations into Australian law by direct reference. Indeed, the Constitution would not permit a single piece of legislation to implement the whole of ChAFTA: section 55 requires that 'Laws imposing taxation shall deal only with the imposition of taxation', and hence legislation purporting to both set tariff rates and (say) regulate foreign investments would unconstitutional.

Although the requirement of legislative authorisation would be an important procedural constraint on Australia's capacity to enter into this kind of agreement, it is not an insurmountable hurdle. The federal Parliament could validly authorise the executive to enter into an agreement containing an ISDS.[72] Furthermore, such authority could be retrospectively conferred: it is quite clear that the federal Parliament has the power to enact retrospective legislation,[73] including so as to authorise executive acts that were invalid at the time that they occurred.[74] Indeed, this occurred shortly after the decision in *Williams*: the Commonwealth Parliament enacted legislation retrospectively empowering the Commonwealth executive to enter into the contracts for the provision of school chaplaincy services, and many other pieces of expenditure that had previously lacked statutory authorisation.[75]

But the fact that the hurdle identified here can be overcome in a relatively straightforward matter does not diminish its importance. If this hurdle does

[72] Such legislation would be valid under the 'external affairs' power (above n 39, and the discussion in the text thereto), as an IIA negotiated by the Australian government would be an 'external affair' in the relevant sense. It would also very probably be valid under s 51(xxxix), which permits the Commonwealth Parliament to enact legislation in respect of matters that are 'incidental to the execution of any power vested by this Constitution … in the Government of the Commonwealth'. In this case, authorising entry into the IIA would be incidental to the Commonwealth government's exercise of power to negotiate such an agreement on behalf of the Australian nation.

[73] See, eg, the Statute of Westminster Adoption Act, discussed above (n 33). Of course, this assumes that the retrospective law otherwise conforms to the Constitution. Retrospective legislation must, for example, be compatible with ch III of the Constitution, which is discussed below.

[74] See, eg, *Plaintiff M68/2015 v Minister for Immigration and Border Protection* [2016] HCA 1, (2016) 257 CLR 42, 110 [180].

[75] In *Williams [No 2]* (n 2), this legislation was found to be invalid as far as the chaplaincy contracts were concerned, but not on grounds of retrospectivity: rather, it was held that the subject matter of chaplaincy contracts was not one in respect of which the Commonwealth Parliament enjoyed legislative power.

indeed exist, then the executive can enter into agreements containing ISDS provisions, but only with parliamentary authorisation by way of the conferral of the requisite statutory power. This would diminish some of the democratic objections that have been levied against clauses of this kind, by ensuring that Australia only agrees to be bound by arbitral awards with the approval of its democratically elected Parliament. We revisit this issue below.

V. THE CONSTITUTIONALITY OF THE ENFORCEMENT OF ISDS AWARDS BY AUSTRALIAN COURTS

The final question this chapter will consider is the constitutionality of legislation that makes ISDS awards enforceable in Australian courts—such as the International Arbitration Act. Because such legislation gives effect to Australia's international legal obligations under the New York Convention and the ICSID Convention, and also gives effect to the United Nations General Assembly resolutions recommending the UNCITRAL Model Law on International Commercial Arbitration,[76] it is prima facie valid, as explained in section III above.[77] However, as was also noted, the legislation will not be valid if it is contrary to Chapter III of the Constitution.

In section IV, we explained the limitations imposed by Chapter III of the Constitution, and concluded that they are unlikely to prevent the executive from validly entering into an IIA that contains an ISDS provision. However, legislation that makes ISDS awards enforceable in Australian courts raises a different Chapter III concern, which was recently addressed by the High Court in *TCL Air Conditioner*.

TCL Air Conditioner concerned the enforcement of an arbitral award between non-state parties. The unsuccessful party challenged the validity of the International Arbitration Act, on two bases: first, that by making arbitral awards enforceable in Australian courts, the International Arbitration Act effectively delegated the judicial power of the Commonwealth to those arbitrators; second, that by requiring Australian courts to enforce an arbitral award, even if the award was attended by an error of law, the Act compromised the integrity of those courts.[78]

[76] Model Law on International Commercial Arbitration of the United Nations Commission on International Trade Law, GA Res 40/72, UN GAOR, 40th Session, 112th plen mtg, Supp No 53, UN Doc A/RES/40/72 (11 December 1985); Revised Articles of the Model Law on International Commercial Arbitration of the United Nations Commission on International Trade Law, and the Recommendation regarding the Interpretation of Article II, Paragraph 2, and Article VII, Paragraph 1, of the Convention on the Recognition and Enforcement of Foreign Arbitral Awards, Done at New York, 10 June 1958, GA Res 61/33, UN GAOR, 61st Session, 64th plen mtg, Agenda Item 77, Supp No 17, UN Doc A/RES/61/33 (4 December 2006).

[77] In particular, it is legislation with respect to Australia's external affairs: above (n 39).

[78] *TCL Air Conditioner* (n 47) 557 [40] (French CJ and Gageler J); 576 [111] (Hayne, Crennan, Kiefel and Bell JJ).

The High Court rejected these arguments, primarily on the basis that the making of an arbitral award is not an exercise of judicial power—that is to say, it is not the exercise of the sovereign power to resolve disputes.[79] Rather, arbitration is a voluntary and binding submission, by the parties to the dispute in question, to the determination of an arbitrator; the resulting award (even if attended by an error of law) is an expression of that agreement between the parties.[80] In particular, the prior rights of the parties in relation to the dispute are, by way of their own voluntary agreement, 'discharged and replaced by the new obligations that are created by an arbitral award'.[81] The arbitration is, in effect, a consensual adjustment of the rights obtaining between the parties; it is these new rights, resulting from the consensual submission to arbitration, that a court may then be called upon to enforce pursuant to the International Arbitration Act.[82]

Four members of the Court repeatedly used the phrase 'private arbitration'[83] to describe the subject matter of their judgment, but they make clear that what they mean by this phrase is:

> [A]rbitration undertaken in fulfilment of an agreement to submit a dispute to arbitration. Private arbitration is distinguishable from arbitration concerned with the enforcement of public rights derived from statute, such as arbitration to resolve industrial law disputes.[84]

The other two justices made a similar point about the phrase 'private arbitration' as it has been used in earlier decisions of the Court:

> The reference to 'private arbitration' was not to a private function, as distinct from a public function, but rather to a function the existence and scope of which is founded on agreement as distinct from coercion.[85]

Thus, there is no reason to think that the Court's analysis of the difference between arbitration and the exercise of judicial power does not apply equally to arbitration when one of the parties is a state. In such a case, also, the state has voluntarily agreed to a means of settling such disputes as might arise between it and some other party, and any resulting arbitral award will operate to discharge those prior rights and substitute for them in accordance

[79] ibid 553–54 [28]–[29] (French CJ and Gageler J); 566–67 [75]–[76], 574–75 [106]–[107] (Hayne, Crennan, Kiefel and Bell JJ).

[80] ibid 555 [31], 555–56 [33]–[34] (French CJ and Gageler J); 566–67 [77]–[78], 567–68 [80]–[81], 573 [101], 574–75 [106], 575 [108]–[109] (Hayne, Crennan, Kiefel and Bell JJ).

[81] ibid 575 [108] (Hayne, Crennan, Kiefel and Bell JJ); see also 555–56 [34] (French CJ and Gageler J); 573–74 [104] (Hayne, Crennan, Kiefel and Bell JJ).

[82] ibid 555–56 [32]–[34] (French CJ and Gageler J); 567 [79], 573–74 [104] (Hayne, Crennan, Kiefel and Bell JJ).

[83] See, eg, ibid 559 [45], 566 [75], 573 [101], 574–75 [105]–[106], 576 [111] (Hayne, Crennan, Kiefel and Bell JJ).

[84] ibid [45] fn 114.

[85] ibid 554 [29] (French CJ and Gageler J).

with the voluntary agreement of the parties. Hence, the enforcement of such awards in Australian courts does not engage Chapter III, and the International Arbitration Act would be valid in relation to such awards.

It might be objected that, when it comes to the sorts of decisions that a government might make which might then enliven a dispute with a foreign investor, the notion of a consensual adjustment of rights, having its origins in private law concepts of interests and agreement-making, is not appropriate. As discussed above (section II.C; section IV.D), the threatened or actual use of ISDS by investors may have a significant impact upon a government's decision-making and its regulatory capacities. These are not the typical subject matter of 'private' agreements.

It is beyond the scope of this chapter to discuss these matters in any overarching fashion. In relation to Australia, however, it should be noted that considerations of this sort reinforce the conclusion reached in section IV above, that the most pertinent question raised by ISDS provisions is about the scope of Commonwealth executive power to enter into IIAs in which such provisions appear.

VI. CONCLUSION

ISDS provisions are now a common feature of IIAs, including ChAFTA. Yet, they raise significant concerns, which might translate into serious questions of constitutional validity in certain constitutional contexts. This chapter has explained the principles of Australian constitutional law engaged by IIAs containing ISDS provisions to which Australia is a party. We have argued that the primary constitutional question raised by these provisions is thus: does the federal executive have the power to enter into IIAs that contain ISDS provisions without legislative authorisation?

For the reasons given in section IV, our answer to this question is tentative, but it is a tentative 'No'. The case of *Williams* stands as authority for the principle that parliamentary approval is required in order to authorise expenditure of public moneys, except that within the ordinary course of government—and arguably, an IIA that contains an ISDS provision is an agreement to pay, analogous to the contract considered in *Williams*, which would not fall within the exception to this rule.

This is not an unsurmountable hurdle to Australia's participation in ISDS. Parliament possesses the power to enact the legislation required. Furthermore, compliance with this procedural requirement provides at least a partial answer to some of the criticisms that have been made of ISDS, by ensuring that the decision to expose Australia to the prospect of ISDS arbitration is one that is taken by the Parliament as the representative of the people, and not simply by the executive acting solely on its own imperatives.

Part V

Insights and Lessons on IEL and the Knowledge Economy

14

E-Commerce in ChAFTA: New Wine in Old Wineskins?

HENRY GAO

> Neither do people pour new wine into old wineskins. If they do, the skins will burst; the wine will run out and the wineskins will be ruined. No, they pour new wine into new wineskins, and both are preserved (The Christian Bible, Matthew 9:17).

I. INTRODUCTION

AS THE WORLD enters the digital age, electronic commerce has become increasingly important. However, due to its outdated rules, the World Trade Organization (WTO) is ill-equipped in the regulation of electronic commerce. While useful discussions have been held in the WTO, no new rules have been agreed due to the overall lack of progress in the Doha Round. Instead, WTO Members have been trying to negotiate new rules on electronic commerce (e-commerce) in free trade agreements (FTAs), with the recently concluded Trans-Pacific Partnership (TPP) Agreement being one of the best known examples.

As one of the latest FTAs concluded by China and Australia, the China–Australia Free Trade Agreement (ChAFTA) has been praised as a 'comprehensive and high-quality' trade agreement.[1] Thus, it is no surprise that the Agreement includes many new issues which so far have been absent from the many FTAs signed by China. One such issue is e-commerce, which takes up an entire chapter in the Agreement.

[1] Ministry of Commerce of China (MOFCOM), '王守文出席中澳自贸协定媒体吹风会并答记者问' ['Vice Minister Wang Shouwen Attended the Press Conference on China–Australia FTA and Answered questions from Reporters'] (19 June 19 2015), fta.mofcom.gov.cn/article/chinaaustralia/chinaaustralianews/201506/22217_1.html.

This chapter provides a comprehensive analysis of the electronic commerce chapter in ChAFTA. It starts by reviewing the unsuccessful attempts made by the WTO Members in bringing e-commerce into the WTO regulatory framework, then examines the main features of the electronic commerce chapter in ChAFTA. To put things into proper perspective, this work will also compare the electronic commerce chapter of ChAFTA with similar chapters in other FTAs concluded by China and Australia, as well as with other FTAs that have been negotiated by the leader in e-commerce regulation, the United States (US). While acknowledging the progress made in ChAFTA, the chapter also notes the shortcomings in the Agreement and explores the reasons for any such shortcomings, and concludes with some thoughts on how further improvements may be made in the future.

II. REGULATION OF E-COMMERCE IN THE WTO

A. Overview of the Regulation of E-Commerce in the WTO

In the WTO, the first effort to regulate e-commerce was made at the Second Ministerial Conference in May 1998, where the Members adopted the Declaration on Global Electronic Commerce (the Declaration).[2] The Declaration recognised the 'new opportunities for trade', and directed the General Council to 'establish a comprehensive work programme to examine all trade-related issues relating to global electronic commerce, including those issues identified by Members'.[3]

In the Declaration, the Members also agreed to 'continue their current practice of not imposing customs duties on electronic transmissions'.[4] This moratorium on customs duties has been extended several times, the latest was in Nairobi with the moratorium in place until at least 2017.[5]

At the same time, the moratorium also left a few questions unanswered. First, it is unclear as to whether the term 'electronic transmissions' refers only to the medium of e-commerce, or to the content of the transmission as well, ie, the underlying product or service being transmitted.[6] Second, if it

[2] Declaration on Global Electronic Commerce (20 May 1998) WT/MIN(98)/DEC/2, docsonline.wto.org.

[3] ibid.

[4] ibid.

[5] Ministerial Decision on Work Programme on Electronic Commerce (19 December 2015) WT/L/977, WT/MIN(15)/42, docsonline.wto.org.

[6] See, eg, S Wunsch-Vincent, *The WTO, the Internet and Trade in Digital Products: EC–US Perspectives* (Oxford, Hart Publishing, 2006). See also, S Wunsch-Vincent and A Hold, 'Towards Coherent Rules for Digital Trade: Building on Efforts in Multilateral versus Preferential Trade Negotiations' in M Burri and T Cottier (eds), *Trade Governance in the Digital Age: World Trade Forum*, 14th edn (New York, Cambridge University Press, 2012) 182.

refers to the medium of transmission only, does this mean that other digital products which are supplied via traditional medium, such as books, music or videos on CDs could be subject to customs duties? Third, does the prohibition apply only to customs duties, or to other fees or charges imposed on the digital products? Fourth, does the moratorium apply only to imports, or to exports as well?

Pursuant to the Declaration, the General Council adopted the Work Programme on Electronic Commerce in September 1998 (Work Programme).[7] Under the Work Programme, 'electronic commerce' is broadly defined to cover 'the production, distribution, marketing, sale or delivery of goods and services by electronic means'.[8] Moreover, the Work Programme also includes under its scope 'issues relating to the development of the infrastructure for electronic commerce'.

As e-commerce cuts across many different areas, the Work Programme divides up the work among different WTO bodies as follows:

— The Council for Trade in Services shall examine the treatment of electronic commerce in the legal framework of the General Agreement on Trade in Services (GATS), which include horizontal issues such as the scope and classification of sectors and access to and use of public telecommunications transport networks and services, the application of both unconditional obligations such as MFN and transparency and conditional obligations like market access, national treatment and domestic regulation, standards, and recognition, as well as measures taken for the protection of privacy and public morals, the prevention of fraud and competition disciplines.[9]

— The Council for Trade in Goods shall examine aspects of electronic commerce relevant to the provisions of General Agreement on Tariffs and Trade (GATT) 1994, the multilateral trade agreements covered under Annex 1A of the WTO Agreement, and the approved work programme, which include not only tariff-related issues such as classification, customs duties and market access, but also non-tariff issues such as rules of origin, customs valuation, import licensing and standards.[10]

— The Council for Agreement on Trade-Related Aspects of Intellectual Property Rights (TRIPS) shall examine the intellectual property issues arising in connection with electronic commerce, which include issues such as the protection and enforcement of copyright and trademarks, and new technologies and access to technology.[11]

[7] Work Programme on Electronic Commerce (25 September 1998) WT/L/274, docsonline.wto.org.

[8] ibid para 1.3.

[9] ibid para 2.1.

[10] ibid para 3.1.

[11] ibid para 4.1.

— The Committee on Trade and Development shall examine and report on the development implications of electronic commerce, taking into account the economic, financial and development needs of developing countries.[12]

These bodies shall report their progress to the General Council on a regular basis.[13] In addition, the General Council is also responsible for the review of any cross-cutting trade-related issues and all aspects of the Work Programme concerning the imposition of customs duties on electronic transmission.[14] In carrying out its work, these bodies shall also take into account the work of other intergovernmental organisations as well as relevant non-governmental organisations.[15]

Since then, the Members have conducted many discussions on e-commerce in the various bodies. However, due to the slow progress in the Doha Round in general, the Members have not been able to reach any decision on the substantive disciplines on e-commerce notwithstanding the ambitious agenda foreseen in the Work Programme.[16]

In the absence of new disciplines, the main obligations on the regulation of e-commerce under the existing WTO legal framework can be found in the GATS Telecommunications Annex, which sets out the basic rights of access to and use of public telecommunications transport networks and services by service suppliers, including e-commerce suppliers.[17] Under paragraph 5.a, the general principle is that such service suppliers shall be accorded access to and use of public telecommunications transport networks and services on reasonable and non-discriminatory terms and conditions. This principle is further elaborated in the following sub-paragraphs, which try to strike a delicate balance between the users' rights (paragraph 5.b and 5.c) and the regulators' rights (paragraph 5.e–5.g).[18]

Beyond the rules in the Telecommunications Annex, the issues concerning the regulation of e-commerce in the WTO fall into the following three main areas.

[12] ibid para 5.1.
[13] ibid para 1.2.
[14] ibid.
[15] ibid para 1.4.
[16] Work Programme on Electronic Commerce: Dedicated Discussion on Electronic Commerce Under the Auspices of the General Council (11 November 2013) WT/GC/W/676, docsonline.wto.org.
[17] Annex on Telecommunications, in General Agreement on Trade in Services. General Agreement on Trade in Services (GATS) (15 April 1994) LT/UR/A-1B/S/1 Annex 1B, docsonline.wto.org.
[18] For a detailed discussion on this principle, see H Gao, 'Commentary on Telecommunication Services' in R Wolfrum and PT Stoll (eds), *Max Planck Commentaries on World Trade Law, Volume VI: 'WTO–Trade in Services'* (Leiden, Brill Publishers, 2008) paras 41–54.

The first is the classification issue. Internet activities could arguably be classified as either goods or services.[19] The distinction is not merely theoretical but has profound practical implications. If they are treated as goods, they could be subject first and foremost to customs duties, as well as Most-Favoured-Nation (MFN) treatment, national treatment, and a whole set of non-tariff disciplines such as those on rules of origin, import licensing, customs valuation etc. On the other hand, if they are treated as services, the Members will not be able to regulate them through border measures such as tariffs, but they would have significant leeway in imposing domestic regulations on e-commerce.

While some activities such as the online delivery of books and audio-visual products could arguably be classified as goods according to the technology-neutrality principle, most activities carried through the internet share more similarities with services trade. For example, many e-commerce activities are intangible and non-storable like services. Similarly, many e-commerce activities are produced with the joint input from both the suppliers and consumers, thus are tailor-made according to the needs of specific consumers like most services.

As it is impossible to provide a comprehensive discussion of both goods and services in such a short chapter, this chapter will mainly focus on the services issues here. Unlike GATT, which applies a uniform set of rules to most products, GATS adopts a different regulatory approach. According to the 'positive listing' approach, WTO Members only assume obligations for sectors that they have included in their Schedule of Specific Commitments.[20] Thus, one has to further determine which sector or sub-sector e-commerce activities fall under and check the respective schedules to see if it is covered.

Second, even for services covered in its schedule, a WTO Member can choose among different levels of liberalisation by inscribing commitments ranging from 'none' (which means 'no limitation' or 'fully liberalised') to 'unbound' (which means 'no commitment') in the market access and national treatment columns.[21] Thus, one has to check the schedule to determine the appropriate obligations for e-commerce activities.

Third, for legitimate policy reasons, WTO Members might need to deviate from their normal obligations. This is possible under both GATT and GATS by citing the 'General Exceptions' clauses.[22] However, as illustrated by WTO cases, the preferred exceptions under each agreement have been rather different. Under GATT, the most commonly cited exceptions are

[19] Wunsch-Vincent and Hold (n 6) 183.

[20] GATS (n 17) Art XVI (Market Access).

[21] Guidelines for the Scheduling of Specific Commitments under GATS (23 March 2001) S/L/92 paras 41–49, docsonline.wto.org.

[22] General Agreement on Tariffs and Trade (GATT 1994) (15 April 1994) Art XX [1867 UNTS 187; 33 ILM 1153 (1994)], docsonline.wto.org; GATS (n 17).

those to protect public health and environment.[23] In contrast, the favourite clause under GATS has been the public morals exception.[24]

Due to their unique nature, e-commerce activities pose special challenges to the GATS regulatory framework on all three issues. In the following sections, I will discuss the regulatory difficulties in each of these areas and, where appropriate, make some policy suggestions on how to address these problems.

B. Classifications

Under GATS, services are classified according to the Services Sectoral Classification List (Classification List), which classifies all services into 12 sectors and 160 sub-sectors.[25] While this system does a good job in classifying most other service sectors, it has not been so useful in classifying e-commerce activities. To start with, the Classification List is outdated as it is based on the United Nations Provisional Central Product Classification (CPCprov).[26] The CPCprov was published in 1990, when the internet was still in its infancy and many e-commerce activities, such as search engines, did not even exist. It doesn't provide direct reference to many e-commerce activities that are common today. Instead, they are often scattered across many sectors. For example, search engine services can arguably be classified under either telecommunication services or computer and related services. Paradoxically, some of the classifications under the Classification List also overlap with each other. For example, under the Classification List, online information processing and data processing share the same code under CPCprov, but are grouped under telecommunication services and computer services respectively.

To better capture the reality of e-commerce activities, the current classification system needs to be reviewed and revamped in a systematic manner.[27] Depending on the nature of the services, different approaches should be taken. On the one hand, for e-commerce activities which have been supplied through traditional channels before the advent of the internet, they should be grouped under the original sector as per the technology-neutrality principle, unless of course their natures have been changed by

[23] GATT 1994 (n 22) Arts XX(b), XX(g).

[24] GATS (n 17) Art XIV(a).

[25] Services Sectoral Classification List (10 July 1991) MTN.GNS/W/120, docsonline.wto.org.

[26] United Nations, 'Provisional Central Product Classification' (1991), unstats.un.org/unsd/CR/Registry/regcst.asp?Cl=9&Lg=1.

[27] For an overview of the classification issues for e-commerce, see generally, L Tuthill and M Roy, 'GATS Classification Issues for Information and Communication Technology Services' in M Burri and T Cottier (eds), *Trade Governance in the Digital Age: World Trade Forum*, 14th edn (New York, Cambridge University Press, 2012).

the online delivery.[28] Thus, online banking services shall be classified under banking services, and online universities shall be classified under educational services etc. On the other hand, the classification of services that only emerged with the birth of the internet is trickier. As the latest version of the Central Product Classification (CPC) includes many such services, it is tempting to simply replace the reference to the CPCprov codes in the Classification List with the corresponding codes in the new version. However, this approach is undesirable for the following reasons. First, as the Classification List is not mandatory, not every WTO Member uses it or includes explicit reference to the CPC codes in its schedule.[29] Second, even for those that do use the CPC, the schedule cannot be simply updated with the new CPC versions. This is because the CPC often reshuffles the code numbers around when the versions are updated, thus the same code numbers under different versions might refer to entirely different services.[30] Third, as cases like *US-Gambling* have shown, it has been a challenge for WTO Members to fully understand even their own commitments.[31] Thus, they will not accept a comprehensive update of the schedules without careful scrutiny.

Because of these difficulties, even just an update of the schedules based on the latest CPC version probably cannot be achieved without major negotiation efforts. In addition, as many e-commerce activities are closely linked together, it is probably better to take a cluster approach in the review and deal with them together.[32]

[28] For a discussion of the application of the technology-neutrality principle to e-commerce activities, see generally, S Peng, 'GATS and the Over-the-Top Services: A Legal Outlook' (2016) 50(1) *Journal of World Trade* 21.

[29] Notably, the United States doesn't use the CPC code in its classification. United States of America, Schedule of Specific Commitments (15 April 1994) GATS/SC/90, docsonline.wto.org. However, while the US schedule makes no explicit references to CPC numbers, it corresponds closely with the GATT Secretariat's list. See United States International Trade Commission, 'US Schedule of Commitments under the General Agreement on Trade in Services' (August 1998) Investigation No 332-354. This issue was also debated in the *US-Gambling* case. Report of the Panel, United States–Measures Affecting the Cross-Border Supply of Gambling and Betting Services (10 November 2004) WT/DS285/R paras 3.41–3.43, 3.65, docsonline.wto.org. It has been modified by Report of the Appellate Body, United States–Measures Affecting the Cross-Border Supply of Gambling and Betting Services (7 April 2005) WT/DS285/AB/R, docsonline.wto.org.

[30] A good example is the classification of data processing services (CPC 843) under CPCprov and CPC Version1, which is discussed in detail in H Gao, 'Googling for the Trade-Human Rights Nexus in China: Can the WTO Help?' in M Burri and T Cottier (eds), *Trade Governance in the Digital Age: World Trade Forum* (New York, Cambridge University Press, 2012) 258–60.

[31] Report of the Panel in United States–Measures Affecting Gambling (n 29) paras 3.44–3.70, 6.135–36.

[32] The cluster approach was proposed by the US and the EU in 2000. Communication from the European Communities and their Member States: The Cluster Approach (22 May 2000) S/CSS/W/3, docsonline.wto.org; Communication from the United States: Framework for Negotiation (13 July 2000) S/CSS/W/4, docsonline.wto.org. This approach grew out of an initial proposal by Dominican Republic, El Salvador and Honduras for an annex on tourism in GATS. C Raghavan, 'To Cluster or Not to Cluster (in GATS)' (19 July 2000), www.twn.my/title/cluster.htm.

C. Obligations

Other than the MFN principle, most obligations under GATS only apply when a Member schedules relevant commitments. For each sector that a Member includes in its schedule, the Member may choose how much market access[33] or national treatment[34] that it is willing to offer. Moreover, such scheduled commitments are also subject to sector or mode-specific limitations.

For e-commerce activities, such regulatory frameworks create the following problems.

First is ambiguity in sectoral coverage. Even though a Member may choose which sectors to include in its schedule, ambiguities could still arise due to imperfections in the classification system. A good example in this regard is the *US-Gambling* case. In this case, the US included in its schedule a sub-sector entitled 'Other Recreational Services (except sporting)'. While the US argued that 'sporting' includes gambling services, the WTO panel disagreed and ruled that sporting doesn't include gambling services and thus should be included in the US commitments.[35] While this problem could arise in any service sector, e-commerce activities are particularly prone to interpretive ambiguities due to the classification difficulties mentioned earlier.

The second problem is confusion on modes of supply. Under GATS, services could be supplied in four modes: 1, cross-border supply; 2, consumption abroad; 3, commercial presence; and 4, movement of natural persons.[36] For e-commerce activities, it is quite difficult to tell if a service is supplied through Mode 1 or 2 as the service is provided in cyberspace.[37] Further complication could arise in cases where the service supplier is located in another WTO Member, but maintains a server in the home country of the consumer. It could be argued that Mode 3 shall apply in such cases.

[33] GATS Art XVI.1: 'With respect to market access through the modes of supply identified in Article I, each Member shall accord services and service suppliers of any other Member treatment no less favourable than that provided for under the terms, limitations and conditions agreed and specified in its Schedule'. GATS (n 17) Art XVI.1.

[34] GATS Art XVII.1: 'In the sectors inscribed in its Schedule, and subject to any conditions and qualifications set out therein, each Member shall accord to services and service suppliers of any other Member, in respect of all measures affecting the supply of services, treatment no less favourable than that it accords to its own like services and service suppliers'. GATS (n 17) Art XVII.1.

[35] Report of the Panel, United States–Measures Affecting Gambling (n 29) paras 3.30–3.70, 6.34–6.138.

[36] GATS Art 1.2: 'For the purposes of this Agreement, trade in services is defined as the supply of a service: (a) from the territory of one Member into the territory of any other Member; (b) in the territory of one Member to the service consumer of any other Member; (c) by a service supplier of one Member, through commercial presence in the territory of any other Member; (d) by a service supplier of one Member, through presence of natural persons of a Member in the territory of any other Member'. GATS (n 17) Art 1.2.

[37] Work Programme on Electronic Commerce (16 November 1998) S/C/W/68 paras 7–8, docsonline.wto.org. See also, Wunsch-Vincent and Hold (n 6) 182.

As a Member may have different levels of commitment depending on the mode of supply, the confusion over mode of supply could lead to illogical consequences.

To address these problems, the author makes two suggestions. First, the WTO Members should agree on a set of scheduling guidelines for e-commerce activities. This would help clarify the meaning of schedules and avoid future complications. Second is the formulation of a set of regulatory principles that sets a minimum regulatory standard for e-commerce activities. In this regard, the Telecommunications Reference Paper[38] provides a really good model due to the close link between the two sectors.[39]

D. Exceptions

The General Exceptions clause allows a WTO Member to deviate from its normal obligations.[40] Under GATS, the most frequently cited exception is the public morals exception. Interestingly, in both the two cases concerning internet services, ie, the *US-Gambling* case[41] and the *China-Publications* case,[42] the respondent cited the public morals exception to defend their measures. In their rulings, WTO Panels and the Appellate Body often accord wide discretion to the national authorities in defining both the boundaries and depth of the exception, but this could lead to bizarre results. For example, in the *China-Publications* case, the Appellate Body encouraged the Chinese government to conduct censorship itself as it is supposedly better than outsourcing to private firms from the perspective of WTO law.[43]

[38] WTO, 'Negotiating Group on Basic Telecommunications, Telecommunications Services: Reference Paper' (24 April 1996), www.wto.org/english/tratop_e/serv_e/telecom_e/tel23_e.htm.

[39] For an example on how the Reference Paper can be revised to apply to internet networks, see, eg, R Kariyawasam, 'Better Regulation of Digital Markets: A New Look at the Reference Paper' in M Burri and T Cottier (eds), *Trade Governance in the Digital Age: World Trade Forum*, 14th edn (New York, Cambridge University Press, 2012).

[40] GATS (n 17) Art XIV.

[41] Report of the Appellate Body (n 29); Report of the Appellate Body, United States–Measures Affecting the Cross-Border Supply of Gambling and Betting Services (20 August 2007) WT/DS285/AB/R/Corr.1, docsonline.wto.org; Report of the Panel (n 29).

[42] See, eg, Report of the Appellate Body, China–Measures Affecting Trading Rights and Distribution Services for Certain Publications and Audiovisual Entertainment Products (21 December 2009) WT/DS363/AB/R 3, docsonline.wto.org. See also, Report of the Panel, China–Measures Affecting Trading Rights and Distribution Services for Certain Publications and Audiovisual Entertainment Products (12 August 2009) WT/DS363/R and Corr.1 261, docsonline.wto.org; Report of the Panel, China–Measures Affecting Trading Rights and Distribution Services for Certain Publications and Audiovisual Entertainment Products (19 August 2009) WT/DS363/R/Corr.1, docsonline.wto.org.

[43] In this case, the US proposed that, instead of having the importing firms conduct the content review of imported publications, the Chinese government shall be given sole responsibility for conducting content review. Both the Panel and the Appellate Body agreed that these

In my view, it is problematic to accord wide discretion on the public morals exception to countries without democratically elected governments as the views of such governments on public morals are not necessarily truly aligned with those of the people. A good way to prevent the potential abuse of the exception is to adopt some universal benchmark on what may qualify as public morals, so that fundamental human rights, such as those enshrined in the Universal Declaration of Human Rights,[44] will not be harmed under the disguise of protecting public morals. As the core competence of the WTO is in trade, it is ill-equipped with this task. Instead, we should consider adopting a mechanism similar to the one under the Sanitary and Phytosanitary (SPS) Agreement,[45] ie, having the standards formulated by another international organisation[46] with competence in public morals issues, and making it mandatory for the WTO to consult them when disputes arise.[47]

E. Conclusion

In conclusion, while GATS, in its current form, is not well suited to the regulation of e-commerce, it has the potential to keep up with the regulatory task. However, to make this happen, we will need new approaches in dealing with e-commerce activities, especially on key issues such as classifications, obligations and exceptions.

In this regard, the WTO might wish to learn from the approaches taken in the various FTAs. In the next sections, we will examine how ChAFTA and other FTAs deal with e-commerce issues.

are reasonably available alternatives. Report of the Appellate Body (n 42) paras 7.869–7.909. For a discussion of the Panel and Appellate Body decisions in the China—Publications and Audiovisual Products case, see, eg, P Delimatsis, 'The Puzzling Interaction of Trade and Public Morales in the Digital Era' in M Burri and T Cottier (eds), *Trade Governance in the Digital Age: World Trade Forum*, 14th edn (New York, Cambridge University Press, 2012) 285–89.

[44] United Nations General Assembly Res 217A (10 December 1948) UN Doc A/810, 71.

[45] Agreement on the Application of Sanitary and Phytosanitary Measures (SPS Agreement) (15 April 1994) LT/UR/A-1A/12, docsonline.wto.org.

[46] It refers explicitly to the SPS standards, guidelines and recommendations made by various international organisations such as the Codex Alimentarius Commission, the International Office of Epizootics, and the Secretariat of the International Plant Protection Convention. ibid para 3, Annex A.

[47] See, eg, SPS Agreement Art 11.2, which gives the right to dispute settlement panels to consult the relevant international organisations on scientific or technical issues. See, also, SPS Agreement Art 12.3, which requires the SPS Committee to 'maintain close contact with the relevant international organizations in the field of sanitary and phytosanitary protection ... with the objective of securing the best available scientific and technical advice for the administration of this Agreement'.

III. REGULATION OF E-COMMERCE IN CHAFTA

While e-commerce is a relatively new issue, the potential for cooperation between Australia and China in this area has long been recognised by both countries. In 1999, for example, the two countries signed the Joint Statement on the Online Economy and Electronic Commerce and the Memorandum of Understanding on Cooperation in the Information Industries and noted the following opportunities for collaboration on e-commerce:[48]

— Encouraging the exchange of information about policies and strategies, including legal and regulatory matters, to foster the maximum spread of benefits from development of information industries within each country.
— Encouraging exchange of information and strategies on the effective use of information technology and telecommunications within Government and in the support of Government service delivery.
— Fostering the effective use of electronic commerce between the two countries.
— The principles of no barriers to trade conducted electronically; the retention of each country's ability to regulate for public policy purposes; and encouragement of trade and investment through further facilitating electronic commerce.[49]

In the Trade and Economic Framework between Australia and the People's Republic of China (the Framework) adopted in 2003, the two countries reaffirmed their commitment and resolved to 'intensify cooperation' on this issue.[50] The Framework also called for the two countries to 'jointly undertake a feasibility study into a possible bilateral Free Trade Agreement (FTA) negotiation'.[51]

In 2005, the two governments concluded the Australia–China Free Trade Agreement Joint Feasibility Study. E-commerce was prominently featured as a section in Chapter 6 entitled 'Implications for Bilateral Cooperation', which purports to 'outline ... sector-specific issues ... of importance to the commercial relationship, and highlight possible areas for cooperation and facilitation to promote further bilateral trade and investment

[48] China FTA Study Taskforce, Department of Foreign Affairs and Trade, Government of Australia, and Department of International Trade and Economic Affairs, Ministry of Commerce, Government of China, 'Australia-China Free Trade Agreement Joint Feasibility Study' (ChAFTA Joint Feasibility Study) (March 2005) 104, dfat.gov.au/trade/agreements/chafta/Documents/feasibility_full.pdf.

[49] ibid 107.

[50] 'Trade and Economic Cooperation Framework between the People's Republic of China and Commonwealth of Australia' (24 October 2003) Annex I, investmentpolicyhub.unctad.org/download/treatyfile/2666.

[51] ibid para 8.

through an FTA'.[52] After reviewing the state of development of e-commerce in both countries and their respective regulatory frameworks, the study suggested that further cooperation on e-commerce may be achieved through the following:

— Maintaining the current moratorium on customs duties on electronic transmissions between the two countries.
— Making publicly available electronic versions of trade administration documents.
— Encouraging the acceptance of electronic trade administration documents.
— Cooperation on appropriate frameworks governing e-commerce that minimise the regulatory burden, support industry-led development, provide protection for consumers equivalent to that provided for consumers of other forms of commerce, and enable each country to tackle problems unique to electronic commerce (such as online gambling and email spam).
— Cooperation on appropriate electronic authentication and work towards the mutual recognition of digital certificates, based on internationally accepted standards.
— Taking appropriate measures to protect the personal data of people using electronic commerce.
— Cooperation to enhance the acceptance of paperless trading bilaterally and internationally.
— Cooperation to combat the spam problem.
— Working towards the mutual recognition of electronic signatures and encourage the interoperability of digital certificates by business.[53]

In view of the strong interest in e-commerce cooperation, the final text of ChAFTA also includes e-commerce as a separate chapter—Chapter 12. The chapter includes a total of 11 articles. Article 12.1 sets out the objective of the chapter, ie, to 'promote electronic commerce between the Parties'. To achieve this, the Parties 'shall endeavour to ensure that bilateral trade through electronic commerce is no more restricted than other forms of trade'. The next article defines eight important terms in the chapter, ie, digital certificates, electronic signature, electronic version, personal information, trade administration documents, United Nations Commission on International Trade Law (UNCITRAL) and unsolicited commercial electronic message. The next seven articles spelt out the substantive obligations. Based on their origins, the obligations can be divided into the following categories.

[52] ChAFTA Joint Feasibility Study (n 48) 7.
[53] ibid 107.

A. Application of WTO Rules

In Article 12.1, the Parties explicitly recognise the applicability of relevant WTO rules to the regulation of e-commerce. In line with this, several WTO rules are incorporated into the e-commerce chapter. For example, Article 12.3 confirms the moratorium on customs duties, as contained in paragraph 5 of the WTO Ministerial Decision of 7 December 2013 in relation to the Work Programme on Electronic Commerce, which is also known as the Bali Ministerial Decision.[54] Similarly, Article 12.4 mirrors the transparency obligation contained in Article X of GATT and Article III of GATS by requiring the Parties to publish or make publicly available e-commerce related measures and respond promptly to requests by the other Party for information on such measures. Also, the provision on the acceptance of electronic versions of trade administration documents in Article 12.9.1 is modelled after Article 10.2 of the WTO Trade Facilitation Agreement.

However, the practical utility of these provisions is rather dubious as they are either repetitive or lack substantive content. Take Article 12.3.1 for example: as the Bali Ministerial Decision referred to therein only extends the moratorium on customs duties until 2015, this article is practically useless. While one may argue that Article 12.3.2 could incorporate later extensions of the moratorium as it refers to 'any further WTO Ministerial Decisions in relation to the Work Programme on Electronic Commerce', it does not create any binding obligation as the article allows each Party to 'reserve the right to adjust its practice' in accordance with such WTO decisions, which means that they have the right, but no obligation, to extend the moratorium. Another example is the transparency provision under Article 12.4, which requires the Parties to 'promptly publish, or otherwise promptly make publicly available' e-commerce related measures and 'respond promptly to all requests by the other Party for specific information' concerning e-commerce related measures. This clause simply copies the provisions under Articles 13.2.1[55] and 13.3.2[56] under ChAFTA. Similarly,

[54] Ministerial Decision on Work Programme on Electronic Commerce (7 December 2013) WT/MIN(13)/32-WT/L/907, docsonline.wto.org.

[55] ChAFTA Art 13.2: 'Each Party shall ensure that its laws, regulations, procedures and administrative rulings of general application respecting any matter covered by this Agreement are promptly published, including on the internet where feasible, or otherwise made available in such a manner as to enable interested persons and the other Party to become acquainted with them'. Free Trade Agreement between the Government of Australia and the Government of the People's Republic of China (ChAFTA) (signed 17 June 2015, entered into force 20 December 2015) [2015] ATS 15, Art 13.2.

[56] ChAFTA Art 13.3.2: 'On request of the other Party, a Party shall promptly provide information and respond to questions pertaining to any actual or proposed law, regulation, procedure or administrative ruling of general application, regardless of whether the requesting Party has been previously notified of it'. ibid Art 13.3.2.

under Article 12.9.1, each Party shall accept the electronic versions of trade administration documents as the legal equivalent of paper documents. This provision is basically the same as ChAFTA Article 4.13.1, which states that '[e]ach Party shall, where appropriate, endeavour to accept paper or electronic copies of supporting documents required for imported goods'.[57]

While one may argue that the inclusion of these provisions in the e-commerce chapter affirms the importance the Parties place on e-commerce, their utilities are rather limited as they have not added anything new in substance. In a way, they are just window-dressing clauses.

B. Application of Non-WTO Rules

In addition to drawing inspiration from the WTO provisions, ChAFTA also includes provisions modelled after non-WTO rules. For example, Article 12.5 incorporates the UNCITRAL Model Law on Electronic Commerce 1996 without spelling out the detailed obligations. Similarly, the provisions on electronic authentication, digital certificates and electronic signatures under Article 12.6 seem to draw their inspiration from the UNCITRAL Model Law on Electronic Signatures (2001).

These issues are not governed by the WTO because they mainly regulate matters under private laws such as contract law, which are outside the scope of coverage of the WTO. The UNCITRAL Model Law on Electronic Commerce 1996, for example, enables private Parties to conduct international trade transactions using electronic means by recognising the validity of electronic messages and documents in such transactions. On the other hand, the UNCITRAL Model Law on Electronic Signatures facilitates the recognition of electronic signatures in fulfilment of various legal requirements under domestic laws such as contracts.

Given the widespread adoption of the two Model Laws by the major economies in the world, the incorporation of these rules in ChAFTA sets a good example and can pave the way for the harmonisation of these rules at the global level.

C. Consumer Protection Rules

The only truly new issue in the e-commerce chapter of ChAFTA is the rules on consumer protection. This is a very important issue as consumers of e-commerce, unlike traditional commerce, often have to provide important personal information and data when they conduct online transactions.

[57] ibid Art 4.13.1.

Without proper regulation, such information could be misused by either the e-commerce businesses, or hackers and other people, for improper or even illegal activities. This issue is addressed in the remaining two articles.

First, Article 12.7 sets out the basic principle for online consumer protection, ie, protection 'that is at least equivalent to that provided for consumers of other forms of commerce under their respective laws, regulations and policies'.[58] One may argue that this doesn't really create new obligations beyond the existing consumer protection rules in traditional commerce. However, given the inherent difference between traditional commerce and e-commerce, which necessitates the collection of personal data such as names, addresses, telephone numbers, IP addresses and credit card numbers, existing rules for traditional commerce might be insufficient. Thus, the confirmation of the same level of protection for e-commerce is a welcome first step. Of course, given the technological limitations and resource constraints, it might not be possible for the regulatory authorities to achieve the same level of protection as in traditional commerce. That is why the same article also provides that the obligation only applies 'to the extent possible and in a manner [a Party] considers appropriate'.[59] This language has watered down the obligation and might make it more difficult for the provision to be enforced.

Second, the next article narrows down to one specific problem in consumer protection, ie, the protection of personal information and data online. Again, the two countries recognise their differences in the existing systems of personal information protection, and do not prescribe a specific set of measures for the protection of personal information. Instead, the Parties are granted considerable leeway to 'take such measures as it considers appropriate and necessary'.[60] To encourage the harmonisation of the relevant standards, the same article also calls for the Parties to 'take into account international standards and the criteria of relevant international organisations' 'to the extent possible'.[61]

Overall, while it is an encouraging move to include clauses on online consumer protection, the two articles do not create specific obligations that can be of much help in practice.

IV. ASSESSMENT OF THE CHAFTA PROVISIONS

As demonstrated by the foregoing analyses, while there are 11 articles in the e-commerce chapter of ChAFTA, they mostly copy from the existing

[58] ibid Art 12.7.
[59] ibid.
[60] ibid Art 12.8.
[61] ibid.

obligations in WTO agreements and the UNCITRAL Model Laws and do not add much to existing obligations. Moreover, these provisions are mainly couched in soft terms that only ask for best endeavours by the Parties in implementation. Finally, as Article 12.11 explicitly excludes the chapter from the application of the dispute settlement mechanism under ChAFTA, the whole chapter falls into a loose collection of non-binding aspirations.

In a way, the disappointing treatment of e-commerce under ChAFTA is not really surprising as it largely follows the approaches taken in the previous FTAs by China and Australia. However, if we compare the e-commerce chapter in ChAFTA with the high standards set by US FTAs, its shortcomings become more evident. These differences are explored below.

A. Comparison with Previous FTAs by China and Australia

As a latecomer in international trade and the WTO, until very recently China has taken a rather cautious approach on non-traditional trade issues in FTAs.[62] Before ChAFTA, China had not included e-commerce chapters in any of its FTAs except the one with Korea, which was negotiated around the same time as ChAFTA and signed only seven days before ChAFTA.[63] The e-commerce chapter under the China–Korea FTA includes nine articles which cover the following: moratorium on customs duties on electronic transmission; electronic authentication and electronic signature; protection of personal information in e-commerce; paperless trading; cooperation; and non-application of the dispute settlement chapter. The China–New Zealand FTA (2008) also mentions e-commerce, but it was only mentioned incidentally in the chapter on technical barriers to trade and the annexed agreement on conformity assessments.

In contrast, Australia has been more receptive to the inclusion of e-commerce chapters in its FTAs. Starting with the 2003 Singapore–Australia FTA, Australia has included e-commerce chapters in eight of the FTAs it entered into before ChAFTA.[64] These FTA chapters usually include the following provisions: moratorium on customs duties on electronic transmission; domestic regulatory framework based on the UNCITRAL Model

[62] For China's approach to the non-traditional trade issues, see, eg, H Gao, 'China's Strategy for Free Trade Agreements: Political Battle in the Name of Trade' in R Buckley, R Hu and D Arner (eds), *East Asian Economic Integration: Law, Trade and Finance* (Cheltenham, Edward Elgar, 2011).

[63] ChAFTA was signed on 17 June 2015, while the China–Korea FTA was signed on 10 June 2015.

[64] These include Australia's FTAs with Thailand (2005), US (2005), Chile (2009), ASEAN–New Zealand (2010), Malaysia (2012), Korea (2014), and Japan (2014).

Law on Electronic Commerce 1996; electronic authentication, digital certificates and electronic signature; online consumer protection; online personal data protection; and paperless trading. In addition, the FTAs with Japan and the US also include a provision on non-discriminatory treatment of digital products;[65] while the FTAs with Korea and Malaysia also include a provision on unsolicited commercial messages.[66] Finally, some Australian FTAs with developing countries[67] include a clause on transparency, which requires the Parties to publish relevant regulations and respond promptly to requests for information.

Overall, ChAFTA seems to have taken a middle ground between the Chinese and Australian FTAs. In other words, it has included all the provisions that are present in the China–Korea FTA and included the common elements of the Australian FTAs, ie, domestic regulatory framework based on the UNCITRAL Model Law on Electronic Commerce 1996; digital certificates; and online personal data protection. While it goes beyond the narrow approach of the Chinese FTAs, it lags behind the more recent FTAs Australia has concluded with more advanced economies such as the US, Japan and Korea. Moreover, some provisions under ChAFTA even fall short of the standard being set under some of the new multilateral agreements. For example, Article 12.9.1 of ChAFTA allows the Parties to refuse to recognise electronic documents as paper documents when 'there is a domestic or international legal requirement to the contrary'. This could potentially violate the obligation to accept electronic copies under Article 10.2 of the WTO Trade Facilitation Agreement.

B. Comparison with US FTAs

The shortcomings of the e-commerce chapter in ChAFTA are even more evident when compared with that of the leading rule-maker in e-commerce: the US. The US first included e-commerce as a joint statement in its FTA with Jordan in 2000. Since then, it has included an e-commerce chapter in

[65] Agreement between Japan and Australia for an Economic Partnership (signed 8 July 2014, entered into force 15 January 2015) [2015] ATS 2, Art 13.4; Australia–United States Free Trade Agreement (signed 18 May 2004, entered into force 1 January 2005) [2005] ATS 1, Art 16.4.

[66] Free Trade Agreement between the Government of the Republic of Korea and the Government of Australia (signed 8 April 2014, entered into force 12 December 2014) [2014] ATNIF 4, Art 15.9; Malaysia–Australia Free Trade Agreement (signed 22 May 2012, entered into force 1 January 2013) ATS 4, Art 15.10.

[67] Agreement Establishing the ASEAN–New Zealand–Australia Free Trade Area (signed 27 February 2009, entered into force 1 January 2010) [2010] ATS 1, Ch 10, Art 3; Singapore–Australia Free Trade Agreement (signed 17 February 2003, entered into force 28 July 2003) [2003] ATS 16 (Singapore–Australia Free Trade Agreement) Ch 14, Art 2.

all its FTAs. Compared with ChAFTA, these e-commerce chapters are not only broader in scope but also deeper in commitments.

Unlike the e-commerce chapters in many other FTAs, the e-commerce chapters in US FTAs do not merely copy obligations from existing international agreements by the WTO or UNCITRAL. Instead, they recognise the unique features of e-commerce and include many innovative rules. For example, the US–Korea FTA includes a provision on access to and use of the internet for e-commerce, which states that:

> To support the development and growth of electronic commerce, each Party recognizes that consumers in its territory should be able to:
>
> (a) access and use services and digital products of their choice, unless prohibited by the Party's law;
> (b) run applications and services of their choice, subject to the needs of law Enforcement;
> (c) connect their choice of devices to the Internet, provided that such devices do not harm the network and are not prohibited by the Party's law; and
> (d) have the benefit of competition among network providers, application and service providers, and content providers.[68]

This provision is inspired by the existing disciplines under the Annex on Telecommunications and Reference Paper, especially the provisions on access to and use of public telecommunications transport networks and services and competitive safeguards. But the principles have been modified to take into account the different nature of e-commerce, and the coverage is expanded to include not only the hardware infrastructure of the internet but also the software environment. As the result, the benefit has been extended to not only the network providers but also the application providers, service providers and content providers.

Another example is the clause on Cross Border Information Flows, which states that the Parties 'shall endeavor to refrain from imposing or maintaining unnecessary barriers to electronic information flows across borders'.[69] This addresses one of the most important issues in e-commerce, which relies on free flow of information to maintain its viability.

Yet more new disciplines have been included in the newly concluded TPP to deal with regulatory barriers to e-commerce. For example, under Article 14.13, TPP Members shall not require a covered person to use or locate computing facilities such as servers and storage facilities in the host country's territory as a condition for conducting business in that territory.

[68] United States–Korea Free Trade Agreement, Art 15.7, ustr.gov/trade-agreements/free-trade-agreements/korus-fta/final-text.

[69] ibid, Art 15.8.

Similarly, under Article 14.17, a TPP Member may not require the transfer of, or access to, source code of software owned by a person of another Party, as a condition for the import, distribution, sale or use of such software, or of products containing such software, in its territory.

These new rules reflect the concerns of the major US e-commerce providers, which are increasingly subject to various trade barriers in foreign markets. Unfortunately, they are not included in ChAFTA's e-commerce chapter.

V. CONCLUSION

While Australia and China have recognised the importance of e-commerce from as early as 1999, the e-commerce chapter of ChAFTA is rather disappointing. Most of the provisions simply copy from the existing obligations in the WTO and UNCITRAL agreements. Moreover, the enforceability of these provisions is also problematic as they are largely couched in best-endeavour terms and the whole chapter is excluded from the application of the dispute settlement mechanism. In other words, while e-commerce is one of the most important issues in the twenty-first century, ChAFTA has largely taken a twentieth-century approach to the regulation of the sector. This begs the question: why didn't ChAFTA include a more robust chapter on e-commerce?

If we take a closer look at the bilateral trade profile between Australia and China, we will not find such a conservative approach surprising. According to the Ministry of Commerce (MOFCOM) of China, the bilateral trade volume between the two countries was AUD$128 billion in 2014.[70] Among that, services trade accounted for only 16.7 billion, or 13 per cent.[71] Furthermore, natural resources have accounted for the bulk of the goods trade. For example, in 2014, minerals and precious metals accounted for more than 80 per cent of Australia's exports to China. On the other hand, China's exports to Australia consist of mainly mechanical products, textile, furniture and toys. In other words, the bilateral trade between Australia and China is still mainly twentieth-century trade (in manufactured goods) or even nineteenth-century trade (in natural resources and agricultural products). E-commerce between the two is virtually non-existent. Thus, it

[70] MOFCOM, '《国别贸易报告：2014年澳大利亚货物贸易及中澳双边贸易概况》' ['National Trade Report: Trade in Goods with Australia and Summary of Sino-Australia Bilateral Trade in 2014'), countryreport.mofcom.gov.cn/record/view110209.asp?news_id=42741.

[71] MOFCOM, '《中华人民共和国政府和澳大利亚政府自由贸易协定解读》' ['Q&A on China–Australia FTA'] (2 March 2016), fta.mofcom.gov.cn/article/chinaaustralia/chinaaustralianews/201506/22176_1.html.

is no surprise that ChAFTA did not put a lot of effort into the e-commerce chapter.

Of course, this does not mean that the bilateral trade between Australia and China could never harness the great potential of e-commerce. According to the Australian Trade and Investment Commission (Austrade) and the Sydney-based e-commerce analytics company ThinkChina, Chinese online shoppers have big demands for Australian products ranging from packaged snacks and honey, to skincare products and milk powder.[72] However, even if such potential for e-commerce could be realised in their bilateral trade, China and Australia might still be hesitant to upgrade the rules on e-commerce due to their conservative regulatory philosophies.

In the case of China, its online censorship regime has long been regarded as a major obstacle to the free flow of information.[73] In recent years, the Chinese government has been further tightening the regulation of the internet. For example, in 2014, the China Banking Regulatory Commission (CBRC) and the Ministry of Industry and Information Technology jointly issued the *Guidelines on Promoting the Use of Secure and Controllable Technology in Banking Industry (2014–2015)*,[74] which requires IT service providers to establish research and development and service centres in China, and to file their source codes with the CBRC. In 2015, the National People's Congress published a draft of the Internet Security Law, which requires the operators of key information infrastructure to store the personal information of its customers on local servers.[75] On the other hand, Australia also has reservations concerning the US data flow approach due to both the dominance of US companies in global e-commerce and security concerns as revealed by the Snowden affair.[76] Thus, Australia offered alternative approaches in the

[72] Australian Trade Commission, E-commerce in China: A Guide for Australian Business (June 2015) 14–15, www.austrade.gov.au/Australian/Export/Export-markets/Countries/China/Doing-business/e-commerce-in-china.

[73] For a discussion of the online censorship regime in China and its consistency with WTO rules, see, eg, H Gao, 'Google's China Problem: A Case Study on Trade, Technology and Human Rights Under the GATS' (2011) 6 *Asian Journal of WTO & International Health Law and Policy* 347.

[74] China Banking Regulatory Commission (CBRC) and the Ministry of Industry and Information Technology, 《银行业应用安全可控信息技术推进指南》（2014–2015年度）[*Guidelines on Promoting the Use of Secure and Controllable Technology in Banking Industry (2014–2015)*], *Yinjian Banfa* (2014) No 317 (26 December 2014). For a detailed discussion of the Guidelines, see, eg, King & Wood Mallesons, 'China Banking IT Regulation Tightened Up' (16 March 2015), www.chinalawinsight.com/2015/03/articles/finance/new-cbrc-rules-tighten-up-the-security-administration-on-chinas-banking-it.

[75] National People's Congress of China, 《网络安全法（草案） [Internet Security Law (first draft)] (6 July 2015) Art 31, www.npc.gov.cn/npc/xinwen/lfgz/flca/2015-07/06/content_1940614.htm.

[76] G Greenwald, E MacAskill and L Poitras, 'Edward Snowden: The Whistleblower behind the NSA Surveillance Revelations' *The Guardian* (11 June 2013), www.theguardian.com/world/2013/jun/09/edward-snowden-nsa-whistleblower-surveillance last accessed 29 March 2017.

TPP negotiations, which reportedly eventually watered down stronger US approaches.[77]

Given the cautious attitude taken by China and Australia, the e-commerce disciplines under ChAFTA will probably remain rather modest for the foreseeable future. However, such an old-fashioned regulatory approach is unlikely to be conducive to the development of e-commerce. Instead, the two countries should try to craft new wineskins, so that the new wine will be preserved rather than ruined.

[77] 'TPP Countries to Discuss Australian Alternative to Data-Flow Proposal' (6 July 2012), insidetrade.com/Inside-US-Trade/Inside-US-Trade-07/06/2012/tpp-countries-to-discuss-australian-alternative-to-data-flow-proposal/menu-id-710.html.

15

Expanding the E-Commerce Chapter in ChAFTA: A Green Box, Orange Box and Red Box Approach

JIE (JEANNE) HUANG*

I. INTRODUCTION

THE CHINA–AUSTRALIA FREE Trade Agreement (ChAFTA) came into effect in December 2015 and achieved effective and positive results in the first year of its implementation. Eighty-five per cent of products from China and Australia are covered by reduced tariffs, which has brought a significant increase in trade in goods between both countries. It also helped to achieve a 56 per cent surge in Chinese investments in Australia in 2016.[1] On 24 March 2017, the Australian Minister for Trade, Tourism and Investment and the Chinese Commerce Minister signed a Declaration of Intent regarding Review of Elements of ChAFTA during Chinese Premier Keqiang Li's official visit with Australian Prime Minister Malcolm Turnbull at Parliament House in Canberra.[2] Both leaders agreed to commence reviews of the services and investment elements of ChAFTA.[3]

* An earlier version of this chapter was presented at the ChAFTA Conference organised at the University of New South Wales Faculty of Law in June 2016 and the author is obliged to Professor Colin Picker's comments. This chapter is published as a series paper of China National Social Science Fund Project (16BFX202). All errors remain to be mine. FTAs concluded by Australia cited in this chapter are publicly available at dfat.gov.au/trade/agreements/Pages/trade-agreements.aspx. For China's FTA list, see fta.mofcom.gov.cn/english/fta_qianshu.shtml.

[1] 'China to Expand FTA with Australia, NZ' *Global Times* (6 April 2017), www.globaltimes.cn/content/1041184.shtml.

[2] 'Declaration of Intent on Reviews of Services and Investment Commitments Signed in Canberra' (Department of Foreign Affairs and Trade (DFAT), 24 March 2017), dfat.gov.au/trade/agreements/chafta/news/Pages/declaration-of-intent-on-reviews-of-services-and-investment-commitments-signed-in-canberra.aspx.

[3] 'New Agreement with China to Drive Economic Cooperation' (Media Release, 24 March 2017), trademinister.gov.au/releases/Pages/2017/sc_mr_170324a.aspx.

They also witnessed the signing of a number of agreements to boost cooperation in fields such as agriculture and food, which are the most important items of trade between both countries.

In this context, this chapter intends to discuss how to expand the e-commerce chapter in ChAFTA by a comparative study of free trade agreements (FTAs) in China and Australia. The current e-commerce rules in ChAFTA need to be developed for three reasons.

The first reason is that the cross-border e-commerce between China and Australia is booming. China's cross-border e-commerce market values have increased from 53 billion RMB (roughly AUD$10 billion) in 2011 to 626 billion RMB (roughly AUD$122 billion) in 2016.[4] This lucrative market is what Australian businesses cannot afford to lose. ChAFTA is one of the first FTAs concluded by China that included an e-commerce chapter, because e-commerce is significant for trade between Australia and China. It is estimated that Australia is the fourth most popular source of products for Chinese online shoppers behind the US, Japan and South Korea.[5]

Second, China has not developed a consistent approach to regulate cross-border e-commerce. Australia may want to use ChAFTA to lock in favourable regulations for Australian traders. Before April 2016, goods purchased through cross-border online retails were treated as 'personal' so were not subject to tariffs and internal taxes. This significantly boosted cross-border online retails because goods purchased in this channel may be cheaper but have higher quality compared with those sold in domestic markets. However, on 8 April 2016, China announced it would impose on cross-border online retails tough new cross border e-commerce regulations, such as new tax, registration and labelling requirements.[6] This has weakened market confidence and disturbed the growth of cross-border e-commerce between China and Australia. In May 2016, China implemented a transitional period for the new regulations until the end of 2017. Right before Chinese Premier Li's official visit to Australia, in March 2017 China announced that it would

[4] 徐行[X Xu (trans)], '中国推迟跨境电商税改，澳洲保健品商家股价受益'['China Delayed the Implementation of the New Cross-border E-commerce Tax Reform'] (FT 中文网[FT Chinese], 22 March 2017), www.ftchinese.com/story/001071871 (in Chinese).

[5] 'E-Commerce in China' (Australian Trade and Investment Commission, 2017), www.austrade.gov.au/Australian/Export/Export-markets/Countries/China/Doing-business/e-commerce-in-china.

[6] 《关于跨境电子商务零售进口税收政策的通知》[Notice about Tax Policy on Import of Cross-border E-commerce Retail Products] (People's Republic of China) Ministry of Finance, State Administration of Taxation, and General Administration of Customs, Cai Guan Shui [2016] No 18, 24 March 2016 (In Chinese). 《关于公布跨境电子商务零售进口商品清单的公告》[Announcement on Issuing the List of Import of Cross-border E-commerce Retail Products] (People's Republic of China) Ministry of Finance et al, Announcement [2016] No 40, 6 April 2016 (In Chinese).

indefinitely delay the implementation of the new regulations.[7] Namely, goods exported to China via cross-border e-commerce platforms will be continuously classified as 'personal' instead of 'common' trade, which means no additional requirements for local registration or labelling will be imposed on the former.[8] The tax exemption for personal goods annually is 20,000 RMB (roughly AUD$3,916) per person but 'common' trade needs to pay import taxes, consumption taxes and value added tax. This helps to level the playing field for Australian and Chinese companies selling products online. China's Vice Minister for Foreign Affairs, Zeguang Zheng, also indicated that 'we are willing to expand cooperation with Australian companies in cross-border e-commerce'.[9] The favourable e-commerce policies made shares of Australian companies, such as Blackmores, Bellamy's and a2 Milk, a sharp increase.[10] Aldi began to directly sell Australian produce online into China. Chinese c-commerce giants are also interested in the Australian market. In 2017, Alibaba established its office in Melbourne, with the intention to expand in Australia.

Third, cross-border e-commerce regulations between China and Australia are very important in practice but, unfortunately, until now there has been little contemporary scholarship on Chinese e-commerce law[11] that has

[7] A Grigg, 'China Backs Down on Tough New-Commerce Laws in Boost for Aussie Exporters' *The Australian Financial Review* (20 March 2017), www.afr.com/business/retail/fmcg/china-backs-down-on-tough-new-ecommerce-laws-in-boost-for-aussie-exporters-20170320-gv28fe.

[8] ibid.

[9] K Needham, 'China Wants to Expand E-Commerce Trade with Australia' *The Sydney Morning Herald* (21 March 2017), www.smh.com.au/business/retail/china-wants-to-expand-ecommerce-trade-with-australia-20170321-gv2xed.html.

[10] '中国跨境电商新政无限期推迟，澳洲相关公司股价齐飞' ['Indefinite Postpone of China Cross-border E-commerce New Regulation, A Rocket Increase of Aussie Shares'] (金钱抱[Baomoney], 21 March 2017), www.baomoney.com.au/macro/101631.jhtml.

[11] Regarding discussions on Chinese law for e-commerce, see, eg, YP Liu, 'E-Commerce Intellectual Property Rights Protection in China' (2016) 28 *Intellectual Property & Technology Law Journal* 14, 14–16 (discussing e-commerce law of China and on how foreign companies can protect their intellectual property rights); K Luo, 'E-Commerce Laws and Practices in China' (2016) 33 *Arizona Journal of International & Comparative Law* 219, (providing a general view of China's E-commerce laws and the practices); Y Qi, 'Import Duties Relating to Cross-Border E-commerce in a Chinese Context' (2016) 33 *Arizona Journal of International & Comparative Law* 263 (providing suggestions on the balance and harmonisation of the tax burden between e-commerce and non-e-commerce enterprises in China); W Yan, 'The Electronic Signatures Law: China's First National E-Commerce Legislation' (2005) 17 *Intellectual Property & Technology Law Journal* 6. Regarding comparative studies between China and other countries, see, eg, S Shackelford and A Craig, 'Beyond the New "Digital Divide": Analyzing the Evolving Role of National Governments in Internet Governance and Enhancing Cybersecurity' (2014) 50 *Stanford Journal of International Law* 119, 157–64 (comparing China, the EU, India, the UK and the US and arguing that there exists a continuum of governmental interest in and approaches to regulating cyberspace); C Rizzi, *E-Commerce Law in China: The Functioning of E-Commerce in China and the Influence of the EU Model* (AH Alphen aan den Rijn, Kluwer Law International, 2013) (exploring the prospects for e-commerce in China through a comparative exploration of the current Chinese policy approach and lessons

answered the following critical questions: (1) what are the differences and similarities between Chinese international trade law for e-commerce and its Australian counterpart?; (2) how has China used its FTAs to regulate cross-border e-commerce?; and (3) what is the trend for China's FTAs in this field?. This chapter tries to answer these questions, especially in the post-TPP (Trans-Pacific Partnership Agreement) era in the Asia-Pacific region.[12]

This chapter compares FTAs concluded by Australia and China, particularly ChAFTA, the China–South Korea FTA, the Australia–US FTA, the Australia–South Korea FTA and the TPP Agreement.[13] It is because ChAFTA and the China–South Korea FTA are not only the most recent FTAs concluded by China, but also the only Chinese FTAs containing an e-commerce chapter. Australia concluded the US–Australia FTA in 2005, the Australia–South Korea FTA in 2014 and the TPP Agreement in 2016. Although the TPP Agreement will likely not come into effect, it is still worth discussing because examining these three FTAs may demonstrate a historical evolution of an Australian approach to regulation of cross-border e-commerce.

This chapter divides e-commerce regulations into three 'boxes': the Green Box contains new regulations that may be easiest for China and Australia to reach consensus on and include in the expanded ChAFTA; the Orange Box includes new regulations that are important for the healthy development of cross-border e-commerce between China and Australia and a good possibility exists for both countries to include such regulations in the expanded ChAFTA;[14] regulations in the Red Box are difficult for China and Australia

that can be drawn from initiatives from the EU). Regarding China's international trade law for e-commerce in the WTO contexts, see, eg, P Delimatsis, 'Protecting Public Morals in a Digital Age: Revisiting the WTO Rulings on US–Gambling and China–Publications and Audiovisual Products' (2011) 14 *Journal of International Economic Law* 257.

[12] Australia may defer passing any legislation, or amendments to existing legislation, to implement the TPP Agreement. See DFAT, 'Trans-Pacific Partnership Agreement: Latest News' (2017), dfat.gov.au/trade/agreements/tpp/Pages/trans-pacific-partnership-agreement-tpp.aspx; FD Simões, 'Amicus Curiae in the Trans-Pacific Partnership' (2017) 54 *American Business Law Journal* 161, 165–66 (arguing that the TPP Agreement is a '21st century agreement' and potentially set forward a model for FTAs worldwide).

[13] The TPP Agreement is a mega FTA and the other FTA comparators are generally bilateral FTAs. The TPP Agreement is the only mega FTA discussed in this chapter, because the mega FTA that China concluded (ie, the China–ASEAN FTA) does not contain an e-commerce chapter and the TPP Agreement is the only mega FTA to which Australia is a party.

[14] In this chapter, the colour 'orange' is used as distinguished from the 'yellow' lights and the 'amber' box in the WTO Agriculture Agreement. The 'yellow', if using the traffic light example, means cautions. Amber Box in the WTO Agriculture Agreement means demininis. In contrast, this chapter argues that regulations in the Orange Box should be encouraged. 'Orange' represents fruit with a sour and sweet taste. It is suitable for what the chapter argues, that although China and Australia have not included consumer protection in ChAFTA (the sour part), there is a good opportunity for them to do so in the future (the sweet part). The image of orange is healthy, which also corresponds to what the chapter encourages that China and Australia should provide: stronger consumer protection measures in the expanded ChAFTA.

to include in the expanded ChAFTA so the two countries may want to exclude them from their negotiation agenda.

This chapter proceeds as follows. Section II argues that China and Australia should primarily focus their efforts on expanding the e-commerce regulations in the Green Box, which contains regulations for (1) customs duties, fees, other charges and domestic taxes; (2) paperless trade, digital signature and authentication; (3) the adoption of the United Nations Commission on International Trade Law (UNCITRAL) legal instruments; (4) cooperation mechanisms; and (5) a dispute resolution system. The majority of these regulations are directly related to trade in goods. They are important for China and Australia because currently cross-border e-commerce between China and Australia mainly involves tangible goods, such as healthcare products, agricultural foods, wines, skincare products and formula milk. It is also feasible for both nations to expand on the Green Box regulations because some of them are already included in FTAs of both China and Australia. In section III, this chapter proposes that China and Australia may explore the possibility of adopting regulations in the Orange Box, which focuses on consumer protection. Expanding ChAFTA in the Orange Box is possible, since these regulations have been accepted by Australian FTAs and may probably be adopted by China's future FTAs based on the recent development of Chinese domestic legislation. Section IV suggests that China and Australia should stay away from regulations in the Red Box, which include provisions to facilitate free flow of information across borders contained in the TPP Agreement. These regulations do not appear in Australian's FTAs other than the TPP Agreement and are also hard for China to adopt because its political concerns prevail over economic benefits. Section V concludes this chapter, suggesting that China and Australia should focus their negotiations on the Green Box, explore consensus on the Orange Box, and avoid the Red Box. Hopefully, in the near future, the two countries can agree upon an expansion of the e-commerce chapter in ChAFTA.

II. GREEN BOX

Tangible goods are the most important items for trade between China and Australia. For example, although ChAFTA has only been in force for one year, it has increased Australian wine sales in China by 38 per cent, skincare products by 82 per cent and the value of fresh lobster exports by 400 per cent.[15] Therefore, both countries will have an interest in expanding regulations for facilitating trade measures (eg, paperless trade, digital signature and authentication) and improving their domestic e-commerce

[15] 'New Agreement with China' (n 3).

legal systems through use of UNCITRAL legal instruments. These expansions are feasible because the rules are taken from the World Trade Organization (WTO) and UNCITRAL, to which both China and Australia are parties, and are largely adopted by their FTAs. Moreover, China and Australia may consider expanding their e-commerce regulations to digital products, such as exemptions from customs duties, fees and other charges imposed on the border.

A. Customs Duties, Fees, Other Charges and Domestic Taxes

Customs duties, fees, other charges and domestic taxes are traditional measures applicable to international trade. Early in 1998, WTO members agreed to exempt electronic transmission from customs duties.[16] This practice was adopted by the Australia–South Korea FTA.[17] The US–Australia FTA extends exemption from customs duties to fees and other charges in connection with the importation or exportation of digital products.[18] The TPP Agreement does not impose any customs duties on cross-border trade in digital products either.[19] However, fees or other charges imposed at the border that are different from duties are permitted by the TPP Agreement.[20] Nevertheless, in contrast to earlier Australian FTAs, digital products in the TPP Agreement do not include those encoded on a physical carrier; therefore, imposing duties, fees and other charges on the border is difficult, if not impossible, for contents transmitted online. Therefore, although the TPP Agreement does not outlaw fees and charges imposed on the border other than customs duties, this tends to be somewhat irrelevant because it is particularly difficult to apply those fees and charges to cross-border information flows.

Like the Australia–South Korea FTA, ChAFTA and the China–South Korea FTA both exempt cross-border electronic transmissions from customs duties.[21] However, China's FTAs including ChAFTA do not touch upon fees

[16] The Geneva Ministerial Declaration on Global Electronic Commerce WT/MIN(98)/DEC/2 (25 May 1998), docs.wto.org.

[17] Free Trade Agreement between the Government of the Republic of Korea and the Government of Australia (Australia–South Korea FTA) (signed 8 April 2014, entered into force 12 December 2014) [2014] ATS 43, Art 15.3.

[18] Australia–United States Free Trade Agreement (Australia–US FTA) (signed 18 May 2004, entered into force 1 January 2005) [2005] ATS 1, Art 16.3.

[19] Trans-Pacific Partnership Agreement (TPP Agreement) Art 14.3.1, ustr.gov/trade-agreements/free-trade-agreements/trans-pacific-partnership/tpp-full-text.

[20] ibid.

[21] Free Trade Agreement between the Government of Australia and the Government of the People's Republic of China (ChAFTA) (signed 17 June 2015, entered into force 20 December 2015) [2015] ATS 15, Art 12.3; Free Trade Agreement between the Government of the People's Republic of China and the Government of the Republic of Korea (China–South Korea FTA) (signed 1 June 2015, entered into force 20 December 2015) Art 13.3.

and other charges other than duties, as well as internal taxes. These are left to domestic laws. This may be explained by the fact that the US strongly supports exempting customs duties, fees and other charges in connection with the importation or exportation of digital products. This is a standard practice for all FTAs concluded by the US after the Australia–US FTA, such as the US–South Korea FTA.[22] However, China has no FTA with the US, and it is unsurprising that China's FTAs do not exempt fees and other charges other than duties. Nevertheless, China and Australia may consider doing this when expanding ChAFTA. This will increase the competitiveness for products traded by e-commerce in each other's markets.

B. Paperless Trade, Digital Signature and Authentication

Regulations for paperless trade, digital signature and authentication are not only designed for trade in digital products. They also serve trade in traditional tangible goods. The rationales underlying these regulations are the principles of technology neutrality and functional equivalence between paper and digital documents. These regulations are generally included in the e-commerce chapters of the FTAs in China and Australia.

i. Paperless Trade

International trade involves both commercial and regulatory entities, such as importers, exporters, banks, insurers, customs, inspection and quarantine bureaus etc. To make trade happen, documents need to be circulated at three stages: business-to-business, business-to-government, and government-to-government (eg, between different governmental agencies). For example, in a typical import transaction, contracts of sale, bills of lading, invoices, insurance policies and other documents are not only exchanged between business parties but also submitted to customs, the inspection and quarantine bureau and other governmental agencies for importation procedure. Statistics show that paper documentation and procedures represent around 10 per cent of the cost of the goods in international trade.[23] One stage's demand for paper documents may undo the expected benefits of paperless

[22] eg, Free Trade Agreement between the Government of the United States and the Government of the Republic of Korea (signed 20 June 2007, entered into force 15 March 2012) Art 15.3.1.

[23] UN Directories for Electronic Data Interchange for Administration, Commerce and Transport, 'Part 2: Uniform Rules for Conduct for Interchange of Trade Data by Teletransmission (UNCID)', www.unece.org/tradewelcome/un-centre-for-trade-facilitation-and-e-business-uncefact/outputs/standards/unedifact/tradeedifactrules/part-2-uniform-rules-of-conduct-for-interchange-of-trade-data-by-teletransmission-uncid/part-2-uncid-chapter-1-introductory-note.html.

trade in the whole transaction.[24] In this context, the business-to-government document submission is of special significance. Different country requirements for documents and procedures have a direct negative impact upon trade. It complicates business transactions, slows down processes, increases trade costs, and even sometimes functions as a disguised trade barrier. Government initiatives to accept digital documents serve as a springboard for commercial entities to adopt digital transaction between them.[25] Moreover, according to a survey conducted by the UN in 2015, full implementation of cross-border paperless trade is expected to generate US$257 billion of additional export potential annually for the Asia-Pacific region alone.[26] Paperless trade has special significance for small and medium-sized enterprises (SMEs) because the cost and complexity of paper documentation may intimidate or discourage them from conducting international trade.[27] Notably, paperless trade originally comes from the goal to facilitate traditional trade in goods. It is unsurprising that both Australia's and China's FTAs addresses paperless trade requirements between private parties and government agencies.

The paperless trade clause in the Australian FTAs provides that states shall endeavour to provide electronic trade administration documents to the public and recognise trade administration documents submitted electronically as the legal equivalent of the printed versions.[28] The publication of electronic administration documents resonates with Article 7.4 of the Revised Kyoto Convention, which requires that the domestic law of its members shall provide for e-commerce methods as an alternative to paper-based documentary requirements.[29]

Compared with the best effort clauses found in Australian FTAs, including the TPP Agreement, ChAFTA imposes stricter requirements: states shall accept electronic versions of trade administration documents as the legal equivalent of paper documents except in two situations.[30] First, if there is a domestic or international legal requirement to the contrary; or

[24] E Laryea, 'Facilitating Paperless International Trade: A Survey of Law and Policy in Asia' (2005) 19 *International Review of Law Computers & Technology* 121, 123.

[25] ibid 124.

[26] UN Economic and Social Commission for Asia and the Pacific, 'Joint United Nations Regional Commissions Trade Facilitation and Paperless Trade Implementation Survey 2015: Asia and the Pacific Report 2015', www.unescap.org/sites/default/files/UNRCs_TFPT_Survey_ESCAP_Regional_Report_2015.pdf.

[27] Laryea (n 24) 122.

[28] eg, the Australia–South Korea FTA (n 17) Art 15.7; the Australia–US FTA (n 18) Art 16.7.

[29] The revised International Convention on the Simplification and Harmonization of Customs Procedures, adopted by the World Customs Organization in June 1999 and effective in February 2006. Among TPP Members, Australia, New Zealand, Japan, Viet Nam, Indonesia, the US and Canada are parties to the Revised Convention. For more information, see 'List of the Contracting Parties to the Revised Kyoto Convention' (World Customs Organization, 2017), www.wcoomd.org/en/topics/facilitation/instrument-and-tools/conventions/pf_revised_kyoto_conv/instruments.aspx. Most of the TPP Members have ratified the revised Kyoto Convention, except Chile, Peru and Mexico.

[30] ChAFTA (n 21) Art 12.7; TPP Agreement (n 19) Art 14.9.

second, doing so would reduce the effectiveness of the trade administration process.[31] This is a stronger clause than the equivalent in the China–South Korea FTA, which only requires that states try to provide and explore the possibility of paperless trading.[32]

Paperless trade is more than electronic submission of documents, since the former includes electronic/automated customs system, internet connection available to customs and other trade control agencies at the border, e-payment of customs duties and fees, electronic single window system etc.[33] ChAFTA does not impose obligations on these areas of paperless trade. China and Australia may try to explore the possibility of expanding paperless trade to these areas. The reason is that Australia has been seeking to reduce its dependence on exports of mineral resources such as coal and iron ore due to declining global demand. Australia inclines to expand exports of high-quality food and agricultural products to meet the growing middle-class demand in Asia, especially in China.[34] Trade in high-quality food and fresh agricultural products requires efficient custom declaration proceedings. If China and Australia can cooperate in these areas, Australia may be able to export more food and agricultural products to China and Chinese consumers may also be able to enjoy fresh and nutritious Australia food.

ii. Digital Signature and Authentication

Digital signature and authentication are crucial to enhancing security and preventing fraud in e-commerce.[35] They are the basic building blocks of mutual recognition of electronic documents along the entire cross-border e-commerce supply chain. However, according to a UN survey, less than 20 per cent of Asia-Pacific countries fully implemented measures for recognised certification authority.[36] China and Australia, however, have recognised the importance of digital signature and authentication for e-commerce. The TPP Agreement, ChAFTA and the China–South Korea FTA have similar provisions for digital signature and authentication in two respects.[37]

[31] ChAFTA (n 21) Art 12.7.

[32] China–South Korea FTA (n 21) Art 13.6.

[33] UN Economic and Social Commission for Asia and the Pacific (n 26) 19–21.

[34] '《中澳自由贸易协定》生效一周年' ['One Year Implementation of the ChAFTA'] (Australian Embassy, China, 19 December 2016), china.embassy.gov.au/bjngchinese/20161219ChAFTAmediarelease_cn.html (in Chinese) '外媒称澳大利亚农产品对华出口并非一帆风顺' ['Foreign Media Reported that the Australian Agricultural Exports to China Is Not a Smooth Sailing'] (腾讯财经 [*QQ Finance*] 18 November 2014), finance.qq.com/a/20141118/052216.htm (in Chinese).

[35] See the UNECE's website dedicated to UneDocs, www.unece.org/etrades/unedocs.

[36] UN Economic and Social Commission for Asia and the Pacific (n 26).

[37] TPP Agreement (n 19) Art 14.6; ChAFTA (n 21) Art 12.6; China–South Korea FTA (n 21) Art 13.4.

First, to recognise the principle of technology neutrality. It requires that no party may deny the legal validity of a signature solely because the signature is in electronic form.[38]

Second, to permit private contracting regarding digital authentication and signature.[39] Private contracting is a useful way to address the differences between domestic law on digital signature and authentication. Private parties may agree upon specific terms and conditions of signature and authentication for cross-border e-commerce transactions between them. They are allowed to mutually determine the appropriate authentication methods for that transaction, and have the opportunity to establish before judicial or administrative authorities that their transaction complies with any legal requirements with respect to authentication.

Nevertheless, unlike ChAFTA, the TPP Agreement allows its members to specify in their domestic law about the method or standard of authentication in a particular category of transaction.[40] For example, in financial transactions, Member States may provide special methods or standards of authentication to protect transaction security. This is a practical method to acknowledge that members may have special needs in a particular category of transaction. Moreover, it does not go against technology neutrality and private contracting. ChAFTA should consider adopting a similar provision as the TPP Agreement.

C. Adopting UNCITRAL Legal Instruments

The TPP Agreement, the Australia–South Korea FTA and ChAFTA require that their members shall maintain a legal framework governing electronic transactions consistent with the principles of the UNCITRAL Model Law on Electronic Commerce.[41] The TPP Agreement also encourages its members to adopt the UN Convention on the Use of Electronic Communications in International Contracts (Electronic Contract Convention). This Convention was initiated by the US and drafted based upon e-commerce principles

[38] TPP Agreement (n 19) Art 14.6; China–South Korea FTA (n 21) Art 13.4.

[39] TPP Agreement (n 19) Art 14.6; ChAFTA (n 21) Art 12.6; China–South Korea FTA (n 21) Art 13.4.

[40] TPP Agreement (n 19) Art 14.6.

[41] TPP Agreement (n 19) Art 14.5; Australia–South Korea FTA (n 17) Art 15.4; ChAFTA (n 21) Art 12.5. Legislation based on or influenced by the Model Law has been adopted in 67 states in a total of 143 jurisdictions up to 22 May 2016. Australia adopted the Model Law in 2011 and China in 2004. For more information oo the Model Law, see United Nations Commission on International Trade Law (UNCITRAL), 'UNCITRAL Model Law on Electronic Commerce (1996)' (UNCITRAL 2007), www.uncitral.org/uncitral/en/uncitral_texts/electronic_commerce/1996Model_status.html.

found in the UNCITRAL Model Law.[42] It applies to contracts for the sale of goods, services, licences of software, auctions etc.[43] China signed the Electronic Contract Convention in 2006 but has not ratified it yet. This helps explain why ChAFTA only requires its members to enact domestic laws according to the UNCITRAL Model Law.[44] China should consider ratifying the Electronic Contract Convention in the near future. It could help bring Chinese domestic legislation on e-commerce up to international levels.

UNCITRAL has pioneered international laws for e-commerce. Early in 1996, it published the Model Law on Electronic Commerce, which establishes fundamental principles for e-commerce, such as functionally equivalence, non-discrimination, and technology neutrality.[45] These principles share the same idea that paper-based communications and electronic communications with the same purposes and functions should be treated equally. These principles were adopted by the Model Law on Electronic Signatures in 2001 and the Electronic Contract Convention. These UNCITRAL instruments aim to facilitate the use of modern communication techniques and to remove obstacles or uncertainty coming from legislation based upon traditional paper-based communications. The TPP Agreement shares these goals but it goes further in three respects. First, besides focusing on technology, it also emphasises the rights of internet users, such as personal information protection and rights to free flow of information, which will be discussed in the following sections.

Second, the TPP Agreement extends the non-discrimination principle. Under the UNCITRAL instruments, the non-discrimination principle means information shall not be denied legal effect, validity or enforceability solely on the grounds that it is in the form of a data message. In other words, the UNCITRAL instruments compare electronic communication with paper-based communication. But the non-discrimination clause for digital products under the TPP Agreement compares a digital product created, produced, published, contracted for, commissioned or first made available on commercial terms in the territory of another party with other like digital products of a party or a non-party. In other words, under the TPP Agreement the non-discriminatory treatment is not between a digital product and a traditional paper-based product, but instead, it is between a digital product and other like digital products. In addition, regarding consumer protection in the TPP

[42] The United Nations Convention on the Use of Electronic Communications in International Contracts (the United Nations Convention), UNGA Res 60/21, UN Doc A/RES/60/21 (9 December 2005). For comments, see CH Martin, 'The Electronic Contracts Convention, the CISG, and New Sources of E-Commerce Law' (2007–08) 16 *Tulane Journal of International & Comparative Law* 467, 470.

[43] The United Nations Convention (n 42) Art 2.

[44] ChAFTA (n 21) Art 12.5.1; China–South Korea FTA (n 21) Art 12.5.

[45] UNCITRAL, UNCITRAL Model Law on Electronic Commerce with Guide to Enactment (1996), www.uncitral.org/pdf/english/texts/electcom/05-89450_Ebook.pdf, 20–21.

Agreement, the non-discriminatory treatment clause requires that the personal information of e-commerce users and non-e-commerce users should be protected equivalently.

Third, both the UNCITRAL instruments and the TPP Agreement endorse party autonomy in e-commerce, but the former is limited to contract formation by electronic means while the latter goes beyond electronic contracting and encourages industrial self-regulation as being indispensable to positive law regulation of e-commerce. For example, the Model Law on E-commerce embodies the principle of party autonomy in Article 4, which provides that private parties can use consensus to revise its Chapter III Communication of Data Messages. Chapter III is about formation of contracts by electronic means and relevant validity issues. The TPP Agreement, in contrast, recognises party autonomy not only in contracts, but also in developing codes of conduct, guidelines and enforcement mechanisms in private sectors.[46] Notably ChAFTA also requires that parties shall (TPP Agreement uses a best-efforts clause) support industry-led development of e-commerce.[47] Industrial self-regulation or industry-led development of e-commerce regulations reflect the fact that the technology the internet is based upon are protocols and codes established by private groups or organisations, such as the Internet Engineering Task Force, World Wide Web Consortium, Internet Society, the Internet Corporation for Assigned Names and Numbers (ICANN) and the Internet Assigned Numbers Authority (IANA).[48] The internet does not have to be regulated in a top-down manner by state positive law,[49] but rather it supports industry self-regulation that reflects party autonomy.[50]

Australia and China may draw lessons from the above: personal information protection is essential for the development of big data; and a digital product and other like digital products should be treated in an equivalent way, which is a reasonable application of the non-discrimination principle under the WTO.

D. Cooperation Mechanisms in Regulating Cross-Border E-Commerce

Although ChAFTA has a provision for cooperation mechanisms in regulating cross-border e-commerce, both Australia and China should consider enhancing these mechanisms.

[46] TPP Agreement (n 19) Art 14.5(e).

[47] ChAFTA (n 21) Art 12.5.2.

[48] G Schneider et al, *The Internet*, 5th edn (United States, Cengage Learning, 2009), cengage.com.au/product/title/the-internet---illustrated/isbn/9780538750981, 12.

[49] M Mueller et al, 'Making Sense of "Internet Governance"' in D MacLean (ed), *Internet Governance: A Grand Collaboration* (New York, United Nations ICT Task Force, 2004) 110.

[50] J Waz and P Weiser, 'Internet Governance: The Role of Multistakeholder Organizations' (2013) 10 *Journal on Telecommunications & High Technology Law* 331, 331.

First, neither ChAFTA nor the China–South Korea FTA explicitly mention SMEs assistance. E-commerce is of special significance for SMEs as they generally lack the networks to get into international markets. E-commerce can help them to expand their business. However, because of limited financial and legal resources, they may not have sufficient knowledge about FTAs compared with multinational enterprises. Therefore, special assistance for SMEs is necessary.

Second, Australia and China may consider jointly encouraging private parties to develop methods of self-regulation, such as codes of conduct, model contracts, guidelines and enforcement mechanisms and other ways to foster e-commerce.

Third, Australia and China need to highlight cooperation on cybersecurity matters. Cybersecurity is crucial in the internet era.[51] Both the Chinese government and enterprises are also confronted by potential hacker attacks. China's future FTAs should consider including cybersecurity issues in the cooperative mechanisms under e-commerce chapters.

E. Dispute Resolution

The China–Australia FTA[52] and the China–South Korea FTA[53] exclude disputes concerning e-commerce from their dispute resolution chapters. However, the US FTAs are different: a Member State that violates the obligations in the e-commerce chapter can be subject to retaliation measures under the state-to-state dispute resolution mechanism.[54] In other words, the disputes concerning e-commerce between Member States are governed by the dispute settlement chapter, which provides mechanisms such as consultations, good offices, conciliations, mediation and panels to resolve disputes.[55] This is significant, because the dispute resolution mechanism can compel Member States to strictly implement treaty obligations. Nevertheless, investors cannot bring investment arbitration against a state that violates the e-commerce

[51] H Duncan, 'An E-SOS for Cyberspace' (2011) 52 *Harvard International Law Journal* 374, 379.

[52] ChAFTA (n 21) Art 12.11.

[53] The China–South Korea FTA (n 21) Art 13.9.

[54] eg, TPP Agreement (n 19) Arts 14.18, 28.20. A two-year grace period after the TPP Agreement effective date is allowed for Malaysia to waive its obligations under Art 14.4 (non-discriminatory treatment of digital products) and Art 14.11 (cross-border transfer of information by electronic means). A two-year grace period after the TPP Agreement effective date is also allowed for Viet Nam to waive its obligations under Art 14.4 (non-discriminatory treatment of digital products), Art 14.11 (cross-border transfer of information by electronic means) and Art 14.13 (location of computing facilities).

[55] ibid Art 28.3.1(b), which provides this mechanism applies when a party considers that an actual or proposed measure of another party is or would be inconsistent with an obligation of this Agreement or that another party has otherwise failed to carry out an obligation under this Agreement.

chapter unless the state also breaches chapters such as the investment, cross-border supply of services or financial services.

III. ORANGE BOX

The Orange Box contains regulations that Australian FTAs have adopted and China's future FTAs may adopt. This category focuses on consumer protection regulations. Protecting consumer confidence in e-commerce is equally as important as removing trade barriers.[56] These regulations are covered by FTAs in Australia and China, but Australian FTAs have made broader and stronger commitments than their Chinese counterparts. Nevertheless, based on the recent developments in Chinese domestic law and considering that China is also facing similar issues of consumer protection, China and Australia may be able to work together to enhance consumer protection in ChAFTA.

A. Combat Fraudulent and Deceptive Commercial Activities

Different from Australian FTAs, the online consumer protection clauses under China's FTAs focus solely on technology neutrality, namely that online consumers shall be protected in a way at least equivalent to that provided for consumers of other forms of commerce according to the domestic law of a Member State.[57] The Australia–US FTA endorses the importance of adopting and maintaining transparent and effective measures to protect consumers from fraudulent and deceptive commercial activities.[58] Nevertheless, the TPP Agreement is the first Australian FTA that requires its members to adopt or maintain consumer protection laws to proscribe fraudulent and deceptive commercial activities that cause harm or potential harm to consumers engaged in online commercial activities.[59] This behind-the-border measure requires members to make domestic legal reforms. The TPP Agreement defines fraudulent and deceptive commercial activities as practices causing actual harm to consumers or that pose an imminent threat of such harm if not prevented.[60] Examples include misrepresenting material facts, failing to provide products or services to consumers who have made payments, unauthorised charging or debiting consumers' financial,

[56] TPP Agreement (n 19) Art 14.2.
[57] ibid Art 12.7.
[58] The Australia–US FTA (n 18) Art 16.6.
[59] TPP Agreement (n 19) Art 14.7.
[60] ibid Art 16.6.2.

telephone or other accounts.[61] Fraudulent and deceptive commercial activities can be conducted online or offline. With burgeoning cross-border e-commerce transactions, fraudulent and deceptive commercial activities increasingly transcend national borders. In this context, the TPP Agreement requires cooperation between national consumer protection agencies or other relevant bodies on activities related to cross-border e-commerce aiming to enhance consumer welfare.[62]

Combating fraudulent and deceptive commercial activities in e-commerce is a highlight of the newly amended Chinese Law on Protection of the Rights and Interests of Consumers (China Consumer Protection Law).[63] For example, if consumers buy goods online, they have the right to return the goods within seven days of receipt and need not give a reason.[64] This measure can deter online retailers who fraudulently sell low-quality products. The law also requires online sellers to provide consumers with information such as their business addresses, contact methods, the quality and quantity of goods or services, prices or costs, the duration and manner of performance, safety precautions and risk warnings, after-sales service, and civil liability.[65] This requirement can help consumers seek legal remedies against online retailers who commit fraudulent and deceptive commercial activities. The law also significantly increases compensation to consumers: if sellers fraudulently provide goods or services, compensation for a consumer's losses has improved.[66] The old law only imposed double compensation. The new triple compensation aims to build Chinese consumers' confidence in goods and services sold in China, which is in line with China's long-term goal of boosting domestic consumption.[67] Therefore, although currently absent in China's FTAs, Chinese domestic law strongly proscribes fraudulent and deceptive commercial activities and hence it is not unlikely that ChAFTA might in the future include enhanced consumer protection.

[61] ibid.

[62] ibid Arts 14.7.3, 16.6.5, 16.6.6.

[63] The Decision on Amending the Chinese Consumer Protection Law was adopted at the 5th Session of the Standing Committee of the Twelfth National People's Congress on 25 October 2013, and took effect on 15 March 2014.

[64] 《中华人民共和国消费者权益保护法（2013修正）》[Law of the People's Republic of China on the Protection of Consumer Rights and Interests (2013 Amendment)] (China Consumer Protection Law) (People's Republic of China) Standing Committee of the National People's Congress, Order No 7 of the President of the People's Republic of China, Art 25; exceptions include made-to-order goods, perishables, digitalised goods which are downloaded or opened by consumers, and delivered newspapers and periodicals.

[65] ibid Art 28.

[66] ibid Art 55.

[67] 'China Introduces New Consumer Protection Law' *China Briefing* (8 April 2014), www.china-briefing.com/news/2014/04/08/china-introduces-new-consumer-protection-law.html.

B. Minimise Unsolicited Commercial Electronic Messages

The TPP Agreement is the first Australian FTA imposing on its Member States a legal obligation to minimise unsolicited commercial electronic messages, which are defined as messages for commercial or marketing purposes sent to an electronic address through an internet access service supplier, without the consent of the recipient or despite the explicit rejection of the recipient.[68] The TPP Agreement would have required members to adopt measures that require suppliers of commercial spam to help recipients to avoid receiving those messages without their consent.[69] Members should also have provided recourse to the recipients against commercial spam suppliers.[70] Commercial spam is a cross-border issue and can be combated more effectively through international cooperation. Therefore, the TPP Agreement would require members to cooperate to prevent unsolicited commercial electronic messages.[71]

Unsolicited commercial spam is also a thorny issue in China. ChAFTA, although it provides no obligation to minimise unsolicited commercial electronic messages, does require its two members to share information about online consumer protection, including unsolicited commercial electronic messages.[72] The Chinese Administrative Measures for Online Trading and Chinese Consumer Protection Law also bans commercial spam sent without consumers' consent or after a clear refusal.[73] In China, consumers have recourse against commercial spam suppliers if they receive commercial spam without their consent. They can bring tort claims under personal privacy protection law if the spam suppliers illegally access their phone numbers or email addresses. They can allege contractual breaches if a telecommunications service provider promises to diminish commercial spam in a service contract but fails to do so. However, compared with the time and cost associated with litigation, consumers may often decide not to use those sorts of remedies. To tackle this issue, Articles 37.7 and 47 of the Chinese Consumer Protection Law empowers consumer associations to bring class actions on behalf of consumers against commercial spam suppliers or telecommunications companies. These Chinese laws echo the TPP Agreement requirement.[74]

[68] TPP Agreement (n 19) Art 14.1.
[69] ibid Art 14.14.1.
[70] ibid Art 14.14.2.
[71] ibid Art 14.14.3.
[72] ChAFTA (n 21) Art 12.10.
[73]《网络交易管理办法》[Administrative Measures for Online Trading] (People's Republic of China) State Administration for Industry and Commerce, Order No 60, 26 January 2014, Art 18; Chinese Consumer Protection Law (n 63) Art 29.
[74] TPP Agreement (n 19) Art 14.4.

The TPP Agreement does not specify what recourses a state must provide to consumers to reduce commercial spam in its domestic legal system. Therefore, Chinese law would satisfy the TPP Agreement's requirements. Moreover, international cooperation in combating commercial spam benefits Chinese consumers. As such, it is likely that the Chinese government will consider inclusion of these sorts of provisions when expanding ChAFTA.

C. Protection for Personal Information

FTAs in Australia and China both protect personal information of e-commerce users but at different levels. The TPP Agreement defines personal information broadly, as any information, including data, about an identified or identifiable natural person.[75] Personal information protection contains behind-the-border measures and requires Member States to undertake domestic legal reform. The TPP Agreement requires each Member to adopt or maintain a legal framework to protect personal information of e-commerce users.[76] This legal framework can be a comprehensive one covering privacy, personal information or personal data protection, it can also be sector-specific, or in the form of laws enforcing industrial voluntary undertakings relating to privacy.[77] However, it should be in line with principles and guidelines of relevant international bodies. TPP Agreement members should make their laws publicly accessible[78] and apply non-discriminatorily.[79] They should also exchange information about each other's personal information protection law to enhance conformity.[80]

In contrast to the TPP Agreement, other FTAs in Australia and all FTAs concluded by China put personal information protection in the online data protection clauses.[81] Member States in those agreements are encouraged to consider international standards and the criteria of relevant international organisations to improve domestic measures for the protection of personal information and other data.[82] These are best-effort clauses and lack detail for implementation.

[75] TPP Agreement (n 19) Art 14.14 requires that parties shall adopt or maintain measures regarding unsolicited commercial electronic messages and provide recourse against suppliers of unsolicited commercial electronic messages.

[76] TPP Agreement (n 19) Art 14.8. Brunei and Viet Nam are exempted from this article before the date on which their domestic law provides protection for personal data of the users of e-commerce.

[77] ibid fn 6.

[78] ibid Arts 14.8.3, Art 14.8.4.

[79] ibid Art 14.8.3.

[80] ibid Art 14.8.5.

[81] ChAFTA (n 21) Art 12.8; China–South Korea FTA (n 21) Art 13.5; Australia–South Korea FTA (n 17) Art 15.8.

[82] eg, ChAFTA (n 21) Art 12.8, China–South Korea FTA (n 21) Art 13.5.

The main challenge for China to adopt high-level protection of personal information in FTAs is that such protection involves behind-the-border measures but China's domestic law for personal information protection is still developing. Therefore, China has refrained from making any commitments in its FTAs.

'Personal information' has never been explicitly defined in Chinese legislation. The most official definition is provided by the Information Security Technology—Guidelines for Personal Information Protection Within Public and Commercial Services Information Systems.[83] It refers to 'computer data that may be processed by an information system, relevant to a certain natural person, and that may be used solely or along with other information to identify such natural person'.[84] Personal ID number, race, political viewpoint, religion, biometric information, telephone number, birth date, address, financial information, medical records, even geographical location, an address book in a mobile or computing device are all treated as personal information. The Guidelines are the most comprehensive official document to address personal information protection in China. However, it is not law so is not binding. Moreover, its scope is limited because it does not apply to government agencies or other institutions exercising 'public management' functions.

In China, laws concerning personal information protection are fragmented and most of them are found in regulations issued by ministries, rather than being issued from the National People's Congress (NPC) and its Standing Committee. These laws can be divided into three categories.

The first category covers laws regulating collection of personal information, ie, the circumstances in which a state organ or business entity can legally collect personal information. In China, citizens are required to provide personal information, such as national ID number, for transactions in banks, tickets in railway stations, healthcare in hospitals and even access to internet cafes.[85] Authentic identity information must be

[83] 《信息安全技术公共及商用服务信息系统个人信息保护指南 [Information Security Technology—Guidelines for Personal Information Protection Within Public and Commercial Services Information Systems] (People's Republic of China) Standardization Administration and the General Administration of Quality Supervision, Inspection and Quarantine, GB/Z 28828-2012, 5 November 2011. The Guidelines divide personal information into 'personal sensitive information' and 'personal general information'. The former refers to information that would have an adverse impact on the subject if disclosed or altered, and the latter means all personal information other than personal sensitive information. For comments, see 'China's First National Standard on Personal Information Protection to Take Effect' *China Briefing* (4 February 2013), www.china-briefing.com/news/2013/02/04/chinas-first-national-standard-on-personal-information-protection-to-take-effect.html.

[84] ibid, Art 3.2.

[85] Art 23 of the Regulations on the Administration of Business Premises of Internet Access Service provides that Internet cafes shall verify and register the identification cards or other valid certificates of the internet users, and shall record the relevant net information.

provided for conducting most online transactions,[86] including selling computer applications (apps) from internet stores.[87] The general requirement is that collecting and using personal information must comply with the principles of legality, proportionality and necessity.[88] Consumers must be informed about the purpose, method and scope of the information collected and used.[89] If providing personal information is not a compulsory obligation under the law, collecting personal information must be based upon consumers' consent.[90] For example, the 2014, Administrative Measures for Online Trading issued by the State Administration for Industry & Commerce require that online commodity dealers and relevant service providers and their employees should obtain consumers' consent before collecting personal information, must keep that information strictly confidential and may not divulge, sell or illegally provide such information to others.[91] Nevertheless, in order to combat telecommunications fraud and enhance national security, the Chinese government increasingly requires its citizens to provide ID and other personal information when applying for a new telephone number, opening a new internet account or even mailing a parcel through China Post.[92] The growing real name identity authentication requirements potentially increase the possibility of leakage of personal information.[93]

The second category of personal information protection governs the transfer of personal information, namely the circumstances where a state organ or a business entity that legally collects personal information can transfer such information to a third party. In China, some entities that can legally collect personal information currently fail to protect this information. Illegal sale and use of personal information are rampant, and have

The underlying policy is to prohibit minors from accessing internet cafes and also prevent illegal use of the internet. 《互联网上网服务营业场所管理条例（2016修订）》 [Regulations on the Administration of Business Premises of Internet Access Service (2016 Revision)] (People's Republic of China) State Council, Order No 666, 2 June 2016, Art 23.

86 Examples include the real-name system of online stores. 《国家工商行政管理总局关于加强网络市场监管的意见 [Opinions of the State Administration for Industry and Commence on Strengthening the Supervision of the Online Market] (People's Republic of China) State Administration for Industry and Commerce, 6 November 2015.

87 《移动互联网应用程序信息服务管理规定 [Provisions on the Administration of Mobile Internet Applications Information Services] (People's Republic of China) Cyberspace Administration of China on 28 June 2016, Art 7.

88 ibid Art 7.2.

89 ibid Arts 7.2, 8.

90 ibid Arts 7.2, 7.4.

91 Administrative Measures for Online Trading (n 73) Art 18.

92 J Jie, 'Real-name Registration for Express Deliveries' *Global Times* (8 January 2014), www.globaltimes.cn/content/836303.shtml.

93 H Yong, 'Three Features of China's Internet Legislation' (2016) 48 *Chinese Law & Government* 1, 3–4.

frequently caused serious cases of telecommunications network-related fraud.[94] In 2009, the Standing Committee of the NPC made it a crime if any staff member of a state organ or an entity in a field such as finance, telecommunications, transportation, education or medical treatment illegally sells or provides personal information on citizens, which is obtained during the organ's or entity's performance of duties or provision of services, to others and causes serious consequences.[95] In December 2013, the Resolution Relating to Strengthening the Protection of Information on the Internet prohibited the collection of personal data without consent and the illegal transfer or sale of personal information to third parties by internet service providers (ISP) and other businesses.

The third category deals with the deletion or disposal of personal information. Many Chinese laws require ISPs, websites, internet app providers or other entities to keep consumers' personal information for a certain period of time. For example, a mobile internet app provider has to record users' log information and keep it for 60 days.[96] Internet cafes are required to keep information of consumers' identification cards and the relevant internet browsing information for at least 60 days.[97] The records may not be modified or deleted during the period of keeping.[98] However, none of these laws indicate how to dispose of that information after this period. Presumably all this personal information should be properly deleted.

Although China has not built a comprehensive personal information protection regime, its domestic law has clearly gone beyond the personal information protection requirement in its FTAs. Considering the recent development of Chinese domestic legislation, China and Australia may expand ChAFTA to strengthen online consumer protections in three regards: first, it may require members to enhance domestic legislation against fraudulent and deceptive online activities; second, it should require members to minimise unsolicited commercial electronic messages to ensure the healthy development of e-commerce; and third, an expanded ChAFTA may include obligations on personal information protection.

[94] See 《公安部关于印发<打击治理电信网络新型违法犯罪专项行动工作方案>的通知 [Notice of the Ministry of Public Security on Issuing the Work Plan for the Special Campaign of Cracking Down on and Controlling New Telecommunication Network-Related Illegal and Criminal Activities], (People's Republic of China) Ministry of Public Security, *Gong Xing* No 3410 [2015], 4 November 2015.

[95] This person can be sentenced to a fixed-term imprisonment of not more than three years or criminal detention, and/or be fined. 《中华人民共和国刑法》（1997修订 [Criminal Law of the People's Republic of China (1997 Revision)] (People's Republic of China) National People's Congress, President Order No 83, 14 March 1997, Art 253.

[96] Provisions on the Administration of Mobile Internet Applications Information Services (n 87) art 7.6.

[97] ibid, Art 23.

[98] ibid.

IV. RED BOX

The Red Box contains e-commerce regulations for free flow of information where it is difficult for Australia and China to reach an agreement, because these regulations represent the sharpest difference between the e-commerce chapters in FTAs concluded by China and Australia, respectively.

China's FTAs have never touched upon free flow of information. This is because China adopts a sophisticated censorship of the internet.[99] Its 'Great Firewall' filters all online contents via different targets, such as internet content providers, individual consumers and foreign websites' content.[100] The Chinese government plays on fears that the commitment to the free flow of information for e-commerce in FTAs may become a Trojan Horse, extending rights to what China considers to be dangerous political dissidents, and consequently threatening its approach to governance. China maintains a ban on Google, Facebook, Twitter, and the *New York Times* etc. China is also concerned that commitments to free flow of information for e-commerce in their FTAs could ultimately result in its internet censorship regime being challenged as a form of trade barrier.

The regulation of the free flow of information does not appear in any Australian FTAs except the TPP Agreement. The TPP regulations have five components. First, principles on access to and use of the internet for e-commerce benefit consumers, who are the subject of free flow of information.[101] The TPP Agreement provides that consumers can benefit from choosing internet services and applications freely, connecting their end-user devices to the internet as they wish, and have open access to online information.[102] Notably, the TPP Agreement does not define 'consumers'. Australian consumer law interprets 'consumers' broadly, including all individual purchasers of goods or services for their own use.[103]

The second component addresses cross-border transfer of electronic information.[104] The TPP Agreement requires its members to enable a covered person to freely transfer information (including personal information)

[99] C Stevenson, 'Breaching the Great Firewall: China's Internet Censorship and the Quest for Freedom of Expression in a Connected World' (2007) 30 *Boston College International & Comparative Law Review* 531, 537.

[100] JA Lee and CY Liu, 'Forbidden City Enclosed by the Great Firewall: The Law and Power of Internet Filtering in China' (2012) 13 *Minnesota Journal of Law, Science & Technology* 125, 128.

[101] TPP Agreement (n 19) Art 14.10.

[102] ibid.

[103] Small businesses may be considered as consumers in certain circumstances. For example, in Australia, the Unfair Contract Terms Laws has been extended to protect small businesses if certain circumstances are fulfilled. J Paterson, A Robertson and A Duke, *Principles of Contract Law*, 5th edn (Pyrmont, Thomson Reuters Professional Australia Limited, 2016) 402.

[104] TPP Agreement (n 19) Art 14.11.

online and cross-border for the conduct of commerce.[105] In two aspects, this requirement has a broad coverage. First, although the TPP Agreement e-commerce chapter does not define 'commerce', this term has been recognised by international law to have a broad coverage. For example, in the UNCITRAL Model Law on Electronic Commerce, 'commerce' is explicitly interpreted widely so as to cover matters arising from all relationships of a commercial nature, whether contractual or not.[106] Second, the scope of this article should be interpreted in conjunction with the non-conforming measures in Chapter 9 (Investment), Chapter 10 (Cross-Border Trade in Services) and Chapter 11 (Financial Services). These non-conforming measures are in negative lists. Accordingly, if cross-border transfer of electronic information is not forbidden in a certain industry under the lists, no prohibition should be imposed and personal data and other information should be allowed to transfer across borders for commercial purposes.

The third component bans localisation of computing facilities, such as servers, which are the infrastructure to free flow of information.[107] In recent years, with increasing concerns about online security and privacy, some states impose a mandatory requirement to store critical data on servers physically located in their territories.[108] Industry and internet advocates argue that localisation may create a more serious risk of fragmentation of the internet than censorship, because it 'threatens the major new advances in information technology—not only cloud computing, but also the promise of big data and the Internet of things'.[109] In reality, localised data may be lost in the event of a security breach; data that are encrypted and stored based on global best practices may be more likely to be secure.[110]

The fourth component regulates software source codes, which is the technology core for the realisation of the free flow of information.[111] Article 14.17.1 of the TPP Agreement requires that a person of another Member State transfer or provide access to its software source code as a precondition to import, distribute, sale or use such software or products containing such software in its territory.[112] Article 14.17.1 should be read in

[105] ibid.
[106] The UNCITRAL Model Law on Electronic Commerce (n 45) Art 1.
[107] TPP Agreement (n 19) Art 14.13.
[108] E Marel, H Lee-Makiyama and M Bauer, 'The Costs of Data Localisation: Friendly Fire on Economic Recovery' (2014) European Centre for International Political Economy No 3/2014, ecipe.org/publications/dataloc/, 3.
[109] L Clark, 'T Berners-Lee: We Need to Re-Decentralise the Web' *Wired* (6 February 2014), www.wired.co.uk/news/archive/2014-02/06/tim-berners-lee-reclaim-the-web; A Chander and UP Lê, 'Breaking the Web: Data Localization vs the Global Internet' (2014) California International Law Center Working Paper 2014-1, ssrn.com/abstract=2407858.
[110] See United States International Trade Commission, 'Digital Trade in the US and Global Economies (Part 2)' (2014), usitc.gov/publications/332/pub4485.pdf, 84.
[111] TPP Agreement (n 19) Art 14.17.
[112] ibid Art 14.17.1.

conjunction with Article 9.10 of the TPP Agreement, which provides performance requirements in investment. No party shall require the transfer of a particular technology, a production process or other proprietary knowledge to a person in its territory in connection with the establishment, acquisition, expansion, management, conduct, operation, or sale or other disposition of an investment in its territory.[113] To a certain extent, Article 9.10 and Article 14.17.1 overlap because they both prohibit a party requiring the transfer of certain proprietary knowledge (eg, source code) to a person in its territory. However, Article 14.17 goes beyond Article 9.10 by prohibiting the 'access' requirement. Providing 'access' to the source code is equal to releasing it. Moreover, Article 9.10 regulates the process of an investment from establishment to disposition. Article 14.7 focuses on the import, distribution, sale or use of products containing a source code. In addition, Article 14.7 is limited to mass-market software or products containing such software, and does not include software used for critical infrastructure.[114] Mass-market products generally target consumers. The TPP Agreement allows its members to require the transfer or access to source code used for critical infrastructure in order to protect national security of such infrastructure. But Article 9.10 is not subject to this. In conclusion, Article 9.10 and Article 14.7 serve a similar purpose to prohibit local performance requirement, but Article 9.10 is *lex generali* and Article 14.7 is *lex specialis* for software source code in e-commerce.

The fifth component governs internet connection fees, which are the monetary cost of the free flow of information.[115] The TPP Agreement suggests its Member States allow a supplier seeking internet connection of a Member to negotiate charge sharing with suppliers of other members on a commercial basis.[116] The charge sharing scheme may compensate the respective suppliers for the establishment, operation and maintenance of facilities.[117] Notably, this is a best-effort clause. Annex IV (non-conforming measures for state-owned enterprises and designated monopolies) of the TPP Agreement does not apply to e-commerce. If foreign suppliers can have equal access to internet infrastructure as their local competitors, trade in digital products can be better liberalised.

Unlike the WTO or other FTAs, the TPP Agreement has the potential to enhance online freedom of speech through its guarantee of free flow of information regarding trade in digital products. This comes from its five components of free flow of information and is also based upon its

[113] ibid Art 9.10.1(f).

[114] ibid Art 14.17.2.

[115] ibid Art 14.12.

[116] ibid. Suppliers may negotiate compensation for the establishment, operation and maintenance of facilities.

[117] ibid.

negative-list approach for non-conforming measures in trade in services and investment. If the Transatlantic Trade and Investment Partnership (TTIP), the Trade in Services Agreement (TiSA) and the TPP Agreement can adopt similar regulations for free flow of information, they would cover 100 per cent of the technologically advanced countries (other than China and Russia). If these Treaties become effective, China's 'balance' between political stability and internet blocking will come under increasing pressure. However, considering the US withdrawal, the TPP Agreement may not come into effect in its current format. China may try to exert its influence on developing an international trade law for digital products in the Green Box and Orange Box and carve out the regulation of free flow of information in the Red Box. As other Australian FTAs do not contain provisions for free flow of information, it is unlikely that Australia and China will propose the revision of ChAFTA that would include such provisions.

V. CONCLUSIONS AND PROSPECTS

Confronted with similar challenges brought about by the tremendous growth of transnational e-commerce transactions, both China and Australia have gone beyond the WTO multilateral framework and formulated e-commerce chapters in FTAs. Except for the TPP Agreement, Australian FTAs are not significantly different from their Chinese counterparts in the content of their current e-commerce chapters. The revision of the e-commerce chapter in ChAFTA could focus on regulations in the Green Box, seek consensus on the Orange Box, and avoid those in the Red Box. In other words, Australia and China should actively consider the possibility of extending exemption from customs duties to other fees and charges on the border, enhancing measures on paperless trade, digital signature and authentication, establishing broader cooperation mechanisms and state-to-state dispute resolution for e-commerce. They may also explore the possibility of imposing higher standards on online consumer protection. These efforts may help both countries to successful expand the e-commerce chapter of ChAFTA, influence international law-making in the field of e-commerce, and benefit their internet enterprises and consumers.

16

The Ideas Boom: The Innovation Economy in the Post-ChAFTA Australia–China Relationship

KEN SHAO

I. INTRODUCTION

INTELLECTUAL PROPERTY LAW is central to any free trade agreement (FTA) that has been concluded or negotiated in recent years. In the China–Australia Free Trade Agreement (ChAFTA), which entered into force on 20 December 2015, intellectual property is covered under Chapter 11 of the Agreement. When compared with many intellectual property provisions seen elsewhere, Chapter 11 appears to contain little other than to reaffirm the parties' existing international obligations under the Agreement on Trade-Related Aspects of Intellectual Property Rights (TRIPS Agreement). This background, as the author will argue in this chapter, constitutes a strategic facet for understanding the Australia–China relationship in the twenty-first century. This relationship cannot be explored only from an intellectual property perspective, but rather should be examined in line with the boom of the innovation economy in post-ChAFTA China and Australia.

At present, the innovation economy is viewed by China as its most vital economic sector. It is also becoming a priority for Australia, following the release of Australia's brand new National Innovation and Science Agenda in December 2015, the same month ChAFTA became effective. One may reasonably argue that the innovation economy may rise to form a core part of the China–Australia investment as well as trade in goods and services in the ChAFTA era. Examining how China and Australia define and develop their innovation economy therefore is vital in order to understand the direction of the future China–Australia relationship and the extent to which ChAFTA may benefit the two nations.

Section II examines why national innovation systems are much needed in Australia's future economy. Section III goes further to discuss why both

China and Australia intend to establish a flexible, rather than a rigid, intellectual property system for their national innovation objectives. Section IV analyses the background of Chapter 11 (Intellectual Property) of ChAFTA and its similar policy objectives to that of the national innovation policies of China and Australia. Sections V and VI assess future dynamics and challenges seen in post-ChAFTA China–Australia collaborations.

II. THE IDEAS BOOM

The Australian government released an unprecedented National Innovation and Science Agenda (Innovation Agenda) in December 2015, the same month in which ChAFTA came into force. Whilst an immediate connection between the Innovation Agenda and Chapter 11 (Intellectual Property) of ChAFTA may not be established straightaway, it appears that both policies intend to actively promote an open, innovative and dynamic environment for in which the innovation economy can take off. As section II's discussion will show, a proper understanding of the background of the Innovation Agenda may greatly help us to understand how intellectual property is defined in Chapter 11 of ChAFTA and why.

'The Ideas Boom' is a slogan used by the Australian government in the promotion of the Innovation Agenda nationwide.[1] The Innovation Agenda originally included in its campaign materials such specific phrases as 'Building an exciting future for every Australian' and 'There has never been a more exciting time to be an Australian', demonstrating an *unprecedented* shift in Australia's attitude towards its economy, which is traditionally occupied by minerals and resources.[2] This unprecedented shift takes place, as the following argument will show, in an era that Asia, and in particular China, rises as a global innovation centre. It is evident that trading relationships with China safeguarded by ChAFTA will need to have a great focus on the innovation economy.

Whilst the political agendas hidden in the wording of these advertisements were questioned by voters during Australia's 2016 federal election, they cannot change the fact that Australia is yet to have—and in a quite desperate way—an innovation economy.[3] Amid a serious decline in the nation's mining industry, innovation and high technologies have risen to represent a critical sector for Australia to 'deliver new sources of growth, maintain

[1] For its official website, visit www.innovation.gov.au.

[2] Australian National Audit Office, 'Government Advertising Campaign: Welcome to the Ideas Boom' (28 April 2016).

[3] Tom McIlroy, 'Election Slogans: Voters Disagree There's Never Been a More Exciting Time to be an Australian' *The Sydney Morning Herald* (26 June 2016).

high-wage jobs and seize the next wave of economic prosperity'.[4] Even worse, Australia's innovation performance ranking sits unimpressively among Member countries of the Organisation for Economic Co-operation and Development (OECD). It was not until 2014 that Australia began to have a science and technology strategy and Australia was the only OECD country that did not have one.[5] As former Chief Scientist for Australia Professor Ian Chubb stated, 'evidence was mounting that Australia was paying the price for its lack of long-term planning in these areas, and was falling behind overseas competitors on key performance measures'.[6] The Innovation Agenda clearly understands some of the evidence, which includes:

> Australia's rate of collaboration between research and industry sectors is the lowest in the OECD. Only 9% of Australian small to medium sized businesses brought a new idea to market in 2012-13, compared to 19% in the top five OECD countries.[7]

In addition, the Department of Industry of Australia, in its *Australian Innovation System Report 2013*, concluded that most innovation in Australia

> is incremental in nature, comprising the adoption or modification of existing innovations with new-to-the-world innovation being only a small proportion of total innovations. This is in *sharp* contrast to other developed economies that have a much higher proportion of new-to-the-world business innovation and relatively high trade volumes.[8]

In addition to OECD countries, the Asia-Pacific region offers a crucial and perhaps more strategic benchmark for assessing Australia's innovative performance. The twenty-first century is widely regarded in Australia as the 'Asian Century', which, according to *Australia in the Asian Century*, will offer 'a wealth of opportunities, especially for Australia's young people'.[9] Access to those opportunities will however depend upon substantial efforts as major economies in the region, such as Japan, South Korea, Taiwan and now Singapore and Hong Kong, all sit at the top of innovation performance globally, and Mainland China, as a 2015 McKinsey report reveals, 'does have the potential to become a global innovation leader'.[10] This potential is very real—even if we look only at *the Global Innovation Index* 2012 published by INSEAD and WIPO, 'China's performance on the key

[4] Australian Government, National Innovation and Science Agenda, 1.

[5] Chief Scientist, Science, Technology, Engineering and Mathematics: Australia's Future (2014) Commonwealth of Australia.

[6] Nicky Phillips, 'Chief Scientist Releases National Strategy for Science, Innovation and Technology' *The Sydney Morning Herald* (2 September 2014).

[7] National Innovation and Science Agenda (n 4) 4.

[8] Department of Industry, Australian Innovation System Report (2013) 9.

[9] Australian Government, *Australia in the Asian Century* White Paper (2012) 1.

[10] McKinsey Global Institute, *The China Effect on Global Innovation* (2015) 1.

knowledge and technology outputs pillar is outpaced *only* by Switzerland, Sweden, Singapore, and Finland'.[11] By 2015, China's innovation strengths had grown to another level; according to PricewaterhouseCoopers (PwC), Chinese companies now outpace various multinational corporations (MNCs) in advanced research, emerging technologies and trend analyses, and MNCs in China are shifting innovation strategies to align with the Chinese model.[12] The Department of Industry of Australia has already understood this challenging situation clearly and anticipated that there will be 'two factors *fundamental* to successful engagement with Asia—innovation capacity and knowledge of Asian markets'.[13]

It can be argued that the Innovation Agenda represents a *proactive* innovation policy framework that for the first time sets up Australia for a national innovation system, which usually means a network of institutions in the public and private sectors whose activities and interactions initiate, import, modify and diffuse new technologies and ideas.[14] The Innovation Agenda includes initiatives worth AUD$1.1 billion over four years and focuses on four pillars: (i) culture and capital; (ii) collaboration; (iii) talent and skills; and (iv) government as an exemplar. These four sections provide detailed measures regarding tax benefits, diverse funding schemes, insolvency law reforms, researcher–industry partnerships, expanded visa arrangements, policymaking improvement and government procurement. The Innovation Agenda's official website further organises these crucial and exciting themes into functional and even streamlined sections, namely, startups and entrepreneurs, business, young Australians, researchers and universities, and investors. These webpages are designed in a highly engaging and encouraging way.

A similar system fostering an 'Ideas Boom' has existed in China since around 2006. In China, the term 'to construct an innovative country' or indigenous innovation (self-driven innovation) is more widely used than a national innovation system.[15] China's determination to re-emerge as a global innovation leader was triggered by its high dependence on foreign technology, which was an inevitable choice for post-Cultural Revolution China where uneducated cheap labour provided the only gateway for

[11] INSEAD and WIPO, The Global Innovation Index 2012: Stronger Innovation Linkages for Global Growth, 39.

[12] PwC Strategy, 'China's Innovation is Going Global: 2014 China Innovation Survey', 6.

[13] *Australian Innovation System Report* (2013) (n 8) 9.

[14] C Freeman, *Technology Policy and Economic Performance* (London, Pinter, 1987) 1.

[15] K Shao, 'The Cores and Contexts of China's 21st-Century National Innovation System' in K Shao and X Feng (eds), *Innovation and Intellectual Property in China: Strategies, Contexts and Challenges* (Cheltenham, Edward Elgar, 2014) 6. 'Self-driven innovation' is arguably a better term than 'independent' or 'indigenous' innovation; see also K Shao, 'Zizhu Chuangxin and China's Self-driven Innovation: Calling for a Holistic Perspective' [2013] *Cardozo Law Review de novo* 168, 170–71.

China to return to the global market.[16] China's national innovation system includes many components such as higher education and research institution reforms, national policies and their local implementation measures, R&D funding schemes, talent plans, innovation parks, incubators and clusters, government procurement, technical standards, tax and financial benefits, venture capital, schemes supporting emerging industries and startups, technology commercialisation, cultural industries, regional strengths, integrated planning, and national and local intellectual property strategies.[17] Such a complex system is a result of strategic, forward-looking and coordinated planning.

III. INTELLECTUAL PROPERTY FOR CHINA AND AUSTRALIA

What role should intellectual property play under the dynamic national innovation systems of China and Australia? Should they play a role similar to that in the US where intellectual property is simply regarded as a tool for maximising the interests of the stronger party—the US as 'one of the world's most innovative countries'—and for suffocating the weaker party such as China which is viewed, mistakenly, as no more than 'a globally dynamic manufacturing base'?[18] Or, should intellectual property be a catalyst for an open and dynamic innovation economy that needs to be supported by a variety of policies and incentives detailed in the national innovation systems of China and Australia?

It is interesting to see that the term 'intellectual property' only appeared once in the Innovation Agenda and just three times in its 132-page predecessor—the *Industry Innovation and Competitiveness Agenda: An action plan for a stronger Australia* (Action Plan) released in October 2014.[19] The latter even expressed that the government will promote 'intellectual property arrangements that facilitate, rather than *frustrate*, collaboration and commercialization of ideas'.[20] Whilst an exact view on intellectual

[16] K Shao, 'History is a Key Decoder: Why China Aims at Re-emerging as a Global Leader of Innovation' (2013) 29 *Law in Context* 117, 124–26.

[17] Shao, 'The Cores and Contexts of China's 21st-Century National Innovation System' (n 15) 4. A milestone of China's national innovation system is *the Guidelines on National Medium- and Long-term Program for Science and Technology Development* 2006–2020 (the *Guidelines*). The Ministry of Science and Technology of China, www.gov.cn/jrzg/2006-02/09/content_183787.htm.

[18] US International Trade Commission, *China: Intellectual Property Infringement, Indigenous Innovation Policies, and Frameworks for Measuring the Effects on the US Economy* (2010) USITC Publication 4199 xiv.

[19] Australian Government, *Industry Innovation and Competitiveness Agenda: An action plan for a stronger Australia* (2014).

[20] ibid 76.

property is not outlined in the Innovation Agenda, its overall tone endorses an open and innovative culture. This, as we will show in section IV, also underpins the policy focuses of Chapter 11 of ChAFTA, which seems to coincide with the position held by the abolished Action Plan.

To understand how intellectual property may frustrate innovation in countries like China and Australia, we need to know that for over two decades intellectual property has played a key political and economic role as a trade-off in negotiations between developed and developing countries, with weaker parties asked to agree to higher protection levels that may be unsuitable for the level of their domestic development.[21] Whilst China has been developing its national innovation system for over 10 years, as a recent study published in 2014 shows, a high level of dependence on foreign sources of technology is ongoing in China.[22] When Deng Xiaoping reopened China's door to the rest of the world in 1978, China's technological capacity was nowhere close to that of any industrialised nation.[23] The 1980s and 1990s saw China attempt to attract technology transfer from multinationals to local Chinese firms through the innovative model of joint ventures. This model has been proven to be unsuccessful as global corporations always go to significant lengths to retain their intellectual property within the confines of the corporation's boundaries.[24] Even worse, as Peking University law professor Zhang Ping articulated, collaborative agreements prepared by the foreign parties often require the transfer or termination of Chinese intellectual property assets, leading to diminished well-known Chinese brands and innovative potential of various Chinese firms.[25] This situation has made China wary of any regional or bilateral agreements or free trade agreements that implement standards higher than those of the TRIPS (TRIPS-plus standards).

The situation in Australia is not vastly different. As we have already shown in section II, innovation is a weak link for Australia's long- and short-term global competitiveness. Such weakness acts as an immediate driving force behind Australia's timely shift to an innovation economy under its Innovation Agenda. This situation explains why Australia is primarily a consumer and net importer of intellectual property from more industrialised nations,

[21] For how political and economic factors have played in the arena of global intellectual property law, see P Drahos with J Braithwaite, *Information Feudalism: Who Owns the Knowledge Economy?* (London, Earthscan, 2002); SK Sell, *Private Power, Public Law: The Globalization of Intellectual Property Rights* (Cambridge, Cambridge University Press, 2003).

[22] S Grimes and Y Sun, 'Implications of China's On-Going Dependence on Foreign Technology' (2014) 54 *Geoforum* 59.

[23] Shao, 'History is a Key Decoder' (n 16) 124–26.

[24] Grimes and Sun (n 22) 61.

[25] Zhang Ping, 'Intellectual Property Safeguards Interests But Not Necessarily Protects Innovation' *China Business News* (27 December 2013).

and the economic impact on Australia of the extension of intellectual property protection has received very little attention.[26]

This dire reality might have enabled the Australia–United States Free Trade Agreement (AUSFTA) to impose, or at least attempt to impose, TRIPS-plus obligations that may hinder Australia's national interest.[27] This negotiation process, as Melbourne University law professor Andrew Mitchell highlighted,

> provides an illustration of the outcomes that countries with relatively little bargaining and economic power can expect from an FTA with the US. It also serves as a warning of how even an economically successful developed country may end up sacrificing its welfare, public policies and democratic processes.[28]

Therefore, Australia's position in the global innovation and intellectual property arena is as disadvantaged as that of China, or even worse. In a recent study, Christoph Antons and several other scholars have pointed out that the conventional dichotomy of developed and developing countries is no longer adequate when one looks at how Asia-Pacific nations have performed in regional free trade agreements negotiations concerning intellectual property.[29] To that end, Australia is indeed a developing country with weak innovation capacities and disadvantaged intellectual property positions in global competition. China as a much larger economy may be more competitive than Australia in the long run, but it faces similar challenges at least in the short term.

So, how should countries like China and Australia develop their intellectual property policies that may foster dynamic innovation and a good catch-up? It is noteworthy that robust innovation requires the open and energetic dissemination of knowledge instead of rigid intellectual property systems, as knowledge innovation is inherently cumulative. This, in the view

[26] A Capling and J Ravenhill, 'Australia's Flawed Approach to Trade Negotiations: and Where Do We Sign?' (2015) 69(5) *Australian Journal of International Affairs* 503; see also R Gregory, 'The Australian Innovation System' in RR Nelson (ed), *National Innovation* Systems: A Comparative Analysis (Oxford, Oxford University Press, 1993) 324.

[27] C Arup, 'TRIPs as Competitive and Cooperative Interpretation' in J Malbon and C Lawson (eds), *Interpreting and Implementing the TRIPS Agreement: Is It Fair?* (Cheltenham, Edward Elgar, 2008) 20.

[28] A Mitchell, 'The Australia–United States Free Trade Agreement' in R Buckley, V Io Lo and L Boulle (eds), *Challenges to Multilateral Trade: The Impact of Bilateral, Preferential and Regional Agreements* (The Hague, Kluwer Law International, 2008) 116. However, Australia in the end managed to retain certain substances of its public policy mechanisms. A Mitchell and T Voon, 'Australia–United States Free Trade Agreement' in S Lester and B Mercurio (eds), *Bilateral and Regional Trade Agreements: Case Studies* (Cambridge, Cambridge University Press, 2009) 42.

[29] C Antons and RM Hilty, 'Introduction: IP and the Asia-Pacific "Spaghetti Bowl" of Free Trade Agreements' in C Antons and RM Hilty (eds), *Intellectual Property and Free Trade Agreements in the Asia-Pacific Region* (New York, Springer, 2015) 4.

of American intellectual property law professor Julie Cohen, is the 'sociology of creative practice' where creativity 'at its most creative is messy, free-wheeling, and opportunistic; people seize inspiration where they find it and pursue it wherever it leads'.[30] This applies in particular to modern technologies as there is a high degree of cumulativeness, in the sense that each innovator builds on prior developments and discoveries. Cumulativeness is even sequential in many modern industries such as computer software and biotechnology as inventions in those fields are often piled on top of each other. A rigid intellectual property system rewards early innovators extensively for the technological foundation they provide to later innovators but leaves little to the latter. This is not to mention the general public interest in such fields as access to medicine, which is highly regarded by the general public in Australia.[31]

IV. CHAPTER 11 OF ChAFTA

The global complexity of intellectual property noticed under the national innovation systems of both China and Australia may, to a great extent, have informed the writers of Chapter 11 of ChAFTA. Solid evidence can be found in the different attitude expressed towards the above-mentioned AUSFTA's TRIPS-plus intellectual property standards and Chapter 11 of ChAFTA, for the latter has been 'praised' in a 2015 report issued by the Joint Standing Committee on Treaties of the Parliament of the Commonwealth of Australia.[32] The Committee noted that a balanced view of intellectual property is essential for the prosperity of innovation, economic and social development and international trade liberalisation.[33] This attitude clearly reveals the position Australia, as a 'developing country in innovation', intends to take when dealing with global intellectual property and trade-related issues.

When reading the wording of Chapter 11, readers who are familiar with international intellectual property provisions will recognise that many of those articles can be found in the World Trade Organization (WTO) administered TRIPS Agreement. As Members of the WTO, both China and

[30] JE Cohen, 'Copyright, Commodification, and Culture: Locating the Public Domain' in L Guibault and B Hugenholtz (eds), *The Future of the Public Domain: Identifying the Commons in Information Law* (Alphen an den Rijn, Kluwer Law International, 2006) 146, 153.

[31] For the cumulative nature of modern innovation and the inadequate response from patent law, see S Scotchmer, *Innovation and Incentives* (London, MIT Press, 2004) 127.

[32] Joint Standing Committee on Treaties of the Parliament of the Commonwealth of Australia, *Report 154: Free Trade Agreement between the Government of Australia and the Government of the People's Republic of China* (Canberra, 15 June 2015) 22.

[33] ibid 22–24.

Australia shall, as Article 11.4 of Chapter 11 articulates, affirm their commitment to the TRIPS Agreement.[34] This commitment includes the provision of national treatment (Article 11.5) under which 'each Party shall accord to nationals of the other Party treatment no less favorable than it accords to its own nationals with regard to the protection of such intellectual property rights';[35] border measures (Article 11.22) by which 'each Party shall ensure that the requirements necessary for a right holder to initiate procedures to suspend the release of goods suspected of being counterfeit trade mark or pirated copyright goods shall not unreasonably deter recourse to these procedures';[36] and criminal procedures and penalties (Article 11.21) 'to be applied at least in cases of wilful trademark counterfeiting or copyright piracy on a commercial scale'.[37]

Whilst Chapter 11 affirms the parties' TRIPS obligations, its *structure* is quite different from that of the TRIPS Agreement. This is most evident at the very beginning of Chapter 11 under 'Article 11.1: Purpose and Principles' where five out of the seven sub-articles focus on the possible role of intellectual property in a broader technological, social and international context. After providing affirmation for 'maintaining adequate and effective protection and enforcement of intellectual property rights' and that 'intellectual property protection promotes economic and social development' in Article 11.1 (a) and (c) respectively,[38] the rest of Article 11.1 focuses heavily on the public function of intellectual property. It attributes the aim of intellectual property to 'the promotion of technological innovation' and 'the transfer and dissemination of technology', stating that intellectual property 'should support open, innovative and efficient markets', and rejects the view that intellectual property prevails over other rights even when they 'become barriers to legitimate trade'. Appropriate measures, it claims, may be needed to 'prevent the abuse of intellectual property rights' and to 'protect public health and nutrition'.[39]

In stark comparison, the TRIPS Agreement differs strongly in structure. The Preamble, although recognising 'the underlying public policy objectives of national systems for the protection of intellectual property, including developmental and technological objectives', nevertheless focuses on the

[34] Department of Foreign Affairs and Trade, www.dfat.gov.au/trade/agreements/chafta/official-documents/Pages/official-documents.aspx. Of course, such commitment also includes 'any other multilateral agreement relating to intellectual property to which both Parties are party' (ChAFTA) (Art 11.4 of ch 11).

[35] See also Art 3 of the TRIPS Agreement. WIPO, *Agreement on Trade-Related Aspects of Intellectual Property Rights*, www.wto.org/english/tratop_e/trips_e/t_agm0_e.htm.

[36] ibid s 4.

[37] ibid s 5.

[38] ibid Preamble.

[39] TRIPS Agreement (n 35); ChAFTA (n 34) art 11.4 (b) and (d)–(g).

'effective enforcement' of intellectual property as 'private rights' and the provision of 'adequate standards', which made the TRIPS Agreement the most powerful, or perhaps the most aggressive, international intellectual property treaty, prior to the rise of more aggressive regional and bilateral agreements such as the Trans-Pacific Partnership (TPP).[40] To date, the TRIPS Agreement has attracted wide criticism, such as that TRIPS standards and enforcement measures conflict with key global agendas in the fields of public health, climate change, environmental protection, biodiversity, food security, cumulative innovation and information freedom.[41] In a 2014 book, six leading American jurists and economists jointly held that the global intellectual property practice under the TRIPS framework hinders developing nations' catching-up opportunities as well as future development capacities of the US and other developed nations.[42]

Notwithstanding a flexible approach to intellectual property, protecting intellectual property still remains a strong focus under the national innovation systems of both China and Australia and Chapter 11 of ChAFTA. No doubt the enforcement of intellectual property rights remains a great concern for Australian businesses in China. Nevertheless, in a 2007 survey report of more than 2,100 Australian enterprises that have business dealings with China, Kimberlee Weatherall and others concluded that intellectual property issues, whilst problematic for some Australian firms, were not significant enough to outweigh the benefits of doing business with China, and there was no evidence to support the idea of nominating intellectual property as the highest priority in Australia's FTA negotiations with China.[43]

Weatherall's conclusion, made 10 years ago, may still hold certain value in the ChAFTA era. In recent years, intellectual property protection and enforcement in China have changed dramatically, though challenges in the areas of trade secrets, patents, copyrights, rewards and remuneration for service inventions, and trademarks continue to exist. As reported by *the American Business in China White Paper 2016:* 'A majority of respondents view patents, copyright, and trademark laws and regulations as being effective

[40] ibid Preamble.

[41] There are numerous books on these agendas: see, eg, T Wong and G Dutfield (eds), *Intellectual Property and Human Development: Current Trends and Future Scenarios* (New York, Cambridge University Press, 2011); RL Okediji et al (eds), *Intellectual Property Rights: Legal and Economic Challenges for Development* (Oxford, Oxford University Press, 2014).

[42] Okediji et al (n 41) 503–04; 508–09. Note the amendment to TRIPS which entered into force on 23 January 2017 intends to ease poor countries' access to affordable medicines. This is one of the recent efforts that aim to mitigate the TRIPS impact. It gives legal certainty that generic medicines can be exported at reasonable prices to satisfy the needs of countries with no pharmaceutical production capacity, or those with limited capacity. For details see, www.wto.org/english/news_e/news17_e/trip_23jan17_e.htm.

[43] K Weatherall et al, 'In the Shadow of the China–Australia FTA Negotiations: What Australian Business Thinks about IP' (2007) Melbourne Institute Working Paper Series Working Paper No 26/07, 22.

(in China). Nine in 10 respondents believe that China's enforcement of IPR has improved over the last five years'.[44] It is noteworthy that a flexible approach to intellectual property taken by Chapter 11 of ChAFTA must also be assessed against China's massive development of the nation's state-level intellectual property strategy. Unlike Australia's Innovation Agenda that does not allocate intellectual property a specific role, China's popular entrepreneurship and innovation initiative views intellectual property as a core business strategy. Following China's state-level *Outline of the National Intellectual Property Strategy 2008*, intellectual property has become a fashion in China.[45] To encourage commercial transactions of intellectual property assets, China intends to establish a national intellectual property public service platform. Intellectual property enforcement, legal aid and dispute resolution mechanisms will further be improved. Punitive damages, especially for repeated or wilful infringements, will be explored.[46]

To utilise the market value of intellectual property assets, China is also developing innovative solutions such as intellectual property financing, which include allowing startups to use their intellectual property assets to obtain pledge loans.[47] Some of these agendas have already been covered by various intellectual property policies such as the National Patent Development Strategy (2011–2020) (the Patent Strategy) issued by State Intellectual Property Office (SIPO) in 2010. The Patent Strategy supports tax benefits and incentives to inventors, patent pledging, and the establishment of a multilayered patent utilisation system that assists the commercial transaction of patents as a type of property. Chinese enterprises with strong patent portfolios are encouraged to seek financing via public listing on the stock market, equity transactions, bond markets and securitisation.[48]

Australian businesses need to be aware that in the ChAFTA era increasingly there can be more Chinese firms seeking intellectual property protection in Australia. The growing passion of Chinese firms in intellectual property rights should not be underestimated. In 2015 alone, there were 149,238 newly accepted intellectual property cases in Chinese courts and 142,077 concluded ones, accounting respectively for an 11.49 per cent and

[44] The American Chamber of Commerce in China, *The American Business in China White Paper 2016*, 12–14.

[45] The State Council, *Outline of the National Intellectual Property Strategy* (issued on 5 June 2008), www.wipo.int/edocs/lexdocs/laws/en/cn/cn021en.pdf. A balanced view of intellectual property is supported by the *Outline of the National Intellectual Property Strategy*.

[46] The State Council, *The State Council's Opinions on Measures for Strongly Promoting Popular Entrepreneurship and Innovation* (11 June 2015) Part 3.3.

[47] The State Council, *The Guidelines for Developing Incubators and Promoting Popular Entrepreneurship and Innovation* (2 March 2015) Part 2.6.

[48] SIPO, *National Patent Development Strategy (2011–2020)* (issued on 11 Nov 2011), www.sipo.gov.cn/ztzl/ywzt/qgzlsyfzzltjgz/noticeps/201311/t20131113_879257.html.

an 11.76 per cent increase from 2014.[49] The overwhelming proportion of these cases, as Indiana University law professor Xuan-Thao Nguyen concluded in recent research, are usually brought by Chinese firms.[50] Many leading Chinese firms, such as Alibaba, Tencent and Huawei have established intellectual property protection offices. In December 2015, the former Vice President of Pfizer, Matthew Bassiur, was appointed by Alibaba as Vice President, Head of Global Intellectual Property Enforcement, showing Alibaba's attempts as China's e-commerce giant to lead the industry in the fight against counterfeiting and protecting intellectual property rights.[51] One may suspect that challenges will remain amid ChAFTA's very broad intellectual property coverage; but the above trend, followed by a commitment from China and Australia to continue working together to enhance intellectual property examination, registration and enforcement systems under Chapter 11, intellectual property will become a strategic element in the future two-way economic exchanges between Australia and China.[52]

To summarise, when Australia's National Innovation Agenda and Chapter 11 of ChAFTA are assessed jointly against the background of global intellectual property concerns and China's innovation strategies, it is clear that the flexible approach to intellectual property taken under Chapter 11 of ChAFTA intends to foster open and dynamic innovation in both China and Australia. It is reasonable to predict that Chapter 11 may support the two nations' mutual interest in facilitating 'open, innovative and efficient markets' by 'maintaining *adequate* and effective protection and enforcement of intellectual property rights', 'the promotion of technological innovation' and 'the transfer and dissemination of technology'.[53] It is only by focusing on these crucial expressions that capture well the fundamental nature of cumulative innovation, that we can understand and analyse 'the Ideas Boom' which is being energetically supported by both the Chinese and Australian governments.

V. FUTURE DYNAMICS

If intellectual property under both the Innovation Agenda and Chapter 11 of ChAFTA does not intend to create hurdles for the innovation economy

[49] The Supreme People's Court of the People's Republic of China, *Intellectual Property Judicial Protection White Paper of China Courts 2015*, the official website of State Intellectual Property Office (SIPO), www.sipo.gov.cn/ztzl/ndcs/qgzscqxcz/xwfb/201604/t20160422_1264240.html.

[50] X-T Nguyen, 'The China We Hardly Know: Revealing the New China's Intellectual Property Regime' (2011) 55(3) *St Louis University Law Journal* 773.

[51] Lehar Maan, 'Alibaba Appoints Matthew Bassiur as Head of Anti-counterfeiting, IP unit' *Reuters News* (21 Dec 2015).

[52] TRIPS Agreement (n 35) Art 11.9; ChAFTA (n 34) Art 11.21.

[53] TRIPS Agreement (n 35); ChAFTA (n 34) Art 11.4 (b), (d)–(g).

of both China and Australia, then what will represent the future dynamics that may connect numerous innovation efforts taking place in China and Australia in the ChAFTA era in which a friendly intellectual property environment sits under a wider backdrop of reduced tariff and non-tariff barriers to trade in goods and services, investment, e-commerce, movement of natural persons and technical standards?

The first future dynamic is China's 'Internet Plus' economic model not seen anywhere else in the world. This major economic focus was formally announced by China's Prime Minister Li Keqiang in his *Report on the Work of the Government 2015*, which stated that China will

> develop the Internet Plus action plan to integrate the mobile Internet, cloud computing, big data, and the Internet of Things with modern manufacturing, to encourage the healthy development of E-commerce, industrial networks, and Internet banking, and to guide Internet-based companies to increase their presence in the international market.[54]

The concept of Internet Plus includes but is not limited to e-commerce, which has already been very successful in China owing to the economic miracle created by Alibaba, the New York listed company founded by Jack Ma just over 13 years ago. Alibaba is one of the key driving forces behind Internet Plus and defines it as the wide application of the entirety of internet technologies, such as the mobile internet, cloud computing and big data, in all economic and social sectors.[55] For instance, Uber and Didi Dache—the Chinese giant mobile platform taxi-calling app that acquired Uber's China operation on 1 August 2016—are relatively new business models in the Internet Plus era, as these apps must use the mobile internet, cloud computing and big data to instantly process the location of a passenger, the fee and its payment. Through the platforms supported by Internet Plus technologies, traditional industries such as taxi services can all be up on mobile.

In essence, China is moving into an Internet Plus era where new infrastructures (cloud computing, internet and smart devices), new factors of production (big data) and new divisions of labour (such as e-commerce) may support intelligent manufacturing, large-scale personalised products, modern agriculture, intelligent energy, internet finance, online public service, medical services and ageing services, online education, intelligent logistics, B2B e-commerce and export, transportation network management, and more.[56]

[54] L Keqiang, *Report on the Work of the Government* (2015) under 'Section IV. Balancing Steady Economic Growth and Structural Improvement'.

[55] Ali Research Institute, *Internet Plus Research Report of Ali Research Institute* (2015),. www.i.aliresearch.com/img/20150312/20150312160447.pdf, 4. For Alibaba's recent development in Australia, see Tony Yoo, 'Jack Ma just opened Alibaba Australia' *Business Insider Australia* (4 February 2017).

[56] The State Council, The Action Plan for Actively Promoting 'Internet Plus' (1 July 2015). Ali Research Institute, Internet Plus Research Report of Ali Research Institute (n 55) 12.

Within the complex structure of China's Internet Plus economy, We Media (or self-media) is a rapidly rising star on the horizon. Blogs, including *Weibo*, represent the first generation of We Media. All social media apps on smart devices can be viewed as We Media.[57] Particularly relevant to the context of our discussion is WeChat. We Media such as WeChat, motivates users to spread information, and more importantly, this communication effect is directly linked to e-commerce. WeChat is a Chinese mobile app with over 700 million monthly active users accumulated from only as far back as 2011.[58] Developed by Tencent, one of China's three largest internet companies, WeChat acts as a messenger, a phone, a public social media platform, a private network, an online shopping platform, an online game machine, a banking tool, and much more. In an article published by *Harvard Business Review* in 2014, Jeffrey Towson rightly pointed out that WeChat is 'a little like what you would get if you combined AOL, Facebook, Skype, Yahoo, Gmail, Norton, and Twitter—under one roof'.[59]

Since 2015, numerous We Media platforms have started to emerge on WeChat, creating a huge challenge to paper, PC-based and mobile media. One commercially successful example is Luoji Siwei (logical thinking), which is a WeChat platform established by Luo Zhenyu, a Chinese online celebrity (*wanghong*). Luo attracted millions of fans (*fensi*) via his brilliant online talk show programmes that introduce a book a day to fans. Luo then expanded this freebie into an online bookstore, which benefited from WeChat's all-in-one e-commerce functions and his 500 million subscribed WeChat users. Luo's WeChat store has now expanded to include other business sectors such as accessories, stationary, household products and online education. In October 2015, Luoji Siwei completed Series B financing and was valued at over AUD$600 million.[60] With WeChat's all-in-one social and economic functions, We Media is fast becoming a commercial reality in China.

ChAFTA contains a specific chapter that encourages 'cooperation on electronic commerce' (Chapter 12). It states that 'customs duties on electronic transmissions between the Parties' shall not be imposed, and 'cooperation in research and training activities that would enhance the development of electronic commerce, including by sharing best practices on electronic commerce development', is encouraged.[61] Chinese e-commerce giants have already

[57] For an introduction, see Wei Wuhui, 'The Evolution of We Media in China' *TMTPOST* (13 June 2015).

[58] For an up-to-date number of WeChat users, see its official website: www.weixin.qq.com.

[59] Jeffrey Towson, 'Why Facebook Should Worry About Tencent' *Harvard Business Review* (3 April 2014).

[60] Su Su, 'Luioji Siwei completed Series B Financing' *163 News* (20 October 2015), www.tech.163.com/15/1020/08/B6BUQV4D000915BF.html.

[61] ChAFTA (n 34) Arts 12.1, 12.3, 12.10.

taken this opportunity. Jack Ma, the founder of Alibaba opened Alibaba's Australian headquarters in Melbourne in February 2017 as he believes that Australia's clean environment is the next 'gold mine'. In Australia, up to AUD$1 million worth of air has been bottled and Alibaba could be another opportunity for air farmers to expand their businesses.[62] However, for Australian business to access the fashion and complexity of China's e-commerce and Internet Plus model, they need to accept that although ChAFTA has created a supportive environment for them there is a substantial learning process ahead if they are ever to understand China's economic transformation into the Internet Plus era, how We Media operates and that they should not merely sell Australian goods to China via Jack Ma's e-commerce platform, but also try to innovate by themselves in the ChAFTA era.

The second dynamic is regarding China's vast amount of venture capital and huge growth rates in Chinese outbound investment. Venture capital investment activities are very robust in China. Although reports from KPMG and Dow Jones indicate that Chinese venture capital fundraising and investment activities dropped from late 2015 to early 2016 as part of the global decline of venture capital activities, Chinese investors as well as Chinese government funding are still very actively looking for good projects.[63] Professional online investment platforms such as 36kr and Chuangtou Quan (vc.cn) intend to create effective linkages for startups and investors.

Looking at Chinese investment activities more broadly against the backdrop of total global foreign direct investment (FDI) flow declining at an 8 per cent annual rate from 2011 to 2014, China's outbound direct investment (ODI), benefited from its 'Going Global' policy, and increased at a compound annual growth rate (CAGR) of 16 per cent.[64] The strongest growth was not in mining but in health (188.5 per cent growth) and information as well as in computer services and software (59.8 per cent growth).[65] In 2015, Chinese investment into Australia grew more than twice as strongly as the global trend, with investment into Australia's renewable energy and healthcare sectors significantly outperforming that into mining.[66] Such a trend will likely grow following the further implementation of China President Xi Jinping's new initiatives such as 'One Belt One Road' and the Asian Infrastructure Investment Bank.

[62] For Alibaba's recent development in Australia, see Tony Yoo, 'Jack Ma just opened Alibaba Australia' *Business Insider Australia* (4 February 2017); 'Chinese businessman Jack Ma reveals what China really wants from Australia' *News.com* (6 February 2017).

[63] KPMG, Venture Pulse Q2 (2016) 94; Dow Jones, Venture Capital Report: China Q5 (2015) 2.

[64] Ernst & Young, *Riding the Silk Road: China sees outbound investment boom: Outlook for China's outward foreign direct investment* (March 2015) 2.

[65] KPMG, *Demystifying Chinese Investment in Australia* (2016) 8.

[66] ibid 6, 11.

ChAFTA has a very detailed chapter on investment (Chapter 9: 27 pages). It covers a wide range of investments including intellectual property, and accords to investors of the parties 'treatment no less favourable than that it accords, in like circumstances, to its own investors' and 'treatment no less favourable than that it accords, in like circumstances, to investors and investments in its territory of investors of any non-Party'.[67] Chinese investment has been a striking phenomenon in Australia–China relationships for over 10 years. Having benefited from Chapter 9 of ChAFTA, Australia has already set up a gateway to China's investment frontier. Under the Innovation Agenda, the Australian government supports five 'landing pads' in San Francisco, Tel Aviv, Shanghai, Berlin and Singapore.[68] These landing pads are administered by Austrade and act as a mentor and facilitator for Australian firms, and in particular startups in the global market.[69] Among them, the Shanghai landing pad was opened in December 2016 and is described as 'a gateway to China's innovation ecosystem'. The location offers Australian startups with 'immediate opportunities to accelerate their business development' because 'Chinese investors are actively looking for technology investment opportunities and strategic alliances with international companies'.[70]

The third dynamic is related to Australia's unprecedented plan for boosting the commercialisation capacities of university research. Following its recognition that 'Australia's rate of collaboration between research and industry sectors is the lowest in the OECD', the Innovation Agenda promises to 'introduce, for the first time, clear and transparent measures of *non-academic* impact and industry engagement when assessing university research performance'.[71] Such a project can only happen if the traditional 'publish or perish culture' is overhauled. For that purpose, the Innovation Agenda intends to reform funding patterns to boost research–industry collaboration.[72]

Research–university collaborations are often arranged via public/private sector partnership and by establishing physical R&D centres. These models have a long history of implementation in leading economies such as the US and the UK. Examples include the US' Small Business Technology Transfer (STTR) programme that expands the public/private sector partnership to include joint venture opportunities for small businesses and non-profit

[67] ChAFTA (n 34) Arts 9.1 and 9.4.

[68] ibid Art 11.

[69] Australia Unlimited, www.www.australiaunlimited.com/LandingPads/about-landing-pads.

[70] Australia Unlimited, www.www.australiaunlimited.com/Landing-Pads/locations.

[71] Australian Government, National Innovation and Science Agenda (n 4) 4, 11.

[72] ibid.

research institutions, and the UK's Catapult centres where leading businesses, scientists and engineers work side by side on late-stage research and development projects.[73] China has been trying to develop similar models, including innovation parks and university R&D centres, for a number of years. Australia's Innovation Agenda has a clear focus on promoting public/private sector partnerships 'by streamlining and refocusing a greater proportion of research block grant funding toward collaboration'.[74] Since 2015, Australia has invested AUD$248 million over four years in six Industry Growth Centres that are independent not-for-profit companies. One of the four themes of those Centres is to improve engagement between research and industry.[75]

Funding schemes that mainly focus on R&D collaborations at the institutional level, however, may not incentivise knowledge commercialisation to a great extent, or be highly inclusive. *Pecuniary* incentives to *individual* researchers deserve more attention. 'Robust, fit-for-purpose and balanced' incentives for research–industry collaboration, as recognised by a recent Universities Australia report, are essential.[76] Such incentives should well accommodate the interests of researchers and not be limited to more research grants or expanded prestige. The *Boosting the Commercial Returns from Research* report released by the Australian government in 2014 recognises the importance of 'generous *pecuniary* benefits for commercialisation' to researcher entrepreneurship. This will first require many Australian universities to review their intellectual property asset ownership tradition so improved financial incentives are accessible to researchers.[77]

From a comparative perspective, China's approach to rewarding researchers is worthy of mention here. China is one of the few countries that specifically provides legal protection to employee-inventors. Article 16 of China's Patent Law 2008 prescribes that an employer shall reward the inventor of an employment invention; after such patent is exploited, the inventor shall be given a reasonable amount of remuneration according to the scope of application and the economic results.[78] Since 2012, China has been drafting the Employment Invention Regulation that aims to provide better and more protected incentives to employee-inventors and researchers.[79]

[73] For details, see www.sbir.gov/about/about-sttr#sttr-program.

[74] National Innovation and Science Agenda (n 4) 11.

[75] For details, see www.www.industry.gov.au/industry/Industry-Growth-Centres/Pages/default.aspx and www.catapult.org.uk/about-us/about-catapult/.

[76] Universities Australia, Submission to the 'Boosting the Commercial Returns from Research' Discussion Paper (2014) 5.

[77] Australian Government Department of Education & Department of Industry, *Boosting the Commercial Returns from Research* (2014) 7, 20.

[78] The Patent Law of the People's Republic of China, www.www.wipo.int/wipolex/en/details.jsp?id=5484.

[79] For its text, see www.www.sipo.gov.cn/ztzl/ywzt/zwfmtlzl/tlcayj/201403/t20140331_925616.html.

Whilst the Regulation is pending approval, on 3 August 2016, China's Ministries of Education and Industry jointly issued a Policy on the commercialisation of university researches. The Policy requires no less than 50 per cent of the net profit gained by the university from the technology transfer or licensing to be given to the researchers or employee-inventors; if the technologies are used to acquire company equity, no less than 50 per cent of the equity obtained should be given to the researchers or employee-inventors. The rest of the profit will be retained by the university, not by the government, and shall be used only for future research commercialisation. To further encourage university researchers to commercialise their inventions, the Policy allows a university researcher who has met their performance review targets to work part-time in the company that commercialises the invention or to leave the university for no more than three years to set up his own startups.[80]

A similar incentive model should be considered by Australia. But at present, the unsatisfactory commercialisation level of intellectual properties owned by Australian universities and low incentives may lead Australian universities and researchers to seek alliances with their Chinese partners and investors in the ChAFTA era. Under Australia's Innovation Agenda, a new AUD$200 million Commonwealth Scientific and Industrial Research Organisation (CSIRO) Innovation Fund is created to co-invest in new spin-off companies and existing startups that will develop technology from CSIRO and other publicly funded research agencies and universities. Jiangsu Industrial Technology Research Institute (JITRI), a leading institute located in China's economic centre in east China, has already sensed opportunities with the CSIRO model. In March 2017, Jiangsu Province signed a collaborative agreement with CSIRO and established a AUD$6 million JITRI–CSIRO Strategic Collaborative Fund for facilitating the introduction of quality CSIRO research projects into China for commercialisation.[81] JITRI plays a crucial role in promoting and supporting the industrial technology research and commercialisation of the advanced technologies in China. Its latest collaboration with CSIRO should be viewed as China's quick movement towards seizing Australian technologies in the ChAFTA era, as China may provide a far more supportive and financially rewarding environment for Australian researchers to commercialise their technologies.

[80] China's Ministry of Education and Ministry of Industry, *Several Opinions on Improving the Commercialization of Technological Outcomes in the Higher Education Sector* (2016), Parts 2, 5 and 6, www.most.gov.cn/tztg/201608/t20160817_127255.htm.

[81] For the latest news announcement of the JITRI–CSIRO Strategic Collaborative Fund, see www.www.jitri.org/archives/1405/. Another example is the Torch Innovation Precinct of UNSW. As it is stated, 'UNSW is championing a major step forward in Sino-Australian relations by launching an ambitious, government-backed initiative bringing the successful Chinese innovation ecosystem—the "Torch" model of Science & Technology Parks to Australia'. For details, see www.www.torch.unsw.edu.au/.

VI. COMBINED FORCES UNDER ChAFTA

The above examples also indicate that the positive effect of the ChAFTA era is often a combined one. The Innovation Agenda clearly operates not only under Chapter 11 but also Chapters 9, 12 and various other chapters of ChAFTA. Australia Unlimited, an exciting new initiative, is another example of the combined force. It represents 'the voice of contemporary Australia, telling inspiring stories of talented Australians, both at home and abroad, profiling their contributions through their creativity, business acumen, scientific, innovative and humanitarian endeavours'. Australia Unlimited showcases and connects research, startups, industries and investors in an engaging and informative way, and contains a specific section that promotes the landing pads.[82] Australia Unlimited is being actively promoted in China by Austrade, which organised a large Australia Week in April 2016 across 12 cities in Greater China to showcase Australian competitiveness and innovation. It was the largest business mission ever organised by Austrade consisting of almost 1,000 delegates from around 750 companies. Austrade even has a professionally maintained Chinese app integrated to China's largest social media platform, WeChat, so it can publish Australian economic and technological news and projects to the wider Chinese public.

Young Australians are set to become the driving force of the Australia–China joint innovation landscape in the ChAFTA era. Austrade's regular WeChat announcements confirm that Australian startups, many of which are focusing on mobile apps, are heading towards China. The Australia–China Youth Association (ACYA) frequently organises seminars and events about China, including its innovation economy. In 2014, a group of young Australians launched the China Australia Millennial Project (CAMP), which has already become an award-winning, design-led innovation experience and community. It connects dynamic, young leaders in bilateral business incubators, providing them with the tools to address real world, global challenges. A typical CAMP programme includes a 12-week online, part-time course designed by some of the leading innovation practitioners in China and Australia, followed by the Sydney Summit—an intensive, face-to-face conference featuring talks and workshops from leading industry experts and some of Australia and China's most exciting companies.[83] These are all good examples of the combined forces in promoting Australia–China free trade that may potentially generate tangible benefits in the ChAFTA era.

However, the extent to which those future dynamics may work to generate desirable combined forces depends on whether each party can show

[82] For details, see www.www.australiaunlimited.com/.
[83] For details, see www.www.australiachina.org/.

a firm commitment to substantial cultural learning. Chinese investors are yet to comprehend Australia's legal and business environment. Australian firms, young entrepreneurs and startups who are keen to access the Chinese market—such as via Australia's newly established landing pad in Shanghai—will need to work hard to understand the concept of Internet Plus and then figure out how to turn the theory into practice in a cross-cultural context. They will need to understand how e-commerce and We Media (or self-media) have already disruptively changed China's media, entrainment and e-commerce industries, and how this disruptive force can help new businesses to popularise and grow.

One immediate example showing cultural challenges is relevant to China's Internet Plus, which is already becoming a major focus for Australian startups going to the Shanghai landing pad. Few Australians have heard that China's innovation is driven by a quite unique Need Seekers innovation model. As PricewaterhouseCoopers's *2014* China Innovation Survey articulates,

> Chinese companies are more likely than others to adopt a Need Seekers innovation strategy, which means they innovate ahead of customers and competitors. There is little truth to the Western image of Chinese companies as followers of others, focusing on low-value-add activities such as copying technologies and products already available on the market. In fact, Chinese companies in mainland China outpace MNCs in high-value add activities such as advanced and applied research, as well as emerging technologies and trend analyses. Furthermore, we see MNCs in China shifting innovation strategies to align with the Chinese model.[84]

To explain this phenomenon, it is argued that in each niche market, the competition is far fiercer in China than in the US. This is further accompanied by more complicated pain points of Chinese consumers, including those rising from China's urbanisation process and middle-class growth.[85] Such a distinctive phenomenon appears to be a consequence of China's unique social, economic, educational and institutional status quo in its 30 years of transition and, to a more subtle extent, China's historical and cultural tradition rooted in creativity and perfection.[86]

Western commentators have only recently realised that China's Need Seekers innovation model has led China to become a front-runner in mobile tech. WeChat offered speedier in-app news articles long before Facebook, developed a walkie-talkie function before WhatsApp, and made major use

[84] PwC Strategy, 'China's Innovation is Going Global' (n 12) 6.

[85] Wang Xinyue, 'Behind American Firms' Copying of Chinese Ideas: China's Four Unique Strengths' *The Paper News* (8 August 2016), www.thepaper.cn/newsDetail_forward_1510044.

[86] K Shao, 'Taobao, Wechat and Xiaomi: How Innovation Flourishes in China's "Fertile Land of Intellectual Property Piracy"' in P Drahos et al (eds), *Kritika: Essays on Intellectual Property* (Cheltenham, Edward Elgar, 2017) 22–43; Shao, 'History is a Key Decoder' (n 16) 118–21.

of QR codes well before Snapchat. Before Venmo became the app for millennials to transfer money in the US, the Chinese were investing, reimbursing each other, paying bills and buying products from stores with smartphone-based digital wallets. Before the online dating app Tinder, people in China used an app called Momo to flirt with nearby singles. As Ben Thompson, founder of the tech research firm Stratechery said, 'the trope that China copies the US hasn't been true for years, and in mobile it's the opposite: The US often copies China'.[87]

Unless Australian business obtains a high-level understanding of Chinese culture and society, their past and their future, the proven 'major challenges' for Australian businesses—namely, the cultural barriers—will only continue to act as the ultimate hurdle.[88] To this end, the supportive environment created by ChAFTA marks only the very beginning of a golden age. The rest is left to individual players to figure out the way in which their adventure can eventually succeed.

VII. CONCLUSION

The innovation economy may soon represent a striking highlight of the post-ChAFTA Australia–China relationship. As we have demonstrated, when Australia's National Innovation Agenda and Chapter 11 of ChAFTA are assessed jointly against the background of global intellectual property concerns and China's innovation strategies, it is clear that the flexible approach to intellectual property taken under Chapter 11 of ChAFTA intends to create an open, innovative and dynamic environment for the twenty-first century innovation economy to take off in both nations. It is reasonable to predict that Chapter 11 may support the two nations' mutual interest in facilitating 'open, innovative and efficient markets' by 'maintaining *adequate* and effective protection and enforcement of intellectual property rights', 'the promotion of technological innovation' and 'the transfer and dissemination of technology'.[89] These potentials may bloom when the benefits of various other chapters of ChAFTA concerning investment, e-commerce, services and so on are exploited. However, as sections V and VI have demonstrated, ChAFTA can only start to work if several future dynamics of China's innovation economy are well understood.

The flow of creative ideas between China and the West is now *two-way*. Silicon Valley experts admitted that China's mobile tech had already

[87] Paul Mozur, 'China, not Silicon Valley, is Cutting Edge in Mobile Tech' *New York Times* (2 August 2016).

[88] Australia–China Young Professionals Initiative (ACYPI) *From Paper to Practice: The Australia–China Relationship* (2015) 5.

[89] TRIPS Agreement (n 35); ChAFTA (n 34) Art 11.4(b), and (d)–(g).

'had an impact on us and our thinking'.[90] Travis Kalanick, co-founder of Uber, said in early 2016 that in the next 10 years Beijing will be Silicon Valley's only competitor.[91] Looking at the future dynamics of innovation economy in China and Australia—such as the five dynamics this chapter has explored—one may even bravely imagine that Australia might become the home of an Asia-Pacific Internet Plus Silicon Valley amid California's increasing need to be closer to Beijing. Benefiting from its top ranking in the world's most liveable cities, world-class research and human resources and perhaps the unique strength of the same time zone (such as in Perth), Australia might justify itself as an 'amphibian location' for Silicon Valley elites, including those China-born who are allured by homesickness and China's great opportunities, but cautious of pollution, materialism and high property prices in Beijing, Shanghai and Shenzhen.

But before we get too excited, let us not forget that high risk is a fundamental character of startups. China's innovation economy is not functioning without challenges.[92] When moving further into the uncharted territories of innovation and Asian cultural literacy, Australia too will encounter obstacles. As China's national innovation system emerged nine years earlier than Australia's, there are lessons that Australia may learn from China. To what extent can incubators, innovation parks, cultural clusters and funding maximise the success rate of startups and small and medium-sized enterprises? How can you make university reforms intending to minimise the traditional gaps between research and commercialisation really work? Will innovation in high-tech sectors overcome the patent barriers already put up by multinationals? Should we review the bandwagon of young entrepreneurship and assess more mindfully the potential impact of certain technologies, such as virtual reality, computer games and e-commerce, on human societies? These questions can hardly be handled by any free trade agreement and ChAFTA therefore should not be viewed as an all-in-one solution. Stakeholders in Australia–China trading are yet to gain specific knowledge and know-how in cross-border collaborations if they want to fully access the benefits provided by ChAFTA.

[90] Quoted from a Silicon Valley-based venture capital investor. Mozur (n 87).

[91] Wang Xinyue (n 85).

[92] For a detailed study, see L Tie and W Jiuyun, 'A Study on Excessive Convergence in the Choice of Regional Strategic Emerging Industries' (2012) 2 *China Soft Science* 115.

Index

www.ingramcontent.com/pod-product-compliance
Lightning Source LLC
Chambersburg PA
CBHW071305180926
51613CB00001B/133